THE BOOK OF THE TORAH

The Book of the TORAH

✳ ✳ ✳

Thomas W. Mann

Second Edition

CASCADE *Books* · Eugene, Oregon

THE BOOK OF THE TORAH
Second Edition

Cascade Books
An Imprint of Wipf and Stock Publishers
199 W. 8th Ave., Suite 3
Eugene, OR 97401

www.wipfandstock.com

ISBN 13: 978-1-61097-895-8

Cataloging-in-Publication data:

Mann, Thomas W. (Thomas Wingate), 1944–

   The book of the Torah / Thomas W. Mann. 2nd ed.

   ISBN 13: 978-1-61097-895-8

   x + 238 p. ; 23 cm. Includes bibliographical references and index.

   1. Bible. Pentateuch—Commentaries. 2. Narration in the Bible. I. Title.

BS1225.3 M34 2013

Manufactured in the U.S.A.

Contents

Tables

Appendices

Preface

IMAGINE THAT YOU ARE reading merrily along in a contemporary novel when one of the characters, "a good-natured girl, no more than eighteen," from a small Midwestern town, suspects that the capitol city is "wicked and exciting, one of the cities of the plain."[1] Or consider the main character and narrator of another novel, set in seventeenth-century New England, who says, "My father was in his seventieth year when I was born. I was his Benjamin, indeed."[2] Or you are reading an editorial piece in the newspaper when the author complains about the over-abundance of candidates on the stage in a recent Presidential debate: "The assumption that every cat and dog must be in the debate means 90 minutes divided by seven will produce Babel."[3]

What all of these literary references have in common are allusions to biblical stories, more specifically, stories from the first five books of the Bible, called the Pentateuch or Torah. The phrase "cities of the plain" alludes to the story of Sodom and Gomorrah, with its immoral sex; the name Benjamin refers to the last born of the sons of Jacob (he had twelve and one daughter), who was the "child of his old age"; and the mention of Babel refers to the story of the *tower* of Babel, and the confusion of multiple languages.[4] You could probably find *Babel* in a standard dictionary, and perhaps even *Benjamin*, but you would need a search engine to find out what the "cities of the plain" are. You'd have to Google that.

On the other hand, if you know the various Bible stories in question, you won't have to Google. Such allusions suggest one reason why it is worth reading the Pentateuch—simply because it contains stories that have enriched Western culture immeasurably. As the novelist Herman Wouk says, "'In terms of narrative, my boy, there's nothing but the Bible for sheer storytelling.'"[5] Alongside novels and newspapers, there are innumerable works of art, literature, music, and dance whose meaning and significance depend on one's knowledge

1. Stegner, *Crossing to Safety*, 116.

2. Brooks, *Caleb's Crossing*, 159.

3. Henninger, "Our Un-Presidential Debates."

4. Respectively, Gen 13:12 (KJV; NRSV: "cities of the valley") and ch. 19; 45:20; ch. 10.

5. Barnes, "At 97," C1.

of biblical stories. In this sense, the Bible is arguably *the* classic text. But, of course, the Pentateuch is also indispensable if one is to understand fully the major religious communities who trace their origins back to these five books—Judaism, Christianity, and Islam. The background of the New Testament and the Qur'an appears in the Hebrew Bible, and especially what all three call the Torah. Muslims named the Jews "the people of the book," and the heart of that book is the Book of the Torah. Knowing what is in the Torah is the foundation of Western religious literacy.[6]

It is my hope that this second edition of *The Book of the Torah* will increase biblical literacy, to the benefit of college and seminary students, doctoral students, and general readers, especially within religious communities like the church, synagogue, and mosque. There is little doubt that such a need exists, for, as one scholar says, "The Bible appears to be the most revered book never read."[7] Even people who consider themselves secular (or, as they often say, "spiritual but not religious"), are inextricably connected to the stories in the Torah by being part of the culture it has helped shape. Both personal and social identity is rooted in narratives of who we are, where we came from, and where we are going. One of those narratives, we could say the meganarrative is the

narrative that stretches from the beginning of time to a future in the promised land. At their deepest level, allusions such as those mentioned at the outset are more than sidelines; they point to the way in which Scripture has provided a "Secondary World" (a phrase of the author, J. R. R. Tolkien) that serves as an imaginative structure for interpreting our *own* world. Such stories teach us how to live.

I am grateful to Westminster John Knox Press for publishing the first edition of this book, for keeping it in print for almost a quarter century, and for remitting the right of publication for a second edition. I am also grateful to Cascade Books, and especially to editor-in-chief K. C. Hanson, who suggested bringing out a revised edition to serve as a companion to its sequel published in 2011, *The Book of the Former Prophets* (on the books of Joshua through 2 Kings).

Although you can read this book on its own, if you do not know the biblical stories well (and perhaps even if you think you do!), it will be most fruitful if you read the biblical text for each section first. For example, my analysis of the story of Jacob's cheating Esau out of his father's blessing (Genesis 27) assumes that the reader knows the basic outline of the story. Moreover, the biblical text often displays artistic subtleties that this book cannot fully cover (and only you, the reader, may perceive). Most sections of the book state the texts that will be under discussion (e.g. Gen 27:1—28:9), and occasionally I will suggest abbreviated readings.

---

6. As Hendel says about just one book of the Torah, "As a story of deliverance from oppression, the birth of freedom, and the divine sanction of human rights and responsibilities, the Exodus story has served as a paradigm for over two and a half millennia" (*Remembering Abraham*, 72).

7. Beal, *Rise and Fall of the Bible*, 33.

Abbreviations

ANET	*Ancient Near Eastern Texts Relating to the Old Testament*, edited by James B. Pritchard. 3rd ed.
AT	Author's translation
BCE	Before the Common Era (i.e., up to 1 AD)
BZAW	Beihefte zur Zeitschrift für die alttestamentliche Wissenschaft
CE	Common Era (i.e., after 1 AD)
FRLANT	Forschungen zur Religion und Literatur des Alten und Neuen Testaments
JAAR	*Journal of the American Academy of Religion*
JPS	Jewish Publication Society translation of the Hebrew Bible
NRSV	New Revised Standard Version of the Bible
GNT	Good News Translation

Introduction

WHEN INTRODUCING THE HEBREW Bible to college students, I used to begin the first class by placing a beautiful handmade wooden box in the shape of a heart on the table before them. I would ask them what they saw, and they would say, "A wooden heart." I would then open the box and take out its contents—also a wooden heart, but in the form of an intricate three-dimensional puzzle, composed of scores of carefully interlocked pieces of wood. I would then ask the students what this object was, and they would again say, "A wooden heart," but I could already see in their faces a glint of incipient discovery. I would then ask them which heart they thought was more beautiful, and most of them would point to the solid box. Finally, I would ask them which of the two they thought more interesting, and all of them would indicate the puzzle. The point of my little demonstration was to introduce an aspect of biblical study applicable to almost any narrative portion of the Bible, but particularly to the Pentateuch. The Pentateuch is a combination of the box and the puzzle. On the surface, it is a beautiful work of art—uncomplicated and whole. But inside, it is a complex puzzle composed of

innumerable interlocking pieces. I believe that the fascination and the beauty of the Pentateuch are enhanced when we recognize both its puzzle- and its box-like qualities.

The following study is an attempt to understand the Pentateuch both in terms of its final form (the box) and its internal complexity (the puzzle). That much more weight is given to the former than to the latter derives from the previous imbalance in pentateuchal criticism, as the following introduction will explain.

The Hebrew Bible is traditionally referred to by the acronym *Tanak*, which stands for the Hebrew words *Torah*, *Nevi'im*, and *Ketuvim*, or, in English, *Law*, *Prophets*, and *Writings*. This sequence of words reflects the sequence of literary materials that constitute the Hebrew Scriptures: the Torah, often called the Pentateuch because it contains the five books of Genesis through Deuteronomy; the Prophets, containing books of Joshua through Malachi; and the Writings, containing Psalms through Chronicles. This order will seem strange to Christians, whose Bible follows an arrangement that, in essence, places the Writings in the middle rather than at the end. Nevertheless, for both Christians and Jews (and, to a lesser extent, for Muslims), Scripture begins with the Torah.[1] For Judaism we could remove the article before the word *Torah* and say that Scripture begins and ends with Torah, inasmuch as the rest of the Hebrew Bible—especially the Prophetic books, but also to some extent the Writings—can be understood as interpretive extensions of the Torah, rather than as portions of equal weight. Thus all of Scripture becomes, in some sense, torah (i.e., guidance), and Judaism itself may be designated as the Way of Torah.

On the other hand, to say that Scripture begins with Torah from a traditionally Christian perspective, means that Scripture begins with guidance (more commonly translated "law"), but only with the purpose of pointing to "something greater" (Matt 12:6), namely, the gospel of the New Testament. Thus, not despite but precisely because of its relativizing of the Torah, the New Testament in many respects would be incomprehensible without some understanding of the Torah. In short, those who want to know fully what it is to be a Jew or a Christian must at some point read the book of the Torah.

The tripartite division of the Hebrew Bible into Torah, Prophets, and Writings is by no means a recent invention. Not only does the New Testament refer to "the law of Moses, the prophets, and the psalms" (Luke 24:44), but the Prologue to the book of Ecclesiasticus (Sirach),

from about 130 BCE, provides a similar division. The further back into history we move, of course, the less precisely can we date the crystallization of the Torah. The reference to Ezra's recitation of "the book of the Torah of Moses" (AT) in Neh 8:1–8 would seem to place the formal designation of the Pentateuch at least as early as c. 450 BCE, after Israel's return from exile in Babylonia. It is even possible that this designation arose almost one hundred years earlier, during the exile itself, but at this point the discussion becomes mostly speculative. The "book" would not have looked like a contemporary book, which is technically a codex (having separate pages that are bound together); it would have been in the form of a long scroll.[2]

Whenever the Pentateuch received its present shape as a literary unit, it was the result of a surgical procedure. While its separation from the Former Prophets (Joshua through 2 Kings) may seem perfectly natural (e.g., the Pentateuch deals with Israel's history from the creation up to the occupation of Canaan), in fact the separation is artificial. The book of Deuteronomy, which at one time served as the introduction to the Former Prophets, has been removed from that position to serve as the conclusion of the Tetrateuch (Genesis through Numbers), thereby forming the Pentateuch. The theological significance of this literary surgery is a subject to which we shall return at the

1. There are references to the Hebrew Bible in the Qu'ran, but they are by no means as integral to it as those in the New Testament. Muslims trace their origins back to Ishmael, one of the sons of Abraham (see the discussion of Genesis 16 and 21).

2. Thus our use of the term *book* for the Torah and for the individual "books" of the Hebrew Bible is somewhat misleading. Our use of the verb *scroll* to describe moving among pages on a word processor or website is a relic of what books originally looked like. Also, biblical chapters and verses were not indicated until around 1200 CE.

end of this study; for now we need only posit the surgery itself.[3]

Those scholars who maintain an originally separate origin and function for the book of Deuteronomy defend their position by a prior claim that the book derives from a different author than the Tetrateuch. From as early as the seventeenth century, it has become increasingly clear that the Pentateuch, traditionally called the five books of Moses, is not the work of a single author at all, much less of Moses, but in fact is a composite document containing a number of literary strands, each probably stemming from a different period of Israel's history. Indeed, it is possible that the gap between the earliest and latest literary strata in the Pentateuch is as much as five hundred years—from about 1000 to 500 BCE.[4] The work of distinguishing these strands—usually referred to as source criticism, or the Documentary Hypothesis—is accomplished by careful attention to differences in language and style, theological emphasis, and logical consistency (e.g., contradictions). The results of many years of research in this area are reflected in a list of code letters: J, E, D, and P. Each of these letters stands for an "author" of the Pentateuch. Thus, *J* stands for the Yahwist—the letter *J* begins the German word for Yahweh—and is thought by some to stem from the time of the Davidic–Solomonic empire (c. 1000–922 BCE), while others

argue for an exilic setting (some 500 years later). The letter *E* stands for the Elohist, usually located in northern Israel around 850 BCE. The two names reflect different names for God (Yahweh and Elohim).[5] The letter *D* stands for the Deuteronomist, found almost exclusively in Deuteronomy through 2 Kings. Chronologically, the Deuteronomist is located between about 620 BCE, a century after the fall of the northern kingdom of Israel, and the period of exile that began with the destruction of the southern kingdom of Judah in 587 BCE. The final strand is designated *P*, which stands for Priestly. Considerable debate continues about the temporal location of this strand, especially vis-à-vis D; some think that P is earlier than D, some that D and P are basically contemporary, while others maintain that the bulk of P is about seventy-five years later, reflecting the exilic period. Sometimes these literary strands are found in separate blocks, such as P in Genesis 1:1—2:4a and J in 2:4b–25, and at other times they are intricately intertwined, as in the flood story in Genesis 6:1—9:19.[6]

5. See Appendix 2.

6. For an extensive introduction to source criticism, see Campbell and O'Brien, *Rethinking*, 1–20. They take a radically different position, arguing that the various repetitions and contradictions do not point to different continuous literary sources but to the way in which the text reflects the oral performance of the stories. The text is more like the script of a play or a musical score that is open to various interpretations by the performers, with directions for such variety provided by the playwright or composer. On such performances, see also Niditch, *Oral World*, 120–30. For a spirited and compelling defense of the traditional Documentary Hypothesis, see Baden, *Composition*. Note especially his argument that P is an independent literary document equivalent to J and E (180–82).

3. The classic work that attempts to demonstrate the original orientation of Deuteronomy is that of Noth, *Deuteronomistic History*.

4. Baden (*Composition*, 225), who refrains from dating any of the documents, suggests at least a four-hundred-year gap between their authorship and the compilation into the Pentateuch.

Some scholars have used the letter *R* to refer to one or more redactors who combined the sources into the present, canonical text, often imposing their own views in the process. However, if we follow one of the most recent studies of the Documentary Hypothesis, we should instead use another letter, *C*, for compiler. In this view, the compiler was not an author or theologically motivated redactor but a preservationist, whose sole discernible intent was to produce a chronologically meaningful combination of the available literary sources.[7]

Until recently, at least, there was a general consensus that each of these "authors" wrote with a particular audience in mind and with a particular message for that audience, and that this historical context was of primary importance in determining the meaning and significance of the text. Walter Brueggemann's synopsis is representative: "To chasten the pride and prosperity of the united monarchy, J recalled to its notice that 'by you the families of the earth will be blessed.' To loosen Israel from the quicksand of Canaanite syncretism, E extolled her, 'fear God.' And to summon her in exile, DtrH [our D] admonished, 'return,' while P, to encourage, told her to 'be fruitful and multiply, fill the land, subdue it and have dominion.'"[8]

The ambiguity of our dating of P is an indication of the complex development that stands behind all of the four literary strands and is easily obscured by the brevity of the preceding paragraphs. In fact, two other critical disciplines—form and tradition criticism—have shown that the Pentateuch is hardly the product of four individual "authors" whose work was done all at once at four discrete points in Israel's history. Rather, each of the major literary strands, while perhaps located at a particular period of Israel's history, also contains many older traditions. Some of these traditions may have been passed on in oral rather than written form, until they found written expression in one (or more) of the literary strands. The transmission of these traditions from the original oral form (hypothetical, of course) to the latest written form is called the history of traditions.[9] Scholars attempt not only to trace the history of traditions but also to establish the "setting in life" (German: *Sitz im Leben*) of the original oral form (or one of the later stages). That is, biblical scholars often seek to determine the social context of the oral tradition.

An example of the combined use of literary, form, and tradition criticism may be helpful.[10] The custom of Passover is described in at least three major literary strands. The Priestly stratum is found in Exod 12:1–20, while the Yahwistic stratum picks up in 12:21–39 (perhaps including passages of E). Another editor (perhaps an early representative of the

---

7. This is the basic thesis of Baden, *Composition*, especially 227–29. See further below.

8. *Vitality of Old Testament Traditions*, 38. For a thorough and insightful introduction to the wide range of biblical interpretation, see Brueggemann, *Theology of the Old Testament*, 1–114.

9 The difference between oral and written is by no means absolute, for an oral culture can continue to influence writing for a very long time, on which see Niditch, *Oral World*. For her critique of how scholars appeal to oral traditions regarding texts, see ibid., ch. 8.

10. See also Appendix 1. For an introduction to all of these methods and more, see Holladay, "Contemporary Methods."

Deuteronomic school) has added material about the associated custom of eating unleavened bread in 13:3–10 and, in addition, a significantly different picture of Passover is presented in Deut 16:1–8. Here is an example of outright contradictions in the Torah: according to J and P, the people are to celebrate Passover in their homes (Exod 12:7, 22), whereas according to D they are to come to a central sanctuary (Deut 16:6).[11] Thus the Passover tradition is crystallized in written form in the three basic literary strata, J, D, and P, and some scholars attempt to trace a development in the tradition chronologically from J to P. Moreover, this history of tradition can be traced behind the earliest written record (J) to a likely setting in life out of which the tradition developed in its oral stage, namely, a herdsman's custom that occurred at the change of pasturage each year. In fact, having traced the tradition backwards, one could then continue to trace it forwards to the practice of Passover among

contemporary Jews—a history of tradition stretching for thousands of years.

As already implied, the influence of form and tradition criticism on the results of literary criticism has been enormous. Above all, the first two methods have established that the major literary strata of the Pentateuch are not at all the products of authors in the contemporary sense of that word. For example, the so-called Yahwist was not an individual who sat down sometime during the Davidic monarchy and wrote an original history of Israel's beginnings. Instead the Yahwist, and indeed all the pentateuchal authors, are more properly understood as editors or redactors. First, they are redactors in that they collected various traditions, arranged them in literary formulations, and gave them a particular style and theological emphasis. Second, these authors were redactors or editors in the more familiar sense—they expressed their opinions about many issues through their writing, sometimes *taking issue* with each other.

To return to the Passover tradition as an example, we can look at the combination of the Priestly author (at least Exod 12:1–20) with the text of J (basically Exod 12:21–23, 29–39). The P text now serves as an introduction to the Passover story, which changes the way in which the reader will approach the J text. Thus, the detailed legal ordinances in the Priestly stratum, given by God to Moses before the actual event of the first Passover, prevent the reader from concluding that the customs surrounding Passover arose accidentally during the departure from Egypt itself (e.g., the Israelites baked unleavened bread simply because they had to leave quickly, before yeast could

11. There are many other contradictions: for example, how many animals does Noah take into the ark, and of what kind (Gen 7:2, 8–9)? Does Jacob travel to his family's hometown because he is afraid of his brother's intent to murder him, or because his father does not want him to marry a local woman (Gen 27:42–43; 28:1–2)? Was it Ishmaelites or Midianites who hijacked Joseph to Egypt (Gen 37:28, 36)? God says to build only a crude, earthen altar (Exod 20:24), but later God says to make it from acacia wood with a bronze veneer (27:1–2). Such contradictions are most easily explained as coming from different authors. Milgrom cites a Midrashic saying: "'Contradictions are thus built into revelation,'" noting the contradictions between the two major literary sources of the book of Leviticus, P (Priestly), and H (Holiness Code) (*Leviticus: A Book of Ritual*, 5).

be added, 12:39). All is done in obedience to God's prior instructions, which prescribe seven *days* of eating unleavened bread (12:15). While we cannot assume that the compiler was motivated by any intent other than chronological sequence, we can look at the result of this editorial fusion as a story that is different from the mere sum of its parts.[12] In fact, the Passover tradition as a whole is contained in a redactional unit that stretches from 11:1 to 13:16, and its inclusion with ch. 11 ties it in with another redactional unit, the plague narrative, which runs at least from 7:14 through ch. 11. Indeed, if we extended our literary horizon, we can see how the rest of the book of Exodus—and ultimately, the Pentateuch—is a composite of a number of redactional units.

We have now come full circle: from, first, the Pentateuch or Torah as a distinct entity within the canon; then to the complex history of traditions that stands behind (or beneath) this entity; and, last, back to the final, redactional form of the whole. In recent years, scholars from widely different perspectives have argued that such a movement toward interpretation of the present form of the text is precisely the direction biblical research ought to be going. As Robert Polzin has put it,

> Traditional biblical scholarship has spent most of its efforts in disassembling the works of a

complicated watch before our amazed eyes without apparently realizing that similar efforts by and large have not succeeded in putting the parts back together again in a significant or meaningful way.[13]

While few, if any, scholars want to abandon the fruits of over a hundred years of research, they are raising cogent questions about the methods and goals of that research. Without disputing the composite nature of the Pentateuch, some scholars wonder about the precision with which we can delineate the classic sources or authors, about our ability to reconstruct their historical context, and about the extent to which such reconstruction should control our interpretation of the present text. Is E really an independent narrative source or, at best, a set of fragmentary editorial additions? Do we really have one or more narrative sources that run continuously throughout the Pentateuch, or a collection of originally self-contained and independent stories (e.g., the ancestral stories of Genesis 12–50 and the exodus story beginning at Exodus 1)? Can we be certain that J wrote during the Davidic-Solomonic empire, and even if we can, should we then base our interpretation of the meaning of, say, his Abraham stories on that historical context? Was P originally a continuous narrative, and did it compete, as it were, with J, or is it an editorial supplement to J? It should at least give us pause that one can easily make much of the call of Abram (Gen 12:1–3) by a J who wrote in the heady days of the tenth century, or one who wrote to the

---

12. Baden, *Composition*, 227: "It is the job of the canonical interpreter to find meaning in the final form of the text; it does not follow, however, that it was the intention of the compiler to create that meaning." Thus here it simply makes sense chronologically for the instructions for Passover in P to come before the *event* of Passover that follows.

13. "The Ancestress of Israel,'" 82–83.

distraught exiles in the sixth, or even to those in postexilic Israel.[14]

Similar questions arise concerning historical events that may (or may not!) lie behind the biblical narratives. Given the nature of the literary materials in the book of Exodus, for example, how successfully can we penetrate to what actually happened? Even if such an analysis can yield reliable conclusions, how should we apply those conclusions to the meaning of the text as it now stands? Were we to conclude (as some scholars do) that the events of the escape from Egypt and the encounter with God at Mount Sinai derive from originally independent traditions and were experienced by different groups of people, what would we then do with the text that connects these events in a narrative sequence? We can ask the same question about the connection between the ancestral stories in Genesis and the exodus tradition.

Hans Frei, among others, has posed most sharply the problems which beset the traditional literary and historical approaches to the text. Frei complains that, in some literary approaches, the biblical stories have been "identified with a reconstruction of the process by which they originated and of their cultural setting," and that in historical approaches "critical reconstruction of the reported events constituted the subject matter of narrative texts."[15] In both cases, "the *meaning* of the stories was finally something different from the stories or depictions themselves"—the meaning lay behind the text, not in the text.[16]

The current focus on the final form of biblical narrative, and especially of the Pentateuch, is shared by representatives of diverse methodological perspectives: New Critics, structuralists, rhetorical critics, and canonical critics, as well as many for whom there is no particular label.[17] Using the terms of modern, secular literary criticism, these scholars frequently speak of their work as primarily synchronic rather than diachronic—i.e., emphasizing the text as a whole rather than its individual components. If we think of the text as the heart-shaped box with which we began this chapter, these scholars want to admire its smooth surface shape rather than its jagged piecemeal structure; if we think of the text as a body, synchronic scholars would rather admire its external anatomy rather than dissect it. Similarly, there is an increasing tendency among such scholars to look at

---

14. For Americans, this would be like the span between 1490 and 1990! The current trend among numerous scholars is to date J much later, perhaps as late at the exile. See Dozeman and Schmid, *A Farewell to the Yahwist?*—and note the significance of the title. The contrast with a *post*exilic time would be even stronger if, as some scholars believe, the concern is to show that Israel can occupy their land *without* a monarchy. But the Davidic–Solomonic dating continues to have its supporters, e.g., Fisher, *Genesis: A Royal Epic*, 6–9; Hiebert, *Landscape*, 144–45 (yet again, the latter two scholars differ in how they understand a figure like Abraham—one as a king, the other as a farmer!).

15. *The Eclipse of Biblical Narrative*, 9 (italics added). In other words, the stories are reduced to *how* they were composed rather than the final *product*. Frei's critique, however, should not prevent our acknowledging the process (see below).

16. Ibid., 11.

17. See the survey of critical methods in Barton, *Reading the Old Testament*. We can adopt in general Hendel's judicious description of the patriarchal stories in Genesis: "a composite of historical memory, traditional folklore, cultural self-definition, and narrative brilliance" (*Remembering Abraham*, 46).

the text as a story rather than as history. Instead of looking for historical referents, we are encouraged to look for metaphorical language, literary themes, and overarching structures. Instead of looking through the text as a window to the historical world, we are invited to look at the text as the representation of its own world. Just as we can talk about the world of Homer or Dickens or Faulkner (who even provided a map for his readers), we can also talk about the "story-shaped" world presented by Scripture.[18]

The preceding paragraph is misleading if it suggests that we are confronted with an either/or situation: either read the text as a composite document reflecting actual historical events and authorial situations, or read it as a seamless narrative that renders a completely fictive world. While the emphasis in many recent studies (and in this one) is clearly on the latter way of reading, this does not mean that we can ignore the significance of the former. To do so would be both foolish and dishonest. The Pentateuch is at once a composite document and a unified narrative. To read it as only one or the other would be to distort its character as a text. The depth dimension of the text is the result of a process of fervent reinterpretation of Israel's traditions in order to meet the theological needs of successive generations. If these voices are completely stifled, we fail to recognize the character of the text as Scripture as well as story. As Gunther Plaut says at the outset of a massive commentary on the Pentateuch, "what is important is to both understand its background and at the same time treat

the book as an integral unit."[19] In short, the documentary sources "tell very different stories," but the compiler's work of composition has produced "a single story."[20] Our task is to attend to both.

Readers may rightly ask of biblical scholars, what difference does it make if the text is not by a single author, written at one time from one place, but a mix of numerous sources? The answer is compound:

- the text is a composite of various voices—polyphonic, not monophonic;

- full understanding of the text, therefore, involves acknowledging the

19. *Torah*, xxiii. Thus Dozeman (*God at War*, 181), who devotes his whole book to distinguishing between preexilic, Deuteronomistic, and Priestly traditions and texts, yet concludes that their very combination in the Pentateuch suggests a hermeneutic: "The goal cannot be to isolate an original voice or any one subsequent voice at the expense of others." Rather, "the aim of any interpreter will always be to strive for the broadest inclusion of canonized traditions." Similarly, in his previous book (*God on the Mountain*, 173), Dozeman concludes that the final redactors (the priestly authors), deliberately "created ambiguity which forces the reader to acknowledge conflicting interpretations in the canonical text," including earlier voices with which they differ. Schmid ("Literary Gap," 49), whose views are similar to Dozeman's, insists that "divergent concepts" like the competing versions of land settlement (peaceful and ecumenical versus militant and exclusivist) "cannot be fully grasped theologically if one regards them *from the beginning* as part of the same logical literary order," that being, by and large, Genesis and Exodus (italics added). Nevertheless, a synchronic reading may *in the end* attend to the "logical literary order" presented by the canonical text.

20. Baden, *Composition*, 247–48. He emphasizes, however, that we should not ascribe any intent to the composition other than the production of a chronologically consistent story. See the next note.

18. See Wicker, *Story-Shaped World*.

process that produced it;[21]

- hearing the polyphony acknowledges the integrity of the various voices who allowed *other* voices to speak, even when they disagreed with each other (the redactors were not ruthless censors);

- the voices may speak from different communities or "parties," reflecting different self-interests (e.g., clergy versus lay, royal versus tribal, agricultural versus urban);

- polyphony points to multiple views of truth, not one absolute view;

- the result may be to hold varying and even contradicting views in tension, rather than harmonizing them or opting arbitrarily for one of the other.[22]

To illustrate the last point theologically, in Genesis alone we encounter portrayals of God as a transcendent, cosmic architect (Genesis 1); as a potter kneeling in the mud (Genesis 2); as a sweaty championship wrestler (Genesis 32); as a discrete, hidden providence (Genesis 37–45); and even as a terrifying tyrant who demands child sacrifice (Genesis 22)! Rather than being dismayed by such variety, readers will do well to consider the richness of the plurality as an encouragement to *think* theologically about what God is like to them (and *not* like!).[23]

Like many other recent studies of the Pentateuch and biblical narrative in general, this book stems from a revived interest in the nature of narrative itself and especially the paramount role that narrative plays in religious discourse. Although most of us have from childhood an intuitive grasp of what a story is, even a cursory survey of recent critical studies concerning the nature of narrative reveals a bewildering complex of interpretive problems.[24] Not only are the various forms of narrative often difficult to distinguish (epic, parable, saga, myth, legend, history, and so forth), but the ways in which they render a meaning

21. Baden (ibid., 228) in fact argues that "the theological intentionality [of the compiler] is not to be found in the text of the compiled Pentateuch, but rather in the very act of compilation itself . . . The competing voices preserved in the Pentateuch are, in fact, complementary, even as they disagree. Only when they are read together is the picture complete." Such an integral reading of the "single story" (see above) protects Baden's view from the full weight of Frei's criticism. See the next note also.

22. Brueggemann (*Theology of the Old Testament*, 317), using the language of the courtroom, grounds his method in the "disputatious propensity of Israel," in which "the process of cross-examination seems to go on in the Old Testament text itself." Thus over against Israel's "core testimony" there is "countertestimony."

23. Jack Miles's popular book, *God: A Biography*, is an exercise in imaginatively transforming the "observed inconsistencies" or "multiplicity" of God, including what is revealed by historical scholarship, "into God's experienced inner conflict" (21). As a result, the voices of different authors seem to collapse into a singular narrative voice. One picture of God ("in one word who God is") is as a warrior (106; cf. 154–57 on the book of Joshua). To see how differently a biblical scholar can handle such a topic, see Hawk ("Truth about Conquest," especially 134–37). In the often appalling stories of Israel's conquest of Canaan in the book of Joshua, he discerns "narratives and counter-narratives." For an imaginative fictional illustration of how an author could combine contradictory versions of a story, see Heym, *King David Report*, e.g., ch. 5 on the two introductions of David to Saul in 1 Samuel.

24 Scholes and Kellogg, *Nature of Narrative*; Crites, "Narrative Quality of Experience"; Stroup, *Promise of Narrative Theology*.

are also frequently intertwined. The complexity in determining the meaning of narratives (and all other genres of texts) is compounded when we consider the role of the reader or interpreter, and what he or she brings *to* the text that affects the significance *of* the text. Simply to use the inclusive expression *he or she* already illustrates the point: feminist readings of texts may well yield different meanings from exclusively male readings, and the same is true of sociologically distinct communities.[25]

As if unraveling the nature of narrative itself were not complex enough, the problems are compounded when we speak of the pentateuchal narrative, primarily because, as we have seen, the text is not the product of a single author but of numerous authors over a very long period of time. When we refer to the pentateuchal narrative in the following chapters, therefore, we shall mean the text as we have it now before us, but which we also recognize to be the product of a long history of traditions and editorial activity. While our emphasis will fall on the literary integrity of the present text, we shall also at times refer to the traditional authors (e.g., J and P) or at least consider those places where different literary sources appear to be joined together. Our

major purpose, however, will be twofold: 1) to delineate the internal literary (i.e., redactional) cohesiveness of larger units (e.g., Gen 1:1—11:9, or the Jacob cycle, or Numbers 1—10); and 2) to delineate the narrative integrity of the Pentateuch as a whole, i.e., how the larger units constitute what we today call books, and how the sequence of these books makes sense.[26]

The integrity of the pentateuchal narrative, however, derives not only from the form of story but also from literary types that are not inherently narrative, especially law. Law is an essential element in the plot of the Pentateuch, and without that element the story would be incomplete. Indeed, even the discrimination between story and law, however appropriate in terms of distinguishing literary forms, can suggest that narrative texts only recite, whereas legal texts only command. To deny an imperative force to story, however, is to ignore the motivational nature of biblical narrative, that is, its "rhetoric of command."[27] Similarly, to limit the meaning of law to its imperative force and its content is to ignore that its meaning and authority are partly dependent on its narrative context. The word *torah* in its widest sense means "guidance," "instruction," or "discipline,"

---

25. Thus, African Americans may well read a text (e.g., the law of the slave, Exod 21:2–11) in a radically different way from those whose heritage does not include slavery (or, more so, whose heritage includes slave-*owning*!). For an introduction to such reader-oriented interpretation, see Silva, "Contemporary Theories of Biblical Interpretation," especially 116–22, and note the various communities represented in the essays between pages 150 and 187. In the same volume, see Holladay, "Contemporary Methods," especially 143–45.

26. The term *biblia*, from which we get the word *Bible*, refers to books in the plural; but the use of the term *book* itself is misleading, for the Hebrew word *sefer* originally referred to a scroll that was rolled out (as is still the case with the Torah scroll in contemporary synagogues). Thus one could not look at a scroll and see separate books the way one could look at a collection of contemporary volumes side by side on one's bookshelf.

27. The phrase is Frye's, *Great Code*, 211; cf. 216. On the general relation between law and story see Sanders, *Torah and Canon*, 1–4

and only in its most narrow sense "law." The Torah is the definitive guidebook of ancient Israel, and it guides in the form of both narrative and law so that the two become inseparable and indispensable. We shall therefore devote considerable attention to Leviticus, Numbers, and Deuteronomy. These books are often neglected or even ignored as part of the Pentateuch, due to a truncated concept of narrative that implicitly relegates law to an inferior status.[28]

Our observation that the biblical authors are better understood as editors may have led to the unfortunate conclusion that these nameless literati were not artists at all but merely pedantic technicians who spliced texts together with little or no imagination. This is far from the case. Not only do the biblical authors display considerable artistry in the composition of individual stories, but even in the larger redactional process they display impressive literary and theological sensitivity. The scope of the present study will not allow us to do a close reading of every passage. It is important, therefore, that the reader have at the outset a grasp of the artistry of biblical narrative to aid his or her reading of the biblical text.[29]

In an introduction to an anthology of biblical literature, the novelist Reynolds Price described his youthful fascination with the biblical characters as portrayed in the pictures of *Hurlbut's Story of the Bible*. In those pictures he found himself confronted not with your average "Sunday-school confections" but with "credible ancient orientals, hairy and aromatic."[30] Because the biblical authors persistently refuse to moralize, their characters are adamantly earthy creatures. Far from being cardboard stereotypes of moral virtue—or vice—they are "credible" men and women of great and ultimately impenetrable complexity. As Alter has put it,

> We are compelled to get at character and motive . . . through a process of inference from fragmentary data, often with crucial pieces of narrative exposition strategically withheld, and this leads to multiple or sometimes even wavering perspectives on the characters. There is, in other words, an abiding mystery in character as the biblical writers conceive it, which they embody in their typical methods of presentation.[31]

Whereas in our retelling of the biblical stories (especially for children) we tend to convert the characters into types of good and bad, the text itself refuses to make such neat distinctions. Even Pharaoh of Exodus, who comes as close as one can to being an outright villain in the Pentateuch, remains in the end a character of intricate and inscrutable

---

28. For a recent study that emphasizes the centrality of law, see Watts, *Reading Law* (45): "The story alone may inspire, but to no explicit end. The list [law] alone specifies the desired actions or beliefs, but may not inspire them." The combination of narrative and law will become especially prominent in the covenant traditions of Exodus and Deuteronomy.

29. Still one of the best short introductions to Hebrew narrative art is Auerbach's classic discussion of Genesis 22 in *Mimesis* ("Odysseus' Scar," 3–23). For a full-scale development of Auerbach's approach see Alter, *Art of Biblical Narrative*. Alter refers to the overall redactor as

"the biblical Arranger" in *Five Books*, 167.

30. Price, *A Palpable God*, 11.

31. Alter, *Art of Biblical Narrative*, 126.

motivations. In short, it is precisely the mystery of biblical characters that makes them so realistic.

This abiding mystery of human characterization is a result not simply of a sophisticated literary aesthetic, or even a probing anthropology, but also of the "monotheistic revolution" in ancient Israelite thought.[32] Even when God is not directly involved in a particular story, the way in which the story represents reality is profoundly theological. The reticence of the biblical authors that produces a pervasive ambiguity in their human characters extends even to the divine. This ambiguity in turn results from the authors' perception that the world of human experience is a mixture of what Flannery O'Connor called "mystery and manners," by which she meant the way in which the divine will works in and through the most ordinary (indeed, for her, "grotesque") human motivations

and aspirations.[33] The world of the pentateuchal narrative is a world of constant tension between the divine will and human will: the biblical characters are free to act on their own, yet they are subject to the sovereign designs of God.[34] As Auerbach has put it, "The sublime influence of God here reaches so deeply into the everyday that the two realms of the sublime and the everyday"—O'Connor's mystery and manners—"are not only actually unseparated but basically inseparable."[35] The biblical characters "are bearers of the divine will, and yet they are fallible, subject to misfortune and humiliation—and in the midst of misfortune and in their humiliation their acts and words reveal the transcendent majesty of God."[36]

32. Ibid., 154.

33. O'Connor, *Mystery and Manners*, 103, 153, 202–3.

34. Cf. Alter, *Art of Biblical Narrative*, 33.

35 *Mimesis*, 22–23.

36. Ibid., 18.

ONE

Genesis

The Book of Generations

THE PRIMEVAL CYCLE (1:1—11:26)

Introduction

GENESIS 1–11 IS COMPOSED of individual stories that, at least in their original form, we must understand critically as myths. Unfortunately, people often use the word *myth* to refer to something that is not true, usually in opposition to facts. But here the old proverb applies: never let facts get in the way of a good story. Myths are good stories that contain profound truths, albeit fictional. Myths are not about what once happened in history but what always happens in human experience. One might compare another familiar literary form from the Bible—the parable. No one would say that Nathan's parable that traps King David in his crime is factual, but it is certainly a true analogy for David's behavior (2 Sam 12:1–6); no one would argue that

the Good Samaritan is a real person, but the story tells us something essential for how we understand our relationship to others (Luke 10:25–37). Just so, the myths in Genesis 1–11 tell us about the reality of the world both ancient and modern. These stories do not have historical persons or events as referents but describe the origin of aspects of the world that are timeless, e.g., the dominance of humankind as a species, the distress of work, the hostility between siblings, the ambivalence of urban culture, and the multiplicity of languages. In short, these stories are etiological.[1]

---

1. Of course, the truth of the stories goes beyond such etiologies (including why snakes do not have legs, 3:14) to explore the origins of alienation between humans, between humans and nature, and between humans and God. Other literary types can be etiological as well, and there are many in the Hebrew Bible (e.g., the founding of the place Bethel, Gen 28:10–22, on which see Appendix 1).

Moreover, for a long time scholars have recognized that many of these stories are not unique, but are related to earlier traditions recorded in ancient Near Eastern literature: in the story of Adapa, one man's offense brings ill to humankind, as does Adam's; in the story of Atra-Hasis, a tremendous flood covers the earth, though one man is saved through the help of one of the gods—a story obviously very similar to the flood story in Genesis; traditions concerning characters before the flood resemble the genealogy in Genesis 5. There are also connections between the account of creation in Genesis 1 and the Mesopotamian story of creation called *Enuma elish* ("When on high"), and between the garden of Eden story and the Mesopotamian Epic of Gilgamesh, and his futile search for immortality.[2]

Despite the similarities to these ancient Mesopotamian texts, we can show that the biblical versions of these stories are significantly different, not only individually, but also and especially when each story is read in the context of the series that runs to the end of Genesis 11, on into the rest of Genesis, and beyond. A collection of such stories within one text of such magnitude is unknown elsewhere in the ancient Near East. Thus, the story at the opening of ch. 6 about the sexual union between the "sons of God" and human women has a blatant mythological background, but its original purpose (to explain the existence of giants on the earth) has dramatically changed to introduce the flood story. The context of the story gives it a moral and theological significance far greater than what the story itself could bear.

The linking of originally independent stories into a progressive series means that a fundamental change has taken place. Each story is not simply an incident that occurred in primordial timelessness, and the meaning of each story is no longer limited to a description of the way we are. The meaning of the individual stories is now significantly augmented in that the stories have become the prologue to the rest of the Pentateuch. Although we still cannot say that these myths have converted into history, we can say that they are transformed into a kind of history-like narrative. In other words, they are no longer self-contained short stories; they are now the opening chapters of a historical novel (so to speak), and as such they provide the dominant themes that will guide our reading of that novel.

There are two ways in which the individual stories are tied together. First, they share a number of themes and motifs, the repetition and transformation of which constitute a major dimension of the plot of the extended narrative. As we shall soon see, the most important and overarching themes are introduced in Genesis 1.

Second, the individual stories are connected by the familial sequence imposed on them, that is, by a genealogical structure. Thus from Adam and Eve we move to their sons, Cain and Abel, after which the extensive genealogy in ch. 5 brings us down to Noah, the chief

2. For a brief survey of this literature, see Parker, "Ancient Near Eastern Literary Background of the Old Testament." All these texts are found in Pritchard, *Ancient Near Eastern Texts* (*ANET*). For overviews of each of the books of the Pentateuch in relation to ancient Near Eastern literature, see the essays by William W. Hallo in Plaut, *Torah*.

character in the flood narrative. Subsequent genealogies bring us to Abraham and thus connect Genesis 1–11 with chs. 12–50. Without some such connection between the characters, there would be no continuing narrative at all, only a juxtaposition of self-contained stories, each with its own internal plot, a plot with no bearing on the story that follows. We can, of course, imagine such a collection of isolated stories (contemporary collections of short stories offer a rough analogy) and can even imagine how such a collection could have thematic unity, providing a picture of the primeval world, a world that contained alienation, murder, violence, and ethnic diversity. But such a world would have no story; it would simply be the sum of incidents only accidentally related to each other, and perhaps not related at all.

The genealogical structure of the pentateuchal narrative, on the other hand, portrays a "story-shaped world,"[3] a world shaped by the causal relationships between characters who represent successive generations of a single family line. Consequences resulting from the actions of both divine and human characters determine the development of a plot extending beyond the limits of each individual story. Thus the story of Cain and Abel is not simply an illustration of the animosity between siblings, or even of religious hatred; it is also an illustration of how the alienation between God and humankind, and within the human community—introduced by Cain's parents—has spread to the second generation.

The genealogical connections between the characters not only provide the foundation on which the pentateuchal narrative is constructed, but also mark the points of major transitions in the narrative. Thus ch. 5, which lists the generations from Adam to Noah, marks the transition from the antediluvian world to the flood story; ch. 10 marks the transition from the flood story to the international political picture portrayed by the tower of Babel story (11:1–9); and 11:10–26 follows one line of the family of Noah down to Abraham, marking the transition to the ancestral stories. Moreover, a member of the Priestly school adapted a genealogical formula ("these are the generations of X") and used it to mark divisions throughout the narrative, not only for Genesis 1–11, but also for chs. 12–50.[4]

Careful examination of the function of this formula in each context reveals two purposes. When the formula is followed primarily by genealogical material, it serves to conclude a preceding narrative segment (5:1; 10:1; 11:10; 25:12; 36:1, 9), whereas when it is followed primarily by narrative material it serves as an introduction to that story (2:4; 6:9; 11:27; 25:19; 37:2). In fact, in several of the latter cases, the word rendered as "generations" is best translated "story" (2:4; 25:19; 37:2). Although the formula is not employed with exacting consistency, it seems that the pentateuchal narrative of Genesis is divided into at least five, and perhaps six, parts: a prologue (1:1—2:3), the story of heaven and earth (2:4—11:26, perhaps the story of Noah is a separate part beginning at 6:9), the line of Terah

---

3. The phrase is that of Wicker, *Story-Shaped World*.

4. See 2:4; 5:1; 6:9; 10:1; 11:10, 27; 25:12, 19; 36:1, 9; 37:2.

(11:27—25:18), the line of Isaac (25:19—36:43), and the line of Jacob (37:1—end).[5] Thus I have provided Genesis as a whole with the descriptive title "The Book of Generations," taken from 5:1.

It should be clear by now that the traditional separation of Genesis 1–11 from chs. 12–50 is at best imprecise, for the redactors signal a transition not at 12:1 (the call of Abraham) but at 11:27.[6] Moreover, in neither 11:27 nor 12:1 do the redactors indicate a major break in the narrative that warrants a division of Genesis into two independent units. The redactors have marked off 11:27—25:18 (the story of Abraham and Sarah) only as part 3 (or 4); they have not marked off chs. 12–50 as part 2.[7] This observation has theological implications. However important the call of Abraham may be (12:1–3), it does not represent a radical disjunction within the pentateuchal narrative. Yahweh has spoken before to humankind and will speak again. Human beings have responded to Yahweh before (sometimes with integrity, usually not), and this too will happen again. In short, the call to Abraham is simply one more step in Yahweh's attempt to come to terms with the created world. The biblical redactors did not choose to present us with two separate collections of stories—one in which the problem is raised, and another in which the problem is answered. In truly realistic narrative, things can never be that neat and tidy. If we approach the text from such a simplistic

perspective, we shall fail to appreciate the rich complexity of the pentateuchal narrative, in which the problems of human existence before God and the possibilities for some solutions to those problems are always fraught with ambiguity and uncertainty. With perplexing frequency, a new step in the right direction will be followed by two steps in retreat; Abraham was not the first, and certainly not the last, to be a master at both the one-step and the two-step routines.[8]

As we turn to a contextual analysis of the primeval cycle, a schematic outline of the material will help to focus our discussion (see Table 1.1, below).

1. "In the beginning" (Genesis 1:1—2:4a)

To the reader unfamiliar with the scholarly study of the Bible, the intricate debates that we have sketched in the preceding pages may seem pedantic, if not even silly. It is easy to ridicule theories of composition that propose a list of literary sources such as J, E, D, and P, not to mention Jg, Pg, Ps, DtrH, DH, KD, and KP. Nevertheless, scholarly debates are honest attempts to wrestle with the ambiguity that becomes apparent upon even the most cursory investigation, and

---

5 This is essentially the division followed by Plaut, *Torah*, ix–xi.

6. Cf. Clines, *Theme of the Pentateuch*, 76–78.

7. The traditional chapter divisions are late (i.e., Christian) additions to the text.

8. Carr (*Fractures*, 240–41) argues that the non-Priestly primeval history reaches a resolution in which God has come to terms with human rebellion, and civilization has emerged, and chs. 12–50 therefore do not represent an answer to any problem raised in 1–11. He does not see any development originally of "the crucial theme of divine mercy and provision for broader humanity" continuing in 12–50. However, he comes back to the view that, in the canonical text, one *can* see in 12:3 "God's answer to" the cosmic problems raised in 1–11 (323).

Table 1: The Primeval Cycle			
1:1—2:3	**2:4—4:26**	**5**	**6:1—9:19**
Creation	Family failure	Descendants of Adam	World failure—chaos
			New Beginning
			Covenant
	9:20–27	**10**	**11:1–9**
	Family failure	Descendants of Noah	World failure
			11:20–26
			Descendants of Shem

the first three words of the Bible provide a remarkable example (Gen 1:1a, to be exact). Readers of the NRSV will see no less than three possible translations: (1) "In the beginning when God created"; (2) "when God began to create"; and (3) "In the beginning God created" (see note a to the text; the JPS lists the latter two as well). What difference does it make? It makes all the difference in the world, and rather literally—that is, cosmologically. Translation number 3 is perhaps most familiar, but it presents a problem: why would God create "a formless void" (v. 2)? An alternate for this phrase itself—"formless and desolate" (GNT)—helps illustrate the problem. Why would God create something that is "desolate"? Actually, the Hebrew phrase seems to refer to chaos, so, again, why would God make chaos? But if we adopt possibility number 2, then the chaos or "formless void" or desolation was already there when God *began* to create, and that seems to contradict what most people probably think, namely, that "in the beginning" there was nothing (the traditional Latin

expression accordingly is *creatio ex nihilo*, "creation out of nothing"). In short, the alternatives (3) and (2) suggest that when God created the world, either God made a mess of things, or a mess was already there, and neither of these alternatives seems altogether attractive. As for translation number 1, it is simply a compromise between the other two, which solves nothing.

The ambiguity of the opening phrase derives from the Hebrew vowel markings that, in fact, combine two grammatically incompatible words. Translation 1 actually reflects this incompatibility, even though it is not apparent to readers unfamiliar with Hebrew. It is as if the ancient rabbis who provided the vowel markings for the consonantal text[9] could not decide on *how* to begin the Bible, and thus

9. Originally Hebrew texts were composed of consonants only, and the vowel markings were added later. Thus the consonants (e.g., *dbr*) could have different related meanings (a verb meaning "he spoke," or a noun meaning "word"), or entirely different meanings (another verb meaning to "turn away").

encapsulated their ambivalence in the first two words.

Given parallels with other ancient Near Eastern creation texts (such as *Enuma elish*), possibility 2 is the most likely original. If that is the case, then the biblical author was not interested in what we call creation out of nothing *philosophically*. Rather, the text seems to be more concerned to show that, in creating the world, God is bringing *order* to a pre-existent chaos. There is, in fact, a mess already there, and what God does is to make the mess into something meaningful. The mess essentially is water—"water, water, everywhere," to recall a famous expression (from *The Rime of the Ancient Mariner*). In some ancient creation stories (both biblical and extrabiblical), water is identified with a chaos *monster*, but here, at most, that tradition is only hinted.[10] God creates the world by *separating* water and making a space with water above and below, something like a cosmic bowl with a lid, upside down (on day 2, v. 6). Now there is sky and ocean. But the rest of the water does not go away; after God creates the earth ("dry land") under the dome, the water remains above the earth and below it (vv. 9–10), presumably extending infinitely, although the author does not engage in such astrophysical questions. The cosmology is radically different from our understanding of the cosmos, but only in what constitutes the space, not in its bizarre appearance. In place of water, modern physics postulates an eternally expanding universe—indeed, the possibility of a *multiverse*, i.e., many universes. Add this to black holes, string theory,

and dark energy, and you have a picture equally baffling as the notion that the universe is full of water.[11] (We will see the *return* of these waters in the flood Story.)

But before everything else there is light to illuminate the darkness. The world and the Torah begin with a command. The first words reported of God are an executive order, hurled into the unfathomable darkness of that watery chaos: "And God said, 'Let there be light.'" The world and the Torah also begin with a response to the command totally in conformance to God's will: "and there was light." The terseness of the initial command/execution sequence (only four words in Hebrew)—"be light, light was"—is without parallel in the following verses, but the message is the same throughout. "God said . . . , and it was so." The Priestly author here introduces us to a view of God and the world and *how* the world ought to be. Everything fits and works the way it ought to because everything follows what God says. All of this the text expresses, again with dignified brevity, in v. 31: "And God saw everything that God had made, and indeed, it was very beautiful" (AT).[12]

10. Ps 74:12–15; 77:16–8; 89:9–10; 93:3–4; 97:1–5; Isa 27:1; 51:9–11.

11. See, for example, Greene, *Elegant Universe*. For an intriguing study of the "virtual parallels" between modern science and the biblical understanding of creation (one that is not "creationist"), see Brown, *Seven Pillars*, especially chs. 3 and 4.

12. The Hebrew word can mean "good" but also "beautiful." The Priestly view of the sublimity of the universe here would fit well with the view of contemporary physics. As Greene puts it, "The elegance of rich, complex, and diverse phenomena emerging from a simple set of universal laws is at least part of what physicists mean when they invoke the term 'beautiful'" (*Elegant Universe*, 169).

> "Nature works, Raphael learned, because it has order, and from order, it has beauty." "In time he understood that nature was not something outside the human world. The reverse is true. Nature is the real world, and humanity exists on islands within it."[13]

The orderliness and harmony of the world are evident not only in the process by which creation takes place, but also in its structural design. The parallelism of the days of creation provides the literary structure of Genesis 1. Thus the origin of light on the first day parallels the appearance of the heavenly lights on the fourth; the separation of the cosmic waters on the second day (forming sea and sky) parallels the creation of sea and air creatures on the fifth; and the formation of earth and vegetation on the third day mirrors the origin of animals and humanity on the sixth. Finally, the Sabbath day (not explicitly mentioned by name) constitutes the capstone of the created order. The orderly structure of the author's work reflects the orderly design of the cosmos (see Table 2, below): every part of the world appears before us in perfect balance and symmetry, majestic and wondrous.

Order is thus the main theme of the Priestly author's account of creation. This emphasis on harmony with the will and commands of God extends far beyond Genesis 1, forming a nucleus of themes and motifs that continue throughout the pentateuchal narrative and into the rest of the Hebrew Bible. From beginning to end, the Pentateuch will be preoccupied with a world in which order derives from responsibility to the divine will, and disorder from irresponsibility. Our observations about Genesis 1, therefore, not only delineate local literary features but also a fundamental theological presumption that governs the rest of the Torah. As Robert Alter writes,

> All this reflects, of course, not only simply a bundle of stylistic predilections but a particular vision of God, man, and the world. Coherence is the keynote of creation . . . Law, manifested in the symmetrical dividings that are the process of creation and in the divine speech

---

Table 2: The Orderly Design of the Cosmos

Day 1 Light	Day 4 Lights (Sun, moon, stars)
Day 2 Sky/Oceans	Day 5 Sky and sea creatures
Day 3 Earth	Day 6 Earth creatures
Day 7 Rest (Sabbath)	

---

13. Wilson, *Anthill*, 122, 140.

that initiates each stage of creation,
is the underlying characteristic of
the world as God makes it.[14]

The correspondence between creation and divine will is not coercive, however, but cooperative. Thus literally when God says, "Let the earth grass grass" (v. 11), then the earth "grasses grass"—the earth does "what comes naturally" and participates in the creation process.

Alongside the harmony resulting from responsibility to the divine will, Genesis 1 announces a second theme that will preoccupy the pentateuchal narrative: the role of human beings in relationship to the earth they inhabit. The distinction of humankind is expressed by the divine soliloquy in Gen 1:26: "Then God said, 'Let us make humankind in our image, after our likeness; and let them have dominion over the fish of the sea, and over the birds of the air, and over the cattle, and over all the earth, and over every creeping thing that creeps upon the earth.'" Human beings reflect something of the divine nature. That the image is both "male and female" (v. 27) suggests that God's being includes both as well. As Niditch says, "For feminist readers of scriptures, no more interesting and telegraphic comment exists on the nature of being human and on the nature of God."[15] But the main aspect reflected here is God's sovereignty. Humanity is, as it were, the vice-regent of God on earth, the little lord of the universe. Of course, this in no way questions the ultimate sovereignty of God. The very fact that human beings are creatures—i.e., created by God—enforces their utter dependence. Nevertheless,

next to God (and perhaps the angels) humankind enjoys the status of the highest link in what medieval philosophy called the chain of being (cf. already Psalm 8). Humankind's power and control over the earth is unquestioned and—it would seem—limitless (but see below).

Like the theme of order and responsibility, the theme of humankind's relationship to the earth is not limited to Genesis 1. The cosmic perspective of this chapter will pervade the primeval cycle, where the interest is in the whole planet, just as the anthropological focus is on human beings in general. Yet, by the time we reach the end of the cycle, we will have seen a steady narrowing of the focus, so that "earth" (Hebrew 'eres) points more and more to particular lands, just as the characters will increasingly represent not Everyman and Everywoman (as Adam and Eve do), but particular nations and ethnic groups. Beginning with Genesis 12, the primary interest will be the promised land, the land of Canaan. Nevertheless, it would be a grave mistake to conclude that what happens on the earth of the primeval cycle is only background for what will happen in the land of Canaan, for the pentateuchal narrative makes the radical claim that what will take place in the land over the Jordan will be of crucial significance for all of the lands beyond the Jordan.

Finally, Genesis 1 introduces a third theme and associated motifs that will continue throughout the pentateuchal narrative. Following the report of the creation of humankind in vv. 26–27, God pronounces a blessing that, in part, repeats the declaration of humankind's dominion over all other creatures. In

14. *Art of Biblical Narrative*, 143–44.

15. Niditch, "Genesis," 16a.

addition, God pronounces the following words: "Be fertile and increase, and fill the earth and subdue it" (cf. v. 22). For the ancient world, the basic meaning of blessing had to do with fertility—fertility of crops and herds, as well as human fertility. In the middle of winter an ancient Israelite could not go to the local supermarket and buy canned tomatoes, not to mention fresh tomatoes. The failure of a fall crop could mean starvation. Infertility, therefore, could be virtually synonymous with death, and was consequently associated with the antonym of blessing, curse. By extension, blessing also connoted material security, health, and peace: adequate shelter and food, the absence of disease, freedom from violence and war. The meaning of blessing is irreducibly concrete, even materialistic, stubbornly refusing to be converted into a purely spiritual category. For this reason the pentateuchal narrative will often point with ingenuous delight to the great possessions of its characters—numerous children, large herds of sheep and cattle, ample gold and silver; for these things are seen not so much as the rewards of hard work as the gifts of a beneficent (if also inscrutable) God. Blessing is a mark of divine grace.

Genesis 1:28 informs us that blessing does not exclude human work; indeed it clearly requires some human effort. The pronouncement of blessing is phrased in the imperative mood: be fertile, increase, fill, subdue, rule. Here is one of the most peculiar and interesting features of the blessing. On the one hand, by blessing humankind God empowers them to fulfill the content of the pronouncement of blessing. On the other hand,

the pronouncement of blessing itself is couched as a command, implying that human beings are to a significant degree responsible for effecting the blessing. The divine blessing, in other words, is a kind of charge, in two senses of the word. In the first sense, the blessing charges the recipient with a special kind of energy or force; in the second sense, the blessing charges the recipient with a task and a responsibility. Both senses must be kept in mind, for to exclude one or the other would be to distort the meaning of blessing. To exclude the first sense would be to make blessing a merely human achievement; to exclude the second sense would be to make blessing a magic power, a type of *mana*.

Given the two senses of blessing as charge, the theme of blessing clearly overlaps with the themes of order and responsibility we have discussed above. Blessing is rooted in the creative power of God and, at the same time, is expressed as a command. This overlap is only one among many, as we shall see throughout our analysis of the Pentateuch. The various themes and motifs that we shall trace are not rigid categories easily separated from each other, much less independent of each other. It is precisely the inextricable intertwining of these themes that makes the pentateuchal narrative so fascinating.

In the contemporary world, plagued with ecological disasters like climate change, the language in this first account of creation, describing human "dominion" over the earth easily becomes part of the problem.[16] As the "image of God,"

16. See the issue of the journal *Interpretation* 65/4 (October 2011) on the topic of *Creation*

humans seem to be totally elevated above all other creatures—indeed, above nature itself. Their charge to "subdue the earth" sounds like a warrant to exploit natural resources without regard for ecological consequences, such as the pollution of air, soil, and water. But in other ancient cultures, "image of God" described the unique way human *kings* (and occasionally queens) represented the divine. Here *all* humans represent God in a unique way, so their rule should mirror the way God has created the world, that is, with infinite concern for harmony, cooperation, and beauty.[17] The divine *economy*—literally, "household rule"—supersedes human economy, even as the human economy is often understood as though development and making money were the sole criteria.[18] Similarly, subduing the earth may mean nothing more hostile than the activities necessary for agriculture—clearing land, plowing, and irrigation.[19] Moreover, the second story of

creation and its aftermath in 2:4b—3:24 will provide a perspective that is even more earth friendly, as we shall see.

The Pentateuch is one people's understanding of its corporate identity, wrought from the struggle to comprehend its relationship to the rest of the world, to grasp the meaning of divine blessing and curse, and to come to terms with the agony of human failure. The themes announced or at least intimated "in the beginning"—divine command and human responsibility, people and land, blessing and curse—continue to the end, where Israel stands "beyond the Jordan," listening to the last words of Moses, which are also the words of God: "If you obey the commandments of Yahweh your God . . . then you shall live and increase, and Yahweh your God will bless you in the land which you are entering to take possession of it" (30:16, AT).[20]

2. East of Eden (2:4b—3:24)

With the Priestly author's majestic exordium behind us, we can turn to the Yahwistic narrative of creation in Gen 2:4b—3:24. Julius Wellhausen once drew a graphic distinction between the literary style in Genesis 1 and Genesis 2–3.

Groaning for essays and references to numerous other resources on this topic.

17. Brown, *Seven Pillars*, 39–42, suggests that the structure of Genesis 1 (see above) not only reflects the order of the world but also mimics the spatial architecture of the typical ancient temple, and that humans represent the statue of the divinity that would have been in such temples; but humans "are not conquerors of creation" (47), rather we are called to imitate God's "care-filled stewardship" (77).

18. Wendell Berry in particular has developed this contrast, see *Art of the Commonplace*, especially 219–354: "Two Economies."

19. Otherwise the word most often refers to military conquest. That even animals can subdue nature is evident to anyone who has seen a beaver dam! Some Native Americans were appalled at Europeans who tilled the soil, thereby tearing open the skin of Mother Earth. But some contemporary Native Americans build golf courses in the Southwestern desert in a desperate attempt

---

to promote "economic development."

20. My use of the term *theme* is different from that of tradition critics such as von Rad and Noth (e.g., Noth, *History of Pentateuchal Traditions*, ch. 7; von Rad, *Genesis*, 13–27). On the other hand, I obviously do not agree with Clines (*Theme of the Pentateuch*, 20) when he insists that there can be only one theme to a work. For him, that theme is the partial fulfillment of the promise to Abraham. Since that promise is a triad of posterity, divine-human relationship, and land, we are in close agreement despite our theoretical differences.

When we move from the one to the other, he said, we cannot help but notice "the fresh early smell of earth [that] meets us on the breeze."[21] By this he meant that the second account of creation is a much more earthy story than that of the Priestly author in Genesis 1. Wellhausen's observation was perceptive, because earthiness plays a central role in Genesis 2–3. Whereas ch. 1 is interested in the earth (ʾereṣ) as "planet," as well as in the sea and sky, chs. 2–3 focus only on earth (ʾadamah) as "ground" or "soil." In fact, the relationship between humanity and the "ground" dominates 2:4b—4:16, and the term ʾereṣ does not reappear until near the end of this unit. In 2:7 the author moves immediately to the creation of "the human," Hebrew ha-ʾadam.[22] Unlike the majestic sovereign of Genesis 1, here the LORD God (Yahweh Elohim) is pictured as a farmer and potter who forms the human out of the ground and blows into him the breath of life. The intimate relationship between the human and the ground is even more obvious in Hebrew, for the author uses the word ʾadamah as a counterpart to ʾadam; compare Latin *humus* and *humanus*, or English "earth" and "earthling." The ʾadamah is arable soil suitable for agriculture. But the garden is not a vegetable patch, as it were, because so far there are no field crops or herbs, or even rain (v. 5); the garden is an orchard consisting of fruit trees (v. 9), watered by a stream from underground (v. 6), and the human's calling is to "tend" it (v. 15).[23] To

eat—a key word throughout—all the human has to do is pick fruit off the trees.[24]

Just as medieval theology proudly placed human beings immediately below the angels in a chain of being (see above), so much religious anthropology has understood human beings as apart from nature rather than a part *of* nature. In particular, humans supposedly have souls, and animals do not. Indeed, this is also one way to understand the prior expression "image of God."[25] Yet the description of God's creative work as a potter and the animation of the clay statue suggest a more subtle relationship between humans and other life. Just as God "formed the man from the dust of the ground" (2:7), so God makes to grow "every tree" in the garden of Eden "out of the ground" (2:9), and when it comes time to make a partner for the man, God's first attempt is to form "out of the ground . . . every animal of the field and every bird of the air" (2:19). In short, in this account, all earthly life comes "out of the ground." What we distinguish as animal, vegetable, and mineral, in this anthropology are all intimately and inextricably related. Human beings are "mud kin" with all other earth creatures (*fauna*), and with the trees of the orchard (*flora*).[26] And just

---

reverence and care (again, over against exploitation and abuse).

24. Note that the word for "eat" occurs five times in 3:17–19 alone; humans are vegetarians until the change in 9:3

25. An example of an alternative understanding of "image of God" would be McFague's expression: "We are the self-conscious aspect" of the cosmos (*Body of God*, 124).

26. I have addressed this relationship more fully in *God of Dirt*, especially 11–12. See Hiebert, *Yahwist's Landscape*, 62–68.

21. *Prolegomena*, 304.

22. The *name* Adam does not clearly appear until 4:25.

23. The Hebrew for "work" can be translated "serve," which would add the connotation of

as humans in their bodies are kinfolk with other creatures and with the trees, all these creatures also share the same divine breath. The commonality is implied in the description of the human becoming a "living being" and the animals each becoming "a living being" (2:7, 19, AT).[27] Other texts are more explicit: all creatures have the "breath of life" (Gen 6:17; 7:15, 22); all are "created" by God's "breath" (Ps 104:29–30; cf. Eccl 3:19).[28] Not only is there no dichotomy between body and soul in humans; there is also no clear ontological distinction between humans and animals, for all their obvious differences. With our scientific knowledge of photosynthesis, we could go a step further and say that the very breath that we breathe in is also the breath that plants breathe out.[29] Thus we are not only "mud kin" with *flora* but also *spiritual* kin as well. This profound anthropology of relationship is the basis for all biblically based ecology, and another reason to reject any misreading of Genesis 1 that would allow for ecological abuse.

After the man and the woman have tasted of the tree of knowledge, the relationship between the man and the ground is radically distorted. We learn of this in 3:17–19:

> And to Adam Yahweh Elohim said,
> "Because you have listened to the voice
>   of your wife, and have eaten of
>   the tree
> of which I commanded you,
>   'You shall not eat of it,'
> cursed is the ground ('adamah)
>   because of you;
>   in distress you shall eat of it all
>   the days of your life;
> thorns and thistles it shall
>   bring forth to you;
>   and you shall eat the plants
>   of the field.
> In the sweat of your face
>   you shall eat bread
> Until you return to the ground
>   ('adamah),
>   for out of it you were taken;
> you are dust,
>   and to dust you shall return."
>   (AT)

27. This commonality is obscured by the NRSV translation of v. 19, where the Hebrew phrase (*nepeš hayyah*) is the same (except singular rather than plural). Cf. Milgrom on Lev 17:11 (where "life/lives" is the root *nepeš*): "Both animals and people have a *nefeš*, 'soul'" (*Leviticus: A Book of Ritual*, 190).

28. In all these citations the Hebrew word is *ruah* (note the alterative translation in the NRSV footnote to Ps 104:30, the same word that is used in Gen 1:3, and see the translation alternatives there). Thus, unlike English, Hebrew can use the same word for "wind," "breath," and "spirit" (cf. Greek *pneuma*). In fact, "spirit" is an abstraction that is already rarified. On such abstractions, see Abram, *Becoming Animal*, 146–50, 272–73.

29. Margulis, "Talking on the Water," 72. For a poem on "soul" in nature, see Oliver, "Some Questions You Might Ask," in *New and Selected Poems*, 65.

> "It never seems to occur to [those who propose human dominion over nature] . . . that Nature's object in making animals and plants might possibly be first of all the happiness of each one of them, not the creation of all for the happiness of one. Why should man value himself as more than a small part of the one great unit of creation? And what creature of all that the Lord has taken the pains to make is not essential to the completeness of that unit—the cosmos? The universe would be incomplete without man; but it would also be incomplete without the smallest transmicroscopic creature that dwells beyond our conceitful eyes and knowledge.
>
> From the dust of the earth, from the common elementary fund, the Creator has made *Homo sapiens.* From the same material he has made every other creature, however noxious and insignificant to us. They are earth-born companions and our fellow mortals."[30]

the transition from fruit to bread represents the fundamental categories of raw and cooked, to which we may add intimacy with nature versus enmity toward it, and nudity versus clothing.

Despite the many ambiguities in this story, one thing at least is clear: alienation sets in when the man and woman break the commandment of God (3:1–7). As in ch. 1, the first words spoken by God to humankind are a command, in this case a prohibition: "of the tree of the knowledge of good and evil you shall not eat" (2:16–17).[32] Among the various motivations for breaking the command (see v. 6), the determinative one appears to be the possibility of becoming like God. But—the reader may quickly object—according to Genesis 1 humankind already *is* like

In other words, the man is alienated from the ground, and his work as orchard keeper now becomes that of subsistence farmer—agriculture—growing the very "plants of the field" that before had been unnecessary (2:5). Moreover, his work, which had been relatively effortless, now will be hard and distressful.[31] Culturally,

30. Muir, *Nature Writings*, 826.

31. The garden of Eden is an orchard oasis, including at least figs (3:7) and probably olives

and pomegranates. The subsistence agriculture typical of the Palestinian highlands and dependent on rainfall does not appear until 3:17–19. This is implied in Rosenberg's NRSV annotation to 3:17–19. See Hiebert, *Yahwist's Landscape*, 52–62, who suggests that the lush Jordan valley is in mind (13:10). Compare Meyers, *Discovering Eve*, 104; and Friedman, *Genesis*, 28 (on 4:11). Contrast Fretheim, *The Book of Genesis*, 364a. After all, the author does not say that God brings rain or field crops after noting their *absence* in the circumstantial clause of 2:5.

32. Thus there are three arboreal entities here: the fruit trees, the tree of life (not reappearing until 3:22), and the tree of knowledge. "Good and evil" is an umbrella expression rather than an exclusively moral one, something like "A to Z." Cf. Deut 1:39, where it refers to adult consciousness contrasted to childlike ingenuousness. Thus some interpreters have seen a "fortunate fall" here in the sense of maturation necessary for full adulthood, with the woman boldly leading the way. Note there is no reference in this story to an apple, or even to sin, much less the devil. For a dialectical reading of Genesis 2–3 in which there is only one tree with two sides (cf. breath/dust; male/female, etc.) see LaCocque, *Trial of Innocence*, 68–79.

God, created in God's image and likeness (v. 26). Why is this likeness affirmed in ch. 1 and then repudiated in chs. 2–3 (cf. especially 3:22–24)? One answer, of course, is that two literary sources are involved, but there is a deeper dimension as well.

The relationship between God and humankind is properly that between one who commands and one who obeys. The maintenance of this relationship—and of all its benefits symbolized by life in the garden—requires that human beings not step beyond the limits imposed on them by the command. Yet the man and woman are clearly free to do precisely that. They are not puppets manipulated by a divine puppeteer. To be human is to be capable of rebellion against God, yet to submit to the divine will. But the woman and the man, prompted by the serpent, do not want to be human in these terms; they want to be superhuman.[33] Thus the alienation we have already observed between the man and the ground reflects his willful repudiation of his natural being as a creature in an attempt to become like the creator. We shall see this attempt on the part of human beings to become like God again as we move through the primeval cycle.[34] Reaching a crescendo in the story of the tower of Babel (11:1–9), the attempt to step beyond the limits of human nature provides a framework for

"the story of heaven and earth" (2:4), and how the original goodness of the created order disintegrated into chaos.

We have penetrated into only three chapters of the primeval cycle, yet already an enormous shift has taken place. Despite the fact that Genesis 1 and 2–3 derive from different authors, in their present juxtaposition these chapters are united by a common concern for the central themes we have delineated. The pentateuchal narrative is certainly not J or P, nor is it even J and P, for the combination of these two units has created a new narrative that includes but also transcends both units. Theologically, God is "as close to us as breathing" (Genesis 2) but also "distant as the farthest star" (Genesis 1).[35] Anthropologically, human beings are the image of God (Genesis 1) but also made of clay (Genesis 2) and stubbornly rebellious.[36]

In ch. 1 the pattern of command/execution portrayed the perfect order of creation according to the divine will; in chs. 2–3 the irresponsibility of the serpent, woman, and man to the divine command propels the world into disorder and alienation. The way things *are* as described in 3:14–19 results from human denial of how they *ought* to be.[37]

---

33. Hence the ironic title of a book by Sallie McFague, *Super, Natural Christians*. Cf. LaCocque (*Trial of Innocence*, 21): "the desire for infinitude and self-divinity."

34. So also LaCocque (*Onslaught against Innocence*, 127): "There is indeed in J's [i.e. the Yahwist's] narratives on the primeval era a remarkable consistency, the leitmotif of becoming like God (see Gen 3:5)." Cf. also LaCoque, *Trial of Innocence*, 189.

35. These two phrases are part of a Eucharistic prayer in the United Church of Christ *Book of Worship*, 69.

36. Carr, *Fractures*, 318, emphasizes the tension: "these two narrative worlds are juxtaposed without being resolved into each other," reflecting the ambiguity of our own world.

37. Meyers (*Discovering Eve*, 118) joins others who argue that 3:14–18 originally was independent of the surrounding prose and thus the "prescriptions" were not "penalties" for wrongdoing but more descriptions of the way things are.

The dominion that humanity has been given over the earth and all its creatures is threatened and qualified. Humankind is alienated from the ground, the source of sustenance, and attempts to subdue it will be frustrated. Moreover, a permanent enmity has now arisen between one of the creatures (the accursed serpent) and humankind as a result of the woman's implicit denial of her role as co-vice-regent. Finally, a curse seems to overshadow the blessing because of the man. The marital relationship erodes when the man blames the woman (v. 12, and implicitly God!); harmony becomes hierarchy when the man *"dominates"* the woman (3:16b, AT). For her part, the woman's increased pregnancies will make her work as the farmer's wife all the more "distressed," just as his work in the field is "distressed" (3:16a).[38] In short, responsibility is replaced by in-fidelity; community (with God, in nature, within the family) is broken; blessing must compete with curse.

The position of humankind within the world is now fraught with uncertainty and anxiety. With the expulsion of the man and woman from the garden (3:23–24), that alienation deepens, and the pentateuchal narrative is thrown into suspense. Human beings are permanent exiles from the pristine space and time of Eden. There is no way back and the way ahead is uncertain. The plot of the pentateuchal narrative, to its very end, will be concerned with the attempt to find another way human beings can live with integrity before God, at home on the earth, and within the security of divine blessing. For much of Western culture, at least, this adventure sets in motion what will become the quintessential quest story.

38. Here I follow to some extent the interpretation of Meyers, *Discovering Eve*, especially 103–21. The major change from traditional readings is in 3:16a, which she translates "'I will greatly increase your toil and your pregnancies," where "toil" has nothing to do with childbirth but with the extensive household work of a farmer's wife. Instead of "toil," I use "distress" (cf. her p. 105) because it can refer to emotional strain due to physical exhaustion, and because "distress" fits with the use of the same word in 3:17 referring to the strain of the man's work, and again in 5:29 referring to *relief* from such strain for Noah. The root word also occurs again at the end of 3:16a (NRSV "pain") and at a key place in 6:6 to refer to God's "distress" (NRSV "grieved"), on which see below. Regarding 3:16b, Meyers argues that such domination was not systemic misogyny but necessary as a social sanction to insure that women bore enough children to maintain labor in farming. Otherwise, the marital relationship was largely "egalitarian" (p. 169; cf. 1:26–27; 2:18, "a helper as his *partner*," without whom the man is incomplete). Of course, traditionally this verse in particular has been used to condone the subordination of women, if not outright abuse.

3. Two Murderers (chs. 4–5)

The story of Cain and Abel in 4:1–16 is permeated with references to the ground. Cain is the firstborn of Adam and Eve, and, like his father, is a tiller of the ground. When Cain's offering from the ground is not accepted, he murders his herdsman brother Abel while in the fields (Cain's "home turf"). Yahweh learns of the murder because the ground has soaked up Abel's blood, which is crying from the ground. Cain's response to God's question actually blames God, who is often described as the "keeper" of Israel.[39] Alongside the theme of the ground, the author introduces the theme of the

39. Cf. Psalm 121, and compare Cain's father's words in 3:12. Thus illimitable sermons on being the "brother's keeper" are misinterpretations!

curse. Cain is cursed from the ground. This is a dramatic shift from Genesis 3, where the ground was cursed because of the man. Any attempt to till the ground at all will fail—the ground will not simply yield thorns and thistles as with Adam. Adam and Eve were banished from Eden, and from intimate communion with God; Cain is banished from the ground and hidden from God's presence (v. 14). Cain is forced to become a vagabond, a wanderer on the "earth" (Hebrew: 'eres).[40] LaCocque puts it vividly: "he is like a space capsule lost in the emptiness of the universe."[41]

The reason for Cain's punishment is obvious: he is the first fratricide. What is not so obvious is why God acknowledges Abel's sacrifice and not Cain's. It is unlikely that Abel's was more worthy; indeed, both are probably firstlings sacrifices intended to secure divine blessing on crops and herds.[42] God does not explain why the younger brother will, in effect, be blessed and the elder not (introducing an element of the blessing theme that we shall see many times in Genesis). The divine will is inscrutable, but nonetheless clear. Cain's task is to submit to the divine will rather than to the power of sin (v. 7). Emphasizing Cain's freedom and capacity to master sin ("you must rule over it"), the text affirms his responsibility as a hu-

man being. Yet Cain refuses to be human. He is not only the first fratricide, but the first who murders for *religious* reasons. The murder of his brother represents not only a failure to heed God's instruction, but also an attempt to wrest the control of blessing from God. In this sense, Cain's sin suggests a continuation of his parents' desire "to become like God."[43]

Thus the story of Cain and Abel presents an augmentation of the estrangement and disorder that began in ch. 3. The separation between humans and ground now goes so far that Cain is banished from the ground entirely; the irresponsibility that was evident in ch. 3 is now explicitly labeled as submission to sin with its resulting guilt (vv. 7, 13). Finally, the curse that in ch. 3 afflicted only the serpent and indirectly the ground now afflicts Cain. The theological alienation that began in ch. 3 and infected the relationship between husband and wife is now compounded by the radical alienation between brothers. Sociologically, the hostility between them is not so much the archetype of farmer versus herdsman, for both occupations were combined within the typical highland household. Rather, sibling rivalry, common to virtually every family, here is compounded by the custom of primogeniture—the older being the one to inherit the father's land (cf. Deut 21:15–17). But God's favoring the younger's sacrifice threatens to upset the sibling order, and Cain responds to the threat with violence.[44] Such rivalry

40. As White points out, the place-name Nod comes from the root word for "wandering." Thus Cain is banished to "the cursed, metaphorical 'land of wandering,' a permanently liminal state of existence" (*Narration and Discourse*, 168).

41. LaCocque, *Onslaught against Innocence*, 31.

42. See Westermann, *Genesis 1–11*, 295. On the combination of both agriculture and animal husbandry in the same household, see below.

43. It is also possible to read Eve's comment at the birth and naming of Cain ("I have created a man with the help of Yahweh," 4:1, AT) as continuing her former act of imitation in 3:5.

44. Hiebert, *Yahwist's Landscape*, 38–41, 75–76; Hopkins, "Life in Ancient Palestine,"

between older and younger brothers will be central to the story of Jacob and his family (chs. 25–50).

It is significant that the curse on Cain did not follow as a result of God's rejection of his sacrifice. Instead, the curse was a result of Cain's negative response to the blessing of another. This situation foreshadows what will become a major issue in the rest of the pentateuchal narrative, beginning with Genesis 12: the attitude of those who stand initially outside the blessing will determine, in part, whether they themselves will eventually participate in that blessing or not. Moreover, explicit references to divine blessing are far more frequent than references to cursing, and in the latter the authors appear to avoid active formulations with Yahweh as subject. For example, Yahweh blesses Adam and Eve directly (1:28), but seems more to state the result of Cain's own behavior when announcing his curse (4:11; cf. 3:14, 17). It is as if Yahweh is always willing to bless, but some people bring on themselves a curse.

Although Cain is exiled and must leave God's presence, God spares his life and does not leave him helpless. Since Cain now has no kinfolk to protect him, God provides him with a protective mark, accompanied by a law: "If anyone murders Cain, it will be avenged sevenfold" (v. 15).[45] The commandment

regarding vengeance plays a key role in the brief and rather enigmatic passage that follows (4:17–24). In its present context this passage traces the family line of Cain through six generations,[46] and describes the growth of civilization—the first city, cattle herdsmen, musicians, and smiths. The context suggests ambivalence to culture, but with its positive side: sandwiched in between Cain's violence and that to follow in vv. 23–24 there is the sound of the "lyre and pipe," perhaps suggesting a redeeming aspect of civilization, "a powerful rhythm within life that works for good."[47] But the focus of this unit falls on Lamech and the link drawn with his great-grandfather several times removed, by means of the reference to Cain being avenged sevenfold (v. 24). Lamech's poetic recitation reveals a bombastic bully rippling his muscles before his wives and bragging about the youth he has killed simply for striking him. For all his heroic posturing, however, what Lamech really represents is an increase in unrestrained violence and an extension of revenge "seventy-sevenfold." Lamech supplants God's law with his own, and thus stands in the line of his ancestors, who also wanted to be "like God," providing a kind of climax to the literary unit 2:4—4:26. The movement in the narrative is described succinctly by von Rad: "First the Fall, then fratricide, and now the ex-

---

220–21; cf. Cotter, *Genesis*, 43: "it is brother-ness itself that is at play here." See also LaCocque, *Onslaught against Innocence*, 59–61.

45. See Westermann, *Genesis 1–11*, 295. The mythic dimension of the story appears in the unanswerable question of who is present in the world at this point other than his parents? (and the related question, where does Cain find his wife, 4:17?)!

46. For the parallels to the Sethite genealogy in ch. 5 (P), see Plaut, *Torah*, 54. Note that J refers to the Sethite line in abbreviated form in 4:25–26.

47. Fretheim, *The Book of Genesis*, 377. For a probing analysis of the ambiguity of urban culture, see LaCocque, *Onslaught against Innocence*, 122–30: "a nest of brigands and a haven for the lonely" (126).

ecution of vengeance (which God has reserved for himself!) is claimed by man."[48] And yet, the invocation of Yahweh frames the entire unit (vv. 1 and 26).

Whatever function the genealogy in ch. 5 may have served originally,[49] its juxtaposition with the preceding material is itself dramatic. The lineage of humankind that ran from Adam through Cain and down to Lamech saw a number of cultural advancements, but ended with a figure of reckless irresponsibility and homicidal violence. In contrast, the Sethite line of Adam represents a new beginning, already anticipated by J in 4:25–26.[50] The effect of 5:1–5 in light of the preceding chapters is to reiterate the positive themes announced in ch. 1: the creation of humankind in the image of God and the blessing placed on man and woman. In addition, the corollary motif of fertility is dramatically affirmed by the ensuing list of generations—the man and woman indeed have been fertile and increased! The redactional position of this chapter thus serves an intriguing theological function in the ongoing narrative. Despite the radical disorder that has grown since ch. 2, the author reminds us of the unique position of humankind within the world, thereby injecting a note of hope. The author implies that, despite human failure, humankind's original status "in the image of God" is transmitted to successive generations, for Adam's son is

born "in his own likeness, after his image" (cf. 1:26–27). A similar note of hope also sounds near the close of the chapter when the Yahwist looks ahead to Noah (*noah*) who will be the agent of a new beginning after the ravages of the flood (5:29): "This one will bring us comfort [root *naham*] from our labor and from the *distress* of our handiwork with the *ground* that Yahweh has *cursed*" (AT).[51] Also, since the Sethite line begins with Enosh ("humankind") and ends with the only family to survive the flood, ch. 5 moves in effect from one "new Adam" to another. Such a transition is highly appropriate since the flood story (6:1—9:19) marks the central turning point of the primeval cycle.

4. The Flood Story (chs. 6–9)

The flood story is a combination of the two sources J and P, each having a different literary and theological agenda. The Yahwistic version focuses on the motifs of the human heart and the cursed ground, whereas the Priestly stratum focuses on the role of blessing and covenant in the context of a movement from creation to chaos to re-creation. Their fusion has resulted in a narrative of increased depth and richness.

Preceding the flood story we have the mythological tale in which the sons of God married, and thus had sexual intercourse with, human women. Retrospectively, this tale now represents the most serious—indeed,

---

48 *Genesis*, 108.

49. A list of antediluvian figures leading up to the protagonist of the flood story is also known from Mesopotamian sources (e.g., the "Sumerian King List"). See Speiser, *Genesis*, 41–42; and Plaut, *Torah*, 54.

50. The name Enosh (given to the son of Seth) is a synonym for Adam ("humankind").

51. The name Noah attempts a pun with the word for "comfort." Note the allusion to the key italicized words in 3:17. The resolution to this hope comes in 9:20, but, as we shall see, it is immediately compromised.

metaphysical—possibility of human beings becoming "like God," only "from
the top down," as it were. Instead, God
decrees a further limitation on human
longevity (cf. 3:22). In addition, by juxta-
posing this tale with the beginning of the
flood story, the redactor has directed its
etiological function away from the origin
of giants (the Nephilim) toward the motivation for the coming divine judgment.

The prologue to the flood story
(6:5–8) is linked to the preceding tale
by catchwords eliciting familiar themes.
Humanity has indeed "begun to increase
(*rabab*) on the face of the ground" (v. 1),
yet this is accompanied by divine-human
"mixed marriage" and corresponding increase (*rabab*) of human wickedness on
the earth (v. 5). Thus Yahweh decides to
wipe humanity *off* the face of the ground
(v. 7). In describing Yahweh's decision,
the author suggests that the evil of the
human heart has inflicted "distress" in the
heart of God, thereby drawing a connection to the Eden story (AT, cf. above on
3:16–17). Such an authorial observation
of the inner thoughts and feelings of God
is as bold as it is poignant. Only rarely
do biblical writers allow themselves such
freedom.[52] Here the depiction renders a
character of both pathos and indignation—indeed, a God who is vulnerable to
human unrighteousness, who can be hurt
by human sin. Consequently, we cannot
construe the flood as the heartless and
brutal act of an uncaring deity. Here there
is a tragic element even in the inner life
of God, for in order to restore creation to

its original goodness, God must all but
destroy it.[53]

The next passage (vv. 9–22) begins
with the Priestly author's slant on the
"wickedness" of v. 5, and an apparent answer to the question, why does God vow
to destroy not only those wicked humans
but all land creatures? (In telling the story
to children, narrators normally do not
raise this troublesome question.) The
answer is in 6:11: "Now the earth had destroyed itself in God's sight, and the earth
was filled with violence. And God saw
that the earth had destroyed itself, that all
flesh had destroyed its way on the earth"
(AT). Here "all flesh" has gone astray.
What could this mean? Most likely, the
Priestly author understands not only humans but also all land creatures originally
to be vegetarian, for explicitly God has
only given them plants to eat (1:29–30).
This diet will change after the flood, certainly for humans and presumably for
animals (see below on 9:2–5). But the
animals have already reverted to being
carnivores (however natural that seems
to us), and their killing of each other is
part of the "violence" that fills the earth
(6:11). As a result, God vows to destroy
"all flesh . . . along with the earth."[54]

On the other hand, God again re-
lents, not only regarding humans, but

---

52. Usually thoughts are rendered by speech
(e.g., 6:7; 1:26; 8:21; 11:6). See Alter, *Art of Biblical Narrative*, ch. 4.

53. This inner turmoil is one result of the
monotheistic perspective, for in the Mesopotamian flood stories different gods decide to inflict
the flood on humans and to save them from it.

54. See Gardner, "Ecojustice," 118–22. The
vegetarian Paradise reappears in the eschato-
logical prophecy of Isaiah (11:6–9). Note that
sea creatures, of course, will survive the flood
(whether or not they are vegetarians!). The Yahwist narrative, in contrast, already assumes the
killing of animals by humans (4:4, 20; 8:20) and
even, apparently, by God—3:21!

also all land animals; as the human species will be saved, so will all others. While the previous passage ends with Yahweh "taking a personal liking" to Noah (6:8), in this passage Yahweh promises to establish his *covenant* with Noah (v. 18). A covenant—or better, "treaty"—is a formal agreement or contract between two parties. The resolution of the flood story will entail both a movement within the heart of God and the completion of a diplomatic process initiated by Yahweh's pledge. In fact, by the artful arrangement of the J and P sources, the redactor probably intends us to see one movement taking place, rather than two separate occurrences. The granting of a unilateral peace treaty by God is rooted in the divine heartache over creation. Nevertheless, the anticipations of divine mercy in 6:5–22 do not prevent the judgment that follows. The waters that God had separated from the earth in creation God now unleashes, drowning all land animals and returning the entire earth to watery chaos (cf. 6:17; 1:7). Solitary and silent, the ark floats on the surface of the dark deep, bearing the remnants of all animal life (7:18; cf. 1:2). A wooden box without sails, oars, or a rudder, it is utterly dependent on God's protection.[55]

The turning point in the story comes when God "remembers" Noah and all the animals with him in the ark (8:1; cf. Exod 2:24). The movement from creation to chaos is now reversed, and a re-creation takes place: the drying up of the waters, the landing of the ark, and ultimately the restoration of peace among God, humankind, and the world. It is quite a

New Year's Day celebration (8:13)! God's remembering is the manifestation of God's character as one who is faithful to a promise—in this case, the pledge of the covenant previously made to Noah.

Cleansed by the flood, the earth now appears pristine, as it did "in the beginning," and Noah emerges from the ark as a new Adam. Just as the flood story has revealed new depths to the character of Yahweh, so it renders an equally complex character in Noah. On the one hand, God seems to befriend Noah completely out of grace, unrelated to any merit (6:8); on the other, Noah is described as a "righteous man" (*ṣaddiq*), the only one in his violent generation who lives with "integrity" (6:9). At this point in the story, the differences could be explained by recourse to J and P, but the story as a whole is more subtle.

To say that Noah is righteous is to say that he lives responsibly, in accordance with the divine will, and it is worth remembering that he is the first character we have met in the primeval cycle of whom this is said. Noah is the first character who *has* character. His righteousness is rendered by the way the story is told. Since Hebrew narrative usually prefers dialogue to develop character and plot, it is striking that Noah never utters a word throughout the entire story. The narration consists only in the speech of God and the words of the narrator. Of Noah, we are only told that he "did all that God commanded him" (6:22; 7:5, 9, 16). In a wider context, Noah is the only character so far in the primeval cycle who remains completely speechless, and it is not coincidental that he is the only character so far who listens to what God says.

---

55. Friedman, *Genesis*, 39, pointing out that the ark is really a box, not a boat.

If God's selection of Noah is initially unconditional, it is also true that Noah rises to the occasion. His first act upon leaving the ark is to offer a sacrifice of reverent gratitude. At the same time, as an expiatory sacrifice it represents the first and only expressed desire within the primeval cycle for reconciliation with God.[56] In fact, Noah's gesture is the immediate motivation for resolution within the heart of God, for it is in response to the sacrifice that God resolves "in his heart, 'I will not again curse the ground because of humankind . . . nor destroy every living creature'" (8:21, AT). The promise is not to lift the curse of 3:17, only that there will be no *additional* curses like it,[57] which is to say universally against the whole earth because of all humans, nor will God destroy all creatures. The coinci-

dence of human righteousness and divine grace has diminished the alienation that began in Eden—but only in part, for, as God adds, "the inclination of the human heart is evil from youth" (8:21; cf. 6:5). God has changed, even though human beings remain the same! As Fretheim puts it, "God thus decides to take suffering into God's own self and bear it there for the sake of the future of the world."[58] Accordingly, God now confirms the seasonal regularity of nature that makes agriculture possible (v. 22).

In a sense, the flood has been a failure in that it has not eradicated the "evil inclination" that was its cause. The epilogue (9:1–17) reflects a similar resignation. The opening section is framed by the repetition of the blessing at creation—"be fertile and increase" (vv. 1 and 7). Here, for the first time, the blessing includes specific laws governing humanity's dominion over the animals, which will live in "fear and dread" of humans who are now allowed to eat them (v. 3; cf. again 1:29), and yet God prohibits the animals from dining on humans! Anyone—animal or human—who sheds human blood will be guilty of homicide (v. 5).[59] Law necessarily accompanies blessing in the "new creation" because of the human tendency toward evil, a problem amply demonstrated by the homicidal Cain and Lamech.[60] Corresponding to law as the

56. On this sacrifice, see Milgrom, "Sacrifices," 769.

57. There is some tension between 8:21 and 3:17 in that the latter at least originally seems to describe the status quo of agriculture (different words for "curse" are involved as well). The suggestion of some "relief" from the curse in 5:29 further complicates the picture (see on Noah, below). One might wonder if the relief means the end of "thorns and thistles," but that is unlikely. Hard toil remains, nonetheless. Hiebert (*Yahwist's Landscape*, 45–48) notes that the verb in 8:21 can mean "not again" or "not continue to." He refers to "alleviation of the dreadful toil of subsistence farming," or moderation, or relief, then goes so far as to say that Noah's integrity has "moved God to *terminate* the curse on arable land" (47, italics added; cf. 68–70). But this seems to go too far, as if we are back in the garden of Eden. Moreover, in the larger context of the Pentateuch, the possibility of divine curse on the *agricultural land of Israel* will become very real in the framework of the Sinai covenant. Note especially Deut 28:16–24, where God will curse "the fruit of your ground ['*adamah*]," and send drought such that the rain turns to dust (and contrast Gen 8:22!).

58. Fretheim, *The Book of Genesis*, 396.

59. Even humans are not allowed to eat animal meat with the blood in it (e.g., steak tartare), out of respect for the life of the animal (there is more detail on such dietary laws in Leviticus). For homicide by an animal, cf. Exod 21:28. The supposedly new permission to eat meat seems to ignore Abel's apparent diet (4:4).

60. On the role of law here, see von Rad,

	Table 3: The Primeval Cycle		
Family Failure	Genealogy	World Failure	New Beginning
chs. 2–4	ch. 5	6:6–13	9:1–17
9:20–27 (Noah)	ch. 10	11:1–9 (Babel)	

concrete form for human responsibility under the blessing, Yahweh now fulfils the pledge of a peace treaty with Noah and all living creatures. It is a unilateral, "everlasting treaty" (v. 16), advertised, as it were, in the "sign" of the rainbow. At the end of the rain, God's weapon hangs in the sky to show that it will never again be used for cosmic destruction. Although animals are now prey for humans, "every living creature" is a beneficiary of God's Noachic covenant of protection. Indeed, the covenant is with the earth in its entirety (note that "*every* living creature" and "*all* flesh" occur nine times in vv. 8–17). Along with the garden of Eden, the rainbow sign is the root of a biblical ecology.[61]

"Noah and the geological record tell us that sea level can change, and relatively quickly. The fastest way is through the melting of ice. And melting ice is precisely what is going on right now." "Sea level rise becomes the single greatest natural danger threatening civilization as we know it."[62]

The plot of the Pentateuch will be marked by a succession of covenants between God and human beings—first with Noah and all creatures, then with Abraham and Sarah (chs. 15 and 17), and finally with Israel (Exodus 19–24), demonstrating again that the story of Israel is part of a larger world story (see Appendix 3).

The world now stands at the threshold of a new beginning, yet the text has recognized an aspect of the human will that is resistant to a life of integrity before God. The realism of that pessimistic note will soon be confirmed. Rather than a fresh start on the new way of blessing that God has opened, we see a reversion to the old way that leads to a curse. In fact the rest of the Primeval Cycle suggests

Genesis, 129, and Westermann, *Genesis 1–11*, 64–65.

61. Thus protection of all species is part of this covenant—indeed, even ritually impure creatures were brought into the ark (e.g., 7:2, "unclean"). Again, there is more on such natural distinctions in Leviticus.

62. Ward, *Flooded Earth*, 22, 30, citing a recent scientific study that associates ancient flood stories with cataclysmic inundation of the Eastern Mediterranean due to prehistoric global warming ("the Holocene thermal maximum").

a cyclical repetition of what happened in between creation and the renewal of blessing. We can see this correspondence most clearly in an outline (See Table 3, above).

5. From Noah to Babel (9:20—11:9)

Despite numerous problems of interpretation raised by 9:20–27, the contextual significance of this story about Noah the vineyard owner is fairly clear. On the one hand, Noah presumably brings some "relief" from the burdensome curse on agriculture (3:17; 5:29) by planting a vineyard, apparently because, like the orchard of Eden, it requires less work. On the other hand, Noah seems to have taken too much comfort in wine, for he is also the first recorded drunk, leading to a scandalous if puzzling incident of sexual impropriety by his son, Ham.[63] As a result, Noah places a curse on Ham's *son*, Canaan, while Noah's other two sons receive a blessing. Why a curse is pronounced on Canaan goes unexplained, as unfair as it is, but it will certainly not be the last time children will suffer for the wrongs of parents (see below).[64] While Noah commits no grave offense, his drunkenness hardly befits his role as the potential new Adam. When we add this story to those in ch. 3 and 4:1–16, we thus have a complete disruption of the family (again, the basic structure of human community): between husband and wife, between siblings, and now between parents and children (and, for that matter, grandchildren).[65]

At the same time, however, this story introduces a change in characterization. From here on, individual characters in Genesis often will represent political entities as well as family members (e.g., Canaan and the Canaanites), and the themes we shall be tracing will rarely, if ever, occur without some political connotation—and polemical presentation. Thus the theme of humanity and the earth shifts to political or ethnic groups and territorial lands—and the theme of blessing and curse shifts with it.[66] Already in our present story about Canaan it is at least implied that the political subjection of a particular people within its own land is a result of a curse pronounced on its founding father as a punishment for moral turpitude. The Canaanites will come to embody all that is alien, "pagan," and immoral to Israel's ancestors—the quintessential Other.[67] No doubt Canaan-

---

63. Most likely Ham commits some kind of incestuous sexual offense with (or against) his father (cf. Lev 18:6–7).

64. The problem appears in the Ten Commandments, Exod 20:5; cf. Exod 34:7; Deut 24:16; Ezekiel 18.

65 See Westermann, *Genesis 1–11*, 66–67. Along with other scholars, Westermann sees here an originally independent story of a Noah different from that of the flood story. Such familial blessings and curses were considered to be ineradicable, becoming a major problem in the story of Jacob and Esau (ch. 27).

66. Hiebert, *Yahwist's Landscape*, 48.

67. Note again, as one example, Lev 18:2, 24–30, in which the illicit act of Ham is identified as commonplace among Canaanites. European settlers in the Americas similarly saw Native Americans as savages, even though both peoples were quite capable of savagery. A comparable etiology of incestuous sexual origins for the Moabites and Ammonites will appear in the Sodom and Gomorrah story (cf. 19:30–38). Alter (*Five Books*, 620) rightly refers to "a widespread reflex of projecting uncontrolled sexuality onto the cultural other," including "blacks in America."

ites would describe their origins quite differently, had they a chance to speak!

> "In explanation of the chasm between white and black, some Evangelicals turned to their dog-eared Bible to elaborate upon earlier scriptural defenses of slaveholding. They based the blacks' inferiority upon the will of God which . . . was revealed . . . in the curse of the drunken Noah upon the descendants of his son, Ham (Africans), because of an invasion of the patriarch's privacy."[68]

The political configurations introduced by the story of the curse on Canaan are also reflected in the "Table of Nations" in ch. 10. This material, of course, picks up where the genealogy of ch. 5 left off, now tracing Noah's offspring to the line of Shem, which will later produce Abraham. Although many of these names remain obscure, it is clear that they represent geopolitical entities: Egypt, Canaan, Assyria, Aram, and so forth. By giving us these names, and by specifying geographical borders (e.g., vv. 5a, 10–11, 19, 30), the text presents us with a verbal map of the ancient world, categorized by the repeated refrain, "These are the descendants of *X* by their families, their languages, their lands, and their nations" (v. 31; cf. vv. 5b, 20). Overall, Genesis could be seen as an extended genealogy, or an ethnic etiology, explaining the origins of virtually all the peoples of the world, but especially those in the geographical

proximity to Canaan (Palestine).[69] As the summary notice in v. 32 puts it, this is the way "the nations spread abroad on the earth after the flood" (cf. already 9:19). In the context of the pentateuchal narrative, therefore, the table of nations represents a fulfillment of the renewed blessing on humankind—they have been fertile, increased, and filled the earth. However, ch. 10 must be seen not only as a fulfillment of what precedes, but also as an anticipation of what follows—the story of the tower of Babel. Chapter 10 tells us that human beings spread over the earth; 11:1–9 tells us why.

The story of the tower of Babel will make little sense unless we first understand what is wrong about the actions of the builders. On the surface there would seem to be nothing wrong in building a city or a skyscraper. Surely such a massive project would grow out of and continue to nourish a desirable sense of community. Yahweh's frustration of the building project thus appears whimsical and even childish, a result of divine jealousy and resentment at what human beings are capable of doing on their own.[70]

It is not surprising, therefore, that differing interpretations abound. Nevertheless, there are several factors suggesting that the fault lies in an attempt to become independent of God. The context of the story leads us to expect such an attempt, for most of the other protagonists

68. Mathews, *Religion in the Old South*, 171.

69. As Hendel notes, "One's place in the genealogy is a sign of cultural self-definition more than it is a sign of biological descent" (*Remembering Abraham*, 10).

70. For a probing analysis of how the characterization of Yahweh in the wider context of the Pentateuch rules out such an interpretation, see Wicker, *Story-Shaped World*, 88–91.

in some way or other have attempted to achieve superhuman status (Adam and Eve, Cain, Lamech, and the divine-human marriage partners). What they all have in common is the desire for *autonomy*—literally "self-law"—which is, in effect, a desire to be like God. In the Babel story, this desire for self-government occurs for the first time on a corporate, political level, for the subject of this story is not an individual or even a family, but a city-state.

What the builders of the skyscraper want, and why they want it, is described most clearly in v. 4. They want a city and a tower "with its top (literally "head") in the heavens." They want to construct, on their own initiative and authorization, "a physical link between the divine and human realms."[71] The city-state will have a transcendent dimension, but only as a facade. Thus the tower represents an attempt to escape the limitations of the human condition. At the same time, by constructing the skyscraper the people express a need to "make a name for ourselves." In other words, the tower signifies a sense of communal identity founded exclusively on human will and effort.

The clearest expression of the purpose of the tower occurs at the end of v. 4: "lest we be scattered abroad upon the face of the whole earth." The word "scatter" occurs three times within the nine verses of the story (vv. 4, 8, 9), each time with "over the face of the whole earth." The emphasis on this motif suggests that the primary motivation for building the tower is not outright rebellion against God (who is never mentioned in the speech), nor an assault against heaven, nor even arrogance. The real reason for the project is fear. The builders are insecure.

But whence this fear of being scattered? Within the confines of the Babel story, it appears inexplicable and irrational, a manifestation of group paranoia. The people perceive a threat when none is there, yet their insecurity leads to precisely the situation they had hoped to prevent—scattering. The significance of this chain of events is heightened by the connotation of the word "scatter," which elsewhere most frequently refers to banishment or exile of a people from its land.[72]

Still, we cannot fully appreciate the significance of this story apart from its context. The geopolitical and linguistic diversity of the world that seemed quite natural in ch. 10 now appears to be the result of human failure and divine punishment—or perhaps divine coercion. For we must now ask, what is it that human beings have failed to do? The answer can only be that they have failed to populate the whole earth in conformance to the divine will (1:28; 9:1). To be sure, the story of Babel makes no explicit reference to the divine command to "fill the earth," but the juxtaposition with ch. 10 and the various expressions for filling the earth there, and the way in which ch. 10 itself follows upon the renewed charge to Noah (9:1), point to such a connection.[73] Un-

---

71. Sarna, *Understanding Genesis*, 11. My interpretation is also in basic agreement with that of Fokkelman (*Narrative Art*, 14–17). Cf. also LaCocque (*Onslaught against Innocence*, 144), who refers to "the megalomaniac builders of the Tower of Arrogance" (cf. also 134–35).

72. With few exceptions (including 10:18). See Ezek 11:17; 20:41–42; 28:25; 29:13; 34:12–13.

73. So also Sarna, *Understanding Genesis*, 67 and 72; Fokkelman, *Narrative Art*, 18 n. 12; and

satisfied with the earth as the field of their dominion, human beings refuse to "know their place," and aspire to something higher.[74] To them, filling the earth meant being "scattered." Rather than spread out, they would build up.[75]

> "THEN Yertle the Turtle was perched up so high,
>   He could see forty miles from his throne in the sky! . . .
>   I'm Yertle the Turtle!
> Oh, Marvelous Me!
>   For I am the ruler of all that I see!"[76]

Finally, our understanding of the Babel story is enhanced in light of the cultural world of ancient Mesopotamia to which the story itself refers. A popular urban structure in that region was the ziggurat, a step-tower that served as a worship and civic center. In fact, the Babylonian creation epic, *Enuma elish*, to which we have referred before, concludes with the construction of a "stage-tower" of cosmic proportions, with the god Marduk enthroned at its top.[77] It is quite possible that the primeval cycle, which begins with creation and ends with the construction of the tower of Babel, is in part a polemic directed against Babylon's temple. *Babylon* signifies babble; the "Gate of the gods" is gibberish. An exilic audience *living* in Babylonian captivity no doubt would have relished the irony.

6. The New Way (11:10—12:3)

The narrative of the primeval cycle takes us from human beings as the "image of God" to human beings as alienated from God, from humankind's dominion over the earth to its "scattering" over the earth, from the garden of Eden and the communal unity of the family to the fragmentation of the nations, from blessing to curse.

The pessimism with which the primeval cycle ends is all the more striking when we observe that up to this point there were signs that Yahweh's gracious care for all creatures would override the growing disorder: clothing for Adam and Eve, a protective mark for Cain, and for Noah, the rainbow in the sky.[78] After the tower of Babel, however, there is no immediate sign of Yahweh's grace. The genealogical material in 11:10–30 opens "section 6," the ancestral saga, which brings us down to Abram and Sarai (whose names are later changed to Abraham and Sarah). Yet even this section includes a depressing note: "Now Sarai was barren; she had no child." The creation and blessing of humankind in Genesis 1, with its accompanying motif of fertility, has come to sterility. At the close of

---

Kikawada and Quinn, *Before Abraham Was*, 69, 71, 81 n. 16. Note also the similarity between 10:6b and 3:22.

74. Cf. Fokkelman, *Narrative Art*, 17; and Miller, *Genesis 1–11*, 24. Cf. Isa 14:13–14.

75. Note that "spreading abroad" is part of the mission with which Israel's ancestors are charged in 28:14.

76. Dr. Seuss, *Yertle the Turtle*, no page number, spoken by Yertle shortly before his tower of turtles collapses into the mud.

77. See Speiser, "The Creation Epic," in *ANET*, 69a, line 62 of Tablet VI. For details on historical ziggurats and the monarchs who built

them, see Sarna, *Genesis*, 83.

78. Cf. most recently Kikawada and Quinn *Before Abraham Was*, 51–52.

the narrative (vv. 31–32) there is merely the added report that Abram's father has taken him away from southern Mesopotamia (Ur of the Chaldees), has migrated toward the land of Canaan (and the people cursed in 9:25), but has settled in the place called Haran,[79] in northwestern Mesopotamia. Abraham is on a journey with a goal (Canaan), but with no stated purpose. It is in this context—the context of a world without God—that God again speaks directly to one man, as he once spoke to Noah (12:1–3):

> Now Yahweh said to Abram, "Go from your land, and from your home, and from your paternal family, to the land that I shall show you, so that I may make of you a great nation, bless you, and make your name great. So be a blessing, so that I may bless those who bless you, and the one who belittles you I may curse, and by means of you all the families of the earth may be blessed." (AT)

While this passage represents a radical shift from the primeval cycle, it is also a bridge joining the primeval stories with the Abraham cycle that follows. In fact, unless we see how the story of Abram and Sarai is also a continuation of the primeval cycle, we shall fail to understand the full significance of their story as a new departure. In other words, while the speech to Abram produces a critical turn in the pentateuchal narrative, it is only a turn, not a new plot. The pivotal function of the speech is evident in its content, forged out of the thematic elements that

79. Though they are spelled the same in English, the place-name is different from the personal name Haran (11:31) in that the place-name begins with the hard *h*.

run throughout the primeval cycle: a journey from an old land to a new land, a movement from curse to blessing, and a new divine charge that both empowers and commands.

With Abram comes the promise of a new land, indeed, a new world (made explicit in 12:7). He will not find this land as a banished fugitive, wandering aimlessly (Cain), nor as a result of forced exile ("scattering"), nor even as a result of ordinary migration (ch. 10; 11:29–32). Rather, Yahweh will show him this land. From now on, one specific geographical space will be fraught with divine purpose. The tie between Abram and this particular land also implies the creation of a new community (v. 2). In contrast to the city-state named Babel, the community named Israel will be made by God and, at the same time, represent the continuing relation of all of humankind to God. This is the bedrock of the biblical understanding of election, but the promise is not solely about a new land (*'eres*); it is also once again about the whole earth (*'adamah*; cf. 26:4; 28:14). Although the focus from here out will be on the former (as Canaan), the latter appears here once again as the ultimate concern. In this sense the charge to Abram *continues* the theme of humankind and the earth from the primeval cycle.

Verse 2 of ch. 12 has already introduced our second theme, that of blessing and curse. The life of humankind in the world began with a divine blessing, a blessing repeated in 5:2 and 9:1, but by the end of the primeval cycle curse appears to predominate. At this point Abram is singled out as the object—and medium—of blessing: "So be a blessing, so that I may bless those who bless you, and the one who belittles you I may curse, and by means of you all the families of the earth (*'adamah*) may be blessed."[80] The end of this verse may be translated "will be blessed" or "shall bless themselves." We shall settle for a rather broad generalization: the blessing on Abram and his people involves other peoples as well. The blessing on Abram "also concerns those on the outside who adopt a definite attitude toward this blessing . . . man's judgment and salvation will be determined by the attitude he adopts toward this work that God intends to do in history."[81]

Will Abram, in fact, live so as to be a blessing? This is the central question that will hang over all of the Abraham cycle (chs. 12–24). The primeval cycle is marked by a cyclical failure of human will in relation to divine will. What human beings consistently lack (with the partial exception of Noah) is integrity and character—in a word, righteousness. To be righteous is to be genuinely human; to be unrighteous is to be inhuman. One may become subhuman, reverting to a status and behavior beneath the dignity of the "image of God," or one may attempt to become superhuman, trying to "become like God." For the primeval cycle (and

the Hebrew Bible in general), the latter is usually the problem. In various ways throughout these stories human beings attempt "to blur the distinction between the human and the divine,"[82] and they remain human only by divine coercion that necessarily entails tragic and "distressful" consequences (e.g., 3:16–17).

The theme of human responsibility is also prominent in the so-called promise to Abram. This promise, after all, is initially expressed in the form of a command: "Go from your land . . . to the land that I shall show you." Moreover, the syntax of the second verse indicates that the consecution of the promise of nationhood and blessing is predicated on Abram's response to this command: "So that I may make of you a great nation."[83] In other words, the successful fulfillment of the promise to Abram is intrinsically linked to the response of the human will; Abram must, after all, respond to the divine command if the promise of nationhood and blessing is to see fruition. In short, the promise calls for human obedience. We can therefore refer to Gen 12:1–3 as a charge—a word connoting command and responsibility as well as promise. The charge is reminiscent of the divine blessing in ch. 1, expressed as both promise and command: "Be fertile and increase." Thus at the beginning of the ancestral stories, there is the clear implication that obedience to the divine command is the way out of human failure, and that this way—implicitly for

---

80. The first phrase here ("so be a blessing") is actually verse 2b and is usually translated "so that you will be a blessing." The verb, however, is pointed as an imperative, and I have translated it accordingly. Read that way, it continues the force of the initial imperative in verse 1, on which see below. The word for "belittle" can also be translated with "curse" but is different from the other word for that here. ("Belittle" is the word used in 8:21 as a synonym for the other, from 3:17.) For more, see my study, "All the Families of the Earth."

81. Von Rad, *Genesis*, 155.

82. Sasson, "The Tower of Babel," 216.

83. For this construction using the imperative mood see Lambdin, *Introduction to Biblical Hebrew*, 119 (§107b). For a particularly close analogy see 1 Kgs 1:12.

all humankind—is the way of Abram.[84] When Abram sets out, he is committing himself to a *relationship* with Yahweh that is *prior to* the promise of land and progeny, a relationship that will often be sorely tested.[85]

Abram and Sarai now depart on a magnificent new adventure. Here is the sign of Yahweh's grace that was lacking after the tower of Babel. Suddenly the whole world—and indeed, we the readers—direct our attention to this man and woman. The future of this one couple holds the only hope for the life—the blessing—of the whole world. "Yahweh said . . . Abram went." Yahweh commands, Abram obeys. This is the way the world, and the Torah, began, and now we begin to see the new way of faith that will become the way of Torah.

THE ABRAHAM CYCLE (11:27—25:18)

Introduction

"A wandering Aramean was my father; and he went down into Egypt and sojourned there, few in number." The Israelite confession of faith contained in Deut 26:5–10 begins with this cryptic summary of the ancestral stories of Genesis. Although the confession appears to refer specifically

to Jacob, it is an appropriate formulation for all the stories, for they are framed on either end by a descent into Egypt (12:10; ch. 46). The frame suggests that Genesis 12–50 forms an interim within the pentateuchal narrative: on the one hand these chapters provide a retrospective and somewhat ironic link to the primeval cycle; on the other, they furnish a prospective and prophetic connection to the section that follows. In relation to the primeval cycle, these stories represent the new reality God intends for the world; at the same time, the stories point beyond themselves to the central event of the Torah—the redemption from Egyptian bondage and the formation of the covenant community. In the end, the great-great-grandchildren of Abraham and Sarah, the couple summoned from the "old world" of Mesopotamia to the "new world" of Canaan, find themselves as resident aliens (albeit highly favored) in the strange land of Egypt (47:11). But the descendants of Abraham and Sarah (highly unfavored) will have to be "brought out" of Egypt "with an outstretched arm and with great acts of judgment" (Exod 6:6).

For convenience, I shall refer to all of Gen 11:27 to the end as the ancestral saga, *saga* meaning a long story that follows the life of a particular family as it unfolds over numerous generations.[86]

---

84. Cf. LaCocque (*Onslaught against Innocence*, 81, 144; cf. 123, 141): Abram is "the one man after God's desire" in whom "a new humanity emerges from East of Eden." Cf. LaCoque, *Trial of Innocence*, 22–23.

85. See White, *Narration and Discourse*, 111–12, with references to von Rad: Abram "is thus called into a primary intersubjective relation, the material consequences of which, though real, are very much secondary."

86. I am using the term to designate an extensive redactional unit rather than individual stories in terms of form criticism. Actually, the entire book is really a saga in this sense. So also Coats (*Genesis*, 5–7, 28–29, 14–15), who sees the whole Pentateuch as a saga since he terms Exodus–Deuteronomy "the Moses saga." The use of the term *saga* is hardly without debate, however. For a review of various scholars' work, see Whybray, *Making of the Pentateuch*, 142–69; and Coats, ed., *Saga*, especially chs. 1 and 2.

Whereas the primeval cycle often leaps over several generations and ultimately includes all nations in its scope (Gen 4:17—5:32; 10:1–32; 11:10–26), the ancestral saga concerns only five generations, from Abraham and Sarah to the children of Joseph. Although we can trace the genealogical connections from Adam and Eve to the children of Joseph, Israel later saw itself as peculiarly related to the ancestors of chs. 12–50, and especially to Jacob, whose alternate name *is* Israel (Gen 32:28).

As we have seen in our analysis of the charge to Abraham in 12:1–3, the themes announced at the outset of the ancestral saga are continuations of those that run throughout the primeval cycle: the relationships between divine will and human responsibility, humanity and the earth, and blessing and curse. The repetition of this thematic charge in formal divine speeches throughout chs. 12–50 serves as a structural pillar supporting the entire narrative edifice.[87] The promises are adumbrated no fewer than five times to Abraham alone (e.g., 13:14–17; 15:1–7, 18; ch. 17; 18:9–19; 22:17–18), but they also form the redactional connection to the Isaac and Jacob cycles, interweaving stories that quite likely were originally unconnected (see Appendix 1). Thus the brief Isaac cycle (chs. 26–27) is introduced by a repetition of the promises (here called an "oath"), now made directly to Isaac:

Then Yahweh appeared to him and said . . . "Reside in this land as an alien, and I will be with you, and will bless you; for to you and to your descendants I will give all these lands, and I will fulfill the oath that I swore to your father Abraham. I will make your offspring as numerous as the stars of heaven, and will give to your offspring all these lands; and all the nations of the earth shall gain blessing for themselves through your offspring." (26:2–4, AT)

Similarly, the promises are continued with Abraham's grandson Jacob:

"I am Yahweh, the God of Abraham your father and the God of Isaac; the land on which you lie I will give to you and to your descendants; and your offspring shall be like the dust of the earth . . . and all the families of the earth shall be blessed in you and in your offspring." (28:13–14; cf. 28:3–4; 35:9–12, AT)

The divine promises are never given directly by God to Joseph, an omission that demonstrates remarkable reserve on the part of the redactors, who apparently refused to violate the distinctive narrative configuration of this cycle in such a manner. Instead the promises are repeated once again to the aged Jacob, now at the moment of his "descent into Egypt" (46:1–4). Later, on his deathbed, Jacob invokes the blessing of the God of his ancestors on the sons of Joseph (48:15–16).

We now narrow our focus to the Abraham cycle. Throughout the centuries many Jews, Christians, and Muslims would have agreed with Søren Kierkegaard: "though Abraham arouses my admiration, he at the same time appalls me

87. For a convenient collection of discussions on the thematic unity of Genesis 12–50, as well as the historical issues involved, see the articles of Baker, Goldingay, Wenham, and Wiseman in Millard and Wiseman, *Essays on the Patriarchal Narratives.*

. . . He who has explained this riddle has explained my life."[88] The one who attracts us because of his singular obedience is also the one who—for the same reason—shocks and repulses us. The man of faith is also the man who would slaughter his own son (ch. 22). We cannot explain the story of Abraham in the sense of solving Kierkegaard's riddle; we can only open the story so that we may see more clearly the mystery it holds.

On the surface the central issue of the cycle concerns the birth of a son and legitimate heir to Abraham and Sarah. Yet the remarkably brief account of Isaac's birth (21:1–7) immediately suggests that the issue involves far more than the completion of a biological process. The real issue has to do with the son as gift of God, how the benefactors live in anticipation and receipt of it, and how they die looking beyond their own lives to the future of the one who embodies the gift. The signification of the son—anticipated, embraced, released, and endowed—transcends the biological plane, becoming something much more than the boy Isaac. The son has become the "seed" of the promise to Abraham, especially the promise that he will become a great nation possessing the land of Canaan, and thus by extension the son has become the bearer of the possibility of blessing for the entire alienated world of the primeval cycle. Of course, this will be true for Jacob as well, and then for his twelve sons, and we could even trace the underlying concern back to the treatment of Seth (4:24—5:3). But only in the Abraham cycle is the issue of the son stretched out,

as it were, to become the focal point of an entire redactional unit.

1. "Go from your country" (11:27—14:24)

The preface to the Abraham cycle in 11:27–32 gives us three items of information to prepare us for what follows. First, in connection with the customary "generations" formula, it specifies in exacting detail the family relationships of Abram and Sarai. Second, we learn that Sarai is infertile (v. 30); and third, the story of Abram and Sarai begins with an uncompleted journey to Canaan, initiated by Abram's father for reasons unknown.

These few verses (not to mention the entire primeval cycle) provide a rich and ambiguous prelude for the story that follows. When Abram accepts the charge, his journey to Canaan becomes a mission to the promised land. Yet to gain this land and be the founder of a "great nation" he must abandon the land of his birth and leave his brother behind. He must become an alien, without the protection of kinfolk or the rights of a permanent resident (not altogether unlike Cain!). Moreover, he who would be the "father of a multitude" is the husband of a barren woman, and they are already old (Abram, seventy-five; Sarai, sixty-five).[89]

Following the charge to Abram, 12:4–9 opens with Abram's unquestioning obedience to the divine charge, as we have seen above: "So Abram went, as Yahweh had told him" (v. 4aα, AT). Yet

---

88. Kierkegaard, *Fear and Trembling*, xvi, 89–90.

89. Clearly the age of this couple is not realistic but legendary exaggeration. Abraham will be one hundred before he fathers a child by Sarah, and she well past menopause (21:5; cf. 17:17).

immediately in v. 4a we are told that "Lot went with him." Although it does not say that Abram *took* Lot with him, nevertheless his allowing Lot to join him means that Abram has not *completely* left his "father's house" (v. 1).[90] While we should not make too much of this, it does raise a question at the outset that will become increasingly complicated: is Abram completely obedient or not, trusting or not, and therefore *trustworthy* or not? Thus the mere half verse of 1a encapsulates the tension in Abram's character that will take us to the climactic ch. 22.

Abram's initial move becomes a geographical survey of places that figure prominently in the ensuing stories. When Abram arrives at Shechem, Yahweh appears to him and says, "To your descendants I will give this land." The "land that I will show you" (12:1) is now utterly concrete: "the place at Shechem, at the oak of Moreh," as are the inhabitants: "At that time the Canaanites were in the land" (v. 6; see Appendix 3). Moreover, the reaffirmation and specification of this promise is presented as the content of the first formal self-revelation of Yahweh in the Hebrew Bible ("appearance"). Yahweh is seen only in what Yahweh says and does, which is to say that Yahweh's identity is expressed only in terms of the story in which Yahweh is the chief character. The reaffirmation of the promise is also significant in that the recipient of the land is specified as Abram's *descendants*. Thus Abram's obedience to the original charge is not so much for his own sake as for the sake of future generations, and his renewed acceptance of the charge is

represented by his constructing an altar to Yahweh, "who appeared to him" (v. 7; cf. v. 8). Here at the outset the divine promise extends beyond the horizon of the chief human protagonist (becoming even more explicit in 15:13–16).

No sooner has Abram toured the land of promise than he is driven from it by famine, and forced to "sojourn" in Egypt (vv. 10–20). Fearful of the ostensible jealousy of the Egyptians over Sarai, he lies about their relationship and hands her over to the pharaoh's harem and apparent adultery (v. 18).[91] Abram's abandonment of Canaan was unavoidable, an external threat to the promise that, while unexplained, is nonetheless real. His abandonment of Sarai, on the other hand, is a cowardly act constituting an internal threat to the promise. Although there is a damsel in distress here, Abram is no knight in shining armor. The situation is rectified only by Yahweh's imposition of a plague on Pharaoh's household, with the consequent expulsion of Abram and Sarai from Egypt.[92]

The opening chapter of the Abraham cycle thus portrays a remarkably intricate web of circumstances and characterization. Precisely because of the way the story takes us from the high point of the divine charge and its acceptance, and plunges us into the utterly ambiguous

90. Cotter, *Genesis*, 91. "House" here means "household," not a building.

91. It is true that, in 20:12, with a repeat of such an incident, Abraham says that Sarah is his half sister, but we don't know that he isn't lying there, and here he asks her to pretend that she is *not* his *wife*.

92. This story obviously foreshadows the story of Israel's descent into Egypt due to famine, the plagues against the pharaoh, and Israel's deliverance and return to Canaan, an exodus pattern.

situations in which the charge begins to work out, ch. 12 functions as a kind of prologue to the entire ancestral saga that follows. Abram is at once the one who responds to the divine charge with trust and obedience, and the one who immediately loses his integrity in the face of difficulties both real and imagined. One can, of course, sympathize with his predicament. He has been promised a land, yet he learns that it will truly belong only to his descendants. As for Abram himself, he arrives in the land "only to walk, so to speak, straight through it and out the other side."[93] The altars he establishes are marks, as it were, of his claim, but Abram remains essentially an alien.[94]

If the themes of responsibility and land appear fraught with ambiguity, so does that of blessing. When the land of promise proves to be a land of famine, there is little evidence of divine blessing.

93. Clines, *Theme of the Pentateuch*, 46.

94. Hiebert (*Yahwist's Landscape*, 89) argues that only the Priestly author portrays the ancestors as *gerim* ("resident aliens") when in Canaan, and that for J they are "landed people at home in the Israelite highlands" (whereas outside they are aliens, e.g., 12:10; 20:1; 21:23, 34; 26:3). Thus the ancestors are also not "seminomadic pastoralists," as many have suggested, largely because of the references to Abraham and others dwelling in tents (e.g., 12:8; 13:3, 5; 18:1–10; 24:67; 25:27; 31:25; in 26:2–3, 6, and 17 there are four different words for dwelling). Nevertheless, it remains the case that the *promise* of land possession continually projects fulfillment into the distant future, even in J, as Hiebert acknowledges when he refers to "territorial claims . . . characteristic of a landed kingdom *such as the Israel of J's time*" (96, italics added), which is "the age of the Davidic monarchy" (145; cf. 100). At the end of Genesis, the ancestors will legally possess nothing more than some water wells at Beersheba (21:25–34; 26:23–33) and a cemetery plot in Hebron (ch. 23), on which see below.

Still, Abram (or more properly, Sarai) enjoys the special protection of Yahweh, and even Abram's mendacity pays off in considerable wealth (v. 16)! Also, rather than serving as a source of blessing for others, Abram's actions have led, in effect, to a curse, however temporary (v. 17). Nor does Yahweh's involvement in the plot escape ambiguity. In order to preserve Sarai, Yahweh must scourge the hapless pharaoh, who, in fact, is the only one who comes away from this story morally untarnished.

In chs. 13–14 the focus of the narrative turns to the relationship between Abram and his nephew, Lot, with explicit foreshadowing of the Sodom and Gomorrah episode that will conclude the story of Lot (18:16—19:38). Abram has returned to the altar at Bethel, where he again invokes the name of Yahweh. Both he and Lot possess such great herds of livestock that they must separate in order to resolve contention over grazing lands. In effect, bountiful blessing requires further division of the family of Abram. At first one wonders if Lot has not gained the upper hand, for he takes advantage of Abram's magnanimous offer and chooses the fertile Jordan valley as his territory. Yet the fact that this land is described as similar to the "garden of Yahweh" and the well-watered land of Egypt does not augur well (cf. 3:22–24), nor is the necessity to "journey East" auspicious, judging from the primeval cycle (3:24; 4:16; 11:2) Lot is a man headed in the wrong direction, as the anticipation of ch. 19 warns.

In contrast, ch. 13 ends with another divine speech in which the promises to Abram are renewed and again expanded. Now Yahweh promises to Abram and his descendants "all the land" that he can see in every direction, a gift "forever," and Yahweh orders him to "walk off" the boundaries as if he were doing a real-estate survey.[95] The expanded geographical scope almost appears a consolation in the face of Lot's immediate gratification. In addition, the motif of "descendants" (literally "seed") is amplified by the metaphor of the "dust of the earth." The vastness of the land will be matched by the multitude of Abram's offspring, again a mark of divine blessing.

In ch. 14 the error in Lot's choice of land already begins to show. Following the defeat of Sodom in a regional war, Lot is taken away as a captive and must be rescued by his uncle, who uncharacteristically appears as a military hero (vv. 1–16). Yet the redemption of Lot is hardly the primary thrust of the chapter (which bristles with oddities), for Abram achieves a greater victory on a sacerdotal level (vv. 17–24). As a returning victor, Abram receives a divine blessing mediated by the Canaanite priest Melchizedek and pronounced in the name of his god, El Elyon ("God Most High," see Appendix 2). When Abram is approached by the king of Sodom regarding the spoils of war, he refuses any of the booty, declaring

that he has sworn an oath to that effect to "*Yahweh*, God Most High, Creator of heaven and earth." In one stroke Abram has accepted the blessing, exalted Yahweh to the status of God Most High, and rejected any deals with the king of Sodom (which we already know to be Sin City, 13:12). Thus the "point of the story according to the closing discourse is to teach the virtues of courage, loyalty, and piety by Abraham's example."[96] If Abram lost his integrity at the end of ch. 12, he has regained it by the end of ch. 14.

2. Righteousness and Subterfuge (chs. 15–16)

The juxtaposition of chapters 14 and 15 suggests a loose connection between the Abram who refuses a reward from the king of Sodom and the Abram who is now promised a reward from Yahweh. The text immediately turns to the question of a son (vv. 1–6), and subsequently to the question of possession of the land (vv. 7–20). Commentators have often observed the apparent contradictions in chronological sequence in the chapter (cf. vv. 5, 12, 17). In fact, in its present form all the action and dialogue takes place in a dream-like state, for vv. 1–11 occur in a "vision," and vv. 12–21 take place in a "deep sleep" (cf. 2:21). From this we should not infer that what transpires is unreal; on the contrary, the language of vision and dream conveys "a feeling of awe and mystery" before the disclosure of ultimate reality.[97] What happens in this chapter is an unprecedented meeting of the divine and the human—

95. Some argue that here Yahweh gives Abram *de jure* title to the land, and Fretheim suggests that "it is *actually given* to him" now, translating "'I am giving'" (*The Book of Genesis*, 434b, italics original). However, the future tense still seems more appropriate; compare the participle of the verb in a similar context in Moses' survey of the land, Deut 32:49. For the perfect tense, "I have given," see 15:18. In either case, Israel does not "possess" the land de facto until the book of Joshua. As Fretheim says later (458b), "he lived in the land, but could not yet consider it his. The promise was for the future."

96. Van Seters, *Abraham in History and Tradition*, 306.

97. Speiser, *Genesis*, 115.

Yahweh and Abram—a moment in which the divine will and the human response stand in full accord. In a word, this is a moment of righteousness.

There has been no previous dialogue between God and Abram; now for the first time Abram speaks directly to God twice, each time in the form of a question that, though deferential, is nonetheless bold and even skeptical. Yahweh promises Abram a great reward, to which Abram responds, "What will you give me, for I continue childless, and the heir of my house is Eliezer of Damascus . . . a slave born in my house?" (15:2–3).[98] Indeed, v. 3a sounds like an accusation: "you have given me no offspring." Yahweh replies with the first definitive promise of a son and heir. He then takes Abram outside and tells him to look up at the stars in the sky, for his offspring will be just as innumerable. And then Abram "trusted Yahweh, and he accounted it to him as righteousness" (AT).

The transition from Abram's strident questioning to inner trust, unexpressed by word or gesture, is remarkable, all the more so because there seems to be little new evidence of *Yahweh's* trustworthiness (cf. 13:16). Again, it is only that "the word of Yahweh" comes to him in a vision that heightens the cogency of the promise, even if it does not guarantee its certainty.[99]

In a video titled "Who is God?" Madeleine L'Engle talks about being a child whose parents would take her out at night to look up at the stars, when she gained a glimpse of something "awesome and wonderful"—in a word, "numinous." Then when she became a parent, she would take her own children up to the top of a mountain to look at the stars whenever there were tragedies in their lives. They would "try to put whatever it was in the context of a universe created by a loving God. So," she says, "whenever I have attacks of faithlessness, which I think we all get, if I can go see stars, that will almost always bring me back."[100]

The primary movement in the chapter so far has been that of Abram's commitment to Yahweh. In vv. 7–11 the focus is on Yahweh's commitment to Abram. The section opens with Yahweh's self-introduction as the one who brought Abram from Ur to Canaan.[101] Mention of the land as gift prompts Abram to pose another question: "Lord Yahweh, how am I to know that I shall possess it?" (AT). Both the bizarre ritual that follows and the divine speech that appears to interrupt the ritual (vv. 13–16) provide a response to Abram's request for assurance.

98. Apparently Eliezer could be Abram's legal heir, but v. 2b is muddled and notoriously difficult to decipher. Strangely, there is no reference here to Lot.

99. Cf. Jer 7:1; 11:1; 18:1; Num 12:6; 24:4, 16; 2 Sam 7:4, 17. The persuasiveness of drawing attention to the stars, and implicitly to God's power as creator, may have the same rhetorical effect as that in Isa 40:25–31, addressed to the exiles in Babylon.

100. L'Engle, *Questions of Faith.* I have referred to this quotation with regard to Second Isaiah in "Stars, Sprouts, and Streams," 150–51.

101. The phrase "who brought you out" is often used for the exodus from Egypt.

The arrangement of the sacrificial elements now functions as a preparation for the speech. Abram falls into a "deep sleep," and the language emphasizes the awe and mystery of the moment: "a deep and terrifying darkness descended upon him." Yahweh now tells Abram the future that stretches not only to his own death but far beyond, a future that includes the exodus of Israel from Egypt ("a land that is not theirs") and the return to Canaan. This prediction is offered as the assurance Abram seeks that he will possess the land (note "know this for certain" in v. 13), even though he will not possess the land in any ordinary sense of the word.

Thus, with some irony, Yahweh confirms the commitment to Abram by showing that the promise is only part of a larger purpose in which Yahweh's own future, as it were, is invested. The importance of that investment transcends any personal fulfillment within the life of Abram. What is at stake is Yahweh's purpose for the future *nation* of Israel, and, in the wider context (12:3b; 26:4; 28:14), for the whole world. At the same time, Yahweh's prediction provides the greatest possible certainty to Abram that his relationship to Yahweh is trustworthy, for this is a moment of apocalypse, that is, an "unveiling" of a future reality, disclosing the validity and trustworthiness of a present hope.

The narrative now proceeds to the completion of the sacrificial ritual that will also provide a seal of Yahweh's righteousness. Customarily, those who pass between the animal parts invoke upon themselves the grisly fate of the animal, should they fail to keep the terms of the agreement (cf. Jer 34:18–20). Here it is

Yahweh who performs this action, represented by the "fire pot and flaming torch," and who then makes a covenant, including the most geographically extended promise of land in the Pentateuch (see Appendix 3). By his participation in the ritual, Yahweh is bound to the words already spoken (vv. 13–16) and to the specific promise of land that follows, at the risk of . . . of what? Dismemberment and death? We cannot press such a symbolic story beyond its semantic limits, but it is clear that Yahweh has voluntarily become vulnerable, opening to an element of risk, in order to commit to the fulfillment of the promise that is made. The movement of the chapter as a whole, therefore, establishes a reciprocal relationship between Yahweh and Abram marked by both mutual risk and mutual commitment.

"And Sarai, Abram's wife, bore him no child." The economy of Hebrew narrative style is especially jolting in this opening line to ch. 16. By sheer juxtaposition we are transported from the visionary to the utterly mundane, from the promise of offspring to infertility, from an instance of unparalleled righteousness to an incident replete with the ambiguities of human desperation, pride, jealousy, and cruelty. Ten years have passed since Abram and Sarai came to Canaan. Now for the first time Sarai appears as a character in her own right rather than a passive victim of circumstances, and she is anything but passive. An admirably determined and resourceful woman, she is willing to face the reality of her situation head-on with whatever methods are at her disposal, and in this regard she resembles a number of remarkable women who follow her, not the least of whom will be her daughter-in-law Rebekah (Gen 25:19–23; Genesis 27) and granddaughters Rachel and Leah (30:1–13). On the other hand, Hagar represents women as victims. She is—by name—"the Alien," and the unjustness of her oppression is the opposite of what the later covenant law will require (Exod 22:21; Deut 24:17). Ironically, then, Hagar and Ishmael are the rejects from the future people of Israel, but socially and ethically the very ones that Israel will be commanded to love as God loves (Deut 10:18–19).

Note the objectivity and forcefulness of Sarai's opening speech: "Look, Yahweh has prevented me from bearing children; have sex with my slave girl; it may be that I shall obtain children by her" (16:2, AT). Sarai does not mince words. We have known about her infertility since 11:30, but never has the problem been seen from her perspective nor bluntly attributed to Yahweh's doing. She is more interested in overcoming the problem than ascribing blame, and quickly moves to her solution: she will obtain children by Abram's having intercourse with her slave girl, Hagar—a suggestion with which Abram willingly complies. In fact, Sarai's ascription of her infertility to Yahweh is compatible with ancient Israelite theology,[102] and the arrangement with Hagar was accepted custom (and law) at certain periods in the ancient Near East, however immoral and unjust it may seem to us (it amounts to coerced maternal surrogacy). But apart from according to our own standards of morality, in what sense are the characters culpable?

If we look at the story by itself, it is clear that none of the characters is flawless. Sarai's treatment of the pregnant Hagar is hardly charitable, and Abram's reticence is equally irresponsible. Even Hagar's contempt for Sarai, though understandable, is unnecessarily abrasive and certainly foolhardy. She flaunts her raised status as "wife" (16:3).[103] Yet the possibility of a deeper significance to the characters' motivations and actions arises when we look at the wider context of the story. Although no reference is made in the chapter to Yahweh's promises to Abram, we cannot read the story without those promises in the background. Yet even here caution is in order. We might assume that Sarai knows of the promises, but we have not been told that explicitly. Moreover, the promise of a son—which is obviously central here—has never specified that Sarai will be the mother. Of course there appeared to be no other candidate, but now one appears. Will Hagar's child, who, if a male, could legally be Abram's heir, really be the "child of the promise"? Are Abram and Sarai culpable for attempting to circumvent Sarai's condition, which Sarai explicitly identifies with Yahweh's will, and so produce the promised child solely by their own efforts?[104] Previously, Abram's actions had put his paternity of the promised child in jeopardy (12:10–20); now Sarai in effect does the same thing for the child's mater-

102. Cf. 20:18; 29:31; 30:2; 1 Sam 1:5.

103. Hagar has moved up from slave girl of Sarai to concubine to wife. As Sarna suggests, "in the course of time the distinction in social status between the two often tended to be effaced (*Genesis*, 208). See also Niditch, "Genesis," 20–21. For further reading, especially from a feminist perspective, see the bibliography in Van Wijk-Bos, *Making Wise the Simple*, 137 n. 9.

104. There is a certain similarity here to Eve's actions and Adam's response in 3:17.

nity. In the end, the context of the story leaves us with serious questions about the integrity of the characters—especially Abram—but offers no definitive answers.

The text does clearly suggest two things. First, Ishmael will not be the child of the promise. The description of him as a contentious "wild ass of a man" (v. 12) seems to exclude his candidacy as Abram's true heir, and this will become explicit in ch. 17. Second, though Ishmael is excluded from the divine promise, he and his mother are not excluded from the blessing that accrues to the line of Abram. The promise of numerous offspring to Hagar (v. 10) is the same promise granted to Abram (13:16; 15:5). The very name of the child—Ishmael, "God hears"—is an expression of Yahweh's gracious response to Hagar's suffering. Even though the child is destined to live in continual conflict with his kinfolk, he will remain stubbornly independent. Here again, Ishmael is more than an individual character; he is also the eponymous ancestor of the Ishmaelites, a people directly related to the Abrahamic line but not sharing in the full privileges of the promises to Abram.[105] What is remarkable about this story and its sequel in 17:18–21 and 21:8–21 is that it is not a triumphant celebration of Ishmael's exclusion, but an attempt to wrestle with the painful and tragic circumstances in which the divine purpose had to be worked out. Although God's messenger attends to Hagar's "affliction," she is ordered to return to it and

"submit."[106] While the text represents Ishmael as an example of how the blessing of Abraham will benefit "all the families of the earth" (12:3), it does not flinch from the ambiguities that make it a blessing well disguised. Irony only compounds the ambiguity when Ishmael's descendants (presumably his grandchildren) buy Abram's grandson Joseph as a slave and take him to Egypt, the original home of Hagar the slave woman (16:1; 37:28).

3. "The sign of the covenant" (ch. 17)

Abram's advanced age, the delay in the fulfillment of the promises, and the maturation of Ishmael provide the setting for a fresh clarification of the relationship between Yahweh and the Abrahamic line. This chapter is by far the longest and most important Priestly contribution to the entire ancestral saga. What happens here is a new and definitive disclosure of the identity of God, as well as of Abram and Sarai, and an indication that the nature of the relationship between God and these characters (and their descendants) defines the constitutive content of the covenant. Accordingly, in the opening scene Yahweh's self-revelation to Abram introduces a new name: "I am El Shaddai: follow my ways and be blameless,[107] so that I may grant a covenant between me and you, and multiply you exceedingly." The name El Shaddai is understood by

---

105. Arabs and Muslims often trace their origins back to Abraham through Ishmael and can rightly point to the divine blessing of their ancestor in 17:20.

106. The words "dealt harshly" (v. 6), "submit" (v. 9) and "affliction (v. 11) derive from the root word 'nh. The succession of four speeches by the messenger suggests redactional activity.

107. For this translation see Speiser, *Genesis*, 122. The covenant offer of v. 2 is also seen as a reward by Van Seters, *Abraham in History and Tradition*, 288.

Genesis 51

the Priestly school to be that portion, as it were, of Yahweh's identity associated with the ancestral saga as a distinct epoch (cf. Exod. 6:2–3). Who is El Shaddai (see Appendix 2)? Of course, he is the one who makes the familiar promises of numerous progeny, land, and nationhood. But what stands out in the Priestly formulation of the promises, and therefore in the identity of El Shaddai, is the pledge to become the God of Abram and his descendants (vv. 7b, 8b).[108] The identity of Yahweh as El Shaddai is wrapped up in the covenant relationship with the descendants of Abram. As an epithet, El Shaddai may mean "God of the Mountain" or "God Almighty"; in the context of ch. 17, it has a demonstrative meaning—El Shaddai is "*their* God." In other words, the identity of God is redefined in terms of this relationship to Abram and his descendants. Just as the personal identity of husband and wife is very much determined by their relationship, and even seems to require a change of name (now frequently for both partners), so the identity of Yahweh is very much determined—"for better or for worse"—in relationship with the ancestors and their descendants, namely Israel. The emphasis on mutual identity formation in ch. 17 requires the introduction of a new name for God and, correspondingly, new names for Abram and Sarai. Most important, this is "an everlasting covenant" (17:7, 13). Although Abraham's "blamelessness" in v. 1 suggests a precondition for the initiation of this covenant, once made with

Abraham it signifies El Shaddai's pledge to be Israel's God "throughout their generations" (17:7). Thus the Abrahamic covenant, as it is called, is the bedrock of a theology of grace, a promise of divine blessing irrespective of human merit (see Appendix 3).[109]

The opening address in vv. 1b–2 suggests the correlation between Abram's righteousness and Yahweh's granting of the covenant: In the second unit (vv. 9–14) Abram's responsibility to "keep" the covenant—that is, to watch over, guard, and maintain it—is delineated. Quite literally, the mark of this new covenant identity is expressed by the rite of circumcision. While the literal applicability of this custom has obvious limitations (particularly for women), symbolically it suggests that covenant identity involves the "whole person" and, moreover, that the recipients of the covenant are responsible for its transmission from one generation to another. Even more remarkable, circumcision, and thus membership in the covenant community, is not restricted to kinfolk, for even a "foreigner who is not of your offspring" must be circumcised. Here the Priestly formulation of the way the blessing pronounced on Abraham can include non-Israelites achieves an "ecumenical spirit."[110]

109. However, some texts can reformulate God's promise in terms of Abraham's merit (22:16; 26:5). There is already a reference to the continuation of this covenant with Isaac as a reward for Abraham's obedience in 26:5, a text that uses language more at home in the Sinai (Mosaic) covenant tradition (cf. also 19:29).

110. Van Seters, *Abraham in History and Tradition*, 293. Circumcision is a prerequisite for participation in the Passover ritual in Exod 12:44, 48. On the other hand, it goes unmentioned in the liberal view of community

108. For a study of the full covenant formula to which these verses are related ("I will be your God and you shall be my people"), see Good, *Sheep of His Pasture*, 65–85.

It is difficult, if not impossible, to reconcile the ecumenical implications of the second unit with what transpires in the third (vv. 15–22). Here for the first time the promise of a son to Abraham specifies Sarah as the mother. Now we know why her role, whether passive (12:10–20) or active (16:1–6), has been so important and will be again (18:1–15; ch. 20; 21:1–7; ch. 23). When the ancestress is in danger, the promises are in danger. Abram's response is bewilderment, if not mockery. In fact, he falls on his face laughing! What a contrast to verse 3a, where the same gesture expresses the conventional act of humility. Abraham cannot help but snicker at the suggestion that he and Sarah, at the ages of one hundred and ninety respectively, will have a child. So certain is he of the impossibility of such a miracle that he immediately suggests an alternative: let Ishmael be the son of the promise. What was apparently an attempt to circumvent Yahweh's will in ch. 16 is now explicitly so. Yahweh rejects this alternative, reiterates that Sarah will be the mother, and now dictates the name of the son: Isaac, "he laughs."

What now of Ishmael? The oracular saying in 16:11–12 has already implied that Ishmael will not be the son of the promise, and now that implication is confirmed. But, as before, that is not the last word for Ishmael. The divine blessing, expressed by the motif of progeny, is also confirmed and extended to include a regal destiny. Ishmael will become the "father of twelve princes," and a "great nation." Even

so, the covenant will be established with Isaac, the son of Sarah, and not with Ishmael, the son of Hagar. The text does not confront the apparent contradiction that Ishmael is circumcised, and thus bears the sign of the covenant (vv. 25–26), yet is excluded from the covenant. Perhaps this avoidance is due to the distinctive Priestly understanding of the nature and content of the covenant that pervades the entire chapter. If, like Abraham himself, Ishmael receives a divine blessing, will father innumerable descendants, and will be the founder of a great nation, yet will not be the bearer of the covenant, what is the content of the covenant? The answer can only be possession of the land of Canaan and the promise "to become your God, and the God of your descendants after you" (v. 7b, and together in v. 8).

4. Divine Visitors (chs. 18–19)

The precedence of the annunciation in ch. 17 cannot rob the story in 18:1–15 of its ingenuous charm. While the Priestly author was interested in the eternal significance of Isaac's birth (e.g., 17:19), the present story functions more on the level of plot, heightening our expectation of an imminent resolution ("in the spring"), and thus pointing towards a climax.

Part of the charm comes from the way we see the elderly couple scrambling "in the heat of the day" to welcome the three passersby and prepare some refreshments. The reader knows from the outset that this is a visitation from Yahweh (v. 1), but the characters do not begin to intuit this until midway through (v. 9). At least, Sarah senses something uncanny (and therefore frightening) when the

---

membership in the postexilic text of Isa 56:1–8, where Sabbath observance predominates. By the second century BCE circumcision had become a defining characteristic of (male) Jewish identity.

mysterious visitor seems to know what she's been thinking ("to herself," vv. 12, 15). In the context of ch. 17, her skeptical laughter echoes that of Abraham (17:17), and thus compounds the ironic wordplay of the name "Isaac" ("he laughs," 17:19).

There may be something to the proverb derived from this story about those who "entertain angels unawares" (Heb 13:2), that is, in some sense Abraham and Sarah are rewarded for their generous hospitality to strangers, although the repeated promises to Abram that now precede the story tend to dull such an effect. Still, hospitality to the stranger represents the most elemental form of human righteousness. Since hospitality is here rendered unwittingly to God in disguise, perhaps we should see this story of divine visitation as part of that "testing" of Abraham that pervades the entire cycle. And perhaps we should infer more than a coincidental connection with the scene immediately following, in which God takes Abraham into confidence. Moreover, the ancestors' hospitality will soon be repeated by Lot, and together their friendly reception of the divine visitors will cast into stark relief the hostile *inhospitality* of the citizens of Sodom (19:1–11).

The prologue and epilogue to the Sodom story (18:16–33; 19:27–29) make Abraham the protagonist instead of Lot, even though Abraham never appears in the action of ch. 19. This framework forces us to look at the story from Abraham's point of view (both literally and figuratively), the point of view of one "looking down on" Sodom as an informed witness. Further, while we might conclude from 19:1–15 alone that Lot saved himself by

also "entertaining angels unawares," v. 29 insists that Lot's salvation is really due to Abraham's favor with God.[111] Thus the prologue and epilogue convert the Sodom story into a piece that connects with the thematic unity of the Abraham cycle: Abraham's role as witness derives from the charge that he has received from Yahweh (18:17–19); Lot's salvation ultimately derives from the blessing placed on Abraham, on the basis of which God's mercy overrides God's justice (18:23–33). Moreover, as the sequel to the story suggests (19:29–38), the blessing of Abraham does indeed extend to other peoples (the Moabites and Ammonites), even if their origin is not one of which to be proud![112]

We may now look at Abraham's role in more detail. The reason for selecting Abraham as the informed witness is given in terms not only of the promises of nationhood and blessing, but also of a specific responsibility to "charge" (*sivah*) his descendants in the way of "righteousness and justice." The explicit purpose clauses in v. 19 are the clearest indication so far of the responsibility that comes with the promises. Indeed, the logical order of the verse ("that he may charge . . . so that Yahweh may bring . . .") suggests that the realization of the promises in the future

---

111. In its current context, Abraham's negotiating in 18:23–33 could be motivated in part to save Lot, even though Lot does not appear all that righteous by the end of the story. Still, since apparently ten righteous people were not to be found in Sodom, it is not Abraham's negotiation with Yahweh that brings about Lot's rescue, but God's remembrance of Abraham as the agent of his blessing (19:29).

112. The sexual impropriety performed when Lot is drunk reminds us of the story of Ham, the "father of Canaan" in 9:20–27.

will depend in part on Abraham's attention to his responsibilities.

Abraham's unique role is emphasized in the opening of v. 19 by an unusually direct expression of his election: Yahweh has "recognized" him, which is to say "singled him out" (JPS) as one with authority and a special purpose.[113] Whether or not Abraham hears the words of vv. 17–19, the reason for his appointment as a witness is all the more crucial when we realize that there is, in fact, one other informed witness to what happens, namely, Lot. He too knows who is destroying the cities and why, because the angels tell him (19:13) in words that may have provided the basis for 18:20. Lot survives the disaster, and presumably he too could relate its theological lesson. But Lot is hardly a man of integrity, for he is willing to hand over his daughters to rapists (19:8, see below), and, in the sequel to the disaster story, Lot allows himself to become so drunk that he unconsciously commits incest with them. Such a man is not a worthy representative of the way of Yahweh! Thus Abraham remains the witness who is informed and divinely appointed, but also whose integrity corresponds to his selection. Appropriately, the story concludes with Abraham returning to the spot of his conversation with Yahweh and looking down on the eerie, smoking ruins of Sodom and Gomorrah (19:27–28).

The sin of Sodom and Gomorrah first appears in 18:20–21. Given the etymology of the word *sodomy* for a sexual act, readers often assume that sodomy is the "very grave" sin of Sodom, and equate

sodomy with male homosexuality. Such a connection, however, is not supported by the text. The word "outcry" is used two times here, but that word usually refers to a distress call resulting from oppression or violence.[114] Apparently some kind of social injustice is involved. In fact, within the story, the real sin of Sodom is the threat of *forced* sodomy—i.e. homosexual rape—with the potential victims being the visiting angels (usually portrayed as male)![115] In short, the depravity of Sodom is not homosexuality but injustice and inhospitality of the worst kind.[116]

So far Yahweh has allowed Abraham to be a witness because he is the trustee of the promises, responsible for inculcating the lesson of Sodom as part of his teaching the way of righteousness and justice. For this reason, Yahweh has drawn Abraham into confidence and entrusted him with the knowledge and significance of what is to happen. Still, at this point, Yahweh's decision to include Abraham in the plan is based completely on Abraham's

---

113. NRSV "chosen." Cf. von Rad, *Genesis*, 208–9; and Brueggemann, *Genesis*, 171.

114. Two synonyms are used here (*z'q* and *ṣ'q*; also 19:13). Cf. Exod 3:7–9; 22:23; Deut 22:24 (involving rape).

115. The words for "outcry" fit with such violence, but not with homosexuality as a loving, consensual relationship between two men, which is hardly what "all the people to the last man" are after (19:4). Thus the Sodom story should not be understood as a kind of illustration of the prohibition in Lev 18:22, whatever one does with the latter. See Appendix 6. (It also makes no sense demographically for every male in the town to be gay!) For a similar and even more gruesome story of attempted homosexual rape, see Judges 19.

116. Hospitality, expressed most vividly by the phrase "the shelter of my roof" (19:8), is more than politeness; in this culture it involved protection of one's guest from all danger and enemies (what the psalmist experiences in Ps 23:5).

ex-officio status and not on his personal integrity. The rest of the prologue (vv. 22–33) functions to demonstrate that Yahweh has made the correct decision in the latter regard as well.

In a sense, Yahweh gets more than bargained for. Apparently Yahweh had intended merely to inform Abraham of what was to happen, because of his status as the trustee of Yahweh's way. Now Abraham demonstrates his acceptance of responsibility, not only by receiving the information, but by questioning Yahweh about divine righteousness and justice: "Shall not the Judge of all the earth do what is just?" (18:25). Yahweh's designated witness now also assumes the role of counselor. With considerable courage, Abraham lives up to the confidence Yahweh has already placed in him. Indeed, by his willingness to question Yahweh's righteousness on behalf of the unrighteous, Abraham confirms his own righteousness with respect to Yahweh. Correspondingly, in Yahweh's agreement to Abraham's questions an important principle is established: Yahweh's righteousness transcends a mechanical system of reward and punishment. That this principle may stand in some tension with the ensuing story in which Yahweh annihilates entire cities does not lessen the significance of what is here revealed about Yahweh's character.[117] Moreover, the potential for mercy within Yahweh's righteousness must be balanced against the depravity of an entire citizenry, who *assaulted* angels unawares (19:4).

---

117. Cf. von Rad, *Genesis*, 208–9; and Brueggemann, *Genesis*, 171. As Sarna notes, "This is no longer an appeal to the attribute of justice but a call for divine mercy" (*Genesis*, 133).

5. Resolutions: Ishmael, Abimelech, and Isaac (chs. 20–21)

In chapter 20 we find Sarah in trouble yet again, much as she was in the incident in Egypt (12:10–20), but now the potential consequences are heightened. With Sarah in a pagan king's harem, the possibility of offspring through Abraham is jeopardized, a problem more troublesome than before, because now we know that Sarah is to be the "mother" of Israel (ch. 17). Similarly, Abraham again finds himself an "alien" in a land that is not his, Philistine territory (cf. 21:34). Yet these problems are resolved as well as they can be: Sarah is released (untouched) from Abimelech's harem, and Abraham is given permission to dwell in Gerar.

What is not so easily resolved is Abraham's behavior. While the present account in some ways attempts to exonerate Abraham, in the wider context of the story his actions remain irresponsible. In fact, he announces that Sarah is his sister at the outset, but *before* there is any apparent threat to him, so Abimelech "takes" her. Within the story his culpability appears all the more striking in contrast to the probity of Abimelech. When God appears to Abimelech in a dream and warns him of imminent danger, Abimelech proclaims his innocence: "Lord, will you destroy an innocent people? . . . I did this in the integrity of my heart and the innocence of my hands" (20:4, 5b). What an ironic contrast this scene makes in comparison to that of Abraham's prior discourse with Yahweh, when he defended the righteous and *un*righteous in the face of Yahweh's judgment (18:22–33)! Here it is not the patriarch but a Philistine king who appears to be the paragon of virtue. In his confrontation with Abraham, Abimelech presses his case even further. It is not he but Abraham who is the cause of sin. In short, Abraham has committed the elemental act of unrighteousness—he has "done that which ought not to be done" to another (v. 9).

In response, Abraham explains the truth behind his apparent lie: Sarah is, in fact, his half sister. Even if we grant the veracity of this claim,[118] surely it will not excuse Abraham's action, which has again put not only Sarah and Abimelech but also the promises of God in grave danger. Further, in the face of the "fear of God" that Abimelech and the Philistines have shown (v. 8), Abraham's attempt to justify his action by portraying the Philistines as *not* fearing God is both hypocritical and self-righteous (v. 11). Abraham even seems to intimate that the whole affair is God's fault for having "led him astray" in the first place (v. 13).[119] God's gracious guidance (12:1) has suddenly become misleading, and Abraham's following it, misguided!

Abraham hasn't made things easy for God either. Once again God has to scramble to preserve the bearers of God's purpose for the world. At the same time, God acts with deliberate restraint, in recognition of the integrity of Abimelech (v. 6). Even so, we learn in the end that God had made the Philistine women temporarily infertile—in effect, accursed

(vv. 17–18). The one who ought to have been the channel of blessing to the world (as indeed he has been before) has instead been the agent of sterility and potential death. Nevertheless it is through the intercession of Abraham (the prophet!) that fertility and life are restored. In short, Abraham's righteousness is again fraught with inconsistency, and the cycle resumes the tension with which it began.

In the space of only seven verses the text now reports the long-awaited arrival of the son of Abraham and Sarah (21:1–7). Only in the last two verses is this momentous event celebrated with a party, when Isaac is at least several years old, and even here the focus is the pun on *laughter*, connecting this unit with the following story about Ishmael (v. 9, where "playing" also derives from ṣaḥaq).[120] Repeating numerous phrases from ch. 17 and 18:1–15,[121] vv. 1–4 emphasize two points: first, Yahweh has done what was promised (vv. 1–2); and second, Abraham has done as he was told to do (vv. 3–4, naming and circumcision). Thus, in a laconic way, the author represents the birth of Isaac as a divine promise fulfilled and a covenant responsibility maintained.

In context, the following story about Hagar and Ishmael (vv. 8–21) is

---

118. There is no suggestion of this relationship in 11:28–30. Sarah apparently repeats the subterfuge (v. 5a).

119. Cf. the same verb in Isa 30:28 ("lead astray"); 63:17 ("make stray"); Ps 107:40; Prov 12:26; and especially Jer 50:6. It is also used in 21:14b for Hagar's aimless wandering!

120. The text and wordplay in 21:9 are ambiguous (see the NRSV note). The word can mean "laugh," as we have seen, but also "play" in the sense of sexual dalliance (cf. 26:8, "fondling"). Since "with her son Isaac" is missing from the Masoretic text, it is even possible that Ishmael is laughing *at* the celebration, similar to the connotation of the word in 19:14 ("jesting," and cf. 39:14, 17 [NRSV "insult"]).

121. Note the parallels to "time," "old age," and "laughter" in 17:17, 21; 18:11, 13–15. Note also the emphasis in vv. 1–2: "as he had said," "as he had promised," "of which God had spoken."

the logical conclusion to ch. 16 and especially to 17:20–21. Yahweh's purposes are worked out within the harsh reality of human rivalry and jealousy, although here the focus is solely on progeny (21:12b). Having ordered the coerced surrogacy of Hagar before (16:1–2), Sarah reverses herself now that she has her own son, and orders the ostracism of both Ishmael and Hagar. Indeed, God even overrides Abraham's objection to the "banishment" (*garaš*) of Ishmael, and Abraham sends them off into the wilderness. When their scarce provisions are depleted, Hagar's despair is wrenching (v. 16). Yet, as before, God cares for Ishmael because he too is the "seed" of Abraham (v. 13). Although he and Hagar are social rejects, and Ishmael is not a full son of the covenant, they are not the object of *God's* curse but the beneficiaries of God's blessing. Thus the angel of God comes to Hagar and Ishmael as they are near death, opens Hagar's eyes to the source of sustenance, and sets the rejected mother and son on the road to becoming a "great nation," a promise that echoes that in 17:20 and is fulfilled at the end of the cycle (25:12–18). Almost as if to embrace a new and separate destiny, when Ishmael grows up, Hagar chooses a wife for him from her own country, from Egypt (v. 21; cf. 16:1).[122]

With the problem of Ishmael finally resolved, the text turns to Abraham's relations with the native inhabitants, in this case Abimelech (21:22–34). The passage highlights two themes: blessing and land. Abimelech approaches Abraham with the

observation, "God is with you in all that you do." Abraham's success and affluence signify blessing, and Abraham quickly learns the truth of the proverb, "wealth brings many new friends" (Prov 19:3). Abimelech proposes a formal agreement affirming mutual honesty and integrity, and Abraham agrees. The arrangement is beneficial to both—a potential share of Abraham's blessing for Abimelech, and for Abraham, the chance to improve on his status as an alien by gaining legal recognition from a native. In fact, the actual ratification of the treaty appears as the means for resolving a dispute over well rights, and Abraham seems to insist on *paying* Abimelech in order to gain legal title to his first piece of Canaanite soil, the well at Beersheba (cf. with Sarah's grave, 23:11–13).

In short, a lot has happened in this little unit. The Philistine king, who had every right to eject Abraham from the land (ch. 20), has instead treated this alien with honesty and magnanimity, however self-serving his motivation. Thus he stands to benefit from Abraham's charge: "those who bless you, I will bless" (12:3). And Abraham, although still an alien, at least has legal recognition and a piece of the promised land. As if to mark his claim, Abraham plants a tree in Beersheba and invokes the name of Yahweh—El Olam, God Everlasting—reminding us of the altars he built earlier (12:7, 8; 13:18; on the name, see Appendix 2).

6. The Test (ch. 22)

You would think that a man of well over a hundred years would deserve a little rest from the trials of life, but such is not

---

122. The story in 21:15–19 seems to assume that Ishmael is much younger than his apparent age of sixteen.

the case with Abraham. Indeed, as ch. 22 tells us, he faced the greatest trial of all at just such a ripe old age. This is a test of unimaginable horror, and it makes for a story that is one of the most inscrutable—and most beautifully told—in the entire Hebrew Bible.[123] For some interpreters, the text represents literary art at its most sublime, and an ideal vision of the nature of God and humankind. For others, the writer is a sadist whose God is the devil and whose human protagonist is a madman.[124]

The test is set apart from its immediate context by the phrase "after these things" (vv. 1, 20). The entire story is about a journey that begins and ends at Beersheba, but something about this journey transcends spatial and even temporal definition. This is a journey whose beginning reaches back to the initial charge to Abraham, and whose destination leads into the future of Israel. The journey to Moriah is the consummation of a larger pilgrimage that is Abraham's life, and it is only because he makes this journey that there will be an Israel to continue in his way.

Together with the opening words of the original charge to Abraham in 12:1, the command to sacrifice his son forms the framework for the cycle: "Go (lek-leka) from your country and your kindred and your father's house to the land that I will tell you" (AT). "Take your son, your only son Isaac, whom you love, and go to (lek-leka) the land of Moriah, and

offer him there as a burnt offering upon one of the mountains that I shall tell you." The one command is full of promise and hope; the other, full of doom and despair. Obedience to the first command led to the birth of a son; obedience to the second would lead to the death of the son.

Both commands are issued by the same God, but they do not come to the same man. The Abraham who answered the first command is not the one who hears the second, for the Abram of 12:1–3 was little more than a name (a name soon to be changed, at that), while the Abraham of ch. 22 is the complex character rendered by the narrative of chs. 12–21. The latter is an altogether human character, capable of that complete conformity to the divine will for which the text reserves the word "righteousness" (15:6; 18:19; cf. 6:9),[125] yet alternately misdirected by fear and diffidence, and capable of such irresponsibility that even pagan kings find him repugnant (12:10–20; chs. 16; 20). This is the man who demonstrated the deepest trust in God, yet who could fall all over himself laughing at the preposterousness of God's promise. He is also the father who was troubled by sending away his son Ishmael (ch. 21). If there is any answer to the question of why God tests Abraham, ultimately it must take into account the context of the entire cycle. God tests Abraham in order to know, once and

123. See the classic analysis of Auerbach, *Mimesis*, 3–23.

124. One need only recall newspaper stories of people who have murdered their own children because they heard a voice telling them to do so.

125. As a result of the redactional combination of stories, there is an ineluctable tension between the Abraham who questions God's righteousness in destroying Sodom and Gomorrah (18:17–33) and the Abraham here who voices no question about the order to kill Isaac. "But," as Hendel says, "in the plural representations of the text, it is all one Abraham," who "exceeds our grasp" of understanding (*Remembering Abraham*, 40–41).

for all, whether or not Abraham trusts in God completely. "It is not a game with God. God genuinely does not know."[126] And the means of the test—the sacrifice of Isaac—is dictated by the fact that Abraham's most questionable behavior has occurred precisely in situations in which he irresponsibly jeopardized, circumvented, or distrusted the promise of a son.

Along with the reason and means for the test, we must also determine its meaning and significance within the context of the cycle as a whole, and not simply within ch. 22. In ch. 22, God demands that Abraham kill his only son; within the context of the cycle, God demands that Abraham kill the promises God has made, and thus return the world to its state at the end of the primeval cycle. Of course, son and promises cannot be separated, but the weight of meaning lies in the fact that Isaac is a gift who embodies God's promise of blessing, land, and nationhood. The test is one of obedience and trust. In essence, it is a test of Abraham's relationship with Yahweh. It asks whether Abraham's trust is really in God, and not simply in what God has promised. Abraham has built altars before and sacrificed to this God, when God renewed the promises (12:7–8; 13:18). Is he willing now to build an altar and sacrifice the promises themselves, embodied in his son, in order to demonstrate his unswerving trust in the God who stands behind the promises? In ch. 15 a sacrifice was the means by which Yahweh demonstrated adamant commitment to Abraham. Now the demand that Abraham kill his son as a sacrifice is the most radical reinforcement of the fact that the son is a gift from God, a gift that,

in sovereignty and freedom, God can call back. Abraham's corresponding willingness to relinquish the son he has waited so long to embrace signifies his utter dependence on the one who has given the son. Abraham cannot possess the promises; they are his by privilege and not by right. They are most truly his only when he "offers them up."[127]

Abraham's obedient response to the divine command in v. 2 is all the more remarkable because he does not know that this is a test. Only we, the readers, know this, and the difference is crucial. The most effective test is one in which those who are being tested are not aware of their situation. Imagine how much more telling a test of our civil defense network would be if those occasional radio announcements did not include the words "this is only a test," and went on to describe some imminent disaster! Abraham does not know that he is being tested, and must take the command with utmost seriousness; we do know that he is being tested. The author has winked at us, as it were, inviting us to identify more with the author than with the protagonist. Although our collusion with the author does not mean we know in advance the outcome of the tale, it means we can observe the action with a detachment unavailable to Abraham.

The skill of the narrator is again evident in the staccato succession of verbs used to describe Abraham's obedient responses on hearing the command (v. 3) and on arriving at the designated spot (vv.

126. Brueggemann, *Genesis*, 187.

127. As Cotter points out, the phrase "whom you love" (v. 2) is the first occurrence of the word *love* in the Hebrew Bible, making Abraham's relinquishment all the more poignant (*Genesis*, 177).

9–10). Without melodramatic flourishes the text leads up to the moment when we see the ritual knife poised over the neck of Isaac. This is the turning point of the story, marked by the reentry of God in the form of the angelic voice that repeats the initial summons: "'Abraham! Abraham!' And he said, 'Here I am'" (v. 11; cf. v. 1). The silence that has pervaded the story between God's command and this call has been broken only by the brief and ironic conversation between father and son. There has been no subsequent word from God explaining the macabre order, nor has there been any utterance from Abraham about his agony—indeed, the author does not even tell us if it *is* agony. Apart from its context, it would be entirely possible to read the story and conclude that Abraham followed the order with a joyful heart and a radiant smile. Avoiding any description of motivation or thoughts or feelings, the story focuses on one question: will Abraham do what God has told him to do? When he raises the knife over Isaac, we know that the answer is yes. In retrospect we can see that it has been so from the very beginning when Abraham responded to the initial summons by saying "Ready."[128]

Abraham has done what God told him to do, and, both in terms of the content and context of this story, his action represents the supreme moment of righteousness in the pentateuchal narrative up to this point. If the first step on the way out of the primeval world of alienation was taken in ch. 12, the final step (for Abraham) is taken here. Abraham

has demonstrated that he "fears God" (v. 12), which refers not so much to fright as it does to reverence and resultant obedience. In one sense, therefore, the story could end with the etiology in v. 14. That it does not end here. but is followed by a renewal of the promises, is of great significance. First, the addition of the promises indicates a crucial aspect of the purpose behind the test. The test was posed, not only to evaluate Abraham's personal trust in Yahweh, but also to establish the trustworthiness of the one through whom Yahweh's promises are mediated to the world. The story's greatest significance lies not in the fact that Abraham is the father of Isaac, but that he is the "father of a multitude"—the father of Israel—and thus the father of the promises. Yahweh's main purpose in the test was to establish that the trustee of the promises was worthy of his office.

The second point is implicit in the first. Yahweh's promises now come to Abraham as a reward for his righteousness. The author makes this explicit at the beginning and end of the divine speech: "because you have done this . . . because you have obeyed my voice." Never before in the cycle has there been such a clear causal connection between obedience and promise. A hierarchy among the major themes we have traced is apparent here: the theme of responsibility is primary. The significance of this development for the meaning of the pentateuchal narrative is eloquently expressed by Mordecai Kaplan:

> These words place the Abrahamic promise in a totally different light. For, while hitherto the promise given to Abraham is mainly an

---

128. Speiser, *Genesis*, 161. The identical phrase is used in verses 7 and 11, each with a different nuance determined by the context.

expression of divine favor, it now comes for the first time as an acknowledgment of Abraham's worth. *This is the point where divine effort meets with full response in the human being.* It is toward this goal, first in Israel and then in all of mankind, that all divine efforts from the viewpoint of the Torah tend.[129]

The formulation of the promises here thus stands in permanent balance—and tension—with the formulation at the beginning of the cycle (12:1–3): on the one hand the promises of nationhood, land, and blessing are a gift of God prevenient to any worth on the part of the recipient; on the other hand, the continuation and fulfillment of those promises is contingent on the responsibility of the recipient. This is a tension that will pervade the Torah from now to the end, but will not achieve its fullest expression until Israel as a people arrives at the mountain of Sinai (Exodus 19).

Finally, the significance of the renewed promises is indicated by the fact that Yahweh's speech takes the form of an "oath" (v. 16a). The use of the formula adds a solemnity to the promises similar to that evoked by the covenant ceremony in ch. 15. But an even greater significance of the oath here in ch. 22 is that it becomes one of those few redactional threads highlighting the continuity of the pentateuchal narrative in its entirety. At a number of critical points a retrospective reference to Yahweh's oath will serve to indicate Yahweh's faithfulness to the promises made to the ancestors.[130] Thus

Abraham's exemplary obedience and Yahweh's corresponding oath represent, not only the climax of the Abraham cycle, but also one of the literary pillars of the Torah, and the theological foundation of hope.

Epilogue (chs. 23–24)

The brief passage at 22:20–24 provides a transition to the epilogue by referring to Abraham's family in Haran (including Uz and Buz!) and especially to Rebekah, who, of course, will become the wife of Isaac in ch. 24. The position of these verses demonstrates the role of the preceding story as part of the framework to the Abraham cycle (i.e., chs. 12 and 22), for these verses have their counterpart in the prologue preceding Abraham's charge (11:27–30). The text then immediately turns to the subject of Sarah's death and burial. The point of the story in its context is that now Abraham holds legal title to a piece of the land of Canaan. Indeed, the purchase of the burial plot is narrated as the report of a legal transaction, as if we had before us a court stenographer's notes and the accompanying deed.[131] The action takes place in the city gate (vv. 10, 18), which served as the courtroom in ancient Israel (cf. Ruth 4), and includes repeated references to the presence of formal witnesses ("in the sight/hearing of," vv. 11, 13, 16, 18). In the lively bartering between Abraham and Ephron, Abraham insists on buying the land. As if the point

---

129. Quoted from an unpublished manuscript in Plaut, *Torah*, 153 (italics added).

130. See Gen 24:7; 26:3; 50:24; Exod 13:5, 11;

Num 14:16, 30; 32:11; Deut 1:8, 35; 6:10, etc. See Rendtorff, *Pentateuch*, 75 (German edition).

131. For example, see the Ugaritic (thirteenth-century) land sale document in Hallo, *The Context of Scripture* 3:256.

were not yet clear, the author concludes the chapter with a deliberately redundant summary reemphasizing the legality of Abraham's title.[132] Now Abraham—"a stranger and alien"—has a "possession" (literally a "hold") on the land of the promise, minimal though it may be.[133] By the end of the ancestral saga, all of the patriarchs and matriarchs will be buried in the cave at Machpelah (except Rachel): "in death they were heirs and no longer 'strangers.'"[134]

The remainder of the epilogue is dominated by a concern comparable to that of securing a portion of the land, namely, finding a wife for Isaac and thus insuring that Abraham will become the "father of a multitude." Things would not work well if the son of the promise remained a bachelor.

The story of Abraham began with a journey from Haran to Canaan, and it ends with a journey from Canaan to Haran and back again. When this journey is over, Abraham's life will be complete, even though he will then take another wife and have six more sons through her (25:1–4). Like Ishmael (and Eliezer), these are not the sons of the promise.[135] Abraham will give these sons "gifts," but he will give "all that he has" to Isaac

(25:4–6a; cf. 24:36). Abraham will send them away "eastward to the east country" (25:6), but he will bring the wife for Isaac *from* the east country. This is not a journey Abraham himself will make, but it is a final movement in that spiritual journey that is the story of his life.

The initial scene suggests that Abraham is nearing the point of death, a scene that will recur with Isaac, Jacob, and, more briefly, with Joseph.[136] From the outset, the search for Isaac's wife takes place without any divine initiative. Abraham's commissioning of the servant is not in obedience to a divine command rejecting a Canaanite wife or demanding a wife from kinfolk. Abraham is acting on his own. However, the opening scene is the only place in the cycle where Abraham quotes the divine charge:[137] "Yahweh, the God of heaven, who took me from my father's house and from the land of my birth, and who spoke to me and swore to me, 'To your descendants I will give this land,' he will send his angel before you, and you shall take a wife for my son from there" (v. 7, AT). Thus Abraham understands what he is doing to be in conformity with his status as trustee of the promises. That status is the core of his narrative identity, and what he does now is an expression of that identity, or in other words, consistent with his character.

When Abraham refers to Yahweh's "oath," he limits the content to the promise of land. This emphasis is all the more

---

132. The verb for "made over" in v. 17 is used in legal real-estate transactions in Lev 25:30; 27:14, 17, 19.

133. The word for "property" and "possession" in vv. 4 and 9 is the same.

134. Von Rad, *Genesis*, 245.

135. Formally, the Abraham story concludes with the genealogy of Ishmael (25:12–18), just as the Jacob cycle will conclude with the genealogy of Esau (ch. 36). Thus the text goes out on a limb with each one (as it were), only to return to the trunk and the chosen ones (cf. Hendel, *Remembering Abraham*, 36).

136. Genesis 27; 47:29—49:33; and 50:24–26 respectively. Note especially the same custom of taking an oath in 24:1–4 and 47:29–31.

137 Except 20:13, which, however, does not refer specifically to the promises and even appears to be critical of Yahweh's guidance (see the discussion and accompanying note above).

striking since the promise of land was the weakest part of the divine oath in 22:15–18. The focus on the land promise arises in response to the servant's question—should he take Isaac back to Haran (presumably to stay) if the suitable fiancée will not leave? Abraham vehemently rejects this possibility, for if Isaac were to return to Haran it would represent a complete reversal of Abraham's life, a repudiation of the promise of land. Indeed, it would amount to a renunciation of the charge Abraham had first obeyed. While Abraham cannot prevent Isaac's own repudiation of the promises, he can at least arrange his marriage in such a way that repudiation will be less likely. This he does by forbidding the servant to take Isaac back to Haran.

Of course if Isaac could marry a Canaanite, there would be no threat to the promise of land. In fact, his status as an alien might even improve (cf. ch. 34). A long history of revulsion against Canaanite culture and religion stands behind the prohibition of this solution (beginning with 9:20–27). Throughout Israel's history, marriage with Canaanites was understood to be the cause of disloyalty to Yahweh, and thus ultimately of loss of the land.[138] The primary concern is not ethnic but theological purity.[139] If,

as seems likely, ch. 24 fits within this tradition, then Abraham's refusal to allow a Canaanite marriage is intended to protect not only the son of the promise but also the promise itself.

Abraham's strictures are twofold: no Canaanite wife, no wife even from kinfolk unless she will come to Canaan. When we combine these two, an interesting result appears. The wife who may not be a Canaanite must come to Canaan. Consequently the new matriarch will in a way share Abraham's story even more than Isaac does, for she too will be told to "go from your land and your kinfolk and your father's household, to the land that I will show you" (12:1). The future matriarch is marrying the son of an alien, and must therefore become an alien herself. Moreover, at the very moment that she says, "I will go," she receives the traditional family blessing, "be the mother of thousands . . . and may your descendants possess the gate of those who hate them" (24:58, 60). The latter part of that blessing is almost identical to part of Yahweh's "oath" in 22:17b.

While Rebekah's declaration, "I will go," is not in response to a direct command from God, it is portrayed as a response to the divine guidance of events that has led to this moment. As her father and brother proclaim after hearing the servant's story, "The thing comes from Yahweh" (v. 50, AT). From the moment the servant receives his commission, the entire story moves according to incredible coincidences of the divine will, making it unlike any other story in Genesis.[140] But the fantastic quality of the narrative

138. Cf. Exod 34:11–16; Deut 7:1–5. Religious and ethnic exclusivity became a major issue in the postexilic community, on which see Ezra 8; Neh 10:28–30; 13:23–30. However, as Meyers points out (*Discovering Eve*, 70–71, 183–84), exogamy was also practiced in Israel's history, notably by Moses and David. See Appendix 3 regarding the problem of xenophobia in connection with covenant theology.

139. So Plaut, *Torah*, 161, in contrast to Redford (*Biblical Story of Joseph*, 247), who suggests that the search involves not only "religious" but also "racial exclusiveness."

140. Despite similarities to the Joseph story, where God is often providentially "with Joseph," making his way prosper.

should not detract from its function, which is to demonstrate that God has confirmed Abraham's actions. In a sense this story is about human initiative and a divine response, human conviction and divine confirmation, human responsibility and divine faithfulness. What Abraham does here is not only consistent with his own character, it is also consistent with Yahweh's character, as Abraham himself predicts at the outset (v. 7).

"Go from your land and from your kinfolk and from your father's household, to the land that I shall show you"; "Go to my land and to my kinfolk and take a wife for my son Isaac." The climax of the Abraham cycle may come with the binding of Isaac, but its consummation comes with Abraham's charge to his servant. In this charge, Abraham's identity is now complete—he knows who he is, not only in terms of the past and the present, but also in terms of that future that extends beyond his life.

THE JACOB CYCLE
(GENESIS 25:19—36:43)

1. Prologue: The Dysfunctional Family (25:19–34)

We might call Isaac the shadow, for he appears as an independent character only in chs. 26 and 27. In the former he is little more than a reflection of Abraham, and in the latter he is already an old man on his deathbed. Jacob is really the protagonist of the story of Isaac that runs from 25:19 to the end of ch. 36; thus we call this unit the Jacob cycle.

Already in the prologue we can see the distinctive thematic focus of the Jacob

cycle in contrast to the Abraham stories. Like Sarah, Rebekah is barren, but this problem, which persists for twenty years, disappears within the space of one verse (25:21; cf. vv. 20, 26)! Similarly, the problem of who will be Isaac's legitimate heir, a problem which begins in utero, reminds us of the young Isaac and Ishmael. But in the Jacob cycle the problem is one of overt rivalry, which was never the case before. Here the two boys are not only full brothers but twins, and much of the tension in the plot derives from the fact that the younger supplants the older, who should have the privilege of primogeniture (cf. Deut 21:15–17). Indeed, this problem continues to the end of Genesis.

If before we thought that Yahweh's purposes had to work out through human agents whose integrity was often questionable, we quickly find that with Jacob we have to reckon with an even more unscrupulous character. Moreover, from the outset the cycle resists any attempt at discerning whether the corresponding inscrutability in the character of Yahweh comes as a result of having to deal with such shady people or, on the contrary, whether it is Yahweh's incomprehensible will that invisibly directs the human characters. In the prologue, the first words from God are an oracle delivered to Rebekah: "Two nations are in your womb . . . ; the elder shall serve the younger." In this reading the oracle, standing at the outset of the cycle, appears to determine the fate of Esau and Jacob as it unfolds in 25:29–34 and ch. 27.[141] However, the latter phrase could mean the opposite: "the elder, the younger shall serve." Just as

141. For a discussion of the role of fate in biblical narratives, see Gunn, *Fate of King Saul*.

in Greek mythology the meaning of the Delphic oracle was not always plain, so in this biblical oracle, both readings are possible, making the events about to unfold ambiguous as to their correspondence with the divine will.[142]

Indeed, the oracle comes as an interpretation of Rebekah's suffering caused by the two fetuses "crashing together" in her womb.[143] The struggle between the elder and younger brothers has already begun before the oracle is spoken. Moreover, one can see at the outset how parental favoritism can trigger family dysfunction: the parents each love one son or the other, easily exacerbating natural sibling rivalry (25:28). The Jacob cycle is a story of constant wrangling and wrestling, an extended and sometimes potentially violent family feud that spills over into the Joseph cycle, and even there is not fully resolved. As one pastoral theologian has commented, "Probably in no other context of human life does our sinfulness show as clearly as it does in the family."[144] Here the characters seem the victims of their own cussedness rather than the helpless pawns of fate. When Jacob emerges from the womb gripping Esau's heel, he may be fulfilling a divine destiny, but he is also acting out of his own nature. While the newborn Esau seems to be an innocent victim of his brother's jealousy, if not of fate, in the following episode he succumbs as much to his own boorish stupidity as to Jacob's wily ploys. Jacob has a sharp mind and no conscience, but Esau is all belly and no brain.

Here is one of the best examples of the way in which personal characters represent national entities. Indeed, the oracle does not even refer to individuals, but to "two nations" and "two peoples." The oracle is about political factions, not fetuses. Esau is Edom and Jacob is Israel, two people that often were hostile toward each other, if not also at war.[145] And clearly the portrait of Esau here is unflattering. He emerges from the womb looking like a furry animal ("all of him like a coat of hair," 25:25, AT), an image confirmed when he wolfs down that stew. The red color in the etymology refers not to the name Esau but to the name Edom and the red rock of that country ("red" is identical to "Edomite").[146] Jacob emerges

---

142. Friedman (*Torah*, 88) has promoted this reading, apparently from a suggestion of David Noel Freedman. Thus Jacob in the following incident and in ch. 27 (there along with Rebekah) could be either advancing God's will or opposing it! Niditch argues that Rebekah "is the one who knows and fulfills what God wants" and represents "a trickster heroine" ("Genesis," 22b, 23b). Cf. White (*Narration and Discourse*, 221), for whom Rebekah is "the intelligent protagonist and instrument of the divine will"

143. See 25:22. The root *rss* usually means "crush." Here it is often translated by "struggled together," which is appropriate but does not convey the more violent connotations of the root.

144. Anderson, *Family*, 97.

145. The region of Edom is south of the Dead Sea. Cf. 36:1; Exod 15:15; Num 20:14–21; Amos 1:11–12; Jer 49:7–22. In 27:40 the subservience could refer to David's subjection of Edom in 2 Sam 8:13–14, and the breaking loose to Edom's rebellion in 2 Kgs 8:20. Edom's rejoicing over the destruction of Jerusalem appears in Ps 137:7–9. For more positive views, see Deut 2:1–8a; 23:7a.

146. Sarna (*Genesis*, 180) points out that the word translated "red" here is "ruddy" when ascribed to David (1 Sam 16:12), apparently an attractive feature. Here the image resembles the contemporary offensive slang word "redneck." Also, one would expect a wordplay between "hair" (*śēʿar*) and the place name "Seir," located in Edomite territory. Cotter (*Genesis*, 189) offers the amusing names "Hairy and the Heel"!

Table 4: The Jacob Cycle

25:19–34 Prologue

26 Isaac and Canaanites: Conflict and covenant

27 JACOB AND ESAU: DECEPTION

28:10–22 Bethel: Departure

29—31 Jacob and Laban: Deception and reconciliation

32:1–2 Mahanaim

32–33 JACOB AND ESAU: RECONCILIATION

34 Jacob and Canaanites: Deception and enmity

35 Bethel: Return

36 The Edomites

---

already "grabbing," which explains *his* name, "Heel Grabber."

> "He acts like an *animal*, has an animal's habits! Eats like one, moves like one, talks like one! There's something even sub-human—something not quite to the stage of humanity yet! . . . There he is—Stanley Kowalksi—survivor of the stone age!" Blanche Du-Bois in *A Streetcar Named Desire*[147]

In short, when Esau and Jacob "crash together" in Rebekah's womb, they set in motion the predominant tension in the Jacob cycle. But already the oracle suggests that this struggle involves more than personal characters. It is not by coincidence that the people of Israel identify themselves with Jacob. His name approaches both in etymology and connotation a contemporary pejorative epithet—Jacob is a "heel." But his new name "Israel" (not given until 32:28) has several meanings. Literally it can mean "God (El) struggles" or "rules," although 32:28 makes God the object—Jacob is "he who struggles with God." The ambiguity may be deliberate. If the Jacob cycle is the story of a family feud, it is also the story of Jacob's struggle to come to terms with the God who befriends him despite his perversity, then fights with him despite his friendship. The Jacob who grabs the heel of Esau is also the Israel whom God wounds in the thigh.

While the structure of the cycle is not completely concentric, there are corresponding sections that an outline reveals (Table 4, above).

In 25:30, Esau ineloquently refers to "that red, red stuff."

147. Williams, *A Streetcar Named Desire*, 88 (Scene 4).

2. The Isaac Stories (ch. 26)

The story that focuses on Isaac him-self begins almost where Abraham's began, with a famine in the land (cf. 12:10–20). Isaac moves to Gerar, the city of Abimelech, king of the Philistines. Immediately Yahweh appears to Isaac and admonishes him *not* to go down to Egypt (as Abraham did), but to "settle in the land that I shall tell you" (cf. Gen 12:1).[148] Then follows a repetition of the blessing and promises of Abraham (vv. 3–5) with explicit references to the cli-max of the Abraham cycle (ch. 22), for the promises descend to Isaac as a fulfill-ment of Yahweh's "oath" to Abraham, and "because Abraham obeyed my voice and kept my charge, my commandments, my statutes, and my laws." The continuation of Yahweh's blessing and promises for the world is a gift only Yahweh can grant, but that now also comes as a divine response to the righteousness of Abraham (cf. 19:29).

The next incident reveals the truth in the proverb "like father, like son." No sooner has Isaac received the promises than he fears for his life and repeats the "sister/wife" ruse (vv. 6–11). As a result he wins the scorn but also the protection of Abimelech, who, one would think, would have been suspicious from the outset.[149]

Once again a sojourner has irresponsibly brought the natives to near catastrophe yet enjoys undeserved welfare. In fact, in the next passage, Yahweh blesses Isaac so abundantly that the Philistines are in-timidated by his affluence and send him away, apparently to the outskirts of Gerar (vv. 12–17). Although v. 15 seems clumsy, it suggests that the Philistines had already tried to protect themselves from Isaac's expansion by filling up the wells that had belonged to Abraham (21:22–34). In effect, therefore, they have broken the treaty between Abraham and Abimelech.

The rest of the chapter describes the process through which the characters are reconciled and the treaty is restored. The names of the wells Isaac's servants dig trace this development: from Contention and Enmity to Room and Oath. But the determinative factor in the reconciliation is the second pronouncement of divine blessing on Isaac (v. 24). By juxtaposition, the pronouncement effects a dramatic re-versal in the Philistines' attitude; they can now see that Isaac's good fortune is not a threat to them but a potential boon. "We see that Yahweh is with you . . . ; you are now the blessed of Yahweh" (vv. 29–30). The result is a renewal of the treaty and the restoration of "peace" (vv. 29, 31).

Perhaps more than any other part of the ancestral saga, the brief story of Isaac gains its greatest significance from its context. Retrospectively, it affirms Yah-weh's faithfulness to the promises—and to Abraham. Prospectively, it holds up an

148. This land turns out to be where he is, Philistia (i.e., the southeast coastal region), and the land promise refers twice to "lands" in the plural (26:3–4), perhaps because the author wants to be sure that Canaan proper is included.

149. If this is the same Abimelech as in ch. 20, he would be quite old. The connections with 12:10–20 and chs. 20–21 are usually understood as evidence for the existence of two alternative traditions of the same incident, now lodged in two literary sources (J in chs. 12; 26; E in chs.

20; 21). A different approach would see in ch. 26 a deliberate commentary on the earlier stories rather than an independent tradition. For the former view, see the standard commentaries; for the latter, see, for example, Van Seters, *Abraham in History and Tradition*, 167–82.

example of blessing and peace for those who recognize the "blessed of Yahweh"—"those who bless you I will bless" (12:3). We now know Isaac as the one who bears Yahweh's blessing, as well as one who can bequeath his own blessing. Thus, in the next story, when Jacob *steals* his father's blessing, we will wonder if he has stolen Yahweh's as well.

3. Deception (27:1—28:9)

"But Jacob said to Rebekah, his mother, 'Look, my brother Esau is a hairy man, and I am a man of smooth skin. Perhaps my father will feel me, and I shall seem to be mocking him, and bring a curse on myself and not a blessing'" (27:11–12). Jacob's words reveal a central trait in Jacob's character, and also foreshadow the rest of the cycle and the saga as a whole. Like his mother, Jacob possesses that rare and dangerous combination of deceitfulness and cunning, a combination that both serves him well and is the source of unending anxiety. Jacob is a slick character. In collusion with Rebekah, he deceives his father by pretending to be Esau, thereby stealing the patriarchal blessing that rightly belongs to his brother, primarily the right of primogeniture.[150] The deception of Isaac and theft of the patriarchal blessing introduce a tension that is maintained until near the end of the cycle (Genesis 33). From now until his old age, Jacob will be both the deceiver and the deceived, and it will seldom be clear whether his reward is one of blessing or of curse.

The story is told with superb artistry, vividly encouraging us to see, hear, feel, and taste what is happening. It assumes the characterization of the two brothers as a hunter and "man of the field" (Esau) and someone who was "satisfied staying at home" (Jacob, 25:27, AT), and, of course, of Esau as hairy (25:25) and Jacob as smooth skinned. "Elder" and "younger" appear repeatedly. Jacob's deception involves an outright lie and is sealed with a kiss. Yet he is blessed in the name of God, an action understood to be irrevocable. Jacob's predominance over his elder brother takes on a bitter irony also in that (thanks to Rebekah) his disguise makes him smell like Esau and the "field that Yahweh has blessed," but which Jacob had disdained (27:27; 25:28, AT).[151]

The themes of nationhood and land appear in vv. 27b–29a, 39–40. The language about the earth concerns agricultural fertility more than political geography, but the line about nations bowing down to Jacob clearly echoes the oracle of the prologue and refers to Israel as a people. The most obvious of the pentateuchal themes here, though, is that of blessing and curse. At first sight, the story is about a personal blessing belonging to the patriarch and at his disposal. The setting is similar to that of ch. 24 and identical to that of chs. 48–49 (*Jacob's* deathbed blessing). Thus the patriarchal blessing is distinct from the divine blessing, which

150. As the alternate translation in the NRSV suggests (notes e and f, "*of* the fatness / dew"), v. 39 may be read in a positive way, thus making the only difference from Jacob's blessing the subservience of Esau, and even that is qualified in v. 40b (so Alter, *Five Books*, 145). Esau is not cursed (cf. also Fretheim, *Genesis*, 536–37). See also n. 152 below.

151. Alter (*Five Books*, 142) points out that Rebekah has shrewdly anticipated Isaac's need to smell his son.

only Yahweh can grant. Or is it? Suspicion is aroused by Isaac's invoking God as the source of Jacob's blessing (vv. 16, 27–28). In addition, the last half of v. 29 sounds very much like 12:3: "Cursed be every one who curses you, and blessed be every one who blesses you!" Thus we are again left to wonder whether what has happened in this story is merely a result of human actions or also an outcome of the divine oracle of the prologue. Finally, when we consider that the story is about blessing gained by deceit (a deceit that really *does* mock the patriarch and tear apart his family), we realize that the theme of responsibility is also involved. Thus the theological ambiguity of the story increases. A scoundrel has made himself heir to "the blessed of the Lord."

Unlike the gullible fool of the prologue who sells his birthright[152] for a bowl of mush, the Esau in ch. 27 is an innocent victim, and he reacts first with inconsolable despair and then with a consuming hatred for Jacob. Rebekah, who seems to be listening outside everyone's door, hears of Esau's plan to kill Jacob,[153] and she urges Jacob to flee to her brother Laban until Esau's wrath subsides. In the redactional context,[154] her tactic with Isaac

is more devious. How dreadful it would be, she says, if Jacob were to marry one of those Hittite women, referring to Esau's wives (26:34–35). As if on cue, Isaac summons Jacob, blesses him again,[155] and dispatches him to Laban, admonishing him not to marry one of the Canaanite women (cf. ch. 24).

The dismissal scene has an ironic effect on Esau, who has done a little eavesdropping of his own. Realizing his father's disapproval of Canaanite wives, he marries a daughter of Ishmael! He who has sold his birthright and lost his father's blessing and, apparently, the special divine blessing as well, marries a daughter of the one who would share Abraham's blessing but not Yahweh's covenant. Esau never seems to make the right move, at least not yet, and there he is with his Ishmaelite wife, waiting for Jacob to return.

4. Departure (28:10–22)

This passage is the linchpin in the cycle and provides the most explicit connection to the wider literary context. Jacob is on his way to Haran (v. 10), and has come

---

152. The birthright is a legal concept ("right of the firstborn"), the blessing a more overtly religious one. On the former, see Deut 21:15–17. Esau's comment in 27:36 assumes that the two can be separate, but in practice they seem to be synonymous.

153. As White says, "It is only the narrator who can 'tell' Rebekah the inner thoughts of another character [27:41]. This makes all the clearer the identification of the narrator with Rebekah's viewpoint" (*Narration and Discourse*, 228).

154. See Appendix 1. Without 27:1–45, we could see a continuous narrative connecting

26:34–35 (Esau's troublesome wives) with 27:46—28:2 (sending off Jacob to Abrahamic kinfolk to *avoid* taking such a wife), linking 28:6–9 (Esau's Ishmaelite wife from Abrahamic kinfolk) to Jacob's journey and stay in Haran (28:10–32:2). Then Jacob's journey would be much like the search for a wife in ch. 24 (i.e. not a flight from danger). Isaac's blessing in 28:3–4 might be a redactional addition to that, connecting the larger ancestral saga. For a more nuanced view of the redaction here, see Alter, *Five Books*, 147–48.

155. This blessing in 28:1 is probably from a different source than that in ch. 27, but, in context, Isaac is now blessing the one whom he knows to have deceived him!

to "a certain place" where he decides to spend the night (v. 11). He has a dream in which Yahweh addresses him for the first time (vv. 12–15), though not as we might expect. Yahweh says nothing of Jacob's deception of Isaac, much less reprimand him. Instead, Yahweh is introduced as the "God of Abraham your father and the God of Isaac," and immediately offers him the promises of land, offspring, and blessing, emphasizing again that the blessing will be one from which "all the families of the earth" will benefit. In addition, Yahweh promises something peculiarly fitting to Jacob's situation: "Know that I am with you and will keep you wherever you go, and will bring you back to this land; for I will not leave you until I have done what I have promised you" (v. 15).

The Bethel story is to the Jacob cycle what the charge to Abram was to the Abraham cycle (Gen 12:1–3); it provides the foundation for the redactional unity of the narrative (see Appendix 1). In both passages the patriarchs stand at the threshold of a journey, but their points of origin and destination are reversed— Abram is leaving Haran (Mesopotamia) for Canaan; Jacob is leaving Canaan for Haran. Jacob is going where Abraham forbade Isaac to go (24:6, 8), the only patriarch to go east, and in context (ch. 27) he is fleeing from fraternal vengeance. Thus the threshold on which Jacob stands is fraught with danger, both behind and ahead. But the place on which he stands, or lies, is a threshold of a different order; it is "the gate of heaven" (v. 17). Yahweh

is here in this "awesome place."[156] Bethel is both literally and figuratively an intersection of divine and human paths, "reaching" each other.[157] Jacob is standing at a strange door that opens in three directions: behind is his past of failure and alienation; ahead is his future of both hope and uncertainty; and over above, coming down to meet him, is the presence of God.

The explicit *pledge* of divine presence and protection on his journey is distinctive to the Jacob cycle and indicates a concerted redactional effort. The cycle revolves around Jacob's journey from Bethel to Haran and back (cf. especially 35:1–15). At crucial points the text will either reiterate the pledge of divine presence or refer back to 28:10–22. Thus the thresholds that shape Jacob's identity coincide with moments of the self-disclosure of Yahweh.

How shall we interpret the fact that a cheater has become Yahweh's beneficiary and the agent of Yahweh's purpose in the world? First we should remember that Yahweh's previous agents, Abraham and Sarah, Isaac and Rebekah, were hardly above reproach. For that matter, the portrait of Esau in the prologue did not display a very worthy candidate either. We would hardly want the promises in the hands of one who might give them up for a bowl of mush. At least, as Robert Alter has put it, Jacob is a character to whom

156. In v. 11 "a certain place" is literally "*the* place," suggesting its special nature, and the word for "place" is used three times in the verse, as well as in vv. 16–17.

157. The word for "came to" in v. 11 and "reaching" in v. 12 are the same root—Jacob has "reached" the place that "reaches" into heaven.

destiny does not just happen—he knows how to *make* it happen.[158]

At the same time, the selection of Jacob represents the freedom of Yahweh, which has a revolutionary and creative dimension. As Northrop Frye suggests, "the deliberate choice of a younger son represents a divine intervention in human affairs, a vertical descent into the continuity [of normal succession] that breaks its pattern, but gives human life a new dimension by doing so."[159] The text, of course, does not speculate on these questions (partly because the combination of the blessed scoundrel results from *redactional* combinations).[160] As the rest of the cycle unfolds, it is interested only in how Jacob and Esau respond to their respective destinies. Regarding Jacob, the story is not interested so much in a doctrine of rewards and punishments as it is in a process of conversion that takes place over the course of Jacob's life. The word *conversion* here does not connote an instantaneous and powerful emotional experience. It refers to a gradual development towards righteousness, a growth marked by setbacks as well as advances. The scoundrel will never become a saint, but he will be transformed by his struggle with God. As for Esau, in the end he will embrace the brother he had intended to kill (33:4, see below).

Jacob's vow at Bethel is the beginning of his conversion. Already in response to Yahweh's appearance and promises, Jacob erects a commemorative monument, a tangible reference point for the future that lies ahead of him, and he pledges that it will be devoted to God. In response to the divine blessing, he vows a tithe.[161] Of course there is still something of the bargainer in this vow—highly conditional as it is; but Jacob is no longer simply the one who grasps blessing on his own; he is now also the one who receives blessing, promises, and protection as an undeserved gift. Thus "the central thought of the story" is this: "God starts a dialogue with Jacob and Jacob succeeds in giving the absolutely adequate response."[162]

Those who remain impatient for Jacob to receive his just desserts will soon find themselves more than satisfied. Indeed, already Jacob's future lies before him with the hope for a new family, but he leaves behind a shattered family and a brother who waits for the day of reckoning. The one who bears the divine blessing also bears the scars of alienation. The country to which he is headed is the old world, and the place he leaves behind is the promised land.

5. Jacob and Laban (chs. 29–31)

Jacob's arrival in Haran is described in terms of the convention of a meeting at a well, and his serendipitous introduction to Rachel reminds us of the servant's

158. Alter, *Art of Biblical Narrative*, 45.

159. Frye, *Great Code*, 182. Cf. Fokkelman, *Narrative Art*, 111, 115–21.

160. Thus Carr can say, "the reader is left with the task of making sense out of a subversive Jacob, on the one hand, and Jacob the divinely supported and morally justified ancestor of Israel, on the other" (*Fractures*, 300).

161. Fokkelman (*Narrative Art*, 75–76) argues with considerable cogency that v. 21b ("Yahweh shall be my God") belongs with the conditional clauses of vv. 20b–21a, and not with the following result clauses of v. 22. For an example of faith without such conditions see Hab 3:17–18.

162. Ibid., 74.

good fortune in finding Rebekah in ch. 24. The story portrays Jacob as someone who will make a good foreman, as he issues orders to the shepherds and gallantly uncovers the well for Rachel. Along with Jacob's natural abilities, the author also emphasizes his kinship ties with Rachel and Laban (especially 29:10!), for it is primarily on this basis that Laban welcomes Jacob into his household as "my bone and my flesh" (29:14). Jacob has found a new home and a new family.

When Laban offers to pay Jacob for his work, Jacob requests the hand of Rachel. After Jacob has worked six years for her, the "elder/younger" oracle of the prologue assumes an ironic twist. Jacob the trickster has met his match in Laban, a "selfish, greedy, exploiting, suspicious man of wealth, who never fails to observe good manners."[163] By exploiting a wedding custom, presumably a veil, Laban substitutes the elder daughter, Leah, for the younger, and thus "deceives" Jacob (cf. 27:35, root *rmh*)—it just isn't right for the younger to supplant the firstborn (29:26)! So Jacob must serve another seven years for Rachel.

The chronic problem of the matriarchs now frustrates Jacob's favoritism for the beautiful Rachel, for Yahweh opens Leah's womb, but Rachel is barren (30:1–24). The rejected older sister triumphs over the younger, thanks to God's "hearing" her "affliction" (29:32–33, cf. with Hagar, 16:6, 11; 21:27). But Rachel is not to be outdone. Like Sarah before her, she offers Jacob her slave girl as a surrogate mother, and through Bilhah Jacob fathers two more sons (but at least does not then

reject the woman). Now God has heard *Rachel's* voice (30:6). Her naming of the second son continues one of the central themes of the cycle and shows that she really is the perfect match for Jacob: "with God almighty wrestlings I have wrestled with my sister, and have prevailed" (v. 8, AT; cf. 32:28).[164]

Eventually the sisters trade Jacob back and forth enough to produce five more children. They must resort to employing yet another slave girl, and the rejected Leah must even *pay* to have Jacob sleep with her again, such is her need to be loved, and God hears *her* yet again (30:14–17). The last born (until the later Benjamin) is—finally—Rachel's own biological son Joseph: "May Yahweh add (to me another son)!" Jacob, on the other hand, has probably had enough. The point of all this is not to portray Jacob as the world's greatest lover. This frenetic sexual activity is clearly a manifestation of the divine blessing—there is no question that Jacob has been fertile and increased! In addition, Jacob's sons will become the twelve tribes of Israel, and the order of their birth and the identity of their mothers will continue the theme of younger over older to the end of the saga. Israel has emerged out of the intense struggle between Rachel and Leah, just as Israel will emerge from the struggle between Jacob and God in ch. 32.

Having gained the family he had sought, Jacob is ready to return to Canaan (30:25–43). But Laban is reluctant to let go of such a prolific worker and son-in-law, and acknowledges that Yahweh

---

163. Benno Jacob, as quoted in Plaut, *Torah*, 207.

164. The literal phrase is "wrestlings of God," where "God" is used as a superlative (NRSV, "mighty") but with obvious connotations. "Naphtali-Elohim" is thus similar to "Yisra-El."

has blessed himself because of Jacob (cf. Abimelech, 21:22; 26:28). Jacob agrees to continue working for Laban in exchange for a share in the herds, but Laban again tricks him out of his earnings. Now it is Jacob's turn at the game of deception. While his magical breeding methods would make a geneticist smile, the results are not amusing to Laban and his sons. To their dismay, Jacob "grew exceedingly rich." Laban's greed for the blessing, and his unjust treatment of the one who bears it, have produced his own financial ruin and alienated him from Jacob and from his own daughters.

So far Yahweh has not been involved in the story overtly, except for opening and closing wombs. Now in the midst of the rising tension between Jacob and Laban, Yahweh intervenes, speaking to Jacob for the first time since he left Canaan, and ordering him to return home with the assurance that Yahweh will be with him (31:3), an order repeated in v. 13 with an explicit reference back to Jacob's dream experience at Bethel in ch. 28. Moreover, Jacob now claims that *God* was behind all his curious breeding tricks (vv. 10–12). It is a claim that the narrator neither confirms nor denies, but it convinces Rachel and Leah, already feeling abused by Laban, to agree with Jacob's rightful ownership of all the wealth that he has gained. Jacob and family flee and Laban pursues.

The story of Jacob's flight stretches the tension in the unit to its greatest degree (31:17–42). Laban is outraged because he has lost his daughters and grandchildren, but also because Rachel has stolen his "household gods," some kind of idols (less pejoratively, iconic images) that were used in household shrines.[165] "Stealing," already so prominent in the cycle, becomes a leitmotif in this climactic section.[166] Of course, Jacob does not know that Rachel has stolen the household gods, and thus when Laban searches for them in vain (thanks to another savvy piece of deception by Rachel), Jacob's defense of himself is ironic (vv. 36–42).[167] Nevertheless, when Jacob credits his successful escape to the presence of God, his statement is consistent with the divine pledge at Bethel, and also with Laban's own encounter with God (v. 24; cf. 20:3).

The unit now reaches its climax with a nonaggression treaty (vv. 43–55). The pursuit has produced a remarkable change in Laban. It is he who initiates the treaty, in part, of course, out of desperation, but also out of an unusual surge of paternal devotion. While he persists in his claim of ownership of his family and property, he will resist any action that would bring them harm (v. 43). The terms

---

165. Hebrew *terafim*, perhaps associated with the veneration of ancestors. David's wife Michal has one (1 Sam 19:13), and, as here, the image is used comically. Cf. also Judg 17:5; 18:14, 18, 24. At least by the seventh century BCE such images were prohibited, e.g., Exod 20:4. See Appendix 4, and Miller, *Religion of Ancient Israel*, 56; Smith, *Memoirs*, 24–25.

166. Root *ganab*. See 30:33; 31:19, 20, 26 (in the latter two, "deceived" = "stole the heart of"), 27 ("deceived"), 30, 32, 39.

167. His oath (31:33) is more risky than he realizes; cf. Judges 11 with a more tragic conclusion. In fact, Friedman (*Torah*, 119) suggests that this oath (and Rachel's lie about menstruating, since she is pregnant) can explain Rachel's death in childbirth in 35:16–20.

of the treaty are intended to protect the marital rights of his daughters, and Laban even invokes Yahweh, along with the ancestral God, as the witness and guarantor of the agreement (vv. 49–53). At the same time, the story no doubt reflects relationships between the people of Israel and the Arameans, just as previous stories allude to Esau as Edom.[168] The unit ends with a brief and touching scene of benediction, in which the old rascal kisses his daughters and grandchildren, and leaves them with his blessing.

The unit has also produced even more remarkable changes in the character of Jacob. His closing speech to Laban may be ironic, but it is not self-righteous. His opening words, "What is my offense? What is my sin . . .?" are entirely appropriate in the context of the preceding story, where Jacob has resorted to his former trickery only in self-defense (and on the advice of angels, no less). Moreover, if what he now adds about his past dealings with Laban is true (and we have no reason to doubt it), Jacob appears to be a model of integrity. Despite his affluence, he has suffered a great deal, not only from the humiliation of Laban's deceptions, but also from physical deprivations (v. 40). Here his speech sounds like a psalm of the righteous protesting unjust treatment by enemies.[169] What a different Jacob this

is from the one who left Canaan, the victim of his own dishonesty and pride!

Jacob's sojourn in Haran brought him a new family that soon encountered its own problems of deception and jealousy, but from this came a blessing and a renewed affirmation of communal harmony sealed by treaty. Jacob has "struggled with humans and prevailed," and in his struggles God has indeed been with him. When Jacob erects a stone pillar for the treaty (31:45), it also marks an end to the journey that he began when he erected the pillar at Bethel (28:18). Now he stands at another threshold, one that will bring him face to face with Esau, and with God.

6. Jacob and Esau (chs. 32–33)

"Jacob went on his way and the angels of God met him." The little bridge between the Jacob–Laban stories and the sequel to the Jacob–Esau stories is a masterpiece of rhetorical brevity and allusion (32:1–2). Together with the appearance of the angels at Bethel, the encounter forms a frame for the preceding unit. At the same time, the text serves as an introduction to the Jacob–Esau story that follows. The redactor has accomplished his purpose partly by the use of catchwords: here Jacob meets angels (literally "messengers"), and immediately afterwards he will send messengers to Esau (v. 3); here he names the place Mahanaim (literally "Two Camps"), and soon he will divide his family and possessions into two camps (v. 7). But the wider context is even more suggestive. The Hebrew for "meet" in v. 1 can have a

---

168. Note the ethnic references in 31:20, 24. Alter also points to the use of the Aramean name in 31:47 (*Five Books*, 174; see note e to the NRSV text).

169. With the final verse, the speech also sounds like a song of thanksgiving or vindication. Compare Pss 7:3–5; 94:16–17; 124:1–2. Verse 40 has an exact parallel in Jer 36:30 in the context of a divine curse.

neutral, positive, or negative connotation, but most frequently it refers to a hostile encounter.[170] The ambiguity is altogether appropriate, for while the preceding context would suggest that the angels are there to serve as Jacob's protective escort, before long Jacob will be wrestling with a divine opponent. He has struggled with Laban and now faces the possibility of a struggle with Esau, but first he will have to struggle with God.

Jacob's preparations for his reunion with Esau reveal two sides to his character that approach contradiction. On the one hand there is the old Jacob—shrewd, calculating, and cautious, he still thinks he can cope with his relationships by manipulation and barter. Thus he divides his "camp" and sends "presents" on ahead to Esau (in 32:15, amounting to some five hundred livestock!). Perhaps the one who sold his birthright for a bowl of pottage will be appeased by Jacob's generous bribes.

In a passage placed between the report of these tactics, we see the other side of Jacob's character (vv. 9–12), one that had previously emerged in his impassioned speech to Laban in 31:36–42. Whether or not it is redactional, the placement is a masterpiece. In the midst of his frantic precautions, Jacob appeals for help to the one of Bethel who promised to be with him and to provide "offspring as the sand of the sea" (v. 12), and the one who summoned him home, promising to "do him good" (v. 9). Jacob finally confesses what we have known all along: "I am not worthy of the least of all the steadfast love and all the faithfulness

that you have shown to your servant" (v. 10). If there is a moment of righteousness in Jacob's life, it is surely here, where he acknowledges that the blessing he enjoys is not one he has earned, but the gift of a gracious God.

We do not have two Jacobs here; we have only the one man, at once calculating and contrite, an inextricable combination expressed by the position of Jacob's prayer in between his two precautionary maneuvers. First he plans, then he prays, then he plans again. Even in his planning there is irony, for the customarily courteous language in his messages to Esau ("my lord," "your servant") comes from the younger who will still be the master of the older (25:23). Moreover, at one point his strategy of sending successive groups of people and livestock to meet Esau assumes that the first to encounter him will be killed, and the second in the lead (after the slave women and children) is poor Leah (33:2)![171]

With his planning and praying done, Jacob is left alone for the night, much as he was on that night so many years ago at Bethel. But there he was fleeing the wrath of his brother; now he is about to come face to face with him. *Face to face* is the appropriate phrase, for the author has sewn together the central sections of this

---

170. Neutral, 1 Sam 10:5; friendly, Isa 64:5; hostile, e.g., Josh 2:16; Judg 8:21; 15:2

171. There is considerable confusion in the text regarding Jacob's strategy. At one point it seems to involve two groups of people and livestock, but at another numerous such groups. In one version the groups seems to be shields in front of Jacob (32:20); in another, he goes in the lead (33:3). Similarly, the location shifts from being at Mahanaim (32:2, 13?) to the Jordan River (32:10) to "the camp" (32:21), then across the Jabbok (a feeder stream, 32:23), back to the other side, and finally at Peniel, which is also called Penuel (32:30–31).

unit with the catchword "face" (*panim*). Especially when it refers to God, the word is often translated "presence," and thus suggests a major theme of the cycle— "I will be with you wherever you go." The "face" motif begins in v. 16, where Jacob instructs his servants to "pass on before me," that is, "to my face." Then the motif abounds in vv. 20b–21: "For he thought, 'I may cover his face with the gift that is going to my face, and afterwards I shall see his face—perhaps he will lift up my face.' So the gift passed on to his face" (AT). While these verses obviously look ahead to Jacob's confrontation with Esau, they also tie that confrontation to the one that immediately follows. Before Jacob can face Esau, he must first face the mysterious man who wrestles with him in the night, and when that match is over Jacob names the place Peniel, "The face of God," and says, "For I have seen God face to face, and yet my life is preserved."

The interlacing of these passages prevents us from reading each of Jacob's encounters separately. It is as if the redactors were saying, "You may not interpret Jacob's wrestling with the divine being apart from his confrontation with Esau, and vice versa." The result is the same when we come to the latter (33:1–11), and we come to it as did Jacob—instantly. Although the effect is slightly weakened by the etiology in 32:32, Jacob has scarcely left Penuel when he looks up and sees Esau and his four hundred men. Reeling from the Face of God, he turns toward the face of Esau. The connection is pursued when the two actually meet, and Jacob says to Esau, "for truly to see your face is like seeing the face of God—since you have received me with such favor" (33:10).

Seeing the face of his brother is like seeing the face of God. Jacob's simile also applies to the preceding story, only in reverse; seeing the face of God is like seeing the face of Esau. Whereas Jacob had every reason to expect his confrontation with Esau to be hostile, Esau came running to meet him with an embrace and a kiss (the very actions that Jacob had used to seal his deception of Isaac, 27:26). Esau acts like God. Whereas Jacob had every reason to expect that any new encounter with divine presence would be friendly, as it always had been, here God appears as an unrecognizable man who attacks Jacob like a nocturnal demon. God acts like Esau.

Part of the richness of the story is that it tells us absolutely nothing about the motivations of the characters. We do not know why God attacks Jacob, or why Esau welcomes him. Such questions lead us only into a dark mystery. Indeed, the previous paragraph has already oversimplified things, for Jacob's painful struggle with the demonic opponent ends with a divine blessing, and the simile he applies to Esau is equally ambivalent; seeing the face of God is usually terrifying, or even fatal.[172] Yet for all of this ambiguity the heart of the story lies in the revelation of the identities of the characters, identities rendered in terms of their attitude toward blessing.

172. Cf. 32:30b; 16:13; Exod. 33:20. As Fokkelman notes (*Narrative Art*, 220), the expression of deliverance in 32:31b represents a fulfillment of the prayer in 32:11; but this does not obviate the ambivalence, as Fokkelman suggests. Cf. Plaut, *Torah*, 219–20.

The most obvious change in identity occurs with Jacob, for he emerges from his nocturnal struggle with a new name, given by God; now he is Israel, he who struggles with humans and God and prevails. Yet immediately the interpretation of the meaning of the name suggests that this is still Jacob as well, and the story bears this out, for Jacob does prevail over his opponent (v. 25a). He is still one who grasps for blessing. Even in the agony of a dislocated hip, he will literally pin the source of blessing to the ground until it releases its benefits to him—and he succeeds. But while he receives the blessing that he demands, it is a Pyrrhic victory, exacted at the cost of a disabling injury. He leaves the Face of God, "limping because of his hip."

The reverse of grasping takes place when Jacob meets Esau. Jacob tries to protect those dearest to him by placing Rachel and Joseph at the end of his entourage, while he goes in front. Now the younger brother bows down seven times to the ground before the elder. But all this posturing proves to be unnecessary, for before he can even explain it, Esau has embraced the brother whom he had sworn to kill. The context suggests that Jacob now offers the gift he had sent before him, and when Esau refuses the gift, Jacob responds with the simile about the face of God. Jacob has tried to "find favor" with Esau by offering him material goods, but instead Esau receives him "with such favor" gratuitously, just as *God* has "dealt favorably" with him gratuitously (33:11, AT).[173] Then he presses the gift on Esau with an equally significant expression:

"Accept, I beg you, my blessing (*birkati*)." Jacob does not simply offer a "present" (*minhah*, 32:13), he offers his blessing, and at this point Esau accepts. This does not mean that Jacob is now returning all that he had taken from Esau, for that blessing cannot be returned (27:33–34). But it does mean that Jacob here acknowledges the operation of divine grace in his life, and is willing to release his grip on the blessing he had so often grasped. Like Abraham, Jacob has been tested by God and now acknowledges the divine blessing as an unmerited gift.

Jacob's release of his blessing marks the most dramatic conversion of his character up to this point, a process that we have traced from his initial vow at Bethel to his final speech to Laban and his prayer to Yahweh. But his conversion is not complete (true conversion rarely, if ever, is). Even as he releases the blessing he presses a gift on Esau, as if he cannot quite trust the sincerity of Esau's welcome. Similarly, in the sequel (vv. 12–17) Jacob's reluctance to travel with Esau or to accept an escort suggests his fear that his favor with Esau may run out, and in fact Jacob does not continue to Seir as he promises, but makes a permanent detour to Succoth.

Jacob is not the only one whose identity changes before our eyes in this story. There is also Esau, who, we should remember, is the eponym of Edom, Israel's occasional enemy. We last saw him as an outraged victim, bent on murder, but he now appears as a loving brother. Even here we cannot be too sure of the extent of Esau's transformation, or, again, the motivations behind it. Why does he arrive with four hundred men? Is his welcome of Jacob a result of Jacob's gift and

---

173. The word in each case is *hanan*, referring to unmerited grace.

subservient attitude, or does it reveal an intrinsic spirit of forgiveness, or simply a case of time healing all wounds? Is his offer of an escort to Seir really an insidious form of protective custody? We do not know. All we know is that he appears to Jacob like the face of God, and that in his hospitality to his brother—the one who bears the blessing of Abraham—he too receives a blessing (cf. ch. 36 below). Thus in the end the movement of the Jacob cycle is in a direction we could not have anticipated at the beginning; it is perhaps the most dramatic instance in the Pentateuch of the divine promise, "those who bless you, I will bless."

Finally, one more character appears in altered guise, the one who stands behind, as it were, the Face of God. Who is this mysterious being who wrestles with Jacob in the night? All along we have treated this character as if it were transparently Yahweh, but is that the case? Is it really a "man," and not God (v. 24)? Or is it a Hebrew troll who lurks by this river, waiting to devour passersby? In terms of the history of traditions, the character who appears here is probably a little of each of these. But Jacob's declaration at the end appears definitive—he has seen God face to face. Unless we take this identification to be Jacob's alone, and not that of the author, the text affirms that Jacob's encounter at this threshold of his life is an encounter with God—the God of "Israel." Jacob has struggled with humans all along (Esau, Laban), but all along he has been heading for this struggle with God.

The text is nevertheless concerned to maintain the obscurity of this deity. With Jacob a new identity emerges from the struggle, an identity at least revealed in a new name. But his antagonist refuses to reveal a name. At Bethel, Yahweh appeared to Jacob, introduced as the "God of Abraham your father and the God of Isaac." The God who now wrestles with Jacob remains nameless. Even as God appears face-to-face, God is effaced. The character of God reveals a new dimension here, one deriving from the context of this story within the overall cycle; all along, God has appeared as Jacob's friend, even (and especially) when he did not deserve it. Now God appears as Jacob's enemy. Before God protected Jacob on his way; now Yahweh stands *in* his way. No doubt we would have expected it to be otherwise, for God to be an antagonist to the cheat and a protector to the penitent. But the fact that God is otherwise is precisely what is revealed about God's identity.

Jacob has become Israel, he who struggles with God. Yahweh has become an ineffable power who struggles with Israel. The cycle that began with two brothers "crashing together" reaches its climax with Jacob and Yahweh fighting together. Here even God is one who struggles and—at least momentarily—who does not prevail! Yahweh is now not only the one who tests those whom he blesses, but also the one who will fight with them and, if necessary, wound them in order to maintain sovereign freedom. This is the same freedom out of which Yahweh made promises to Jacob at Bethel. If "Israel" means that Jacob "has struggled with God and with humans and prevailed," it also means "God rules."

7. Outrage at Shechem (ch. 34)

Along with the stories about Isaac and Abimelech, those about Jacob's relationships with Laban and Esau portray a movement from contention and hostility to reconciliation, sealed by a covenant or non-aggression pact. The story about Jacob and the city of Shechem represents an antitype to that pattern, especially in contrast to its structural counterpart in the Isaac stories, where the subject is also that of relationships with the native inhabitants rather than kinfolk. Jacob's sons make their first appearance here as full-fledged characters, and they do not get off to a very good start.

The transition to the story in ch. 34 is puzzling (33:18–20). Jacob moves to the city of Shechem, where he purchases a plot of land "from the sons of Hamor," and erects an altar. Yet in the following story Shechem is the name of one of Hamor's sons who is the crown prince, and Hamor offers land to Jacob and sons as if they own none. Moreover, Jacob arrives "peacefully" in Shechem (root *šalem*, 33:18, AT), yet the next story is anything but peaceful. When Shechem sees the sole daughter of Jacob, Dinah, walking around town,[174] he seizes and rapes her, then instantly falls in love with her, and asks for her hand in marriage. We hear absolutely nothing about Dinah's feelings throughout the story, but there are no reasons to doubt Shechem's sincerity.[175] Ironically, his offer to marry Dinah accords with later Israelite law, however oppressive it may seem to us (Deut 22:28–29). In a culture based on an honor/shame code, the law was designed to protect the victim of rape, who otherwise would remain unmarried since she had been "defiled" (v. 27).[176] Dinah's vengeful brothers pretend to agree with the marriage, but on condition that the Shechemite men be circumcised, and, when the men are incapacitated by this surgery, Simeon and Levi[177] slaughter them all, and the rest of the brothers loot the city and take captive the women and children. In the end the sons of Israel are more guilty of "outrage" than the young man Shechem (v. 7), and it is highly questionable if they have acted in Dinah's best interests. Clearly they make Jacob odious to the Canaanites. At the same time, the significance of the story transcends the relationships between the characters as individuals, extending to the social and political relations between Israel as a people and Shechem as a city representing Canaanites in general.

The text itself moves in this direction when the potential union of Shechem and Dinah becomes a

---

174. It is possible to interpret her visiting about town as indiscrete (so Sarna, *Genesis*, 233), but that obviously does not excuse the rape (Friedman, *Torah*, 116, even questions the use of the term "rape"). At the end Dinah is in Shechem's house, perhaps suggesting that she is already considered a daughter-in-law, but nothing is said about her agreement, so we do not know her wishes.

175. Shechem's love for Dinah is certainly not typical of rapists. For a similar assault with the opposite reaction see 2 Samuel 12, especially vv. 12–15. The differing portrayals of Shechem (from rapist to smitten romantic) may reflect two different literary sources.

176. So also Fretheim, *Genesis*, 577b–78ab, although we cannot know that she has "fallen in love" with Shechem. Others would see Dinah as a prisoner.

177. This incident is probably recalled in the criticism of these two in Gen 49:5–7; but cf. 48:22.

precedent for further intermarriage (vv. 9–10, 20–24). From the perspective of the Shechemites, the motivation for intermarriage goes beyond Shechem's love for Dinah to include the possibility of benefiting from the wealth of the family of Jacob (v. 23a). At the same time the arrangement would benefit Jacob by extending his privilege of residing in the land and obtaining more property, thereby improving his status as a resident alien (v. 10). Indeed, both parties agree that intermarriage would lead to the formation of "one people" (vv. 16, 22).

In the context of the pentateuchal narrative the story takes on far greater significance, therefore, than it would if we read it by itself or even within the confines of the Jacob cycle. In the wider context, the story involves the central themes of the pentateuchal narrative: blessing, nationhood, progeny, and land. Will Israel become a great nation by becoming "one people" with the Canaanite population? Will they gain possession of the land by intermarriage (v. 10)? Throughout the Pentateuchal narrative the answer to such questions is usually a resounding no, a refusal that we have already seen with the matrimony of Isaac (ch. 24) and Jacob (27:46). However, Jacob's son Judah will marry a Canaanite (38:2), and Jacob's son Joseph will marry an Egyptian (and a priest's daughter, no less, 41:45; cf also 46:10).[178]

The irony, of course, is that Jacob's sons rightly reject the Canaanite offer of marriage, but for the wrong reasons,

and with irresponsible tactics. For Jacob's sons only the family name is at stake, not cultural, much less religious, differences. Their goal is not reconciliation or even just retribution but cold-blooded revenge, and their method is one that reverberates throughout the cycle: "deception" (v. 13). Rather than resolving their differences with the Shechemites by means of covenant, or simply withdrawing from the scene, Jacob's sons exploit the sign of the covenant between God and Israel (circumcision) as a device for trickery and bloodshed. Rather than coming to peaceful terms (cf. 26:29–31), they pretend to be peaceful (34:21) in order to wage war. There is an ugly contemporary expression for the result: "ethnic cleansing." Here those who seek the welfare of Israel receive a curse rather than a blessing.

8. The Return to Bethel (35:1–15)

Although Jacob never lived in Bethel, when he returns to this place he comes home, and the Jacob cycle comes to its end. The material that follows the story of his return to Bethel is not, however, insignificant (35:16—36:43). It reports the birth of Benjamin, Jacob's second son by Rachel, and Rachel's death. It reports Reuben's sexual misconduct with Bilhah, Jacob's concubine,[179] followed immediately by a complete list of Jacob's sons. With the juxtaposition of the birth of Jacob's last son and the explicit reference to the discrediting of Reuben as Jacob's firstborn, this section repeats the continu-

---

178. Note also that Jacob himself has children through two slave girls who are *not* kin like Rachel and Leah.

179. In some circumstances, sexual intercourse with the spouse or concubine of one's father is not only sexual rebellion but also political (cf. 2 Sam 16:20–23; 1 Kgs 2:13–25).

ing theme of younger over older brothers and foreshadows the Joseph narrative.[180] Finally, there is a report of the death of Isaac, his burial by Jacob and Esau, and a list of "the descendants of Esau, that is Edom" (ch. 36). The latter has its structural counterpart in the Ishmaelite notice in 25:12–18. In its present context it emphasizes the Canaanite origin of Esau's wives, Esau's withdrawal from Canaan to Seir (because the land cannot bear both his and Jacob's possessions, cf. 13:2–12), and his numerous descendants. Though he lives apart from the line of Jacob, his younger brother, and away from the land of Canaan, Esau too has been blessed. He becomes the father of a multitude of peoples, and kings come forth from him (cf. 17:20).

As we have seen, Jacob's departure from and return to Bethel provide the main structural pillars of the cycle. Appropriately, his return takes the form of a pilgrimage, including an initial ritual of purification (v. 2), a summons to "go up" to Bethel (v. 3a), and a vow to construct an altar in gratitude for God's continual presence with him (v. 3b). Although there is no explicit reference to the formal vow that Jacob swore previously (28:20–22), his return clearly functions as the consummation of his original encounter at Bethel. Even though the reference for "foreign gods" is vague,[181] the rejection

of them helps to emphasize the reaffirmation of the God of Bethel (or El Bethel) as *Jacob's* God in accordance with his vow (28:21, there also named as Yahweh). In fact the unusual number of allusions to previous stories in the cycle suggests that the redactor constructed this passage as a conclusion.[182]

In the immediate context, Jacob makes his pilgrimage to Bethel in response to a divine command (cf. vv. 1, 7), and as a result he receives the reward for which all pilgrims fervently hope—a new appearance of God at the shrine, and a blessing (vv. 9–15).[183] But the primary function of the passage in its wider context is not simply to reiterate the divine blessing and promises, but to have them pronounced on Israel, that is, on the character who has changed so dramatically since the original encounter at Bethel. The positional significance of the text thus resembles that of ch. 22 (the testing of Abraham). The one who receives the blessing and promises now is not the scoundrel and cheater, fleeing from the wrath of his brother, but the penitential pilgrim, responding to the call of God.

The Jacob cycle represents a journey with numerous dimensions: geographical, psychological, and religious; individual

---

180. Simeon and Levi have already incriminated themselves in 34:25–31 as the ringleaders of the Shechem massacre (cf. 49:3–4).

181. In context they could refer to Laban's "household gods" (31:19), although this seems unlikely. Jacob's repudiation of them resembles that of Joshua at the conclusion of Israel's settling in Canaan in Josh 24:14, where the reference is to "the gods that your ancestors served beyond

the River" (i.e. the Euphrates, 24:2, and referring explicitly to Terah and Nahor). The rings are reminiscent of Exod 32:2–4, but there they are used to *make* an idol (the "golden calf").

182. Verses 1 and 7 refer to 28:10–22; v. 3 refers to 32:8; and in context, at least, v. 5 may refer to 34:30 (on such divine protection, cf. Exod 15:13–16).

183. The latter verses clearly conflict with 28:19 and 32:28 in that the names Bethel and Israel are introduced as if previously unknown. Verses 9–15 are usually assigned to P (sometimes without v. 14).

and communal; human and divine. It is a journey during which Jacob spent a major portion of his life "beyond the Jordan," away from the land of promise, just as he will spend the end of his days in the land of Egypt. The essential movement of the story, however, has gone from Bethel (the "House of God") to exile and back to the House of God, and at each of the major turning points of this journey from Bethel to Bethel, God has fulfilled the promise to be with Jacob. Now Jacob has fulfilled his vow. The pilgrim has come home to consecrate that place that represents the center of his life. As with Abraham, God has said, "Go to the land that I will show you," and Israel has obeyed.

THE JOSEPH CYCLE (GENESIS 37:1—50:26)

1. The Dreamer (ch. 37)

Much of what happens in this story will correspond to the bitter proverb coined in the situation of Israel's later exile: "The parents have eaten sour grapes, and the children's teeth are set on edge" (Ezek 18:2). Like his father, Jacob favors one son above all. At first it is Joseph, and later his younger brother Benjamin—Jacob's two youngest, and the only sons of his beloved Rachel. Jacob's special love for Joseph produces a deep jealousy among his brothers, and they seize on the first opportunity to get rid of this favorite son. But while they can rid themselves of Joseph, they cannot dispel Jacob's love for him, and the opening story concludes with Jacob's insistence that he will spend the rest of his days in mourning. Although there are signs of redactional blending here and

elsewhere in the Joseph cycle, the story is told with considerable artistry and often a deep poignancy.[184]

Jacob's obsession for the sons of Rachel thus sets the plot in motion, but it is not the only factor involved. While it is not Joseph's fault that he is the object of his father's exclusive devotion, he does little to ingratiate himself to his brothers. In fact, even before the author tells us of Jacob's dotage we learn that Joseph has "brought a bad report" about his brothers' work (v. 2). Joseph is a tattletale. He is also a prolific dreamer who doesn't realize that some dreams are best kept to oneself. Instead, wrapped in narcissistic wonder, he taunts his brothers with the prospect of their bowing down before him (using Alter's translation): "look, we were binding sheaves in the field, and, look, my sheaf arose and actually stood up, and, look, your sheaves drew round and bowed to my sheaf."[185] It is not until his father appears as one of his subjects that Jacob at last rebukes him. In adaptations of the Joseph narrative for children, interpreters often portray the adolescent protagonist as a model of virtue when, in fact, he is a Mr. Goody-Two-Shoes whom almost anyone would want to throw into a pit.

The central theme of family tension that runs throughout the cycle is associated with a cluster of words and motifs introduced in the opening chapter. Many of these had already become central to

184. Here there is confusion about which brother defends Joseph (Reuben and then Judah), and about the part played by the Midianites and Ishmaelites (the latter providing some irony as the part-Egyptian rejects of the family; cf. especially 37:28 and 36).

185. Alter, *Five Books*, 209, the three "looks" "betraying his own wide-eyed amazement."

the larger story of Jacob when he "crashed against" Esau in his mother's womb (25:22–23): rivalry between siblings, subservience of the older to the younger, hatred and jealousy, and, above all, deception. Just as Jacob had used clothing and animal skins to deceive Isaac, so his sons use clothing and animal blood to deceive him (Joseph's fancy coat).[186] Moreover, the motif of recognition, which figures in the latter scene will recur in the following story of Judah and Tamar, and again much later when the brothers appear before Joseph in Pharaoh's court. In addition the motif of buying and selling runs through the cycle, beginning with the sale of Joseph to the caravan bound for Egypt.

In many ways, therefore, the Joseph cycle continues the family feud which began with the Jacob cycle. Yet within the context of the pentateuchal narrative the story also concerns the survival of Yahweh's blessing on this family, and through them, the fate of the world.

2. Judah and Tamar (ch. 38)

The following story about Judah and his daughter-in-law, Tamar, immediately interrupts the plot. The story covers at least fifteen or twenty years in the life of Judah, but does not even mention Joseph. Interpreters have thus often ignored its contextual significance. The story may suggest the problems which arise when a member of Jacob's family marries a

Canaanite, although his nameless wife does nothing beyond bearing children and dying. But there are closer associations as well. Judah has just joined in the selling of his brother as a slave, and now we find him buying his daughter-in-law as a prostitute.[187] Both he and Tamar are masters at the favorite family game of deception, here involving the custom by which a deceased man would be provided with children through a brother (cf. Deut 25:5–10). But when Yahweh kills two of his sons for "wickedness" or disobedience, Judah is understandably wary of losing another, so he withholds his third son from Tamar, breaking his ambiguous promise (vv. 11, 14b). Then Tamar deceives Judah by disguising herself so that he cannot recognize her, and by securing his signet, which he *can* "recognize" (*nkr*, vv. 25–26, cf. 37:32–33; 27:23)—it is like taking his driver's license.[188] Decked out in her whore's veil, Tamar could easily have upstaged Jacob in his goatskin sleeves.

It is all a messy affair (including a punitive deity), but why is it here? First, the story continues the motif of the firstborn, so prominent in the larger Jacob story. Yahweh's killing of the two sons is hardly attractive, but a fundamental issue is at stake; Onan's coitus interruptus abandons his responsibility in continuing the

---

186. Clothing has already become a recurring motif, beginning with Adam and Eve's fig leaves, then Jacob's Esau costume, and soon Tamar's harlot outfit in ch. 38. As White puts it, "clothing is never mentioned as an act of simple description." Rather, it signals "intentional deception and unintentional disclosure" (*Narration and Discourse*, 220).

187. Two different words for prostitution occur in the story (*zonah* and *qedešah*). There is no word for "temple" in v. 21, and that interpretation is quite likely overdrawn (nor do we know of any temple here). Women who resorted to prostitution, even when associated with temple precincts, almost certainly did so for economic, not sacerdotal, reasons. See van der Toorn, "Cultic Prostitution," 512–13. For another story of a prostitute who demonstrates moral integrity, see Joshua 2.

188. Alter, *Five Books*, 217.

divine blessing, "be fertile and increase"; and his refusal is more active but no more effective than Judah's withholding of the third brother. Moreover, while Judah is not Jacob's firstborn, he is destined for preeminence over the later twelve tribes, as the blessing of Jacob will make clear in 49:8–12. Indeed, one of the *twin* sons of Tamar—Perez, and the *younger*, no less!—founds the line that leads to David, himself the founder of the kingdom of Judah (Ruth 4:12, 18–22). Again we hear ironic echoes of the earlier oracle to Rebekah (cf. 38:27–30 and 25:21–26), and see a family tree rooted in sexual impropriety (19:30–38).

But the story has a more immediate significance in connection with ch. 39. In ch. 39, Joseph falls prey to the treachery of a temptress (the wife of his master, Potiphar), not because he accepts her sexual proposition, but because he refuses her. Thus the sexual impropriety of Judah functions as a foil for the integrity of Joseph.[189] At the same time, Judah stands in contrast to Tamar who, he says, "is more righteous than I" (v. 26). The Canaanite woman who married into the family of Jacob and resorted to prostitution to continue the family line deserves the status of ancestor of Israel more than does Israel's son.

3. Joseph's Rise to Power (chs. 39–41)

So far there has been no reference to divine involvement in the story of Joseph. There will be no dramatic interventions, numinous manifestations, or even direct communications between God and

Joseph. But from the moment Joseph arrives as a slave at the house of Potiphar to the day of his death as the viceroy of Egypt, Joseph's life is marked by Yahweh's blessing and guided by Yahweh's invisible presence. In ch. 39 the author tells us of Yahweh's presence at two crucial junctures. First, as an introduction to the initial story of Joseph's experiences in Potiphar's household, we learn that "Yahweh was with Joseph, and he became a successful man." As often elsewhere, "success" or "prosperity" is a manifestation of divine blessing. Everything that Joseph touches turns to gold, including the business of Potiphar. Like others before him (Abimelech, Laban), Potiphar quickly appreciates what a find he has made, and he promotes Joseph to the position of chief of staff. Unfortunately for Joseph, Potiphar's wife has additional duties in mind for the handsome servant. When Joseph rejects her proposition she maliciously accuses him of attempted rape, and Joseph lands in prison. At this critical juncture the author immediately assures us again that "Yahweh was with Joseph," extending him "faithfulness" (*hesed*) and ingratiating him to the prison warden (v. 21). As a result, the warden promotes Joseph to the position of chief of trusties, and again everything that Joseph does "Yahweh prospers" (v. 23).

In addition to the theme of blessing, ch. 39 concerns the theme of responsibility and raises a question about Joseph's identity. Joseph's rejection of Potiphar's wife (v. 9) suggests that the blessing of God and the favorable treatment by Potiphar have produced a sense of commitment and loyalty—in a word, a sense of righteousness. But who is this Joseph, an

189. Alter, *Art of Biblical Narrative*, 10; in general, 3–12; more recently, *Five Books*, 215.

alien and a prisoner, separated from his family and his native land? Will he maintain his identity as one of the children of Israel, or will he remain in the limbo status of an alien, or will he become an Egyptian? At this point the only answer comes in the form of Potiphar's wife's categorization of Joseph as a "Hebrew," a categorization that here appears derogatory (vv. 14, 17).[190]

In the next two episodes (chs. 40–41) Joseph moves from the prison to Pharaoh's palace. Here too his success is the result of divine guidance, though not expressed as Yahweh's being "with him." Joseph is no longer the starry-eyed dreamer; he is an *interpreter* of dreams who could rival any Freudian analyst. Indeed, his reading of dreams goes far beyond the psychological meaning. For Joseph, every dream becomes a crystal ball disclosing the future. When the butler and baker lament their lack of an interpreter, Joseph gives a stunning reply: "Do not interpretations belong to God? Please tell them to me" (40:8)! The apparent presumptuousness in this response is soon dispelled not only by the accuracy of Joseph's predictions, but also by his subsequent acknowledgment that his skill is a divine gift (41:15–16, 25). Even Pharaoh is so impressed with Joseph's interpretation that he extols the divine origin of his skill: "Can we find anyone else like this—one in whom is the Spirit of God?" (v. 38). Joseph the Hebrew has accomplished what "all the magicians" and all the "wise men" of Pharaoh's court could not (41:8, 24; cf. Exod 8:18–19).

190. The term is often used in contexts involving Israelites and non-Israelites; e.g., Exodus 1–2; 1 Samuel 4; 13; 14.

While the story thus emphasizes Joseph's reliance on God for his success, it also brings out an inherent resourcefulness in his character that complements the divine gift. Having contrived an audience with Pharaoh (40:14), Joseph adds his own advice to the interpretation of Pharaoh's dream. If God has revealed the disaster which is about to happen, Joseph will provide the administrative actions that will circumvent the problem (vv. 33–36). The prophet is also a politician. Rarely has the power of suggestion been so potent, and Pharaoh's response seems virtually predetermined: "Since God has shown you all this, there is no one so discerning and wise as you. You shall be over my house" (vv. 39–40a).

But Joseph's remarkable rise to power raises anew the question about his identity. Almost half his life has been spent in Egypt (41:46), and now he wears the signet ring of Pharaoh himself. Indeed, Pharaoh has also given him a new name—an Egyptian name—as unrecognizable as is Joseph himself: Zaphenath-paneah. Does a new identity accompany the new name? Is Joseph now the favorite son of Egypt? So it would seem, for Joseph not only marries an Egyptian (and the daughter of an Egyptian priest, nonetheless) but also names his first son Manasseh, meaning "God has made me forget all my hardship and all my father's house" (v. 51).

4. Joseph and His Brothers (chs. 42–44)

Almost every section of these chapters contains an ironic allusion or connection to the preceding chapters. At the outset,

Joseph has not seen his family for at least twenty-five years. He is now second in command over all of Egypt, and controls the food supply for the entire world. The author has tied chs. 41 and 42 together with the motif of buying and selling. The Hebrew root *šbr* provides the basis for "grain," "buy (grain)," and "sell (grain)" (41:57—42:6). Thus those who sold their brother into slavery come to him (unknowingly) to buy grain. This ironic reversal constitutes the primary level on which the plot will develop until ch. 45. The opening paragraph (42:1–5) also contains a new motif that will become increasingly significant as the narrative progresses. Jacob orders his sons to go to Egypt for grain, "that we may live, and not die" (v. 2). Here his remark is limited to physical survival, but as the story progresses "live and not die" will come to signify the second level of the plot—the survival of God's purpose for the world. Already this universal significance—another manifestation of divine blessing—is evident in 41:57 where "all the world came to Joseph in Egypt to buy grain, because the famine became severe throughout the world."

The rest of Genesis 42 portrays Joseph's first meeting with his brothers when they "bowed themselves before him with their faces to the ground." Joseph's adolescent dreams finally have come true—and yet again, they have not. Throughout this unit the brothers will "bow down" to Joseph in one way or another many times, but *they* do not know that this is Joseph. They are bowing down before Zaphenathpaneah.

Joseph's reaction is not what we might expect. He does not tell them who he really is, and thereby fully savor his victory. Joseph recognizes them (*nakar*), but he plays the role of a foreigner (*hitnakker*)—and the author plays with words. Joseph assumes the identity of an Egyptian, speaking to them only through an interpreter (42:23). Here arises a puzzle that we can solve only as we move through the entire unit. Why does Joseph not immediately disclose his identity, embrace his brothers, and summon his father and Benjamin to Egypt? That is what he will do in the end (ch. 45), so why prolong the reunion? Why, at the very moment when Joseph remembers his old dreams, does he devise a false accusation that the brothers are spies (v. 9)? What motivation stands behind this deception of his brothers, a deception he pursues with increasingly relentless cruelty?

The first clue comes when Joseph tells his brothers that he wants to "test" their claim to have a younger brother at home (v. 16), although he knows full well the truth of their story. Even a confession of guilt—which is precisely what Joseph hears when his brothers say "we are paying the penalty for what we did to our brother" (42:21)—does not satisfy him. Of course, when he hears this (unbeknownst to them), he is overcome with remorse, and must leave the room to weep, a gesture he will repeat (43:30). Apparently his brothers' words have met part of the larger test Joseph has in mind, but not all, for immediately Joseph returns and gives orders to his servants which will bring his brothers even greater dismay.

At this point the most obvious motivation behind Joseph's actions would be revenge: he wants to make his brothers suffer for what they have done to him, and that certainly happens. But when he demands that his brothers bring Benjamin to Egypt, he must surely know what agony this will cause his father as well. Indeed, we have known from the outset Jacob's deep fear that something might happen to Benjamin (42:4). Joseph would know this too, for he and Benjamin are the favorite sons, the only children of Rachel. This, in fact, is the essence of the following scene in Canaan (vv. 29–38). When Jacob hears the ultimatum that Benjamin must go to Egypt, or there will be no more grain and Simeon will remain enslaved, his refusal is adamant. Even when Reuben, the most innocent of the brothers, offers the life of his own sons if he does not bring Benjamin back, Jacob refuses to listen.

Thus if Joseph's ruse is a test of his brothers, it is also and even more so a test of Jacob. The deepest significance of this situation derives from the larger story of Jacob and, indeed, the ancestral saga as a whole. The old deceiver is deceived again, and by his own son, his favorite son. "He who struggles with God" must struggle again. Like Abraham's, Jacob's character is now probed at its most vulnerable spot— his love for Benjamin, who is in effect his son, his only son, whom he loves (42:38; cf. 22:2)—as if the other sons to whom he is speaking do not count! His narcissistic favoritism makes his decision all the more painful. In order for the family to survive, Jacob must be willing to risk the life of Benjamin. If "Israel" is to "live and not die," Jacob must give up the one whom he holds most dear.

Jacob is in no hurry to take this test. Not until his family is again facing starvation does he raise the question of another trip to Egypt (with poor Simeon, the "other brother," languishing in prison

all the while; cf. 43:14). When Judah reminds him of the demand for Benjamin, Jacob upbraids him for disclosing Benjamin's existence. It is only when Judah offers himself as "surety," as the one who will "bear the blame forever" if Benjamin were to die, that Jacob rises above his obsession and grudgingly agrees to the ultimatum. His response to Judah is characteristic. If it must be so, he says, then let's send a "present" (*minhah*) to the Egyptian. Jacob is ever the strategist (cf. for Esau, 32:13–21; 33:10). First he plans, then he prays: "May God Almighty grant you mercy before the man" (43:11–15).

Judah's brief speech (43:8–10) deserves further attention. His words contain a gesture that goes beyond an expression of guilt, for here Judah offers himself as "surety" for Benjamin's safety, thus placing himself in jeopardy for the sake of the family, "that we may live and not die—you and we and also our little ones."[191] What a different Judah this is from the one who suggested selling Joseph to the Ishmaelites. And what a change in character for the one who, out of fear, refused to allow his son to continue the family "seed" (ch. 38).

Judah's offer of himself as security for Benjamin, and Jacob's willingness to release Benjamin, represent the turning point in that portion of the narrative set in Canaan. In both these gestures the characters tear off the shackles that have bound this family in jealousy, guilt, and despair for over twenty-five years. The characters themselves are not aware of what has happened, anxious as they are over the outcome of their decisions. But

191. Note also that the word for "surety" in verse 9 is derived from the same root *'rb* as the "pledge" in 38:17.

when the one, in effect, embraces Benjamin as a true brother, and the other gives him up as his "only" son, the family of Israel begins a process of healing and reconciliation.

Joseph, of course, knows nothing of what has happened in Canaan, except that Jacob has agreed to send Benjamin. The final episode in this unit (43:16—44:34) thus focuses on the relationship of the brothers. When they return to Joseph's house, the steward abruptly dismisses the issue of the money in their sacks, and announces that the brothers will dine with Joseph (43:32-34). The seating is arranged in three sections: Egyptians, Hebrews, and Joseph, since, for the Egyptians, it is an "abomination" to eat with a Hebrew. No doubt there was a sign on one table saying "EGYPTIANS ONLY." But where does that leave Joseph? In the middle. He is a man without a community. He is Zaphenathpaneah, but not an Egyptian; he is Joseph, but no longer identified as a Hebrew as before (39:14, 17; 41:12). His family does not recognize him and in fact assumes he is dead, and he has not identified himself with them. In short, Joseph is a man whose identity is wrapped up in two separate narratives, or in what were two separate narratives, for the two have now collided. Like his father, Joseph must struggle with the conflicting stories that make up his life. What character will emerge from this collision? At this point we do not know, and Joseph may not know either.[192]

The seating of Joseph's brothers also represents the conflict within the family that has so disrupted their lives. On the one hand, the brothers are seated in strict order of succession, but when the meal is served, Benjamin receives five times as much as his brothers! The banquet thus reflects a critical stage both in Joseph's identity and in the identity of the brothers. They wine and dine merrily in Joseph's house, but on the way home will they throw Benjamin into a pit?

The banquet scene leads to the climactic episode in the unit (ch. 44). No sooner is the banquet over than Joseph orders what will be the final test of his brothers. Again he returns their money to their sacks, and now he has his silver divining cup placed in the sack of Benjamin. The brothers depart for Canaan, no doubt with a great sense of relief that their dangerous mission is over. But Joseph's steward quickly overtakes them and accuses them of stealing the cup. The brothers rightly profess their innocence, backed up by a rash vow: if the cup is found all of them will become slaves and the one who has the cup will die. Both the steward and later Joseph mollify this vow (only the guilty one will become a slave), but this modification hardly lessens the brothers' dismay when the steward opens their sacks—"beginning with the eldest and ending with the youngest"—and finds the cup in Benjamin's sack.

The brothers must now confront Joseph one more time. As in the preceding scene in Canaan, Judah emerges as the spokesman and confesses their culpability: "God has found out the guilt of your servants" (v. 16). But what guilt is this? Surely it is not the theft of the cup. Rather, Judah seems to express their corporate guilt in the "theft" of Joseph (40:15; cf. 42:21-22), a theft of which Benjamin, of course, is innocent. But Joseph insists

192. On the collision of narratives in the formation of identity, see Stroup, *Promise of Narrative Theology*, 171–75.

that only Benjamin will become his slave, while the others can go home "in peace" to their father.

At this critical moment, Judah delivers a long and impassioned speech that concludes, "Now therefore, please let your servant remain as a slave to my lord in place of the boy; and let the boy go back with his brothers." Here Judah has made the definitive gesture that reveals the transformation of his character. He has made good on his pledge to his father. He has offered his own life for the life of his brother, and not just any brother, but Benjamin, the favorite son. At the same time, he has voluntarily (but still unknowingly) offered himself as a slave to Joseph, thus fulfilling Joseph's dreams of long ago. The irony of this transformation is evident when we compare the last words of his speech to that opening scene where Judah and his brothers sent the bloody coat to Jacob: "How can I go back to my father if the lad is not with me? I fear to see the suffering that would come upon my father" (44:34).

5. Reunion (45:1—47:27)

Should we condemn Joseph himself as the perpetrator of unnecessary anguish within his family, or does the end justify the means? Certainly Joseph's tactics are not beyond question, but if his objective was to determine whether or not there had been a change in his brothers—and father—the test he devised was as successful as it was torturous. All that he has heard and seen from them he has observed as if from behind a see-through mirror. Jacob has given up Benjamin, the brothers have confessed their guilt, and

Judah has offered himself as a slave—all to Zaphenathpaneah, the viceroy of Egypt, and not to Joseph. If it had been otherwise, if Joseph had immediately disclosed himself to his brothers and they had professed their guilt and repentance for their wrong to him, would he really know if their repentance was genuine? Or, for that matter, would we?

Another significant factor in deciphering Joseph's motivations appears when he reveals himself to his brothers (45:1–15). Once he has told them who he is, Joseph does not demand an apology for their former acts, nor does he insist that they bow down before him as Joseph, Instead, he immediately absolves them of their guilt. Apparently he is not interested in personal vindication. From here on he will treat his brothers magnanimously and perhaps condescendingly; and he will continue to favor Benjamin (45:22), but he will not be to the others as a lord to servants. He will be their brother.[193]

At last Zaphenathpaneah is Joseph. The arrangement of the characters on the stage, as it were, already suggests Joseph's confirmation of his Israelite identity; he removes all the Egyptians from the room before speaking those definitive words to his brothers (for the first time, in their common language)—"I am Joseph." When Joseph embraces his brothers, he also embraces who he has always been—a Hebrew—in the context of who he is— the Egyptian viceroy. Joseph reaffirms his identity within his family, and thus within

193. As White puts it, "The logic of Joseph's strategy is thus to bring the brothers to the point where they can regain their self-respect so as to be able to accept moral parity with Joseph. Judah's speech eloquently achieves this aim, and evokes from Joseph the final collapse of his alien identity" (*Narration and Discourse*, 267).

the larger story in which this family plays the central role.

At the same time that Joseph reaffirms his identity as one of the children of Israel, he also recognizes that his personal identity is relatively unimportant when compared to his role as an agent within the story of "Israel." For the first time in the cycle, Joseph's words provide an explicit statement of the theological purpose that has been at work throughout the narrative. When the author told us earlier that God was "with" Joseph, he did not tell us why. Now Joseph says God was with him, not simply to make him "a successful man" (39:2) and eventually "lord of all Egypt" (45:9). Much more was at stake than his own rise from rags to riches: "For God sent me before you to preserve life . . . , to establish for you a remnant in the land, and to make possible for you a great escape" (vv. 5, 7, AT).[194] The key word here is "sent." We knew that Joseph had been bought and sold, thrown into prison, and exalted to power, but we did not know he was on a mission, much less a mission of God.

Joseph's statement reminds us of the oracle that began the Jacob cycle (25:23). Who are the real "actors" here? Joseph's statement suggests it is God alone: "It was not you who sent me here, but God" (v. 8). But when we look at the narrative as a whole, it is clearly both God and humans who act, and their actions are inseparable, involving a subtle understanding of divine and human causation. The human characters together with God *co*operate in causing events to happen, without reducing people to puppets or, on the other hand, ascribing sole causation to what people do. Joseph's comments here anticipate his words near the conclusion of the book, when he will refuse his brothers' explicit offer to be his slaves. "Am I in the place of God?" he asks. And, in a sense, the question is rhetorical, and the answer is yes. He has been God's representative and thus, *in effect*, his actions have been God's actions. Indeed, here the theology even explicitly includes the good and evil involved in the story: "you intended to do evil to me, [but] God intended it for good" (50:18–20, AT). The statement does not mean that evil (NRSV: "harm") didn't happen, for it did; but it means that in and through the harm God—"with Joseph"—was working for healing.[195]

At this point we, the readers, have every right to ask the viceroy of Egypt a question he might find embarrassing: How do you know all this? By what authority do you claim a divine mission, and how can we know if your claim is true? After all, one of the most distinctive features of the Joseph cycle is that God never appears to Joseph or talks with him; much less does God inform Joseph of his role in a divine plan. A redactor

194. There is some ambiguity here. Joseph seems to be referring to himself as the "remnant" and the means to "escape" for his family. "The land" could be translated more broadly with "on the earth." The words for "remnant" and "escape" occur together frequently (e.g., 2 Kgs 19:31; Isa 15:9; Jer 44:14; Ezra 9:14–15). Cf. 50:20 and the discussion below.

195. As Alter says, here we have "a luminous illustration of the Bible's double system of causation, human and divine" (*Five Books*, 161; cf. also Alter, *Art of Biblical Narrative*, 32–34, 112–13, 176–77). Other illustrative biblical texts are Exod 3:8, 10; 1 Sam 9:16; 17:31–47; 2 Sam 17:14; 1 Kgs 12:15. For other references on the issue see Mann, *Book of the Former Prophets*, 215, n. 123. See also Fretheim, *Genesis*, 646–47.

has provided his own answer in the form of a divine speech to Jacob, the first such speech since we left the Jacob cycle (46:1–4). By this time Joseph has sent word to his father that he is alive and that Jacob should bring all his family and possessions to Egypt. Jacob is at the final threshold in his life (45:28). What happens now will determine not only his own limited future, but also the future of his family, "the sons of Israel" (46:5). As Jacob leaves the land of Canaan, which he will never see again, he stops at Beersheba to offer a sacrifice. It is significant that he goes there, and not to Bethel, for in doing so Jacob invokes a heritage and a God which transcends his own life—"the God of his father Isaac" (v. 1). His gesture almost seems a farewell to this God, as well as to the land of his ancestors.

Now at this threshold God speaks to him in another nocturnal vision and assures him that he will not go down to Egypt alone: "I am God, the God of your father; do not be afraid to go down to Egypt, for I will make of you a great nation there. I myself will go down with you to Egypt, and I will also bring you up again; and Joseph's own hand shall close your eyes" (46:3–4). Though Jacob is not at Bethel, the God of Bethel who went with him to Haran is still with him wherever he goes, even into Egypt. The speech thus serves as a divine confirmation of Joseph's theological interpretation of all that has happened to this family. It also explicitly extends the significance of this story to include the entire ancestral saga, for as Jacob departs for Egypt God repeats the ancient promise to Abram (12:2), adding a very important little word: "I will make of you a great nation *there*."

What an enormous shift this statement represents. God's promise to Abram was a new initiative, a new way out of the old world of the primeval cycle. That new way led to Canaan, and now, near the end of the ancestral saga, it leads to Egypt. From this point the function of the Joseph narrative as a bridge between the Abraham and Jacob cycles and the book of Exodus becomes increasingly clear. From the beginning, of course, Jacob has been both an individual character and the corporate personality Israel; both are present in God's speech. When God promises to go down with Jacob to Egypt, we think of the individual, but when God promises to "indeed bring you up" we think of Israel the nation and the story of the exodus.[196] The following genealogical material points in the same direction. In fact, the opening line ("now these are the names of the descendants of Israel who came into Egypt") has its exact parallel in the opening sentence of the book of Exodus.

Joseph now develops another ingenious ploy whereby his family gains "a possession in the land of Egypt" apart from the Egyptians (47:11).[197] The plan

196. "Bring you up" could refer to Jacob's burial in Canaan, but that is unlikely. Cf. 28:15 ("I will not leave you until I have done that of which I have spoken to you"), which also seems to apply to Israel of the future (i.e., given the content of the divine words in vv. 13–14).

197. There is considerable editorial confusion on Jacob's arrival. Pharaoh has granted them "the best of the land of Egypt" in 45:18; they settle in Goshen (46:28–29), as Joseph had already suggested (45:10). So why does Joseph need to finagle their living there in 46:31—47:6? Joseph announces their arrival to Pharaoh in 47:1, but Pharaoh seems to announce it himself in 47:5. The Septuagint has a different arrangement, but the problem persists. In 47:11 *Joseph*

is another step in Joseph's reaffirmation of his Hebrew identity, as well as a clear manifestation of the blessing that accrues to the family of Jacob, who now enjoys "the best of the land" (45:18; cf. 27:28). Of course, the blessing extends to the Egyptians, who will also "live and not die" (47:19), an extension beautifully symbolized when Jacob pronounces his blessing on Pharaoh (47:7, 10). He who first sent his sons to beg now comes to bless.

Nevertheless, the blessing, first pronounced at creation, continues to be fraught with irony (47:13–26). When the famine continues, the Egyptians run out of money to purchase grain, and they are forced to sell not only their land in exchange for food but also themselves as slaves—"so that we may live and not die." Moreover, they are selling themselves for the very grain that Pharaoh had collected from them to begin with (41:47–49). Here the blessing that Joseph brings is indisputable, but the means of its distribution is despotic (although the author probably does not see it this way). He who became a slave has now become the master, and his family maintains their independence: "Thus Israel settles in the land of Egypt, in the region of Goshen; and they gained possessions in it, and were fruitful and multiplied exceedingly" (47:27). Nevertheless, Israel's primary memory of Egypt will not be as "the land of Goshen" but "the house of slavery" (Exod 20:2).

6. The Blessing of Jacob (Genesis 47:28—50:26)

There is much editorial complexity in the concluding chapters of Genesis, including where the story originally ended (e.g., 47:12 or 47:27 or 50:26). The complexity derives from the number of issues that need resolving: the relationship between Joseph and his brothers (50:15–21; cf. 45:1–15); the tribal designations and hierarchy of the "sons of Israel" (46:8–27; chs. 48–49); the emergence of "Israel" as a people (e.g., 47:27; 50:25); Jacob's final benediction (chs. 48–49), death, and burial in the family plot in Canaan (47:28–31; 49:29–50:14);[198] Joseph's death and future burial (50:24–26); and allusions backward to the ancestral saga and forward to the book of Exodus (47:27b; cf. 1:28 and Exod 1:7; Gen 48:21; 50:24–25, cf. Exod 3:8).[199] The allusions are redactional seams that connect the ancestral stories with the exodus story, a connection that otherwise is not as obvious as one may think.[200] Indeed, the reference to

198. One might ask, why would Joseph not stay in Canaan after receiving Pharaoh's permission to take Jacob's body there (50:4–14), for one chronology suggests that the famine is over (45:11; 47:28). Some scholars think that the story ended that way at one point in the tradition. That would require deleting 50:7b–9, as well as v. 14 (those Egyptian officials would not look kindly on Joseph's remaining, nor would he leave behind his family!).

199. The references to Machpelah figures in here also (49:30–31), again emphasizing the legality of the purchase (ch. 23).

200. Some scholars think it quite likely that the stories of the ancestors in Genesis and the story of the exodus were originally independent. In fact, there are only a handful of references in Genesis *explicitly* foreshadowing the exodus, the most prominent being 15:13–16 and 48:21; 50:24–25 (Gen 12:10–20 could be *implicit*). The

"granted them a holding in the land of Egypt, in the best part of the land, in the land of Rameses."

the bones of Joseph looks ahead not only to Exod 13:19, where they are transported out of Egypt, but also to Josh 24:32 where they are interred, thus tying together the Pentateuch with the Former Prophets (Joshua through 2 Kings).

The deathbed scene that governs all of chs. 48–49 reminds us of its counterpart in chs. 24 and 27 (Abraham and Isaac). In particular, this scene again assumes an ironic significance in the life of Jacob. What Jacob had done to his father (reversing the order of blessing), he now does to his grandsons, exalting the younger, Ephraim, over the older, Manasseh.[201] Indeed, he adopts his grandsons along-side (if not in place of) his two firstborn (48:5). The old favoritism for the children of Rachel again comes to the fore (48:7). But here and in the extended blessing of all the sons in ch. 49, the narrative significance of the characters as persons gives way to the social and historical concerns of tribes ("Ephraim" becomes synonymous with northern Israel, just as "Judah" does for the south).

Despite some less than favorable "blessings" in ch. 49, no one son (or tribe) is displaced from the family tree (like Cain, Ishmael, or Esau).[202] In terms of the plot of the Joseph cycle, the reconciliation within the family is completed in 50:15–21. In a final fulfillment of Joseph's dreams, his brothers fall down before him and exclaim, "we are here as your slaves." Indeed, this is the first time they have bowed down to Joseph as Joseph. Joseph meets their humility with his own: "Fear not, for am I in the place of God?" This maturity in his sibling relationships is matched by the theological maturity with which he views all that has happened: "even though you intended to do harm to me, God intended it for good, in order to preserve a numerous people" (50:20; see the discussion above.)

This unit, which opened with Jacob on his deathbed, closes with Joseph on his, and with Joseph's death. Perhaps the most significant part of Jacob's deathbed statement is not his last will

references in Genesis 15 are also suspiciously redactional in that the list of dispossessed peoples (v. 19) is otherwise attested only within the exodus tradition (e.g., Exod 3:8, 17; 13:5; 23:23, 28; 33:2; 34:11). Conversely, there are remarkably few references to the ancestors in texts outside of Genesis that are transparently preexilic (e.g., Jacob in Hos 12:3–4, 12; later examples include Exod 6:8; 13:5, 11; 32:13). Scholars disagree on which biblical author first combined the ancestral and exodus narratives (J or P), and when. To further complicate matters, some scholars who posit originally independent *narratives* allow for the possibility of a prior connection as an *"idea"* (Pury, "The Jacob Story," 65, italics original), or that they were *"conceptionally* linked" before writing (Erhard Blum according to Dozeman and Schmid, *Farewell to the Yahwist*, 4; italics added), a possibility that seems to bring us full circle! Moreover, a collection of ancestral stories independent of the exodus story almost certainly would have preceded (or accompanied) the addition of the promise of land that connects ancestors and exodus and looks beyond them to a future fulfillment. In any case, the present text obviously presents the Joseph cycle as a connection between the ancestral stories and the exodus stories, even though it is a wonderful story aside from fulfilling that function.

201. Cf. especially 48:19; cf. 17:20; 21:13; 25:23; 27:36; 29:26. Note also the ironic role of blindness (48:10 and 27:1).

202. White, *Narration and Discourse*, 268. Note the discrediting of the firstborn, Reuben (49:3–4; 35:22), and Simeon and Levi (49:3–7; 34:25), and the exaltation of Judah (49:8–12), reflecting the Davidic monarchy. Joseph also receives an extensive blessing (49:22–26). Some of this poetry is likely very ancient, with language that later orthodoxy would disavow (e.g., 49:25).

and testament (his "blessing"), but his testimony to Joseph: "God Almighty appeared to me at Luz [Bethel] in the land of Canaan and blessed me, and said to me, 'Behold, I will make you fertile, and multiply you, and I will make of you a company of peoples, and will give this land to your descendants after you for an everlasting possession'" (48:3–4, AT).[203] Reciting the definitive experience of his life, Jacob transmits the fundamental religious heritage of the ancestors, much as Isaac transmitted it to him (28:3–4). Since the tradition does not include a scene in which God delivers the promises to one of Jacob's sons, Jacob's own testimony is the only way the knowledge of those promises can continue. Within the ancestral saga, Jacob is the last eyewitness to the direct disclosure of the divine will. As he approaches the ultimate threshold of death, he also approaches the moment of his greatest responsibility, which is precisely to testify to that disclosure for all generations to come.

When Jacob assumes the responsibility of telling this story, the process of conversion transforming his identity is complete: he is now Israel, the father of his people. And Israel is this story—past, present, and future. Indeed, it is only because of Jacob's testimony that Joseph can transmit the legacy of the ancestors from his deathbed: "God will surely come to you, and bring you up out of this land to the land which he swore to Abraham, to Isaac, and to Jacob" (50:24; cf. 48:21). This is the first and only time Joseph refers to the divine promises. They are promises he has never heard directly from God. Thus his trust in these promises—and in the God who stands behind them—is perhaps the most exemplary in the entire ancestral saga, for in order to trust in God, Joseph must also trust in the "witness" to God.

We can now see in retrospect how crucial Yahweh's "oath" to Abraham in ch. 22 is to the redactional unity of the ancestral saga. The oath is repeated at critical moments throughout the narrative, in each case at the transition from one generation to another (24:7; 26:3; 50:24), and, as we have already noted, in the last occurrence Joseph's final words also connect the oath to the exodus tradition, which is soon to unfold (cf. Exod 3:7–8). The saga ends with the bones of Joseph resting "in a coffin in Egypt," but the vision of the characters is already directed toward another horizon.

> [Yahweh] established a testimony in Jacob,
>   and appointed torah in Israel,
> which he commanded our ancestors to
>   teach their children;
> that the next generation might know them,
>   the children yet unborn,
> and arise and tell them to their children,
>   so that they should set their hope in God. (Ps 78:5–7a)

203. This passage (along with vss. 5–6) appears to be an insertion within an otherwise self-contained story (48:1–2, 8–22).

TWO

Exodus

Yahweh Reigns Forever

INTRODUCTION

The most important factor in our interpretation of Exodus is the way the text itself forces us to read it as a unity. The process of tradition has accomplished this by collecting all the material together within one book that renders a narrative without any major divisions. It has also accomplished this unity by a number of critical references both prospective and retrospective. For example, Moses' initial encounter with Yahweh, the God of the ancestors, occurs at "the mountain of God," and in his commission he is told that the most significant confirmation of his selection as Israel's deliverer will be when he and all Israel come back to this mountain to "serve God" (3:1, 12). The goal of chs. 1–15 is not simply escape from Egyptian servitude; it is servitude to Yahweh by the covenant community constituted at Mt. Sinai (chs. 19–40). Similarly, the opening words of Yahweh's revelation of the law at Mt. Sinai are predicated on the preceding story and incomprehensible without that predication: "I am Yahweh your God, who brought you out of the land of Egypt, out of the house of bondage" (20:2). Finally, at the end of the book (40:34–38) the tabernacle is erected and at once infused with the theophanic cloud of Yahweh's presence, continuing a theme that began with the "exodus" (13:21–22) and continued at Sinai (19:9; 24:15–18).[1] The conclusion of the Exodus story does not come with the defeat of Pharaoh or with the revelation of the law at Sinai, but with the advent of the glory of Yahweh in the midst of the covenant community.

1. The cloud serves both to reveal God's presence but also to obscure God's self from sight. It is often accompanied by the "glory," which is a kind of fiery effulgence within the cloud (e.g., 40:34). One could compare the way heat lightning looks within dark clouds, especially since the language reflects Yahweh's similarity to storm deities (cf. Pss 18:7–15; 29; 68:7–8; 77:16–18). See below on thunder as God's voice at Sinai (ch. 19).

What type of story is this story called Exodus? Here for the first time the pentateuchal narrative portrays both a hero and a villain—Moses and Pharaoh. Moses' heroic stature results not only from his opposition to Pharaoh and victory over him, but also from his role as the leader of Israel. The patriarchs are Israel's eponymous ancestors, each of them, and especially Jacob, a paterfamilias writ large. Moses, on the other hand, is the founder of a nation. Just as the Pentateuch from Exodus to Deuteronomy focuses on a people and not a family, so too it focuses on a founder and not a father. Indeed, so central is Moses' role in all that follows that we could easily construe these books as the biography of Moses, or as a heroic saga following upon the primeval and ancestral sagas.[2] Overall, then, Genesis functions as a prelude to the Moses story, providing a "world-historical perspective."[3]

While Exodus traces the rise of a hero and a people, it also traces the movement of the deity named Yahweh. That movement is from conflict to victory to the exercise of sovereignty and the enthronement of the sovereign. The movement of the book reaches its midpoint with the defeat of Pharaoh at the sea and the consequent exaltation of Yahweh as victor over Pharaoh and all other gods (ch. 15). It is from this stage in the narrative that I have chosen a title for the whole book: "Yahweh reigns forever" (15:18). The rest of the book focuses on Yahweh and Israel—on the constitution of Yahweh's realm (19:6) and the construction of the tabernacle as Yahweh's throne room where he will grant audiences with the people's representatives (25:21–22; 29:43–46). Those representatives are the priests, but especially Moses, for the movement of the book also follows the process through which he becomes the unquestioned leader of Israel (14:31; 19:9; 34:29–35; 39:43).

The movement of the book therefore results in the exaltation of three characters: Yahweh as the supreme deity in heaven and on earth, Moses as the servant of Yahweh, and Israel as the realm of Yahweh, Yahweh's "special possession among all peoples" (19:5). This combination alone would suggest that the most appropriate genre for the book is that of epic. What the *Aeneid* was to ancient Rome, Exodus is to ancient Israel. But we need not look to the classical literature of Rome as the only analogue. In fact, the movement that takes place in Exodus has a close parallel in a "typology of exaltation," which appears in epic literature of the ancient Near East.[4]

2. Indeed, Coats has suggested that the figure of Moses binds together the entire Pentateuch. See his *Genesis*, 5–7, 14–15. Martin Buber uses the term "saga" to designate both the individual stories in Exodus and also "the Biblical narrative" of Exodus through Deuteronomy as "a continuity of events" (*Moses*, 13, 17). Cf. Coats's use of "heroic saga," and his title, *Moses: Heroic Man, Man of God*, 37. Van Seters sees the J narrative in Exodus–Numbers as "a biography of Moses," suggested by the title of his book, *The Life of Moses* (see p. 2), a form of antiquarian historiography. Cf. also Knierim, "Composition," 371–72: the Pentateuch "*is the vita, or the biography, of Moses*" (italics original).

3. Knierim, "Composition," 355; cf. 378. Cf. the function of Genesis 1–11 with chs. 12–50.

4. Hallo originally suggested this typology in a joint study with van Dijk, *Exaltation of Inanna*, ch. 6: "The Typology of Divine Exaltation." I have used the typology in *Divine Presence and Guidance*, especially chs. 5–7. For Hallo's more recent view, see his comments regarding Exodus in Plaut, *Torah*, 372–77.

One of the benefits of applying the typology of exaltation to Exodus is that it reflects both the final form of the book and the history of traditions that in all probability stands behind it. Thus Yahweh's rise to prominence is highlighted not only by the redactional structure of the book but also appears specifically in a tradition maintained by the Priestly author, in which Yahweh's identity is a new revelation to Moses and the people of the exodus generation (6:2–3).[5]

The delineation of Yahweh's identity is not simply an arcane topic for philologists and historians of religion, whose search leads them far from the biblical text. It may not be so important whether the divine name originally was pronounced "Yahweh" or "Yahwi" or even "Yahoo" (long before the website!). What is important is that the determination of Yahweh's identity and character lies at the heart of the exodus narrative. This development of divine identity is closely correlated with that of Moses' identity, and with the identity of Israel as a people.[6]

In a survey of the book of Exodus as a whole, one notices that numerous critical links serve to connect major traditions as well as narrative blocks retrospectively and prospectively: the ancestors of Genesis; the exodus, Exodus 1–15; constituting of the covenant community (chs. 19–24; 32–34); construction of a sanctuary (chs. 25–31; 35–40); and the wilderness journey to Canaan (Numbers–Deuteronomy):

- Connection with blessing on creation and on Jacob/Israel in Genesis: Exod 1:1–7 (Gen 1:22, 28; 12:1–3; 47:27 etc.)
- Identity of Yahweh as God of the ancestors in Genesis and Israel's deliverer from bondage: Exod 2:24; 3:6, 15–16; 4:5; 6:2; 13:19; 32:13
- Identity of Yahweh as deliverer and as covenant suzerain: Exod 3:12; 19:3–6; 20:2
- Yahweh's presence as deliverer and suzerain in the tabernacle sanctuary (deliverer: 13:21–22; 14:19–20, 24; suzerain: 19:9, 16; 20:21; 24:15–18): Exodus 25–31; 35–40.
- Yahweh's presence and guidance in the wilderness between Sinai and Canaan: Exod 40:36–38 and Num 9:15–23

1. "GO DOWN, MOSES" (CHS. 1–4)

The narrative opens with a description of the transition from the *family* of Jacob to the *people* of Israel, overlapping with Gen 46:8–27 and the reported death of Joseph at the end of the book (Exod 1:1–6). This transitional material concludes with the following notice: "The Israelites were fertile and increased greatly; they multiplied and grew exceedingly strong, so that the land was filled with them" (v. 7). This is not simply a demographic report;

---

5. This clearly contradicts much of the book of Genesis (already 4:1, 26), but it may accurately reflect the background of some groups within Israel who had never heard of Yahweh until they encountered the God of the exodus story.

6. As Meyers puts it (*Exodus*, 11), "the truth of the past encoded in memory lies in the identity it shapes . . . The exodus story would be the kind of narrative that would help form the identity of an emerging people." Such a view of memory provides an alternative to seeing the story as history in the usual sense of that term.

rather, it is the author's way of saying that a fundamental step toward the fulfillment of the divine promise to Abraham has been accomplished—"I will multiply you exceedingly" (Gen 17:2). Moreover, this promise ultimately derives from the blessing pronounced on humankind at the creation: "Be fertile and increase, and fill the earth and subdue it" (1:28). Thus with this one verse (Exod 1:7) the author has stitched together the primeval cycle, the ancestral saga, and the book of Exodus.[7] In sight is God's purpose for the entire world.[8] In fact, the so-called plague cycle in chs. 7–11 portrays a series of disasters that in effect represent the degeneration of Egypt into a precreation state of chaos, reversing Genesis 1, ending in darkness and death, whereas chs. 15–40 will portray Israel as the center of God's new creation, concluding with a new Sabbath.[9]

Yet at the outset the blessing of creation once again proves to be well disguised. In the opening scene in Pharaoh's court, one wonders if even he knows of Gen 1:28, and especially the command, "fill the earth and *subdue* it"! What God intended for the world at creation Pharaoh sees as bent on subversion. He fears the incredible reproduction of the Israelites as a threat to the security of the Egyptian empire. In effect, his reaction to the blessing is to resist and control it, and he therefore subjects those who had come to Egypt as sojourners to the status of forced laborers.[10]

---

7. There is much debate on the redaction of Exodus 1–3 and how (or even if) the exodus story was originally connected to the ancestral story. See n. 200 in the preceding chapter, and Dozeman and Schmid, *A Farewell to the Yahwist?*, for a variety of viewpoints. In 1:7, 20 there are five different words used for "increase," not to mention "very, very much" (AT; NRSV "exceedingly," cf. Gen 17:2; 47:27). Whenever the stitch in Exod 1:7 was sewn in, it now connects with numerous threads in the Pentateuch, including Gen 1:22, 28; 9:1, 7; 17:2; 47:27b; Exod 1:20; Deut 26:5.

8. Fretheim in particular has emphasized the creational perspective of the entire book (*Exodus*, 12–14, 161–70). See also Dozeman (*God at War*, especially ch. 4, "Exodus and Creation"). He argues that the focus on creation (deriving from the Priestly source), shifts away from a focus on the conquest of Canaan as the goal.

9. Zevit, "Priestly Redaction of the Plague Narrative," 210: "A land in which creation was undone." Cf. Smith, *Exodus Pattern*, 199–200, 266–67; Fretheim, *Exodus*, 105–12; Alter, *Five*

Books, 350. The creational reading of the plague narrative fits well with the recent argument of Fantalkin and Tal ("Canonization of the Pentateuch," 4, 17) that the exodus story intends to portray "Egypt as a world of chaos, an antithesis to the world of cosmic order, so central to Persian imperial self-understanding." They place the final redaction to the early fourth century BCE. See below especially in the discussion of Exodus 39–40.

10. This is not chattel slavery, but conscripted labor; Israel's King Solomon used such labor to build the temple and other royal structures (1 Kgs 5:13–14), resentment over which led to revolution. For discussion of the historical verisimilitude of the picture of enslavement here, see Hendel, *Remembering Abraham*, 59–62.

> "Southern states had a history of placing [mostly African-American] prisoners with industries that would bear the cost of guarding and housing them in exchange for their labor . . . renting prisoners to companies by the month, [thereby] extending slavery by another name. . . . It is estimated that in the eighty years following the civil war as many as eight hundred thousand people had faced the South's corrupt system of justice. Huge numbers of those arrested were forced into involuntary servitude."[11]
>
> "Hitler's [armaments] . . . were produced by slaves in conditions of appalling hardship and brutality. Industrial output was sustained only by ruthless exploitation of captive manpower."
>
> "Slave labor alone made it possible for Germany to continue the war until 1945."[12]

of male infanticide, guaranteeing the *loss* of the labor force—*not* a shrewd policy (1:10).

> "In September 1944 Waffen SS troops exacted a terrible revenge on the civilian population [of an Italian town] for local partisan activities. 'All the children were killed in their mothers' arms.'"[13]

In the midst of this desperate situation—but with no explanation of its significance—a child is born and given the name of Moses (2:1–10). Ironically, he is rescued from Pharaoh's decree by Pharaoh's own daughter, who unknowingly gives him to his real mother to be nursed. She even *pays* Moses' mother to mother him. The princess seems not to mind that the boy is one of those *Hebrew* children.[14]

The actions of these two women, along with those of Moses' sister and the Hebrew midwives of ch. 1, represent the only resistance to Pharaoh's villainy so far in the story. Women who "revere God" act

Each step in Pharaoh's policy is as ruthless as it is irrational. Indeed the purpose of his initial policy is not simply to control the population or to provide a labor force but "to afflict them with heavy burdens." Yet each of Pharaoh's ploys meets with an uncanny ability of the Israelites to reproduce, partly because "the Hebrew women" are so "vigorous" in giving birth (1:19)! Thus in desperation Pharaoh arrives at the ultimate solution

11. Pollard, *Slavery by Another Name*. PBS documentary based on a book with the same title, by Doug Blackmon.

12. Hastings, *Inferno*, 470, 490.

13. Ibid., 446.

14. Here the term *Hebrew* (2:6; cf. 1:19; 2:11, 13; 3:18, etc.) appears synonymously with *Israelite*. Historically, there is some connection with a social group called *hapiru*, who appear throughout the ancient Near East variously as outsiders and misfits, even outlaws, rogues, and bandits, the latter in some ways similar to the Robin Hood of English legend. The term *Hebrew* is often used in distinction from some other group (e.g., Gen 39:14; 1 Sam 4:6). The original social reference also appears in such texts as Exod 21:2; Jer 34:9. In the exodus story Yahweh is identified as "the God of the Hebrews" (e.g., 3:18; 5:3; 7:16, etc.).

in the place of God (1:21, AT). Of course readers (both ancient and modern) know full well what this child will become. In fact, such a birth story is a conventional device for describing the origins of a heroic figure. But the narrator leaves the significance of the birth story undisclosed and jumps immediately to an incident occurring after Moses has reached maturity (vv. 11–15a).

The young Moses, who apparently has grown up in Pharaoh's court, one day suddenly realizes the plight of "his people" (2:11–15). In a spontaneous burst of rage, he kills an Egyptian who is beating a Hebrew. The text emphasizes the secretive nature of his actions (v. 12), but they are no secret to the Hebrew for whom he has intervened. When Moses encounters the same man fighting with a fellow Hebrew, he upbraids him, only to be rebuffed. In the light of what will become of Moses in the rest of Exodus, the irony of the man's words is unmistakable: "Who made you a ruler and judge over us?"

Rejected by his own people and hunted by Pharaoh's henchmen, Moses flees from Egypt to the land of Midian (2:15b–22).[15] He stops at a well, which immediately suggests the probability of a romantic encounter (cf. Gen 24:11–14; 29:2–12). The daughters of a man named Reuel (or Jethro, 3:1) appear, and Moses "saves" them from the bullying of some shepherds (2:17, AT). If the would-be hero cannot deliver the Israelites, he can deliver damsels in distress, and Reuel rewards his actions by giving him a wife. (Reuel is a Midianite priest whom we will

see again in ch. 18).[16] She soon bears him a son, whose name signifies Moses' current status: Gershom, which means, "I have been an alien in a foreign land." If there was a glimmer of hope at the birth of the hero, that glimmer has now gone out.

The first two chapters have thus moved with startling speed from the oppression of the Hebrews to the birth of Moses, his failure as a liberator, and his exile in the land of Midian. This material has already raised one of the central questions dominating the book of Exodus: Who is this Moses? He was born a Hebrew but raised as an Egyptian and named and adopted by Pharaoh's daughter. The Egyptian meaning of his name is apparently "son of," but whose son is he really? As a young man, he recognizes his identity as a Hebrew, but his violent attempt at leadership results in rejection by his own people as well as his alienation from Pharaoh's court. In the end, Moses has started a family and gained a new identity, but it is as "an alien in a foreign land." At this point, Moses is nobody.

Here the Priestly author has made a deceptively brief insertion (2:24), informing us of what the people in the story have no way of knowing: "God heard their groaning, and God remembered God's covenant with Abraham, Isaac, and Jacob" (AT). The author thus invokes the divine promise to the ancestors, just as

---

15. A long way from Egypt—presumably across the Sinai peninsula and around to the east coast of the Gulf of Aqabah.

16. Also named Hobab in Num 10:29. There is an intriguing connection between this priest, Moses, and the "mountain of God" in Midian, perhaps going back to the historical origins of the worship of Yahweh, so dramatically introduced to Moses in ch. 3. Midian is a child of Abraham by Keturah in Gen 25:1–2. For a recent assessment, see Meyers, *Exodus*, 12–13.

the blessing was invoked in 1:7. This insertion has a dramatic effect on chs. 1–2 and prepares us for ch. 3. The question, where is God? increasingly haunts the reader of chs. 1–2, where the only divine action in the midst of such desperate circumstances is the gift of fertility to the Hebrew midwives (1:21)! Thus the insertion at the end of ch. 2 assures us that the silence of God in the face of evil is only apparent, and what is about to happen is a result of God's "remembering" God's people. The text affirms the faithfulness of God despite God's apparent absence. At the same time, it alerts us to a crucial theological understanding of the character of Moses as we approach ch. 3. Moses does not "discover" God as if by some accident having more to do with the intent of sheep than the divine purpose; instead, Moses is discovered *by* God and is drawn into God's purpose for Israel, activated by the divine memory (cf. Gen 8:1).[17]

When Yahweh appears to Moses out of the midst of the burning bush Yahweh speaks for the first time in the exodus narrative (ch. 3). These words break the silence which pervades chs. 1–2 and extends backwards for generations to the last divine speech to Jacob (46:1–4). Indeed, as the dialogue with Moses unfolds, it becomes clear that the passing of generations has led to a state in which Yahweh must be introduced anew both to Moses and to the new generation of the Israelites. No one seems to remember

the name of Israel's ancestral God or to know who Yahweh is, and thus the loss of Moses' identity is paralleled in the loss of Yahweh's.

First, Yahweh is introduced simply as the God of the ancestors: "I am the God of your father, the God of Abraham, the God of Isaac, and the God of Jacob" (v. 6). The text then moves immediately to the statement of the divine mission, connecting with 2:23–25. Yahweh has seen the affliction of Israel ("my people") in Egypt, and he has "come down to deliver them" (3:7–9). The severity of Israel's oppression has produced a radical movement on the part of God, not seen since the tower of Babel and the destruction of Sodom and Gomorrah (Gen 11:5, 7; 19:20–21). In effect, the exodus from Egypt will occur because of an exodus from heaven and a direct intervention in the world of human affairs. Thus a fundamentally new dimension to the character of Yahweh appears. In many ways, this God *is* different from the God of the ancestors, and thus the self-introduction here and even more explicitly in 6:2–3 is warranted.

The divine speech concludes with a direct address to Moses (v. 10): "So now, go, so that I may send you to Pharaoh— and bring my people the Israelites out of Egypt" (AT).[18] God has saved the bad news for last. God has come down to deliver Israel but—as the old spiritual puts

---

17. I have paraphrased the classic formulation of Gressmann (quoted by Childs, *Exodus*, 54): "The discoverer (*Entdecker*) has become the discovered (*Entdeckte*)." Gressmann's comment referred to the development of the tradition within Exodus 3, not to the material in 2:23–25, but the effect is the same.

18. Cf. my discussion of the syntax of Gen 12:1–3, Ch. 1, n. 80. In the received text of Exod 3:10 the verb "and bring out" is an imperative. That Moses is the subject of this verb is stunning, since the verb often signifies the exodus as *Yahweh's* act of deliverance (e.g., 20:2). Many commentators argue for two separate sources in 3:7–8 and 9–10; others see a complementary literary style.

it—Moses must "go down" to Egypt as well. Moses is the human agent of divine salvation. The formulation of the commission thus revives a familiar theme of the pentateuchal narrative: divine grace and human responsibility. The two cannot be separated, nor can the exodus be reduced to one or the other. A *cooperation* of divine and human action must occur for there to be liberation. To be sure, the divine intervention is prior to the human act, and without it there would be no deliverance. Without this commission, Moses was a failure (2:11–15) and would have spent the rest of his life as an unknown shepherd in Midian. Yet, like Abram's before him, Moses' response to the initial command—"Go!"—is an essential part of the divine act. If Moses had said no, God would have had to find another to fill his place. What happens in the exodus event is a combination of divine authorization and human agency, an "act of God" coordinated with and dependent on a heroic man. One can argue that such cooperation forms an essential theme in biblical theology in general.[19]

By the time the dialogue is over, Moses will have come very close to saying no. His initial response is perhaps as

close as we will ever get to the original "Who, me?": "Who am I that I should go to Pharaoh, and bring the Israelites out of Egypt?" In response to his, "Who am I?" Yahweh answers, "I will be with you." Moses' identity is defined only in terms of the *I* of God. As we move through the book each of the crucial manifestations of this divine presence will confirm Moses' identity as Yahweh's agent.

Now it is Moses' turn again, and he responds with a request for the name of the deity with whom he is talking (vv. 13–15). We the readers know that this is Yahweh, but Yahweh has been introduced to Moses only as the "God of your father." On the surface Moses' request seems perfectly natural and understandable. After all, if he rallies the Israelites and proclaims himself their divinely appointed leader, yet doesn't even know the name of the God who appointed him, he will not be a very credible figure. On the other hand, the request for the deity's name may be an attempt to gain control of the deity's power, for knowledge of a person's name is a key to knowing his or her essential nature (cf. Gen 32:29; Judg 13:17–18).

Deciphering the motivation behind Moses' request is not any easier after we have read Yahweh's immediate response (v. 14). This verse contains some of the most difficult interpretive problems in the Hebrew Bible.[20] The response, usually translated "I am who I am," and "I am has sent me," seems to be as much an evasion as an answer. Of course, this is followed by verse 15, where "the Lord" (i.e., "Yahweh") is equated with "the God of your

19. See n. 195 in the preceding chapter. Among others, Coats has emphasized this co-ordination, indicated by the combination "heroic man" and "man of God," a "heroic pattern" focusing on the human agent, along with the "promise–fulfillment scheme" focusing on divine involvement. The balance is essential to "the theology of the Pentateuch" in general—"Moses is *both* servant of God *and* heroic giant" (*Moses Tradition*, 42 [italics added], 44; cf. 72–73; cf. his earlier collection, *Moses: Heroic Man, Man of God*, especially ch. 9. Similarly, Milgrom (*Leviticus: A Book of Ritual*, 5) says that the human role is "to be active partners of God in determining and implementing the divine will."

20. Note all caps in NRSV as if punctuated "I-am-who-I-am."

ancestors" (see Appendix 2). On the one hand, Yahweh is identified as the divine protagonist of the ancestral saga; on the other, Yahweh's identity, which remains hidden, is still a mystery.

Whatever the original intention of these verses, in their present position they point away from any revelation of Yahweh's identity in a single and private moment of unveiling, and point instead toward the progressive disclosure of Yahweh's identity as it is rendered by the narrative that follows. Accordingly, another possible translation of God's answer to Moses may be more appropriate: "I will be what I will be," or even "I am what I will be." Yahweh's identity cannot be reduced to a single word—even if that word be a personal name—but can be grasped only in and through the story that relates all of Yahweh's words and deeds. Yahweh's identity is rendered by the pledges of blessing and promise made in the past ("the God of your ancestors"), by the expression of intentions in the present (3:7–10), and by what Yahweh will do and say in the future. As one of J. R. R. Tolkien's marvelous characters says, "it would take a long while [to tell my name]: my name is growing all the time, and I've lived a very long, long time; so my name is like a story."[21] As the divine protagonist of the pentateuchal narrative, Yahweh's character develops as does any character rendered by a story. As another author suggests, "The name which was almost totally open and devoid of denotative content at the beginning, gradually acquires a meaning in most narratives, so that at the end the name has been given a

definition based on the events which have transpired."[22]

We must not forget that something has already happened to God in this story of Exodus. God has been forced (the classical rabbis would say, "as it were") to come down to Egypt, primarily because the enslavement and genocide of Israel threatens to extinguish the blessing pronounced on Israel, and through them, for the whole world (1:7). It would be surprising if such a radical gesture were not accompanied by a change in Yahweh's character. Both from the standpoint of the history of traditions and from the perspective of the text in its present form, the story of the exaltation of Yahweh renders a new God. The central aspect of the divine character that the exodus story reveals has already appeared in Yahweh's announcement to Moses in 3:7–10. Yahweh is a God of justice who champions the cause of the oppressed. "Liberation is integral and intrinsic in Yahweh's very character."[23] Yahweh is a "deliverer" of the unjustly persecuted, and in order to act as deliverer within the circumstances of the ensuing narrative, Yahweh will also have to become a "warrior" (15:3).[24]

Yahweh's answer to Moses' request for Yahweh's name continues in 4:16–21 with a preview of the "wonders" that will

21. As quoted by McEvenue, *Narrative Style of the Priestly Writer*, 141–42.

22. White, "French Structuralism," 113.

23. Brueggemann, *The Book of Exodus*, 737, referring to the divine speech in ch. 6. For liberation readings from the perspectives of various ethnic groups, see *The New Interpreter's Bible* 1:154–80.

24. This difference in theology may well reflect different origins for the exodus story and the ancestral stories, but even in the latter we have seen such differences (e.g., the theophanies for Jacob compared to the discrete Providence for Joseph).

occur in chs. 7–12. The passage has two parallels, one in 4:21–23, focusing on the death of the firstborn, and another in 7:3–5. These three previews are alike in that they occur in conjunction with Moses' commissioning. From his perspective, they serve as a warning that deliverance will not come easily or quickly. From our perspective as readers, however, these previews at first seem to betray the incompetence of the narrators. They are like people who emerge from a suspenseful movie and tell everyone in the ticket line how the movie ends.

On the other hand, these preview passages provide a corrective to our understanding of the purpose of the overall narrative. The authors are not interested in creating a thriller. Their concern is to exalt the figure of Yahweh, and perhaps the most important way of doing that is to show that Yahweh is in control of events in the narrative from the outset. These previews are thus reminiscent of the initial oracle in the Jacob cycle (Gen 25:22–23) and the retrospective interpretation which Joseph gives of the Joseph cycle (45:5–8; 50:20). In fact, the previews in chs. 4 and 7 go even further, for here the coming events are not only foreknown by Yahweh but also predetermined: Yahweh will "harden [Pharaoh's] heart so that he will not let the people go" (4:21; 7:3). Whatever we may have thought of the young Jacob (who had a hard heart in a different sense), we never thought he was programmed. Do we have here in Exodus a form of divine predestination in which Pharaoh is a mere puppet with whom Yahweh plays? A later text will come close to suggesting that (10:1–2).

The theological implications of the hardening of Pharaoh's heart present one of the most difficult problems in the exodus narrative. I have introduced it here because the text forces us to recognize it before the series of "wonders" begins; but in fact we cannot understand the motif adequately until the cycle has run its course—until the firstborn Egyptians are dead and Pharaoh's troops are drowned in the sea. That the Egyptian firstborn must die—that is, that Yahweh will *kill* them (4:23)—compounds the moral problem of Pharaoh's hard heart.

The final unit in the first commissioning of Moses focuses on Moses' increasingly negative reactions to his call (4:1–17).[25] When Moses first asked for some legitimation of his status as Yahweh's agent, Yahweh promised to be with him (3:12), and subsequently predicted that the representatives of the Israelites ("the elders") would obey him ("hearken to your voice," v. 18). Moses now raises the possibility that they will not "believe" him or obey him but will question his claim that Yahweh has appeared to him (4:1). Here the author introduces a motif that will figure prominently in the definition of Moses' character, the verb 'aman. It means "to affirm, to trust or believe in," and is the origin of our English word *amen* (here it refers to personal reliance, not agreement with concepts). The word is used four times in the rest of this passage, accentuating Moses' need for the

25. Much of the commissioning scene reflects similar stories about Israel's military heroes and prophets, especially the diffidence of the commissioned, so that here *God* cries, "Enough!" (4:14). On the parallels, see Judges 6; 1 Samuel 9–10; Jer 1:4–10; Isaiah 6. Cf. especially Exod 3:9–10 and 1 Sam 9:16.

people's confirmation. Even after Yahweh gives him the miraculous signs to confirm his legitimacy, Moses pleads that someone else be commissioned, and at this point Yahweh angrily provides his brother Aaron, not as a replacement, but as a spokesperson.

The recurrence of the "trust" motif at crucial points later in the narrative (14:31; 19:9) indicates a central tension in the book of Exodus: will the people accept Moses as their divinely appointed leader? Will they trust in him and obey him? Perhaps we are so accustomed to Moses' fame as a "man of God" that we fail to see the seriousness of the issue from the perspective of the characters in the story—especially the Israelites.

The issue is not limited to trust in Moses but includes the people's trust in God. Moses is their only medium for knowledge of the divine purpose. After all, God has not spoken directly to them and will not do so until they arrive at the mountain where he first appeared to Moses (cf. 3:12).[26] How would you respond to someone who told you God had appeared to him in a burning bush and appointed him to be your leader? This is the reason Yahweh gives Moses the miraculous signs to demonstrate his claim. Even the signs, as we shall see, eventually prove to be less than convincing. At the end of ch. 4 Moses returns to Egypt and performs his magic tricks before the people. They "believe" him, and bow their heads in worship to Yahweh, but that trust and worship soon prove ephemeral.

"Go down, Moses, 'Way down in Egypt's land, tell old Pharaoh, to let my people go." Traditional Negro Spiritual

"The Spiritual 'Go down, Moses' comes to us neither in the past tense nor the historical present, but in the future tense, which is to say as a moral imperative. Few obeyed; but Moses remained nonetheless one of the constant reminders that, as a maid told her mistress, '*God never made us to be slaves for white people.*'"[27]

2. "LET MY PEOPLE GO" (CHS. 5–11)

In ch. 5 Moses and Aaron have their first encounter with Pharaoh, and it is a complete failure. Moses' demand for a religious holiday results only in a stretch-out. The suggestion that the Israelites want to "hold a feast" to Yahweh in the wilderness is an obvious attempt at deception. It is clear from what has already happened that neither Yahweh nor Moses intends for the Israelites to return (e.g., 3:8). Although Pharaoh is suspicious for the wrong reasons, he will increasingly appear to realize the real motive behind Moses' request. For his part, Moses will hold to his excuse to the end, and for an important reason: a sacrificial feast, he argues, requires that all of the Israelites participate (men, women, and children) and that they take their cattle with them as well (10:24–26).

---

26. Even at Exodus 19–20 the extent to which the people hear Yahweh's words will not be completely clear; cf. Deut 5:4–5, 22–27, and see the discussion below.

27. Mathews, *Religion in the Old South*, 221 (italics original).

Those who fret over Moses' telling a lie miss the import of the motif in the narrative. The pretense of a religious service is a shrewd bargaining ploy, but it also points to a fundamental theological dimension of the plot. Repeatedly Moses' demand for release will be the line, "Let my people go, that they may serve me." But "serve" can refer to political allegiance as well as worship. Thus the demand poses a central issue: whom will Israel serve, Pharaoh or Yahweh?

The question of Israel's true master is accentuated in ch. 5 by Pharaoh's refusal to "acknowledge" Yahweh and thus Yahweh's claim on Israel. Pharaoh's initial response to Moses is, "Who is Yahweh, that I should heed his voice and let Israel go? I do not acknowledge (literally "know") Yahweh, and indeed I will not let Israel go" (AT). Pharaoh's response represents the first direct challenge to Yahweh's authority in the Pentateuch. Moreover, his refusal to acknowledge Yahweh combines with the earlier question about Yahweh's identity ("what is his name?" 4:13). In fact, along with the question of Moses' identity and authority, Pharaoh's question poses the central issue in chs. 1–15: "Who is Yahweh?" The exaltation of Yahweh is a narrative description of Yahweh's identity in terms of sovereignty over the world, and over the Pharaoh's attempt to exalt himself (cf. 9:17).[28]

By the end of this incident, a second issue emerges, an issue already raised in chapters 3–4: "Who is Moses?" When Moses fails to win the release of the

Israelites, their foremen denounce him as a troublemaker whose scheme has put them in grave danger (v. 21). Moses then directs the complaint against Yahweh in a bitter accusation. He wonders why Yahweh commissioned him, and claims that Yahweh, not only has failed to deliver Israel, but has "done evil to this people" (v. 22, AT). Yahweh's response is to say, essentially, "Just wait and see what I will do to Pharaoh" (6:1), and then in effect to renew Moses' commission (6:2—7:13), a block of material that may originally have been a Priestly alternate to ch. 3. Yahweh encourages Moses despite the failure of his initial mission. Moreover, here the introduction of Yahweh's personal name as a new revelation is much more explicit than in 3:14–15. Of course, the author knows that the name is used in the text of Genesis but is not bothered by this apparent contradiction. In context the emphasis on this tradition of a new name is a forceful way of suggesting what was already implicit in ch. 3: what is about to happen in Egypt will disclose something absolutely essential to the identity of God, something unprecedented.

The structure of the divine speech points toward the definitive disclosure. The speech is framed by the stately formula, "I am Yahweh" (vv. 2, 8). The formula occurs again in the middle of the speech, at the pivotal point between past and future (v. 6, note also the *therefore*). Yahweh appeared to the ancestors as El Shaddai, establishing the covenant with them "to give them the land of Canaan." God has heard their groaning and remembered the covenant. Yahweh is faithful to the promises of the past, but now in Egypt Yahweh's definitive identity is

28. Cf. Dozeman (*God at War*, 119): "The motif also transforms the exodus into a polemical story whose goal is to confront Pharaoh and the Egyptians with Yahweh's power as a creator God, who controls all land, including Egypt."

about to be revealed: Yahweh will "bring out," "deliver," and "redeem" Israel (AT), and Israel will become Yahweh's people. Then they will "acknowledge" ("know") that Yahweh is God. The conjunction of the three verbs in v. 6 and the adoption formula in v. 7, concluded by the recognition formula, provides a succinct description of Yahweh's identity—the identity disclosed by the rest of the book of Exodus, where Yahweh "redeems" Israel (chs. 7–15) and adopts them as a covenant community (chs. 19–40, especially 19:5–6). All these promises of a glowing future, however, are not enough to uplift the Israelites, who cannot *hear* of hope "because of their broken spirit and their cruel slavery" (6:9). Similarly, Moses again expresses anxiety over his capability as Yahweh's spokesperson (6:12 and 6:30; cf. 4:10), as if *he* hasn't heard the speech either! The stage is set for some "signs and wonders."

Thus we turn now to the cycle that begins at 7:14,[29] more accurately called disasters rather than the misleading plagues. The disasters are called "signs and wonders" to emphasize that these are not only natural disasters but acts of God in the literal sense (not that of the insurance industry).[30] Three motifs in the di-sasters cycle highlight the questions, who is Moses? and who is Yahweh? The first is the motif of Pharaoh's magicians, and belongs to the P source. In the first three incidents with Pharaoh (rod/serpent, blood, and frogs), the "wise men and the sorcerers" of the Pharaoh are able to duplicate "by their secret arts" the miracles wrought by Moses and Aaron (7:11, 22; 8:7). That in the first instance Aaron's rod devours theirs does not detract from their impressive skills; on the other hand, the author probably relished the irony that their repetition simply compounds the problem! The signs Yahweh gave to Moses to legitimate his position may have worked with the Israelites (4:30–31), but they have not impressed the Egyptians.

However, in the fourth disaster (gnats) the magicians muster their "secret arts" to no avail. Overwhelmed by their defeat, they even suggest to Pharaoh that "this is the finger of God!" (8:18–19). Finally, with the boils, the magicians come to an ignominious end: "the magicians could not stand before Moses because of the boils, for the boils afflicted the magicians as well as all the Egyptians" (9:11). Thus the motif of the magicians is one way in which the problem of Moses' legitimacy is cast in a new light; at first challenged by their occult powers, in the end Moses stands unrivaled in Pharaoh's court. Even the pagan magicians testify

---

29. The verses 7:8–13 resemble 4:1–5 (the "signs"). However, in the present text a more natural break comes in between 7:7 and 7:8. Scholars often divide the plagues into the sources J and P, and suggest numerous patterns (e.g., 3+3+3+1). For other variations see Psalms 78 and 105. For an example of possible doublets within one plague report, consider 7:14–18, 20b–21a, 24 as parallel to 7:19–20a, 21b–23, the latter adding Aaron, holding up the rod rather than striking the river, and extending the plague to all the water in the land.

30. Meyers, *Exodus*, 76–79, who also suggests

that the literary *arrangement* of the disasters points to God's direct activity. Cf. Fretheim, *Exodus*, 109. Compare collectively 7:3 as well as 3:20; 4:17, 21; 7:8; 8:23. The word usually translated "plague" is literally a "blow" or "strike," hence my "disaster," used most prominently with the death of the firstborn. As Baden notes (*Composition*, 173) the "signs and wonders" are from the Priestly writer and point to God's complete control.

to the power of the God of the Hebrews (8:29), then exit backstage, scratching themselves (9:11).

A second motif derives from the Yahwistic stratum, and concerns the concessions Pharaoh makes to Moses. Here is a progression, not only in the stature of Moses, but also in the recognition of Yahweh's power. Up until the invasion of frogs, Pharaoh has remained adamant. Evidently the croaking becomes too much for the royal ears, however; for at this point Pharaoh promises to let the Israelites go if Moses will "entreat Yahweh to take away the frogs" (8:8). Of course, no sooner has Moses complied with the request than Pharaoh stubbornly changes his mind, despite the stench of all those *dead* frogs (8:13–14). A similar course is followed in 8:25–32, where Pharaoh first offers a temporary release in Egypt, then agrees to a short trip outside the land. Once again, however, and despite Moses' intercession for him (v. 28), Pharaoh balks.

The vacillations of Pharaoh become more drastic with the disaster of hail. Pharaoh suddenly becomes penitent: "This time I have sinned; Yahweh is in the right, and I and my people are in the wrong. Pray to Yahweh [and] . . . ; I will let you go" (9:27–28, AT). Nevertheless, with the cessation of the hail, "he sinned once more" and refused Moses' request (v. 34). With the disaster of locusts, Pharaoh will allow only the adult males to leave, then with the onslaught of the locusts he confesses his sin again (10:16–17), only to fall back into his pattern of refusal. In response to the disaster of darkness, Pharaoh will allow all but the flocks of the Israelites to leave. Moses rejects the offer and he and Pharaoh break off negotiations, ostensibly for the last time (10:21–29). After the death of the firstborn, however, Pharaoh "summoned Moses and Aaron by night, and said, 'Rise up, go away from my people, both you and the people of Israel; and go, serve Yahweh, as you have said. Take your flocks and your herds, as you have said, and be gone; and bless me also!'" (12:31–32, AT). At this point—and we are already jumping ahead of the story—the narrative tension involving Moses' abilities as leader, and Yahweh's power over Pharaoh appears to be resolved: Pharaoh has yielded; the people are free.

The motif of Pharaoh's concessions and withdrawals is closely tied to a third motif, the acknowledgment of Yahweh's sovereignty. This motif began with the initial encounter between Pharaoh and Moses, when Pharaoh said "Who is Yahweh? . . . I do not acknowledge him" (5:2, AT). The motif resumes with the disaster of blood, which Moses introduces with these words: "By this you shall acknowledge that I am Yahweh" (7:17, AT). In the next disaster (frogs), a comparative thrust is introduced. Moses has not only agreed to "entreat" Yahweh to end the nuisance, but has allowed Pharaoh to set the time, "so that you may acknowledge that there is no one like Yahweh our God" (8:10, AT). Again in the disaster of flies, the first formula is combined with a spatial expression. Yahweh's ability to "set apart the land of Goshen, where my people dwell," while the land of Egypt is swarming with flies, is for Pharaoh's instruction, "that you may acknowledge that I am Yahweh in the midst of the earth" (8:22, AT).

The author has drawn out the theological implications of the motif in the disaster of hail, 9:14–16:

> For this time I will send all my disasters upon your heart, and upon your servants and your people, that you may acknowledge that there is none like me in all the earth. For by now I could have put forth my hand and struck you and your people with pestilence, and you would have been cut off from the earth; but for this purpose have I let you live, to show you my power, so that my name may be declared throughout all the earth. (AT)

The same theology appears more succinctly in the reason given for the cessation of the hail, "that you may acknowledge that the earth is Yahweh's" (9:29). By controlling the forces of nature, Yahweh has demonstrated sovereignty over all the world. In the beginning, Pharaoh questioned Yahweh's identity and sovereignty; in the end, Yahweh's name will be universally recognized. While the motif of the magicians was resolved with their humiliating defeat, no such resolution of the concession and acknowledgment motifs takes place within the disaster cycle. In the announcement of the final sign, the acknowledgment motif appears again (11:7), and both motifs play a prominent role in the climactic story of Pharaoh's defeat at the sea (ch. 14). In short, the signs and wonders—including the death of Pharaoh's own firstborn—fail to secure Pharaoh's final concession or his acknowledgment of Yahweh's sovereignty. Such is the hardness of Pharaoh's heart (see further below on this motif and the death of the firstborn).

3. "A NIGHT OF WATCHING" (12:1–13:16)

Between release and redemption comes Passover. The final disaster is the death of all Egyptian firstborns—animal as well as human—but God "passes over" the homes of the Israelites.[31] There is one verse in this unit that is remarkable for both its brevity and its profundity: "It was a night of watching for Yahweh, to bring them out of the land of Egypt; this same night is for Yahweh a watching for all the Israelites throughout their generations" (12:42, AT). This is an unusual example of authorial commentary in which the author steps outside the narrative mode in an overt attempt to instruct readers. The "for Yahweh" is ambiguous, perhaps deliberately so. It refers to Yahweh's "watching" for Israel, and Israel's "watching" for Yahweh, in two senses of the term—one, a provision of protection; the other, an expectation of arrival. This "night of watching," the author suggests, is not confined to the past—it is a night that both "was" and "is."[32]

The redaction turns the original story into a play that each subsequent generation of Israelites can enact. As the French would say, *recit* has become *rite*; narrative has become ritual. The seriousness of this transformation is indicated in that it is fixed by law, "an eternal ordinance" (12:14, 24).[33] All future

---

31. The word for "pass over" in 12:13 that provides the name of the festival more accurately means "skip over."

32. The verse consists of two nominal clauses without any finite verbs; thus the tense must be determined on the basis of context.

33. The liturgical intent appears in the root word for "festival," which occurs three times in 12:14 (including "celebrate" and "observe").

generations are commanded to enact this play once a year throughout their lives. Similarly, the *survival* of the firstborn of Israelites is to be commemorated by the festivals of unleavened bread (13:1–10) and by sacrifice of firstborn animals (13:11–16). In each case, law demands repetition of the story, because this particular story has become the narrative core of what it means to be an Israelite. Just as the exodus story represents the definitive identity of Yahweh and Moses, so it represents the definitive identity of the community called Israel. Those who do not perform this ritual cut themselves off from the community and, in effect, cease to be Israelites (12:15, 19). Moreover, the play practice is a *dress* rehearsal: when the celebrants put on their hats and coats and grab their walking sticks (12:11), they are not just pretending to be Israelites in Egypt—they *are* those Israelites—because who they are is defined by the story they are enacting. The Passover service is a "memorial" (12:14; 13:9) to be remembered (13:3), but one reflecting a distinctive understanding of memory. Future generations cannot remember the exodus any more than contemporary Americans remember Washington's crossing of the Delaware, but within the Passover ritual, the participants identify themselves with the story in such a way that they transcend the temporal and spatial boundaries separating them from the original event. Thus in the contemporary Passover ritual, the celebrants say, "*We* were Pharaoh's slaves in Egypt." What they are saying is not so much we *were* there as we *are* there. Or, to put it another

way, exodus is not only then but now, not only past but present (cf. 13:4).[34]

The consequence of this emphasis on the exodus story as the core of Israelite identity appears when we note what has happened to the promise of land. At three places in the text, arrival in the land of promise serves as the setting in which the Passover ritual is to take place (12:25; 13:5, 11). Remarkably, it is not the fulfillment of the promise of land that is celebrated, but the exodus from Egypt. When the Israelites arrive in Canaan, they are not enjoined to tell their children of the promise of the land to Abraham, but to tell them of their deliverance from the land of Egypt. While the exodus story has by no means effaced the promises to the ancestors, it has removed them from the central position they heretofore held.[35] Now one cannot be an Israelite—even in the land of Canaan—unless one remembers this story.

In terms of the text and later tradition, the Passover ritual has thus become the primary medium for the transmission of the entire exodus story. Passover is so familiar (even to non-Jews) that this function may not seem surprising, but the literary context of the biblical story suggests that it is extraordinary. The Passover text represents the end of the signs and wonders and includes Israel's escape

34. Hendel puts it well: "The Exodus, in this sense, is not a punctual past but ongoing, a past continuous" (*Remembering Abraham*, 71).

35. For an assessment of the critical implications of the land promise in ch. 13, see Rendtorff, *Pentateuch*, 77. In 12:25, 13:5, 11, references to the land of Canaan clearly connect with Yahweh's "oath" in Genesis. In contrast, other references (e.g., 3:8) appear to derive from completely different traditions or authors.

from Egypt (12:37, 41, 51). Yet freedom soon proves more apparent than real, for Pharaoh changes his mind and pursues the former slaves. Israel's redemption does not really take place until Pharaoh's forces are defeated at the sea (ch. 14). Thus the Passover ritual celebrates the night *before* redemption, a night haunted with a spirit of fear and excitement. The characters in the story (and therefore the participants in the ritual) are frozen in a moment of incompleteness, between slavery and freedom, death and life. Only on the other side of this night, "in the morning watch" (14:24), will the tension of the exodus narrative finally be broken, and only then will there emerge a new people, a new leader, and, as it were, a new God.

That the author has explicitly lifted up this sense of incompleteness and legislated it to future generations means that when they identify with this story, they too experience this incompleteness. A similar sense of incompleteness pervaded the book of Genesis, where the fulfillment of the promises to the ancestors was left in suspense, but never in those stories did the author step outside the narrative framework and suggest—indeed, demand—such an attitude for the reader. In fact, as we shall see at the conclusion of this book, the Passover text provides a metaphor for the significance of the end of the Pentateuch and thus of the final shape of the Torah as a whole. "A night of watching" is another way of expressing what "beyond the Jordan" will mean in the book of Deuteronomy.[36]

4. "YAHWEH REIGNS" (13:17—15:21)

The narrator has probably woven together two narrative strands here, but our purpose it not to delineate them or to investigate the historical question of what really happened?[37] Rather, we will see how the story serves as a denouement for the preceding narrative.

Two sets of characters make up this story: 1) those who have yet to acknowledge definitively either the sovereignty of Yahweh or the leadership of Moses— the people of Israel and Pharaoh; and 2) those whose legitimacy has been in question all along—Moses and Yahweh. The preceding cycle of disasters repeatedly hammered at Pharaoh concerning his acknowledgment of Yahweh's sovereignty. Ch. 14 brings the issue to a dramatic resolution. In two almost identical phrases (vv. 4 and 17–18) Yahweh declares, "I will get glory over Pharaoh and all his host, and the Egyptians shall acknowledge that I am Yahweh" (AT). Characteristically, Pharaoh never acknowledges Yahweh's sovereignty, although his soldiers come close to it (14:25). In the end, the text seems more interested in demonstrating Yahweh's "glory" to the reader. The narrative description of Pharaoh's defeat is itself a vindication of the God of Israel. Yahweh has fulfilled the promise of deliverance.

---

36. For a more recent and expanded discussion, see Mann, "Passover."

37. For example, one strand seems to assume that the sea is dried up by a strong wind; another that the sea is split at the cue of Moses' uplifted rod, forming a corridor through walls of water. (Both are combined in 14:21). For a recent division of the sources into two independent (often conflicting) narratives, see Baden, *Composition*, 193–213.

Similarly, the element of narrative tension that began at least with Moses' questioning whether the people would "trust" in him (chs. 3–4) is brought to a final resolution. When the people, who think they are free from Pharaoh's power, look behind them and see with utter horror that the Egyptian chariots are bearing down on them, they angrily rebuke Moses for his apparently disastrous leadership: "Is this not the very thing we told you in Egypt, 'Let us alone and let us serve the Egyptians'? For it would have been better for us to serve the Egyptians than to die in the wilderness" (v. 12). In this scene, reminiscent of the end of ch. 5, the people reject the leadership of Moses and the divine deliverance that stands behind it (a problem anticipated in 13:17). Moses had repeatedly gone to Pharaoh with Yahweh's command, "Let my people go, that they may serve me." Now Israel wants to serve Pharaoh—and at the very moment of their salvation! This picture is all the more telling when we realize that the people have scarcely appeared at all as a prominent character before this point in the narrative. Indeed, this is the first time the people have spoken.

To this bitter and despairing cry, Moses responds with a stinging summons: "Fear not, stand firm, and see the salvation of Yahweh, which he will work for you today; for the Egyptians whom you see today, you shall never see again. Yahweh will fight for you, and you have only to be still" (vv. 13–14, AT). With these remarks ringing in their ears, and with divine protection both in front and behind, the people enter the path through the sea. Rabbinic legend rightly extols the first person to step between the walls

of water! But we need not rehearse the events that follow, for the author's main point is contained in the closing verses: "Thus Yahweh *saved* Israel that day from the hand of the Egyptians; and Israel saw the Egyptians dead upon the seashore. And Israel saw the great work which Yahweh did against the Egyptians, and the people feared Yahweh; and they trusted in Yahweh and in Yahweh's servant Moses" (AT). By recapitulating the language of Moses' previous summons ("fear," "see," "salvation"), the author has shown how the act of salvation has brought the people from the fear of Pharaoh to the fear of Yahweh. Even more significantly, by the resumption of the motif of trust, the entire narrative of Exodus up to this point comes to a magnificent conclusion.

Now we have the first part of the answer to the question, who is Yahweh? The answer receives its quintessential formulation in the narrative of Exodus 1–14, which is summarized most succinctly in the opening lines of the Decalogue (20:2): "I am Yahweh your God, who brought you out of the land of Egypt, out of the house of bondage" (AT). Moreover, the predication following this self-declaration also answers the question raised in Moses' commission—what is God's name? The answer can never again be limited to "Yahweh, the God of your ancestors, the God of Abraham, the God of Isaac, and the God of Jacob" (3:15–16, AT), but must also, and primarily, be "Yahweh your God, who brought you out of the land of Egypt." God does not simply have a new personal name, although that lies within the history of the exodus traditions; God also has a new identity.

The closing phrase in ch. 14 rightly places a theological statement, strictly construed, in preeminent position—the observation of Yahweh's act of salvation has led to trust in him. But closely correlated with this is a statement about Moses. The identity of the man who at first did not even believe in himself, the man whom the people increasingly had more reason to doubt than to trust, is finally confirmed. He is the servant of Yahweh. The rest of the book—and the rest of the Pentateuch—will define in increasing detail the nature of Moses' identity as Yahweh's servant. Already the text has cast him in the roles of a deliverer and a prophetic figure, one who bears the message of Yahweh ("Thus says the Lord") to a stubborn and haughty king. If Moses is a hero, his role as prophet and servant will redefine the characteristics of heroism, providing one of the biblical precedents for the phrase "speaking truth to power."[38] For now, the central focus is on Moses' role as an object of the people's trust (14:31). The correlation of trust in a human being and in God is unprecedented and will remain unequaled (though not unchallenged) in the Pentateuch. From now until the end, Moses will become the central model of "what human life might be like if lived to the full."[39] In short, Moses will become the one who responds to the divine will with virtually complete integrity, a man of righteousness, the true "man of God" (Deut 33:1).

What could one add to this, the opening act of the exaltation of Yahweh, other than a hymn of praise? That is precisely the function of Exod 15:1–18, which represents in poetic form what was already implicit in the preceding narrative—the universal significance of Israel's salvation.[40] The theme of the first part is announced in the opening verse: "I will sing to Yahweh, for he is highly exalted; / horse and rider he has thrown into the sea" (AT). The defeat of Pharaoh has disclosed a new dimension of Yahweh's identity: "Yahweh is a warrior / Yahweh is his *name*" (AT).

However troublesome it may seem to describe God as a warrior, the exodus story is not about redemption from sin; it is about liberation from political oppression, and the means to that liberation involves violence, which, one can argue, is part of the historical verisimilitude of the story.[41] The battle is between Yahweh and the historical forces of Pharaoh. On the other hand, what happened to Pharaoh was not simply a divine victory over human power. Rather, this event also had "theo-political" significance,[42] already announced in Yahweh's impending judgment "on all the gods of Egypt" (12:12). The poem employs ancient mythic themes of creation and chaos to reveal the

---

38. For examples of the classic prophetic messenger formula, see Amos 1–2; 2 Sam 7:5; Isa 7:7; Jer 2:2; Ezek 3:11. The phrase ("Thus says the Lord") occurs hundreds of times in prophetic speech. For a series of punitive natural disasters similar to the Egyptian plagues, see Amos 4:6–11.

39. Coats, "The Yahwist as Theologian?," 31. More recently and in general see his *Moses: Heroic Man, Man of God.*

40. See my *Divine Presence and Guidance*, 123–30.

41. Cf. Alter, *Five Books*, 327: "a process of violent oppression to be broken only by violent counterstrokes" (cf. 338).

42. This term was introduced by Buber (*Moses*, 101), originally with reference to the Sinai covenant of ch. 19.

cosmic dimensions of the exodus event.[43] The fundamental aspect of Yahweh's victory is expressed in 15:11: "Who is like you, Yahweh, among the gods? / Who is like you, terrible among the holy ones? / Awesome in praises, wonder worker" (AT). No power on earth or in heaven could compete with the holy warrior of Israel. Thus the liberation of the people has as its corollary the exaltation of their God.

Just as the other gods stand in fear of Yahweh, so the other peoples stand in fear of Israel (vv. 13–18).[44] Thus in the Song of the Sea Israel celebrates the new identity of Yahweh as savior, and at the same time celebrates her own birth as the people of Yahweh (cf. 3:7, 10). The poem concludes with an accolade to Yahweh's exaltation as king: "Yahweh reigns for ever and ever."

The line is not only an appropriate conclusion to the poem; it is also a fitting doxology to the first act of the exaltation of Yahweh, and looks forward to Yahweh's enthronement as covenant sovereign (chs. 16–40). Exodus 15 is thus "the fulcrum-point of the book of Exodus."[45]

The exodus story began with Egypt's leader and its people opposing those who mediated Yahweh's blessing. The oppression in Egypt is the most outrageous example of the mistreatment of the "alien" in the Pentateuch, and it is also the first direct assault against "the blessed of Yahweh." Exodus 1–15 is a grim story that illustrates part of the charge to Abram: "him who curses you, I will curse" (Gen 12:3).[46] Once the Egyptian people recede into the background of the story, they become the victims of their own ruler's despotic evil. Even if we assume that some of the people were complicit in Pharaoh's initial persecution (ch. 1), clearly not all the people were involved.[47] But they

---

43. In Ugaritic (Canaanite) mythology the Sea is a cosmic force of chaos defeated by the god Baal. Just so, dividing the sea in ch. 14 reflects Israel's version of the myth in which Yahweh dismembered the chaos monster (Isa 51:9–11; cf. Ps 74:12–15; 77:16–18; 89:9–10; 93:3–4; 97:1–5; Isa 27:1). Note also the reference to "the floods" and "the deeps," and cf. Gen 1:2; Deut 33:13; Job 12:22; Ps 77:16. Thus in the exodus event, mythical traditions illuminate an historical experience. Some of the most original and creative work on this and related texts has been done by Cross, *Canaanite Myth and Hebrew Epic*, 112–44. For a convenient list of parallels between Canaanite myth and Exodus 15, see Hendel, *Remembering Abraham*, 100–101.

44. The peoples mentioned here correspond to some of the major characters in the ancestral saga: the Philistines, Edom, Moab, and the Canaanites. Here they are perceived as potential enemies, or at least as those who may stand in the way of Israel. Most likely 15:14–17 refers to the settlement of the exodus refugees in Canaan, and possibly to the temple on Mt. Zion (cf. 15:17–18 with 2 Sam 7:10, 13). On the other peoples, cf. also Exod 23:23–33; 34:11–16; Leviticus 18; Numbers 20–25; Deuteronomy 2–3.

45. Smith, *Pilgrimage Pattern*, 207.

46. Thus I would also argue that the theme of blessing and curse pervades chs. 1–12, especially since such disasters like the destruction of crops, the spoiling of water, and the death of firstborn offspring are among of the most prominent manifestations of divine curse—all obviously connected to fertility or its opposite, sterility. Cf. the covenant curses in Lev 26:14–26; Deut 28:15–68; and note in the latter the explicit references to the Egyptian plagues in vv. 27, 60. When the Egyptians threaten to murder all male Hebrew children, they thereby threaten to exterminate the blessing itself (Gen 1:28; Exod 1:7).

47. The complicity of the people is suggested by 1:9, by the plural verbs following in vv. 11–14, and by "all his people" in v. 22. It is also possible to understand the midwives as Egyptians, although they are more likely Hebrews. Nevertheless, certainly "all his people" would not include children, prisoners, housemaids, and the like. Moreover, the Israelites enjoy the

are all affected by the series of disasters, and, in the end, *every household* suffers the death of the firstborn (12:30)—even prisoners, the lowliest housemaid, and animals (11:5), obviously including children as well as adults. Moreover, here God does not act through the agency of Moses, but God acts directly to kill them (13:15), or sends the mysterious "destroyer" (12:23). In the end, Yahweh carries out the threat of 4:22–23, killing all of Egypt's firstborn because Pharaoh will not let *Yahweh's* firstborn go free. The act evokes the horror of blood vengeance. Here God apparently does what Abraham had persuaded God *not* to do, "to slay the righteous with the wicked" (Gen 18:18).[48] After all, Yahweh is a warrior, and that is what warriors inevitably do, deliberately or not. The text thus presents an inescapable moral problem for the reader, which is not easily resolved, but certainly one motif is at the center of the tragedy that happens to the Egyptians—Pharaoh's hardened heart.

On the one hand, events take their course because Pharaoh hardens his own heart and refuses to allow the Hebrews to leave.[49] "Pharaoh is a thinking, arguing, deciding character,"[50] and he has plenty of opportunities to make the right decision

before disaster strikes. But the narrative also attributes the death of the firstborn and Pharaoh's troops, and indeed the entire series of signs and wonders, to Yahweh's coercion of Pharaoh—*God's* "hardening" of Pharaoh's heart.[51] Contemporary readers often find the apparent contradiction between the two causes of Pharaoh's downfall not only intellectually baffling but also morally repugnant. How can Pharaoh and his people justifiably be punished for what Yahweh has predetermined?

It seems the more the authors reflected on Pharaoh's resistance, the less they could understand how a human being could defy the God of Israel with such obduracy. How could a human being—even if the king of Egypt—impudently ask, who is Yahweh? How could it be that the first disaster disproved Yahweh's own words, "By this you shall acknowledge that I am Yahweh" (7:17), and that Pharaoh persisted in his defiance, one disaster after another, even after the death of his own firstborn child? In short, the authors "found it impossible to regard the causes of something so atrocious, such a plunge into madness and ruin at one's own hands, as lying simply on the human and immanent level: in the last analysis they could only be the inscrutable working of the deity."[52] The divine hardening

---

Egyptians' "favor," however qualified this is by the Egyptians' fear (11:3; 12:36).

48. Thus Meyers notes the difficulty of understanding "how the God of justice and mercy, the liberator of the oppressed, can also be characterized as the direct perpetrator of a mass slaughter of many innocent people" (*Exodus*, 94).

49. A better translation might be "strengthened his resolve." Cf. encouragements like Deut 31:6; Josh 1:7, 18; 1 Kgs 2:2, also using the verb *hazaq*.

50. Friedman, *The Creation of Sacred Literature*, 31–32.

51. Concentrated in previews and in the final four disasters: See 4:21; 7:3; 9:12; 10:1 (which resembles the preview texts in scope), 20, 27; 11:10; 14:4, 8, 17 (in the last occurrence the object is the heart of the Egyptians, i.e., the troops). Baden (*Composition*, 199, 205, 207) argues that in J Pharaoh does as he wills, but in P he is *not* free to do so, a motif intended to emphasize God's power and glory.

52. Von Rad, *Old Testament Theology*, 153. There is a parallel between the death of the

of Pharaoh's heart is another expression of the central thrust of the story, the exaltation of Yahweh.

Theologically, the authors appear more willing to throw into question the morality of God than to risk undercutting the sovereignty of God. The hardening motif illustrates the Hebrew Bible's adamant refusal to assign evil to some force outside Yahweh's power and control. Pharaoh may be a villain, but he is not the devil. What is even more remarkable is that the authors accomplished their task without making Pharaoh a mere puppet. If Pharaoh is not the devil, he is also not a wimp. The result is "a drama of cosmic proportions occurring at the same time in the framework of expectable human behavior."[53]

However unsatisfactory the resolution may seem to the moral sensibilities of modern readers, the fate of Pharaoh and his people reveals the dirty side of the earthiness of the pentateuchal narrative. Divine liberation of the oppressed takes place within the ambiguities of human nature, and within an all too realistic world of maniacal persecution that can only result in tragedy. Freedom from such a relentless political system ultimately occurs within grim and violent circumstances; in this case the violence engulfs Egyptian people who are not directly responsible for Pharaoh's actions. "God cannot save the Israelites without killing

Egyptians."[54] In his last encounter with Moses, Pharaoh had finally sought the blessing that could bring life (12:32), but all his actions, previous and subsequent, brought upon himself and his people a curse. In Moshe Greenberg's eloquent words:

> Thus the opposition of Pharaoh is the archetypal opposition of human power, of human authority to the claims of God. Under pressure it will show flexibility and accommodation, even reversing itself—first by crying for help, then by confessing guilt and making concessions. But after all its retreats, it clings to its last redoubt, a core of self-assertiveness and independence, to surrender which would mean the end of its claim to ultimate, self-sufficient power. Here it resists, careless of the cost, unto death.[55]

> "Even in its death throes, the Third Reich proved able to persuade many Germans to display extremes of futile stubbornness."
>
> "Just as Hitler was the architect of Germany's devastation, the Tokyo regime bore overwhelming responsibility for what took place at Hiroshima and Nagasaki. If Japan's leaders had bowed to logic, as well as to the welfare of their own people, by quitting the war, the atomic bombs would not have been dropped."[56]

---

firstborn here and the near sacrifice of Isaac in Genesis 22: in both the larger narrative context reveals a kind of logic of necessity requiring an extreme decision by God

53. Plaut, *Torah*, 454. For similar images of hardened stubbornness, see Deut 2:30; Josh 11:20, on which see Van Seters, *Life of Moses*, 89–90; cf. also Jer 5:3; Ezek 2:4.

54. Fackenheim, *God's Presence in History*, 25.

55. *Understanding Exodus*, 181.

56. Hastings, *Inferno*, 535, 627. Thus modern

5. "A HOLY NATION (CHS. 19–31)[57]

Numerous scholars from various perspectives have argued that the story of the exodus originally was independent of what happens next at Mount Sinai.[58] For some, the exodus originally led directly to settlement in the land of Canaan, without any wilderness period, much less the formation of the covenant community. Significant theological implications would result from such a conclusion (for example, the separation of salvation from covenant law). Nevertheless, the final re-

daction of the rest of the book of Exodus presents a clear structure:

1. 15:22—18:27: The wilderness journey from Egypt to Sinai
2. ch. 19: The charter of the covenant community
3. chs. 20—23: The laws of the covenant community
4. ch. 24: The covenant ratification ceremony
5. chs. 25—31: Instructions for the tabernacle
6. ch. 32: The sin of the golden calf
7. chs. 33—34: Reconciliation and covenant renewal
8. chs. 35—40: Construction and sanctification of the tabernacle

We have now come to the heart of the Torah.

From the moment the escaping Israelites crossed the border of Egypt, their story became one of a wilderness journey, one that would take them from the banks of the Nile to the banks of the Jordan. In fact, the pentateuchal narrative from Exodus 13 to the end of Deuteronomy can be summarized in terms of an itinerary (cf. Numbers 33), one the redactors have used periodically throughout the text to mark the stages of Israel's journey.[59] But, as in the case of the ancestral saga, the resultant narrative is far more than a travelogue. The wilderness journey is also

---

history presents its own horrific moral conundrums. The tragic dimension of the exodus story appears in one contemporary Passover liturgy that says, "Our triumph is diminished by the slaughter of the foe," and it quotes ancient rabbinic tradition: "When the Egyptian armies were drowning in the sea, the Heavenly Hosts broke out in songs of jubilation. God silenced them and said, 'My creatures are perishing, and you sing praises!'" See Bronstein, *A Passover Haggadah*, 48–49. Milgrom suggests that the death of "the 'silent majority'" such as Germans in the Nazi régime comes under the rubric of "collective responsibility" (*Leviticus: A Book of Ritual*, 32–33).

57. An abridged reading of the biblical text is possible for understanding this section: chs. 19–20; 21:1 (introduction to the Book of the Covenant regulations); 24:1–18 (covenant ceremony); 25:1–9 (introduction to the tabernacle specifications); 31:18 (conclusion of the Sinai revelations to Moses). We will look at the content of some of the specific regulations in their Deuteronomic version.

58. For some examples, see the essays in Dozeman and Schmid, *Farewell to the Yahwist?* Such arguments often include the original independence of the ancestral stories of Genesis as well. Nevertheless, in his study of Exodus 19–24, Dozeman (*God on the Mountain*, 172–73) suggests in the end that the final (Priestly) redactor has constructed the narrative in a "canon conscious" manner that focuses the reader on the final text.

59. E.g., Exod 13:20; 14:2; 15:22, 27; 16:1; 17:1; 19:1, with occasional chronological notices (e.g., 16:1; 19:1); cf. Gen 12:5–9. For further discussion of the redactional function of the itinerary notices see below in the introduction to the book of Numbers.

a metaphor for a spiritual journey, guided by God's command (17:1), but it becomes a painful process of learning and testing in which Israel is constantly offered the grace of divine guidance (*torah*), only to reject that guidance in search of an elusive and disastrous autonomy (literally "self-law").

By far the most important stage in Israel's wilderness journey is the one that takes place at Sinai, the mountain of God. In numerous religious traditions, mountains are the connection between heaven and earth, between the divine and the human, and, as we shall see, the tabernacle described in chs. 25–31 is a kind of moveable Mt. Sinai.[60] The preeminent significance of the stage at Mt. Sinai is indicated by the sheer bulk of literary material attached to it—all of Exodus 19 through Numbers 10—a period of some fourteen months. This massive literary unit is surrounded by descriptions of the events in the wilderness before and after Israel's stay at the mountain of God: Exodus 15:22—18:27 and the book of Numbers.[61] The journey to Sinai lends a pilgrimage character to the book of Exodus.[62]

The first three stories concern the people's complaints in the face of thirst and starvation. Life outside Egypt is not easy! Although these are legitimate complaints, the people express them in an increasingly hostile and accusatory manner, charging that Moses has led them into the wilderness to kill them (16:3; 17:3) and wondering "whether Yahweh is among us or not?" (17:7, AT), thus continuing their anxiety at the Red Sea (14:11). Ch. 16 is the centerpiece of these three stories.[63] Having already provided water, Yahweh now provides food: manna with a side dish of quail. It is not bad fare for wilderness survival. Although we assume that manna is a naturally existing substance,[64] the text emphasizes the miraculous circumstances in which it occurs. No matter how much they gather, the people end up with what they need. When they try to keep it overnight (which is against the rules), it rots, but not so on the weekend. No manna appears on the Sabbath.[65] That, after all, is the day when God rests, and when the people should rest, wilderness or no wilderness. So extra manna appears on the day before the Sabbath, and it keeps overnight. Yet some of the people have to have fresh manna, Sabbath or no Sabbath, and again they break the rules.

The manna story thus depicts a God who provides for the people's needs, and a people who are not satisfied with that provision because it is beyond their

---

60. Eventually Mt. Zion (Jerusalem) will be the place of the temple. In Ugaritic mythology Baal occupies a mountain abode, as do the gods of classical Greek mythology (Olympus).

61. There are parallel stories about manna and quail in Exodus 16 and Numbers 11, as well as stories about the selection of community leaders to assist Moses (Exod 18 and Num 11:11–17, 24–29).

62. See Smith, *Pilgrimage Pattern*, e.g., 191.

63. The manna story about food stands in between two stories about thirst (15:22–27 and 17:1–7). In addition, the two thirst stories are preceded and followed respectively by stories about military threats (chs. 14–15; 17:8–16).

64. Presumably the excrescence of some kind of insect, which sounds disgusting until one remembers the source of honey!

65. The Sabbath is an anachronism anticipating 20:8–11; also anticipatory are the glory of Yahweh (cf. 24:16); "covenant" or "testimony" (16:34, probably the ark, cf. 25:22); and "ordinances" (15:26; 18:20, cf. 21:1; 24:3).

control. They are too insecure to rely on "daily bread," so they gather more than they need, hoard it even though it is perishable, and work to get more when they already have enough.

In Israel's unruliness—literally construed—the manna story anticipates the necessity of a community ruled by law.[66] Already in the Marah story Yahweh (or Moses) had given Israel laws and posed a test for them: if they would follow Yahweh's laws, they would be exempt from the diseases with which Yahweh had afflicted the Egyptians (15:25b–26). The laws were given after the provision of water as a condition of their continuing relationship with Yahweh, the source of blessing, their "healer." Now in the manna story, many of the Israelites exhibit their failure to follow Yahweh's commandments. In fact, here the purpose of providing the manna is not only to meet their legitimate physical need but also "to test them, whether they will walk in my law or not" (v. 4). Obviously many of the people fail the test because they are unwilling to trust in Yahweh's promise of daily food.

In short, the manna story demonstrates the failure of ad hoc laws in maintaining the relationship between Yahweh and the people whom he has redeemed from bondage. Many of the people are incapable of integrity when they are governed by rules that apply only to specific situations. For them righteousness is not possible apart from the law—the Torah of the covenant community.

When we look at all the stories in chs. 15–18, we can see the fundamental

problem: the people do not know who they are with respect to Yahweh or to Moses. They are the people whom Yahweh has liberated from slavery under the leadership of Moses, and their immediate past is constitutive for their identity. How, though, does that past impinge on the present and the future? Now that they are free, what is their relationship to Yahweh and to Moses?

The problem appears most clearly in terms of Moses, as it did in chs. 1–14. Here, as there, it becomes increasingly apparent that the people need some public definition and confirmation of Moses' role. They see him acting as a miracle worker who can turn bitter water sweet, and even produce water from a rock with his wondrous wand. Daily they see that his promise of divine sustenance is trustworthy. They observe him as a man of mysterious power who can control the course of a battle by raising or lowering his arms (17:8–16). Yet one thing is missing: they still have never heard God speak to this man and thereby confirm for them that his words truly represent God's words. They came to trust Moses as their liberator because they saw God's act of liberation (ch. 14). What they now need is a public legitimation of Moses' role as their legislator. The situation is strangely reminiscent of a question addressed to Moses long ago: "Who made you a prince and judge over us?" (2:14).

The need for divine confirmation of Moses' role is all the more pressing because Moses is already acting as the people's legislator and "judge" (18:13–17). Note the counsel of Jethro (Moses' father-in-law): "You should represent the people before God, and you should bring their

---

66. There are numerous references to some form of law or commandment in this section: 15:26; 16:16, 24; 18:16, 23.

cases before God; teach them the statutes and the instructions (*torot*), and make known to them the way they are to go and the things they are to do" (18:19–20). The point of Jethro's advice, of course, is to designate Moses as the "chief justice" and thus to spare him all of the relatively petty legal cases, which his newly appointed assistant judges will decide. The story also concludes with Moses enacting the recommended policy.[67] However, the context of the story points again to what will happen at Sinai, for only there will Moses' new role as legislator be publicly confirmed by Yahweh and formally accepted by the people.

In short, the stories of Israel's journey through the wilderness from Egypt to Sinai again raise the question that dominated the narrative of chs. 1–15: who are Yahweh, Moses, and Israel now? To borrow an analogy from American history, the situation is something like that after the defeat of the British in 1783 but before the ratification of the Constitution in 1789. The analogy is one of contrast as well as similarity, for at least the American people had the Continental Congress of 1775 as a guiding body. Israel, on the other hand, is a people without a polity, led by a general without political portfolio, marching under the "banner" (17:16) of a God whose sovereignty over them remains formally unaccepted and undefined.

With Israel "encamped before the mountain" in the wilderness of Sinai, Moses goes up the mountain to meet with God. Yahweh delivers a brief speech to Moses, which Moses then relays to the people. The content of the speech (vv. 3b–6a) is a paradigm of covenant theology, and in its present position it ensures that the peculiar stamp of that theology governs all that follows. This speech encapsulates the new identities of Yahweh, Moses, and Israel that the subsequent narrative will develop in detail. Yahweh is Israel's covenant sovereign, Israel is Yahweh's covenant community, and Moses is the mediator of the covenant.

> Thus you shall say to the house of Jacob, and tell to the children of Israel: "You have seen what I did to the Egyptians, how I bore you on eagles' wings, and brought you to me. Now, therefore, if you will indeed obey me and keep my covenant, you shall be my treasured possession among all peoples, for all the earth is mine; so you shall be to me a realm of priests, and a holy nation." (AT)

The speech opens with a messenger formula,[68] then moves immediately to a recollection of the exodus and Yahweh's careful guidance of Israel up to this point. Everything that follows is based on this recollection, especially of the exodus: "You have seen what I did to the Egyptians." The people have *seen* the action of God that brought about their redemption from slavery (cf. 14:13, 30–31). Before that event, Israel as a people had no concrete referent on which to base their trust in Yahweh's claim to be their God.

---

67. For another perspective on communal leadership, see Numbers 11–12; in Exod 24:14 Moses suggests that only Aaron and Hur are appointed to settle disputes in his absence.

68 This particular formula occurs only three other times in the Pentateuch (3:14, 15; 20:22). It resembles the prophetic messenger formula ("Thus says the Lord"), which in the Pentateuch is limited to Exodus 4–11 (and 32:27).

Now that referent—one the whole people witnessed—has occurred. When the people enter into a covenant relationship with Yahweh, they do so on the basis of their corporate experience of salvation. Becoming the covenant community is an expression of gratitude for Yahweh's antecedent grace, and an expression of the desire to continue in that grace, now that the act of salvation stands in the past.

The rest of the speech specifies what is required of Israel in order to continue in Yahweh's grace. Yahweh has brought Israel to Yahweh's presence. Freedom was the beginning, not the end, of Yahweh's purpose for this people. Thus the speech takes a dramatic turn in verse 5, beginning with the emphatic "now, therefore." The "therefore" indicates that the act of God is leading to a consequence. The people have seen, now they are summoned to obey—literally to "hear my voice"—and to "keep my covenant." The purpose of this covenant is to provide a formal constitution for the relationship that has already existed between the two parties, the relationship that found its primary expression in Israel's liberation. Those who served the Pharaoh now are summoned to serve Yahweh. "Freedom without law would be no freedom at all."[69]

"If you obey my voice and keep my covenant, you shall be my treasured possession among all peoples." This is surely the most explicit transformation of the

theme of the people in the pentateuchal narrative, especially when we compare this speech with the one at the burning bush. There Yahweh said, "I have seen the affliction of my people . . . and I have come down to deliver them" (3:7–8). Israel was already God's people before the exodus, and there were no conditions for that act of liberation. But now there is a condition if Israel wishes to enjoy the status of God's *covenant* people—Israel must accept and obey the *terms* of the covenant.[70]

If keeping the covenant is the condition of Yahweh's offer, the promise of a special status is the result. "You shall be my treasured possession among all peoples, for all the earth is mine." This one sentence is the crystallization of a process that reaches back into the primeval cycle and was already implied with the charge to Abraham. Out of all the peoples of the world, God chooses Israel to be God's "treasured possession." Israel, fresh from the slave camps of Egypt, is God's special people on earth! Yet within the context of the speech, no explanation appears other

---

69. Clements, *Book of Deuteronomy*, 324. Cf. the comment by Brooks regarding American culture ("Age of Possibility," A29): "People are not better off when they are given maximum personal freedom to do what they want. They're better off when they are enshrouded in commitments that transcend personal choice—commitments to family, God, craft and country."

70. There is debate concerning the nature of the conditionality here (see Appendix 3). Some argue that Israel will always be God's people, as some formulations suggest (e.g., Gen 17:7–8, 13), and that breaking the covenant will not sever this bond, even though it may bring severe consequences (so Moberly, *At the Mountain*, 226 n. 4; Campbell and O'Brien, *Rethinking the Pentateuch*, 84 n. 136: "the *relationship* is primary; the *covenant* is an expression of it" [italics original]). On the other hand, some descriptions of the consequences suggest the destruction of Israel (e.g., Deut 28:20, 45–46), and with the prophet Hosea God can say "you are not my people and I am not your God" (Hos 1:9, but contrast the editorial addition in v. 10!). A fundamental tension is inescapable; see further on this in the discussion of Deuteronomy. The continuance of Israel as God's people will soon be jeopardized (ch. 32).

than what follows in verse 6: "You shall be to me a realm of priests and a holy nation" (AT). The first expression means that Israel is to be the sacerdotal domain of Yahweh, the people who serve Yahweh as priests, so rather than *election* perhaps a better word would be *ordination*. Since "all the earth" is Yahweh's, all peoples belong to Yahweh, but Israel is singled out for this special honor and responsibility. The second expression is closely related to the first, and also to the election formula in v. 5, where the Hebrew literally means "from all the peoples." To be "holy" (*qadoš*) means to be "set apart," to be "consecrated" for a particular task (references to holiness abound here).[71] Israel is set apart from all the peoples of the earth to render priestly service to Yahweh, and, in the context of the pentateuchal narrative, to act as priest for the world. Israel is to be the "great nation" promised to Abraham, the community through whom God's purpose for the created world may be renewed. In retrospect, the ancestral saga was a preparation for the founding of this covenant community. "Israel is to achieve through service to [God] what the whole of mankind, even after the

Flood, proved incapable of doing."[72] Israel is to be the community of righteousness.

The first act in Yahweh's exaltation concluded with a song of praise to Yahweh by "the people whom you redeemed" (15:13). The second act is concerned with "a holy nation," a sanctified community. These are not two separate communities, but one and the same, redeemed and consecrated to a particular task. A great deal of the rest of the Pentateuch is concerned with the proper correlation of these two aspects of Israel's corporate identity—redemption and holiness, salvation and sanctification. Sanctification here refers to the realization of God's purpose and intentions for Israel by Israel. Of course, such a realization presupposes the redemption that preceded. But sanctification also points to something the people themselves must do, to their response to the redemptive act. Sanctification—becoming the "holy nation"—means living out the implications of Israel's redemption. The narrative of Yahweh's redemptive act is incomplete without the narrative of Yahweh's instruction—*torah*—and that instruction is not mere indicative suggestion, but an imperative command.

From the perspective of the opening speech, therefore, chs. 19–40 represent an attempt to answer a number of fundamental questions: What does it mean to be the people of Yahweh? How are the people to define their relationship to the God who has redeemed them? What are the responsibilities that result from their redemption? How does their redemption by God affect the way they live with one another? In short, what is the nature and purpose of this newly created

71. Primary is the taboo of the divine, God as unapproachable and invisible (see below). Note the purification ritual in vv. 10–11 and sexual abstinence in v. 15. Although the whole people is portrayed as God's priesthood, there is a distinction between them and the priests (19:22), as between the priests and Moses. Touching the mountain entails death, or even touching those who touched it (19:13). Similarly, God forbids constructing the simple altar in 20:25–26 out of dressed stones (which are unnatural), lest it be profaned. (Contrast the more ornate altar in 27:1–8.) We will look at the nature of holiness more extensively in the book of Leviticus, including the zones of holiness in the tabernacle.

72 Plaut, *Torah*, 541.

community? How is the redeemed community to become the sanctified community, and what is the Torah, or guidance, that enables this sanctification?

In the next section of ch. 19, Moses reports Yahweh's covenant speech to the people, receives their agreement to enter into the covenant, and returns to Yahweh with their reply (vv. 7–9). Already Moses is performing the role of a diplomatic mediator between the two parties of the treaty.[73] Now, in a second address, Moses learns that Yahweh's self-manifestation to the people will confirm the office Moses already exercises: "I am going to come to you in a dense cloud, in order that the people may hear when I speak with you and so trust you forever." By employing the motif of "trust" (*'aman*) this speech recalls the tension in chs. 4–14 that was resolved when the people saw God's presence at work in the cloud and "trusted" in God and in Moses (14:30–31). But still the people have not heard God *talking* to Moses. The emphasis on hearing rather than seeing is altogether appropriate because in what follows Moses will act primarily as the agent of God's words rather than God's actions.[74]

The motif of trust does not recur in the ensuing theophany, but at the height of the divine appearance, accompanied by all sorts of meteorological phenomena, "Moses spoke and God answered him audibly" (v. 19b, AT). For the first time, the people have witnessed direct communication between Yahweh and Moses. To be sure, the text does not specify the content of this communication, or even that it was intelligible,[75] but that Moses speaks and God answers is enough to produce the intended result. Thus, in the sequel to the theophany (20:18–20), the people recoil in terror and appeal to Moses for help: "You speak to us, and we will listen; but do not let God speak to us, or we will die."[76]

Moses' leadership now takes on a new configuration: Moses is not simply the human agent of divine deliverance;

---

73. Knierim ("Composition," 364) sees a six-fold pattern of ascents and descents of Moses in chs. 19–39 that emphasizes his role as covenant mediator.

74. Overall, there are conflicting notions of the visibility of God in chs. 19–24, no doubt partly due to a combination of literary sources. In 19:9 the people will hear God speaking to Moses, and in 19:11 they will see Yahweh's appearance but hidden in the cloud. In 19:21 God warns against the people trying to look, and in 20:18 they see the phenomena of the theophany. However, in 24:9–11 Moses and a few others actually see God (the second occurrence using a special word for having a vision). The Septuagint (ancient Greek Hebrew Bible) attempts to mute

this virtually unique reference to divine visibility by adding the phrase "the place where God stood." In contrast, in 33:18–22, God allows Moses to see only God's back, not God's face, for "no one shall see me and live." References to seeing the face of God in the Psalms probably are more metaphorical (e.g., 11:7; 17:15; 24:6–9) and have an opposite in God's hidden face (e.g., 10:11; 13:1). In Exod 23:15 and 34:20 it is possible to read "see my face" instead of "appear before me" (so Smith, *Pilgrimage Pattern*, 241).

75. The word "audibly" in v. 19 usually means "voice," often used in the plural for divine thunder. Perhaps "in a thunderous voice" would be better. The metaphors of thunder, lightning, cloud, and the like here are descriptive of storm deities (cf. Ps 18:7–15; Psalm 29; 68:7–8; 77:16–18), of which the Canaanite Baal was one.

76. Thus, despite his differences regarding the exaltation motif, I would agree with Van Seters when he says, "In Exodus the whole purpose of the theophany was to *confirm* Moses' role as mediator (19:9) so that the divine speaking was directed toward Moses during the theophany" (*Life of Moses*, 278, italics original).

he is also the covenant mediator between the people and God, appointed by Yahweh and formally elected by the people. It is through Moses that God will make known God's desires for this people, and in turn, Moses will be their official spokesperson before God. From now on, "to look to God meant to Israel to look to this man, to hear God to hear the word of this man, to obey God to follow his direction, to trust God to trust his insight."[77] From now on, "refusing belief in Moses is tantamount to refusing belief in Yahweh."[78]

Moses' response to the people's reaction at the foot of the mountain employs a subtle use of the word *fear*: "Do not fear, for God has come to test you, so that the fear of him may be before your eyes, that you may not sin" (v. 20, AT). The first "fear" has to do with terror, the second with obedience. The purpose of the theophany, Moses suggests, has been to produce the second sense of fear. In the present text, fear as obedience is inseparable from the fact that the Decalogue interrupts the account of the theophany proper.[79] By inserting the Ten Commandments before the people's reaction in 20:18, a redactor has connected reaction and revelation. The overpowering presence of Yahweh is by no means an

end in itself; rather, the theophany lends authority to the commands of God as they are revealed in the Decalogue. By the same token, the people's fear is not simply "a subjective emotion of terror, but the obedience of God's law."[80] As Paul Tillich suggests, "holiness cannot be experienced without its power to command what we should be."[81]

The closing scene in ch. 20 points to the new identity of Yahweh, which includes not only deeds but also words. This correlation is suggested by Yahweh's first words to Moses after his formal confirmation as covenant mediator, again using a messenger formula: "Thus you shall say to the people of Israel: 'You have seen for yourselves that I have talked with you from heaven'" (v. 22). The parallel to 19:4 is obvious: "You have seen what I did to the Egyptians." Together, these two statements refer to the two "root experiences" of Israel—the experience of Yahweh's "saving presence" and "commanding presence."[82] Both of these experiences—the one in the form of deeds, the other in the form of commandments—are essential to Yahweh's identity.

Such a correlation of deeds and words in the identity of a person has an analogue in historic figures. For example, who Martin Luther King Jr. was could

---

77. Barth, *Church Dogmatics* IV/1, 430. Cf. Friedman: "From this moment on, all revelation to Israel is mediated by a prophet. God never speaks directly to the people again in any book of the *Tanak* [i.e., the Hebrew Bible]" (*Torah*, 240). Cf. Knierim ("Composition," 378): the Pentateuch portrays Moses as "the decisive person for all of humanity's history and existence."

78. Coats, "King's Loyal Opposition," 95.

79. See Plaut, *Torah*, 535–36, and the extensive discussion of Childs, *Exodus*, 351–60, 370–71.

80. Childs, *Exodus*, 373. The text does not say explicitly that the people hear the Decalogue, but we may infer so. The syntax of the end of 19:25 usually would demand the substance of what Moses "told them," but then 20:1 has God speaking. Deuteronomy emphasizes that the people heard the words (4:12), although there too some ambiguity remains (5:5).

81. Tillich, *Dynamics of Faith*, 56.

82. The expressions are those of Fackenheim, *God's Presence in History*, 14.

be known from his active attempts to gain liberation for the Black people of America. But King's personal identity was equally revealed by his speeches, and perhaps most of all by his rightly famous "I Have a Dream" speech. "I have a dream," he said, "that one day this nation will rise up and live out the true meaning of its creed: 'We hold these truths to be self-evident; that all men are created equal.'"[83] However much actions may speak louder than words, this dream of King's said as much about who he was and what he was about as did his deeds. Any narrative of his life that left out his "Dream" speech would exclude an essential aspect of King's identity. In the same way, the biblical text asserts that we know as much about who Yahweh is by Yahweh's words as we do by Yahweh's act of liberation. Yahweh's act and word belong intrinsically together as a definition of identity—they cannot be separated, much less placed one over against the other.[84]

There are numerous metaphors we could use to express the new identity of Yahweh, and the necessarily corresponding identity of Israel, but the one that is most appropriate to the text of Exodus is also well established in subsequent tradition—the realm of God. Of course, the political aspect of Yahweh's character was already implicit in the promises of land and nationhood made to the ancestors. But throughout the ancestral saga Yahweh appears primarily as the guide and protector of an extended family, "the God of Abraham, Isaac, and Jacob." In the first part of Exodus, on the other hand, Yahweh appears as a "warrior" (15:3) who fights against a political power for the liberation of an oppressed people, finally winning universal sovereignty (15:18). In the second part of Exodus, the text represents the nature of the realm that Yahweh has established.

The realm of Yahweh is represented initially by two distinct literary units: chs. 20–24 and 25–31. Taken together these two units constitute the polity of the realm, in both senses of that term, namely, the form of government of a social and of a sacral community.[85] While we shall discuss these two aspects of Israel's polity separately, following the order of the text, it is important to remember that they are complementary and inseparable. There is no spiritual or religious community apart from the secular or political community. Both aspects of the polity of the realm are already visible in ch. 19, where Israel agrees to enter into a covenant with Yahweh by verbal commitment (vv. 3–8), and prepares for the encounter with God by liturgical sanctification (vv. 10–15; cf. 24:4b–8).

The polity of the realm as a social organization is presented by chs. 20–24. The primary content of this polity appears in the form of law: the Decalogue and the Book of the Covenant. While the content of these laws is, of course, of great importance in defining the nature of the realm, and therefore the identity of

83. "I Have a Dream," in *Voice of Black America*, 971–75.

84. This dichotomy has at times appeared in various Christian formulations of grace (e.g., salvation) over against law (e.g., *torah*). On narrative and law, see further in the discussion of Leviticus and Deuteronomy below.

85. For a full development of this term as applied to Deuteronomy, see McBride, "Polity of the Covenant People." Cf. Gilkey, "Political Dimensions of Theology," 154–68 (especially section 2).

Yahweh and Israel, we shall postpone any discussion of the content until we come to the book of Deuteronomy. There much of the same material is repeated and interpreted theologically.[86]

Our primary focus will be on the literary form of chs. 20–24. The sequence of the material is clear. At the opening of ch. 20, in a "preamble" to the Decalogue, Yahweh is identified as the God of Israel's salvation (v. 2) and then pronounces the Ten Commandments, after which the people elect Moses as their official mediator. Moses then ascends the mountain to receive the detailed stipulations of the covenant (20:21—23:33). At the end of these stipulations is an admonitory section in which Yahweh warns of punishments for disobedience and promises rewards for obedience. The unit concludes with a ceremony in which the people ratify the covenant (ch. 24).

Numerous studies have suggested that several parts of these chapters may reflect some of the literary elements of political treaties in the ancient Near East (*treaty* being a synonym of *covenant*).[87] The treaties are between a superior king (a *suzerain*) and one who is dependent on that king's support (a *vassal*). The major parallels between such treaties and chs. 19–24 are a historical prologue in which the suzerain recites his past acts of protection for the vassal (19:4; 20:2), and the stipulations of the treaty that the vassal must obey in order to remain in the good

graces of the suzerain (chs. 20–23). Less developed but implied are the deposit of the treaty document (cf. 25:16, 21), and an indication of rewards and punishments (23:21–22, 25–26). However, the parallels between the treaty pattern and chs. 19–24 are limited and lack several important elements.[88] (The treaty pattern is more developed in the book of Deuteronomy, as we shall see.) Nevertheless, even aside from the treaty pattern, it is clear that Israel is Yahweh's realm (traditionally, "kingdom"), obviously a political metaphor. Yahweh is Israel's covenant sovereign, their suzerain; Israel is Yahweh's covenant people, Yahweh's vassal. In feudal language, Israel is Yahweh's fief, demanding Israel's fealty. Surely one of the most profound (and at times revolutionary) implications of the realm of Yahweh is that if Yahweh is Israel's sovereign, then all other sovereignties are relatively demoted. Membership in the covenant community demands a pledge of allegiance to Yahweh that is absolute and unqualified: "You shall have no other gods before me" (20:3).

Just as the metaphor of the realm of God signifies a new identity for Yahweh it also signifies a new identity for Israel, Yahweh's vassal. To be an Israelite now means to be a member of this covenant community. Israel is no longer a people in the strictly ethnic sense, the progeny of one family line, but a "holy nation" whose primary bond is one of covenantal polity rather than kinship.[89] In principle, at least,

86. Following the canonical books, we will also look at the mostly sacerdotal legislation in Leviticus and to some extent in Numbers as well.

87. See Appendix 3. For a brief review, see Plaut, *Torah*, 525 and the example from a Hittite treaty on 528; see also the more extensive discussion of Hallo in the same volume, 374–76.

88. Numerous scholars would agree with Van Seters when he says that seeing "the Hittite model" in Exodus 19–24 is "so strained as to be completely unconvincing" (*Life of Moses*, 253).

89. As Brueggemann says, "Israel's constitution" is not "by blood, language, or territory,"

membership in the community is open to those who commit to the stipulations. The laws of the covenant represent the borders of Yahweh's realm. To step outside those laws is to remove oneself from the protective sovereignty of Yahweh.

Similarly, to be an Israelite means to be a member of a covenant *community*. Each individual Israelite does not and cannot stand alone, but is also bound to the covenant brother or sister. The covenant code even demands a form of justice for the "alien" (sojourner) that is consistent with the covenant community's self-understanding (22:21). Ultimately there is no personal identity apart from one's covenantal identity, no I apart from *we*. Thus the political metaphor of the realm of God insists that "the inclination of humankind for community with God cannot become a reality without the community of each other."[90]

The second aspect of Israel's polity within the realm of God is represented in chapters 25–31. After Moses has conducted the treaty-ratification ceremony, he again ascends the mountain. The uniqueness of his office is emphasized when he actually enters the cloud that conceals the divine presence (24:18). Moses remains on the mountain forty days and forty nights, during which time he receives another set of instructions, now for the building of a sanctuary. We must

not allow the technical detail of these chapters to detract from their narrative significance. Like the covenantal polity of Israel, the ecclesiastical polity is an essential part of the exaltation of Yahweh, soon to be consummated by the enthronement of Yahweh among the worshiping congregation. "Have them make me a sanctuary, so that I may dwell among them" (25:8).

The implications of this sacerdotal aspect of Yahweh's realm are also far-reaching. Here we shall focus on two of them. First, as with the formation of the covenant community, the creation of the ecclesiastical community will provide a new way for righteousness between God and humankind. In fact, the language of "creation" is all the more appropriate here, for these chapters are framed by references which evoke the creation in Genesis 1. When Moses goes up the mountain to receive instructions for the tabernacle, the author tells us that the glory and cloud covered the mountain for six days, "and on the seventh day [Yahweh] called to Moses out of the cloud" (24:16). Similarly, in chs. 25–31, God speaks the tabernacle instructions in seven speeches, concluding with Sabbath observance as a "sign" of Israel's sanctification by Yahweh (v. 13) and of Yahweh's creation of the world in six days, and resting on the seventh (v. 17).[91] The Sabbath allusions will appear again at the completion of the tabernacle (chs. 39–40).

For the Priestly author (who is at work in these chapters) this passage represents the culmination of a process that began with the covenant and sign

---

but by hearing the covenant words (*The Book of Exodus*, 880b). A multiethnic identity may be reflected in the reference to the "mixed multitude" who were part of the exodus (Exod 12:38). Thus now "house of Jacob" and "children of Israel" (19:3) in this sense function more as political terms than familial (contrast Gen 46:27).

90. Pannenberg, "Zur Theologie des Rechts," 17–18 (my translation).

91. See 25:1 and then six times in chs. 30–31. For more details see Kearney, "Creation and Liturgy."

of Noah (the rainbow) and Abraham (circumcision). All of world history has been driving toward this moment when Yahweh would open a new way for humankind through a new creative act. This act is quite literally a revolution in the relationship between God and humankind. For God to "dwell" with Israel is a reversal of the withdrawal of God's presence that figured so prominently in the primeval cycle: Adam and Eve driven from the garden, Cain hidden from God's presence, or, on the other side, God's "coming down" not to dwell in community, but to "scatter" (Babel) and to destroy (Sodom, Egypt). In short, along with the movement toward covenant community, the exaltation of Yahweh also reveals a movement toward sacral community that began with God's coming down for deliverance (3:8). "The book thus recounts the stages in the descent of the divine presence to take up its abode for the first time among one of the peoples of the earth."[92]

The second implication of Yahweh's enthronement as Israel's exalted sovereign has to do with the ongoing life of the community. However much the covenant polity contained in chs. 19–23 may be constitutive for Israel's identity, the text recognizes that the people will need further guidance from Yahweh in the future. Since this community is defined by the words of Yahweh, there must be some way for it to hear those words afresh, and to hear new words in new situations. This is precisely one of the purposes of Yahweh's enthronement. The tabernacle, and more specifically the "ark of the covenant,"[93]

is the place where Yahweh is enthroned and will "meet" with Israel through the representation of Moses: "There I will meet with you [Moses], and from above its top, from between the two cherubim that are on the ark of the covenant, I will speak with you of all that I will give you in commandment for the people of Israel" (25:22, AT; cf. Num 7:89). The function of the ark and tabernacle here is a development of a probably older tradition about a "tent of meeting" (33:7–11).

> "This is what sacred space is: a site where earth and heaven meet, where time and memory merge, and where we have a means to rise and descend through an open door to the unknown and the eternal." "All architecture is a kind of icon, and this is especially true of religious architecture. It manifests an idea in nonverbal form, functioning as a symbol at the most mundane and the most profound levels."[94]

Here is one of the clearest examples of how the two aspects of Israel's polity are in fact one. Yahweh's enthronement in the tabernacle provides the means by which the "commanding presence" can continue with the people on their journey through the wilderness and on into their future in

---

92. Greenberg, *Understanding Exodus*, 16–17.

93. The ark is a portable box that is part of the sacerdotal equipment of the tabernacle For the enthronement see Ps 99:1, 5; 1 Sam 4:4; 2 Kgs

19:15. More precisely, the ark may be the footstool of an invisible throne (Ps 99:5). Especially in Deuteronomic theology, the ark is primarily a container for the covenant document (the Ten Commandments), with less of an oracular function (cf. Deut 10:1–5; 1 Kgs 8:9).

94. Jensen, *Substance of Things Seen*, 101–102, 104.

the land. The king who dwells in the tabernacle is the God of the exodus and the covenant sovereign of Sinai, guiding the people with the Torah revealed to them through Moses.

6. THE THREAT FROM WITHIN (CHS. 32–34)[95]

"Get up and make for us gods who will go before us" (32:1, AT). These are the first words of the people since the covenant ratification ceremony. The last time they spoke their words were quite different: "All that Yahweh has said we will do, and we will be obedient" (24:7, AT). But the situation in which they now find themselves is also quite different. At the conclusion of the covenant ratification in ch. 24, Moses had ascended the mountain to receive the treaty document and the instructions for the tabernacle. Of the latter, the people know nothing. They are not aware of Yahweh's plan to provide a continual meeting place where they can learn of the divine will and benefit from divine guidance. Moses has been on the mountain for a very long time—forty days and nights. For all the people know, when Moses entered the cloud at the top he also entered the "devouring fire," and that would be the last they would see of him.

In their long wait the people have had time to think of other things and, above all, to worry. They are thinking of the arduous and dangerous journey that lies ahead of them through the wilderness and of their ultimate destination, the land of Canaan. They are worried about the

absence and apparent loss of their leader, Moses, and fearful (not without reason) that his absence means the absence of God as well. Thus what they demand of Aaron is a replacement for Moses and for the divine presence and guidance that has sustained them in the past. Their demand for gods who will "go before" them is all the more ironic since Moses has reported God's promise to "send an angel before you" (23:20), functioning very much like the angel and the pillars of cloud and fire in 13:21 and 14:19–20.

The first six verses of ch. 32 report the construction of the calf and Aaron's pathetic attempt to remedy his error by proclaiming a feast to Yahweh (v. 5). But his effort comes too late. Even if the calf is not intended to be an "*other* god" (20:3), it clearly constitutes a breach of the prohibition against an idol (20:4–6).[96] The people violate the treaty even before they have received the written document. The calf story, therefore, marks a major turning point in the wilderness stories that precede, for here the complaint is not a legitimate concern (as for water or food), but a sign of disobedience and infidelity—the people have "sinned a great sin" (32:30). Correspondingly, God's response

---

96. The story has some relationship to that of the first king of Northern Israel, Jeroboam, who constructed *two* golden calves and installed them in sanctuaries to rival the temple of the Southern Kingdom of Judah in Jerusalem (1 Kgs 12:25–33; the word *ĕlohim* in Exod 32:4 could be translated in the singular). The Exodus story may be a polemic aimed at Jeroboam as well as Aaron and the Aaronide line of priests (including the ludicrous comment of Aaron in 32:24!). The calves made by Jeroboam most likely were not considered to be "idols" in the pejorative sense, but symbols of the invisible presence of God (bulls were frequent metaphors for gods; cf. the function of the ark in 25:22).

is not one of gracious caring (e.g., water, manna) but angry judgment (a pattern that will resume in Numbers).[97]

Now in vv. 7–14, composed entirely of speeches between Yahweh and Moses, a stunning movement takes place, one that goes to the heart of Israel's election, and indeed, to the heart of God. First, in informing Moses of what has happened in his absence, Yahweh refers to Israel as "your people" (v. 7), implying that they are no longer "my people." Then Yahweh adds: "Now let me alone, so that my wrath may burn hot against them and I may consume them; and of you I will make a great nation" (v. 10). In contrast to the rest of the story, this passage poses the problem and its solution in the most radical way possible. It is not a question of indiscriminate execution (vv. 27–28), or of a future punishment limited to the guilty (vv. 33–34), or of an immediate but limited curse by plague (v. 35). Instead, here Yahweh is ready to destroy the entire people. Yahweh threatens to return the world to its pre-Abrahamic state of disorder, and to begin all over again with Moses. With a change in emphasis, the promise to Abraham is repeated word for word: "Of you I will make a great nation" (cf. Gen 12:2).

From the author's perspective, the severity of this decree does not suggest an excessive reaction, as it may to the modern reader. As we have already seen, within the covenant polity the people exists as a single corporate entity, not a collection of individuals. The terms of the covenant call for absolute obedience as a people, and the consequences of irresponsibility are equally comprehensive. The totality

of the covenant polity was emphasized in the description of the ratification ceremony: "Moses came and told the people *all* the words of Yahweh and *all* the ordinances; and *all* the people answered with one voice, and said, '*All* that Yahweh has spoken we will do'" (24:3, AT).

One of the great and enduring insights of Israel's political model for the people's relationship to Yahweh is that "a sinful deed is regarded as having objective *social* consequences, consequences menacing and even *fatal* not only to the doer of the deed but also to other members of his group, to his children and his children's children" (cf. 20:5; 34:7).[98] To contemporary Western attitudes, so bereft of a sense of community and so enamored with individualism—in a word, so "narcissistic"—such an ancient view seems "both immoral and primitive; but, unfortunately, it was also true."[99] That is, the *consequences* of all sorts of wrongdoing (from parenting to racism to environmental pollution) have a way of outliving the wrongdoers and claiming countless victims. While other texts will call into question the concept of corporate responsibility and suffering (e.g., Ezekiel 18), it will remain throughout the Pentateuch (and much of the Hebrew Bible) as a permanent fixture in Israel's covenant

___

97. See Childs, *Exodus*, 260.

98. Gilkey, "Political Dimensions of Theology," 160 (italics added). Cf. Friedman (*Torah*, 413): "we learn from the Torah, no less than from Freud, that humans must look back not only at the good that their parents and grandparents did but also at their errors and faults. It is an essential part of understanding how we came to be what we are."

99. Gilkey, "Political Dimensions of Theology," 160.

polity.[100] What is astounding to the author of vv. 7–14, therefore, is not that Yahweh would threaten to destroy Israel; that was expected. What is astounding is that Yahweh finally decided *not* to do so (v. 14).

This is surely Moses' finest hour. His role of mediator, confirmed at the encounter before, is already tested to its limit. The boldness of Moses' reply is staggering. He reminds Yahweh of both Yahweh's identity and purpose, and calls into question Yahweh's otherwise justifiable wrath. First, Moses reflects Yahweh's classic self-introduction by lifting up before him "your people, whom you brought out of the land of Egypt." He then moves to Yahweh's purpose in a way that reminds us of the acknowledgment motif earlier in Exodus. If Yahweh destroys Israel, the Egyptians will claim that Yahweh's purpose with this people was "evil." Thus Moses demands (note the imperative) that Yahweh reconsider the verdict.

Finally, Moses clinches his argument by reminding Yahweh of the promises of numerous descendants and of land to the ancestors. In fact, Moses refers specifically to the "oath" Yahweh swore to Abraham when Abraham was willing to sacrifice Isaac (v. 13; cf. Gen 22:16–17). Once again that moment of human righteousness has far-reaching consequences.

But our text is more concerned with the righteousness of God. Yahweh's agreement to "remember" the ancestors and to honor the promises to them discloses a dimension of character transcending even the standards of covenant righteousness just revealed at Sinai. Righteousness, again, means being "in right relation with." For Yahweh this still means a relationship in which Israel is elected out of grace alone to be God's people. Yahweh's remembering the ancestral oath is in character with that remembering that triggered Yahweh's intervention to begin with (Exod 2:24; cf. 3:6). Yet there is a radical difference here—one that was glimpsed, perhaps, with a figure like the young Jacob, but that now appears to its fullest extent. It is not just that grace is not a reward for righteousness; it is that grace is offered *despite* righteousness. Israel's failure to live up to the conditions of the covenant means a failure to achieve sanctification, but it does not negate Israel's *salvation*. Yahweh is still willing to call them "my people," as before they even knew Yahweh's name (3:7–10). That relationship is rooted in Yahweh's unqualified love for the people and, in the light of the primeval cycle, love for the world, to whom they have been appointed a realm of priests. As severe as the punishment of this people under the divine curse may be, here and subsequently in the Pentateuch, the text will never suggest a final and complete abandonment of Israel by God. In effect, the golden calf story thus represents an identity crisis within the heart of God. In order to be true to that self that swore the oath to Abraham, Yahweh must suppress that self that is the offended suzerain of Sinai. The "everlasting" covenant trumps the conditional.[101]

---

100. The tension between divine grace and divine judgment runs throughout the Former Prophets, in particular, and clearly reached its most profound complexity in the exile. See Mann, *Book of the Former Prophets*, 387–89. Brueggemann puts nicely the ends of the spectrum: "a strict retributionism that confines God to a set of moral statements" or "an easy affirmation that makes God endlessly accepting and forgiving" (*The Book of Exodus*, 951).

101. For a prophet's expression of the divine agony here, see Hosea 11.

What has happened between Moses and Yahweh makes the rest of the story anticlimactic but certainly not insignificant. After all, only we, the readers, have been privy to this mountaintop decision. Israel knows nothing of it. While the people are reveling in a blasphemous religious frenzy, their fate is being determined on top of the mountain. They are saved before they know they were damned.[102]

The rest of the story also points in the direction of a new and different climax to the sin of the golden calf, suggesting that the full significance of this story will appear only in the context of the following chapters. When Moses comes down from the mountain and sees the degrading spectacle, he angrily breaks the tablets of the covenant, thereby symbolizing the broken covenant relationship between Yahweh and Israel. Indeed, Moses pulverizes the tablets and makes the people drink the powder (pardon does not mean the absence of punishment).[103] Similarly, the end of the story and the beginning of ch. 33 suggest that the basis of Israel's sacral polity has also collapsed. The promise of sending an angel before them now appears in the context of a threat (v. 34; cf. 23:20–21). In fact, in 33:1–3, Yahweh abruptly orders Moses to begin the journey to the land of Canaan, again citing the "oath" to the ancestors. Here too Yahweh promises to send an angel before the people, but says, "*I will not go up among you, or I would consume you in the way*" (v. 3). Obviously, God is still angry!

The people take these words as "evil tidings" (33:4, AT), and rightly so; although they remain God's chosen people, the relationship has been pierced, as it were, on the horns of the golden calf. In effect, they are now in the same position they occupied between Egypt and Sinai, only made more tenuous by their sin. The covenant, under which they were to enjoy the protective sovereignty of Yahweh and realize their very identity as a people, lies shattered at Moses' feet. Moreover, although they apparently know nothing of it, Yahweh has ordered Moses to leave Sinai without first constructing the tabernacle, which was to have served as the spatial medium for Yahweh's "dwelling" among them.

In the present context the "tent of meeting" described in 33:7–11 serves a provisional function. Although it represents God's continuing presence with Israel, it is virtually Moses' private institution that he has erected at his own initiative to serve as a temporary substitute for the tabernacle, the plan for which God has apparently abandoned in his order to begin the journey toward the promised land.[104]

---

102. Cf. Childs, *Book of Exodus*, 562–63.

103. Thus the story includes a violent scene of executions by the Levites (32:25–29), a divine threat of punishment of those who are guilty (vv. 30–34, ignoring v. 14), and, finally, a plague (v. 35). The God who pardons is hardly "permissive"! As Brueggemann suggests with regard to 34:6–7, that God both forgives and punishes remains an "unresolved contradiction" (*Book of Exodus*, 947b). Again, in the context of chs. 32–34, forgiveness means that God does not destroy Israel, not that God does not punish.

104. In its original conception, the "tent of meeting" almost certainly reflects a history of tradition different from that of the tabernacle. Compare the role of the tent in Num 11:16, 26; 12:4. The two are clearly combined in texts like Exod 40:2, 19, 34–35. For a different view, see Moberly, *At the Mountain of God*, 171–77.

Moses now directs his attention to an attempt to secure a pledge from Yahweh that *Yahweh*—and not just an angelic *substitute*—will go with the people (33:12–23). In an apparent attempt to bolster his office as mediator, Moses asks for a new revelation of Yahweh's character so that Moses may know God more fully, and he again asks Yahweh to "consider too that this nation is your people" (v. 13). Yahweh responds with the promise for which Moses had hoped: "I myself will go with you" (v. 14).[105]

Now Moses presses his request even further by asking to see Yahweh's "glory," here apparently meaning God's essential nature, something more ontological than the fire-cloud. This, Yahweh says, is too much, even for Moses. No one can see God's "face," God's very being, and live (apparent exceptions like 24:9–11 and 33:11 notwithstanding). In unusually concrete language, Yahweh's glory will pass by Moses, but Yahweh's hand will cover Moses until all he can see is Yahweh's back.

How is God's glory revealed? Before Yahweh fulfills the pledge to proclaim Yahweh's name to Moses, Yahweh issues an unexpected order: "Cut two tablets of stone like the former ones, and I will write on the tablets the words that were on the former tablets, which you broke" (34:1). Yahweh has decided to reinstate the treaty, and thus to reclaim Israel as Yahweh's covenant people.[106] The renewal of the covenant itself is an act of divine grace, for in this decision Yahweh extends to Israel Yahweh's protective and governing sovereignty, despite their breach of the original covenant. In fact, Yahweh's words—"I hereby make a covenant" (34:10)—follow immediately upon Moses' final plea for pardon (v. 9). The granting of the new covenant is at the same time the granting of pardon (again, contrast 23:21).

Yahweh is now reaffirmed as Israel's suzerain, even though Israel is a rebellious vassal. Appropriately, in this context comes a new disclosure of the divine name (34:5–8). Following the covenant stipulations, the rest of ch. 34 proceeds to a reaffirmation of Moses' identity as mediator. In comparison with the previous covenant process (chs. 19—24), the renewal of the covenant occurs with a significant omission: Israel plays no role whatsoever (v. 27). Now the covenant is made through the agency of the mediator alone, without any consultation of the third party. In a sense, Moses not only represents Israel; he now *is* Israel, the faithful servant by whom alone Yahweh can reestablish the realm of God.

Ch. 34 concludes with what appears to be an explicit contrast to Moses' earlier descent from the mountain (31:18). Again Moses stays on the mountain forty days and nights, and again he returns with the treaty document. His previous delay had driven the people to find a substitute for him, one that even made him comparable to a divine figure: "make a god for us . . .

---

105. For this translation of *panim* (literally, "face"), cf. 2 Sam 17:11. For further discussion, see Mann, *Divine Presence and Guidance*, 157.

106. See the discussion of Childs, *Book of Exodus*, 604–9. Contrast Moberly (*At the Mountain of God*, 83–106, 157–61), who argues that the text presented a covenant renewal from the outset. Baden (*Composition*, 227) points out that covenant renewal as forgiveness here "may be the best reading of the canonical text" but cannot be ascribed to the compiler of the literary sources, whose sole concern was narrative chronology.

for we do not know what has happened to this man Moses" (32:1, AT). Now when he returns, he is so physically transformed as almost to warrant the term *apotheosis* (compare his "shining face" to the image of an aura). Moses' exaltation is a result of his talking with God (v. 29), and now he mediates the divine words with a directness previously unknown.

> By placing the story in this form in its present position the author has given an interpretation of how he wants the entire Sinai tradition to be understood. God and the revelation of [God's] will stand at the center. But Sinai is also the story of Moses, the mediator between God and Israel, who continued to function as a mortal man and yet who in his office bridged the enormous gap between the awesome, holy, and zealous God of Sinai and the fearful, sinful, and repentant people of the covenant.[107]

7. THE GLORY OF YAHWEH (CHS. 35–40)[108]

Through the mediation of Moses and the grace of God, Israel has been saved from death (ch. 32) and reinstated as Yahweh's covenant people (ch. 34). The final section of the book now turns to Israel as a sacral community. Ch. 34 represented a covenant renewal, but chs. 35–40 do not represent a renewal of the sacral community, for this community has not yet come into existence. Indeed, the text has

never suggested that the people know of Yahweh's plan for the tabernacle.

What happens now is just as surprising as Yahweh's decision not to destroy Israel, and the decision to renew the covenant. This is the final movement of the divine presence, culminating in the enthronement of Israel's exalted sovereign, but now that enthronement takes place amid a "stiff-necked" people stained by "iniquity" and "sin" (34:9). For this reason, the allusions in the text to Genesis 1 and the Sabbath that evoke the sense of a new creation—already noted at 24:16 and 31:12–17—now take on a deeper significance, framing chs. 35–40.[109] As Dozeman puts it, "The quest of Israel within salvation history, according to priestly writers, is to rediscover the lost world of Genesis 1."[110]

A parallel to the latter passage, that concluded the original tabernacle instructions, now opens the story of the completion of the tabernacle (35:1–3). Moses assembles the congregation and issues yet another Sabbath commandment. The scene provides an ironic contrast to the opening scene in ch. 32, where the people assembled against Aaron and demanded the calf (v. 1). In light of the previous Sabbath commandments (20:8–11; 34:21), another Sabbath commandment would seem unnecessary, but a reminder is in order because the construction of the tabernacle will be the people's work, and that work must be done in strict conformity to the commandments of God. In addition, the Sabbath commandment reminds us

---

107. Childs, *Book of Exodus*, 619.

108. For a shorter version of the text relevant to this section, read 25:1–10, 22–23, 31, 40; 26:1; 27:1, 20; 28:1; 30:1; 31:12–18; 35:1–3; 39:32; 40:16–38.

109. On this and what follows, see Hallo in Plaut, *Torah*, 311; note also the comments of Plaut on 688. See also Blenkinsopp, *Prophecy and Canon*, 62–63, and his *Treasures Old and New*, 160–61; Smith, *Exodus Pattern*, 266–67.

110. Dozeman, *Book of Numbers*, 55.

of the orderly process through which the world came into being, with God speaking and everything happening "just so."

The people respond to Moses' instructions with what can only be called wild enthusiasm (35:20–29). "They came, everyone whose heart was stirred, and everyone whose spirit was willing, and brought Yahweh's offering" (v. 21, AT). In fact they bring such enormous quantities of goods—from gold to goatskins—that Moses has to issue a restraint order (36:2–7)! Although the people are obviously responding to Moses' instructions, their offerings are technically not expiatory in nature (which one might expect), but freewill offerings, which normally are voluntary rather than obligatory. Thus the construction of the tabernacle represents not only a gracious condescension of Yahweh, but also a joyful "lifting up"[111] of the people's gifts to God. Their offerings here offset their previous offerings to construct the golden calf (32:2–3). Now the "tent of meeting" is truly a meeting of the divine and the human will, and the story of its construction and sanctification continues the story of Israel's reconciliation to Yahweh.

As the work of the tabernacle comes to completion, the allusions to Genesis 1 return. As "in the beginning," so now all has taken place according to Yahweh's will: "the Israelites had done everything just as Yahweh had commanded Moses" (39:32; cf. 42–43; 40:16, AT; see Gen 1:31). As "in the beginning" God had "blessed "the creation, so now Moses "blesses" the people (v. 43b). As "in the beginning" God had "hallowed" the Sabbath day at the end of creation, so now

Yahweh orders Moses to "hallow" the tabernacle (40:9, AT; cf. Gen 2:3). The tabernacle is erected on New Year's day (Exod 40:1, 17), and its furnishings are anointed (40:3–11), its priests ordained (40:12–15). All is done according to the "pattern" that God showed to Moses on the mountain (25:9)—something like a heavenly blueprint. God has promised to be present above the ark (25:22), "enthroned between the cherubim" (cf. 1 Sam 4:4; Ps 80:1). Everything is ready.

All that remains is for Yahweh to sanctify the tabernacle personally. Without that presence, the tabernacle—endowed as it is with the people's offerings of silver, gold, and precious stones—is no more than an empty shell, devoid of any theological significance. Thus the enthronement of Yahweh in the tabernacle constitutes the climax of the book, and indeed, of the pentateuchal narrative up to this point: "Then the cloud covered the tent of meeting, and the glory of Yahweh filled the tabernacle. And Moses was not able to enter the tent of meeting, because the cloud abode upon it, and the glory of Yahweh filled the tabernacle" (40:34–35, AT). In the context of the pentateuchal narrative, the enthronement of the covenant lord of Israel in the tent of meeting provides a community of God and humankind that the world has not seen since the first man and woman were driven from Eden. Thus the tabernacle has cosmological significance: it is the center of the world. "I will dwell among the people of Israel, and will be their God. And they shall acknowledge that I am Yahweh their God, who brought them out of the land of Egypt, that I might dwell among them; I am Yahweh their God" (29:45–46, AT).

111. This is the literal meaning of the *terumah* ("offering"), e.g., 35:5

THREE

Leviticus

In the Presence of God

1. LEVITICUS AS NARRATIVE[1]

MANY A PIOUS VOW to read straight through the Bible from cover to cover has foundered in the shoals of Leviticus. It is difficult to think of a book in the Bible that is less inviting to twentieth-century readers. This collection of ritual customs is not only soporific (two chapters one-quarter hour before bedtime) but often seems utterly primitive as well. Consider the ritual in which a living bird, cedar wood, scarlet stuff, and hyssop are dipped in the blood of a slaughtered bird and then sprinkled on a person to signify recovery from "leprosy" (14:4–7). Such passages conjure up the witches' chant in *Macbeth*: "Lizard's leg, and howlet's wing; / For a charm of pow'rful trouble / Like a hell-broth boil and bubble" (IV.i.16–19).

Few people would want to revive such rituals, but many contemporary worship services use the language of

---

1. Suggestions for reading will appear at appropriate places.

"offering" and "sacrifice" to express both thanksgiving and commitment to God. In addition to providing liturgical language, Leviticus also raises theological questions that the various rituals address: How does the production and consumption of food reflect one's spiritual values (to cite a recent book, *The Omnivore's Dilemma*)? Or, to put it another way, what are the religious dimensions of growing cattle or corn, eating beef or cereal? How does someone who feels alienated from God find reconciliation, that is, "atonement"? What sexual relationships are inappropriate within the covenant community? How do the needs of the poor affect the rights of the well-to-do? How can people who go into debt and must sell their homes ever recover? What is the relationship between the territorial sovereignty of a nation and the way it treats its citizens and cares for the land? The questions are as contemporary as they are ancient, and readers may find some of the answers in Leviticus to be surprisingly challenging.

Leviticus is a book about being in the presence of God. Unlike much contemporary spirituality, "priestly religion does not envision God as an intimate friend of individuals."[2] For the ancient world at least, being in the presence of the divine was always an awesome experience, fascinating and terrifying at the same time—but always terrifying, because to be human meant to feel radically unworthy, indeed somehow "unclean" (i.e. impure) in the presence of holiness, and thus threatened by that presence.[3] Leviticus is a manual of instruction on how to remain fit for being in the presence of God, but it is also a major stage within the plot of the pentateuchal narrative. When we consider the complementary functions of instruction (*torah*) and narration, we shall find that the book represents an indispensable development in the characterization of Yahweh and of Israel.

Alongside the archaic customs in Leviticus, the major problem confronting the reader of the Pentateuch is the dearth of narrative. Only chs. 8–10 (and 24:10–23)[4] contain any action that qualifies as narrative in the ordinary sense. Clearly, the redactors did not arrange or compose the material in Leviticus with the purpose of rendering a realistic story. But here we must exercise extreme caution, precisely

2. Dozeman, *Numbers*, 15.

3. The classic analysis of this phenomenon is that of Otto, *Idea of the Holy*. For examples see Gen 28:17; Exod 3:5; 19:24; and Isa. 6:1–5. Since *unclean* can be confused with *dirty* in the sense of "soiled," rather than associated with the secondary meaning of "polluting, obscene, or indecent," I will often use the term *impure*.

4. On this disturbing story about blasphemy and its punishment see below, n. 153.

in our understanding of what it means to read the Torah as narrative. There can be little doubt that a major intention of the redactors of Leviticus was to compile ritual legislation that would meet their contemporary needs. It is also clear that they included the material here in the Torah in order to give it divine sanction; the legislation is represented as the revelation of Yahweh to Moses at Sinai. At the same time, the significance of the material also derives from its narrative context.

First, let us look at the incident in chs. 8–9 (read 8:1–4, 6, 10, 14–15a, 30; 9:1, 7, 22–24; 10:1–2). The first sacrifices take place here; thus this incident presupposes chs. 1–7, where the proper sacrificial procedures are specified. At first sight, chs. 1–9 might appear a mere Appendix to the book of Exodus, one with which we could easily, even enthusiastically, dispense. But that is far from the case. In fact, these chapters represent the completion of the narrative sequence that began with Yahweh's command in Exod 25:8, "have them make me a sanctuary, that I may dwell among them." This command was enacted at the end of Exodus, when the "glory of Yahweh filled the tabernacle" (40:34, AT).

However, the advent of the divine glory represented only a partial fulfillment of the instructions for the sanctuary. While the sacred space of worship was thereby legitimated, the time was not. In other words, the activities that take place in the sanctuary, and the people who perform these activities, were yet to be consecrated—the sanctification of the altar and the ordination of the priests who serve on behalf of the people. The ordination service is outlined in Exodus

29, but does not take place until Leviticus 8–9. Thus chapters 8–9 constitute the climactic moment at which the entire liturgical structure and activity of the people is consummated. Once again the "glory of Yahweh" appears, and now fire comes from Yahweh and consumes the first sacrifice (9:23–24). Just as the descent of the divine presence consecrated the tabernacle, now it consecrates the ritual of sacrifice and those who perform it.[5]

But the significance of the event in ch. 9 is not exhausted with the constitution of the worshiping community. As we have already suggested, human finitude itself makes being in the presence of God an awesome and dangerous situation. In Israel's case, the narrative context of chs. 1–9 poses an even more threatening situation, for this is a sinful people—the people who, along with Aaron the priest, constructed the golden calf, as well as an *unauthorized* altar of sacrifice (Exod 32:5–6). It is this priest, on behalf of this people, who now approaches the legitimate altar, and thus comes into the presence of God. While Yahweh had rescinded the verdict of annihilation for the sin of the calf (32:14), had reinstated the covenant in response to Moses' plea for forgiveness (34:9–10), and had sanctified the tabernacle with the divine presence (40:34–38), nowhere has the text suggested that there was a complete reconciliation. Indeed, that is the irony of the conclusion of Exodus, where

the holy God descends to the tabernacle and sanctifies it, even though the people and their priest remain under the burden of their sin.[6]

Such ironies the redactors of Leviticus do not like. While it was probably not the original intention of ch. 9 to answer the problem of the golden calf, in its present context it functions as the climactic resolution to that problem. In this chapter Aaron and his sons are ordained and the altar of sacrifice is consecrated by a new manifestation of divine presence. At the same time, the sacrifices Aaron performs at the command of Yahweh mediated through Moses, secure "atonement" for him and for the people (9:7). Had this event not taken place, Yahweh's presence in the tabernacle would be in the midst of a "stiff-necked people," stained by "iniquity" and "sin" (Exod 34:9). Such a situation is intolerable. If Exodus 40 represented the climax of the exaltation of Yahweh, it also immediately introduced a new tension in the pentateuchal narrative: how could the holy God dwell in the midst of a sinful people? That tension is resolved in the first nine chapters of Leviticus, and only there. Thus, to ignore these chapters would be to ignore an essential element in the plot of the Pentateuch.

Second, we note that within Leviticus references appear to the preceding story of Exodus, as well as to Israel's future, recalling the larger narrative context. For example, near the end of the chapter on dietary restrictions (ch. 11), Yahweh asserts the authority of the laws

---

5. Thus the reference to "the eighth day" in 9:1 is not to the preceding chapters but to Exodus 40, thereby connecting with the larger narrative. See Ruwe, "Structure of the Book of Leviticus," 61; and Schenker, "What Connects," 175: the framework to chs. 18 and 20 embeds them "into the whole Pentateuchal narrative."

6. Note that Exod 32:34–35 concludes the golden-calf story with an ominous threat of future punishment as well as a plague, the end of which is left suspended.

and the motivation for obedience in terms of the exodus story: "For I am Yahweh, who brought you up out of the land of Egypt, to be your God; you shall therefore be holy, for I am holy" (v. 45, AT; cf. 18:3). Near the end of the book, we shall see that the retrospective goes all the way back to the ancestors of Genesis (26:42). Similarly, the laws applying specifically to the land of Canaan often begin with a reference to Israel's future occupation (18:3, 27–28; 19:23; 23:10).

Further, the final form of the entire book is, in fact, that of a narrative and not a manual. While narration in the usual sense occurs only in chs. 8–10 and 24:10–23, the rest of the book is presented as a series of divine speeches addressed to Moses (and sometimes Aaron). At beginning and end, the redactors have provided a narrative framework: "Yahweh called Moses, and spoke to him from the tent of meeting, saying, 'Speak to the Israelites, and say to them . . .'" (1:1, AT); "These are the commandments which Yahweh commanded Moses for the Israelites at Mount Sinai" (27:34, AT). Periodically, the introductory framework is maintained by the shorter formula, "And Yahweh said to Moses" (4:1; 5:14; 6:1, 8, 19, 24, etc.).

The framework and connecting devices may seem artificial, and the resulting narrative may lack verisimilitude. After all, with the exceptions noted, nothing really happens in the book. But here we must remember our discussion of the Decalogue and the other laws in Exodus. There we concluded that Yahweh's identity and character are revealed as much by words as by deeds. However minimal the narrative structure of Leviticus may be, its presence makes a crucial difference

for what the text represents. "Leviticus is a narrative text."[7]

How different the material in Leviticus would be, for example, if it were not in the Pentateuch at all, but somewhere else in the canon, and without the minimal narrative seams. Such a situation is hardly unthinkable (cf. Psalms and Proverbs), and in fact was commonplace in other ancient Near Eastern libraries, where sacerdotal regulations do not appear in the context of a story, nor are they represented as divine commands.[8] The Near Eastern ritual laws were part of civil and criminal codes, as they are in the Hebrew Bible, but they were promulgated by the king and thus served to undergird royal authority.[9] In contrast, the Levitical laws are represented as the words of Yahweh uttered within a narrative context, and thus further express the character of the God who is rendered by that narrative.

There is a symbiotic relationship between the narrative framework and the rules: the narrative converts the rules into the words, the speech, of Yahweh, and the speech tells us more about the person rendered by the narrative.[10] Here *torah* (instruction) cannot be understood

7. Ruwe, "Structure of the Book of Leviticus," 57, also emphasizing the direct speech.

8. See the ritual texts in Pritchard, *ANET*, 325–26, 331–53.

9. Hallo in Plaut, *Torah*, 746–47.

10. This symbiosis is most apparent as redaction in those collections using the third person ("If anyone"; e.g., chs. 4, 5). Here the introductory framework (4:1–2a) converts the rules into speech. But in many of the other codes, the relationship between rules and speech is intrinsic by virtue of the use of the first and second person. The latter codes thus virtually presuppose a narrative context, whereas the former (without their redactional introduction) do not.

apart from the narrative framework of *the* Torah; but at the same time those narrative portions within the Torah (i.e., those portions characterized by action) are also incomplete without the accompanying divine speeches. Words and deeds, law and story, belong together, and only together do they fully render the person of Yahweh as represented in the pentateuchal narrative. Thus it is also appropriate to describe Leviticus (and much of Numbers and Deuteronomy) as "a narrative of law."[11]

What do these words of Yahweh say about the character of Yahweh? Primarily, they say that the one who brought Israel out of Egypt, who became Israel's covenant sovereign, and who dwells in their midst in the tabernacle, is also the holy God whose presence demands holiness on the part of Israel. By now that may not seem very surprising, but the depth and breadth of this holiness as represented in Leviticus is one of the most distinctive contributions to the pentateuchal description of God, and indeed, of Israel. How different the character of God now appears from that of the one who ate at Abraham's tent and strolled with him as with a friend. After Leviticus, such an ingenuous portrait of the divine character will be both naive and virtually idolatrous unless it appears in tension with the one who says, "You must be holy, for I am holy" (11:45, AT).

---

11. Dozeman, *God on the Mountain*, 2: narrative here is "a means for directing the reader's attention to law." Cf. the quotation from Georg Fohrer by Baden (*Composition*, 174): "'the narrative provides the foundation for the eternal law, and the eternal law justifies the presentation of the narrative.'" In the end (225, 229), Baden assigns higher "status" to the laws.

2. "YOU MUST BE HOLY"

The background for Israel as a "holy nation" was provided in Exodus 19 in connection with the awesome appearance of Yahweh. Before the advent of the holy God, the people were consecrated—"made holy" (*qiddash*)—they washed their clothes, avoided contact with the mountain, and abstained from sexual intercourse (vv. 10–15, 21–24). This sacerdotal preparation provided a complementary counterpart to the covenantal preparation in vv. 1–9.[12] The instructions to Moses here and in Exodus 24 also suggest three spatial zones of holiness with corresponding social boundaries (i.e. areas restricted to certain people): generally, for laity, for priests or officials, and for Moses alone (cf. Exod 19:12–25; 24:1–2, 9–18). There is considerable ambiguity about the zones and who may enter them and when, but the general divisions in terms of authorized persons is relatively clear. The tripartite arrangement for the Sinai theophany also corresponds to the zones of holiness reflected in Leviticus and already intimated in Exodus 25–31. The tabernacle—a moveable Mt. Sinai—is divided into three zones of decreasing size and increasing holiness, each separated by a screen or curtain: the courtyard, with the altar for sacrifices; the holy place, with the altar of incense; and the "holy of holies" or "most holy place," with the ark of the covenant (cf. Exod 26:33–35). The people may enter only the courtyard; only priests may enter the holy place; and only the high priest (initially Aaron) may enter the most holy place, and even then

---

12. Corresponding to Exodus 20–24; 32–34 (covenantal), and 25–31; 35–40 (liturgical).

only once a year, on the day of atonement (Lev 16:2, 29–30). Alongside other ways of dividing the book, one can even determine a tripartite literary structure divided by the two stories of chs. 8–10 and 24:10–23.[13]

The basic meaning of "holiness" (*qodeš*) is "separation." For Israel to be a "holy nation" means to be "set apart" from all other nations. God has created a sacral community by separating Israel from all the other peoples on the earth. Holiness is not an intrinsic quality belonging to the people; rather, they *become* holy only with respect to Yahweh. Thus the text reads "You shall be *for me* . . . a holy nation" (Exod. 19:6). Leviticus emphasizes the same point: "You shall be holy *to me*, for I, Yahweh, am holy, and have separated you from the peoples, to be mine" (20:26, AT).[14] Thus the people's holiness derives only from the relationship to Yahweh. This is because holiness in its primary sense, as an intrinsic quality, belongs only to Yahweh. In fact, holiness in this sense is virtually synonymous with divinity. Again, the connotation

of separation is fundamental: God is by nature majestic, awesome, exalted, "high and lifted up," the "wholly other."[15] The holiness of God expresses the infinite qualitative distinction between divinity and humanity.

In the context of the book of Leviticus, the holiness of Yahweh is intimately associated with the worshiping community. This connection points again to the startling claim made at the end of Exodus: the "wholly other" God of Sinai, whose very holiness means separation from humankind, condescends to "camp" with this people. However, the resulting conception of divine presence is not as crude as it may at first seem. God is not reduced to the level of a fellow Scout on a camporee (whether Boy or Girl). The Hebrew verb for "encamp" (*šakan*, pronounced "sha-kan") implies an impermanent form of dwelling, one that can be moved from place to place.[16] The verb is obviously appropriate for the tabernacle or "tent of meeting," which moves with Israel on the way through the wilderness (cf. Exod 40:36–38). Theologically, the impermanence connoted by *šakan* suggests that God's presence in the tabernacle is not temporally final, ontologically complete, or in any way restricted or contained by the sanctuary. The tabernacle is sacred

---

13. Douglas, *Leviticus as Literature*, 195–97. She also sees the tripartite analogy reflected in the arrangement of sacrificial animals on the altar (78 and Table 4.1 on 79). Most scholars divide the book into two parts (chs. 1–16 and 17–26, with the Appendix 27), corresponding to the presumed literary sources P and H (for "Holiness Code"). Ruwe ("Structure of Leviticus," 61–62) divides the book into two, but separated by the temporal reference in 9:1 (see above).

14. The verb for "separate" here is the same as that used in Gen 1:4, 6, and so forth. For an early representation of such separation, see Num 23:9b. Cf. Milgrom regarding the Holiness Code of Leviticus 17–27: "the very order of the natural world rests on Israel's ability to maintain its sanctity by separating itself from the nations that surround it" (*Leviticus: A Book of Ritual*, 179).

15. The latter phrase was coined by Otto, *Idea of the Holy.*

16. See Dozeman, *God on the Mountain*, 76, 129–30; Friedman, *Torah*, 456. For a different view, see Mettinger (*Dethronement*, 90–97), who disputes the meaning of "to tent." Nevertheless, he notes that "God is depicted as leading his people from campsite to campsite," a picture particularly fitting to an exilic setting. Cf. Exod 40:36–38; Num 9:15–23; 10:11–13 (on which see the discussion in the next chapter); 35:34–35 (for NRSV "dwell").

space only because Yahweh is present, and not vice versa. There is thus a radical contingency to the earthly sanctuary as the place where the presence of God is located: Yahweh's continued presence is conditional on Israel's continual holiness.

"You must be holy, for I am holy." On the one hand, Yahweh's presence is absolutely essential to the people's existence. It is this presence alone that sustains and guides them; it is the source of their blessing (cf. 6:22–26). On the other hand, the presence of the holy God in their midst means that any departure from the people's consecrated state will endanger their continued existence, because the holiness of God cannot coexist with what is unholy, what is impure or "unclean." The ambivalent character of the divine presence is clear from the juxtaposition of chs. 9 and 10. The divine fire that ignites the inaugural sacrifice and thus provides the means for atonement is the same fire that engulfs those who approach the divine presence in an unorthodox or unauthorized fashion, as do Nadab and Abihu (9:24; 10:1–2).[17] Moreover, those who come into the presence of God—i.e. enter the tabernacle precincts, or partake of sanctified food—while in a state of impurity will die, much as someone coming too close to nuclear

radiation would die if unprotected, and Leviticus provides the protective rules. Yet there exists an even greater threat. If impurity spreads unchecked throughout the entire community, God will "pull up stakes" and leave. God will abandon the sanctuary, and thus the people. Defilement of a single individual puts the very life of the entire community in danger (15:31). Contemporary readers deeply affected by the individualism of Western culture must keep in mind this priestly understanding of corporate or communal solidarity, for it explains why a single person's skin disease or food selection (for examples) can threaten the very existence of the entire society. Thus various rules and ordinances that may seem unreasonably strict, if not draconian, to us, are there to protect the *community's* well-being. An individual must be good for the *common* good.[18]

Clearly Leviticus presents a new formulation of the theme of human responsibility before God. Apart from all the peoples of the world, the Israelites enjoy a unique intimacy with Yahweh. Unlike all other sacral communities, not only the king or the priests have access to the sacred precincts or to ritual instructions, but the people as a whole.[19] Yet, as does the covenantal polity, so the people's privileged status brings with it a serious responsibility. The demand for holi-

---

17. Their heterodoxy involves the use of "unholy [literally, "strange"] fire," the nature of which is impossible to determine. Compare the story of the unfortunate Uzzah, whose innocent touching of the ark spells his death (2 Sam 6:6–11; cf. also 1 Sam 6:19 and text note *u*). In Num 4:20, even Levites (Kohathites) who look at the "holy things" (especially the ark) will die. For a contemporary illustration of the danger of holiness and the ark, see my description of the climactic scene from the film *Raiders of the Lost Ark*, in *Book of the Former Prophets*, 118.

18. Friedman (*Torah*, 484) points out that such a view of contagious impurity is operating in the story in which entire families die along with their respective fathers because of the fathers' breach of sacerdotal orthodoxy (Numbers 16, especially v. 32). A similar corporate vulnerability appears in the covenant theology of Deuteronomy.

19. Plaut, *Torah*, 733–34, along with Hallo, *Context of Scripture* 3:745, 748.

ness is another aspect of the demand for righteousness.

The way to remain holy is, of course, to abstain from sin. The predominant understanding of sin with respect to holiness has to do with what is usually called defilement. Here the standard English connotations of defilement are instructive: impurity, pollution, contamination. Such connotations indicate immediately the strong physical or tactile dimension of defilement. Thus the most appropriate analogue for defilement is "stain."[20] To remove the stain requires cleansing.

> Some form of liturgical cleansing ("ablution") appears in various contemporary religious traditions. Before entering into prayer, many devout Muslims will perform a ritual called *wudu*, which involves a detailed washing of hands, face, head, and feet.[21] Similarly, many Catholics will symbolically wash their faces with "holy water" before entering a church sanctuary, which also serves as a reminder of baptism, itself associated with the "remission of sin." Many Protestants begin worship with a confession of sin and absolution, which could include words like Psalm 51:2 (cf. Lev 14:4): "Wash me thoroughly from my iniquity, and cleanse me from my sin."

The nature of sin as defilement may, at first sight, appear strange to the contemporary reader, although many Americans often seem obsessed with a secular version of John Wesley's famous adage, "Cleanliness is next to godliness."[22] We are used to thinking of sin in terms of specific behavior. Consequently, we may speak of a sin or of sins in the plural. A sin is a particular act (or the lack thereof). Sin is connected with doing something. Such an understanding of sin is by no means absent from Leviticus, which includes regulations governing stealing, lying, treatment of the alien, the poor, the disabled and aged, and business procedures; but the most distinctive construal of sin here is that of defilement. The association between defilement and impurity also indicates that defilement is something that not only can but primarily does happen *to* someone. In most cases, sin as defilement is not the result of an act one commits but it is a state into which one is placed as a consequence of something beyond one's control, or something done unintentionally, or even something unknown (e.g., 4:13, 22, 27; 5:14).[23] It can be "caught" by contact with an object that

---

20. Ricoeur, *Symbolism of Evil*, 33–40. The famous line of Lady Macbeth illustrates the indelible guilt of bloodstain: "Out, damned spot! out, I say!" (V.1.39).

21. For a description, see http://islam1.org/how_to_pray/wudu.htm/. If there is no water

(e.g., in the desert) one can use sand. See also Cragg and Speight, *Islam from Within*, 103–7.

22. As Herberg has suggested, the "American Way" as a religion has "an extraordinarily high moral valuation of—sanitation!" ("America's Civil Religion," 79), and Herberg was writing long before bottles of hand sanitizer became ubiquitous.

23. Presumably, the possibility of having sinned would be manifested by some form of malady; the determination of the guilty party would be effected by casting lots (the Urim and Thummim, the "sacred dice," e.g., Lev 8:8; Num 27:21). For an example of such determination, see 1 Sam 14:24–27, 41–42.

itself is unclean, for impurity has a material quality, like "a gaseous substance, a volatile force, a miasma exuded by the source."[24] Such sin is contagious, and can spread from one individual to the whole community, just as a stain may begin on a garment from a single drop of contaminant, but spread to a much wider area. The threat resembles very much the way contemporary people think of the spread of an infectious disease.

What makes a person impure? The answer to this question primarily is a matter of intuitive interpretation rather than explicit textual explanation. The biblical authors do not give us an extensive theory to explain their practice, whether it involves what foods to eat, what constitutes a disease, or how sacrifice effects atonement. As one scholar admits, "There are many imponderables here that almost all interpreters frankly confess are baffling."[25] Nevertheless, we may categorize the various causes of defilement as bodily discharges, scale infections, food, family relationships, and social injustice.

(Read 15:1–2, 13–19, 25–33.) Bodily discharges perhaps represent the most understandable examples of defiling conditions that happen *to* someone. A man who experiences a nocturnal emission of semen is impure until the evening of the next day, and he must bathe. If the discharge is abnormal (e.g., gonorrhea), he must wait for seven days *after* the disease is cured and then offer an expiatory sacrifice (on such sacrifice, see below). Similarly, a woman who experiences her normal menstrual discharge is impure for seven days, and must bathe at the end,

but if the discharge continues beyond the normal time, she remains impure until it stops, after which she must offer a sacrifice. In these cases, anyone who comes in contact with the person while he or she is impure will also become impure. One theory explains the discharge of semen and blood as both signifying the loss of life, and death is incompatible with holiness.[26] That might also explain why other bodily excretions are *not* mentioned as defiling (urination, defecation, sweating). However, here is also a good example of how one theory does not explain all conditions, for normal sexual relations involving an emission of semen (but not a loss) renders a man and woman temporarily impure also. One should not infer from this that sexual relations are in some way bad. The culture that produced the lyric affirmation of sensuality in the Song of Songs could hardly make such a condemnation. Similarly, although childbirth obviously manifests new life, the blood associated with delivery symbolizes death and renders the mother impure for a length of time depending on the gender of the child (12:1–8). While some of these regulations may appear misogynistic to us, clearly both sexes are susceptible to impurity. Also, it may be that declaring

24. Milgrom, *Leviticus: Book of Ritual*, 142.

25. Kaiser, *Leviticus*, 1000.

26. Milgrom, *Leviticus*, 11–12, 41, 123; "for the life of the flesh is in the blood" (see further below regarding both foods and sacrifices). The connection between semen and life is obvious (especially since semen was thought to be a homunculus, i.e. a complete miniature human being). However, loss of blood due to wounds is not defiling, even though one could bleed to death. No doubt universal "primitive" notions of *genital* taboos stand behind such rules (cf. Exod 19:15). Friedman (*Torah*, 352) argues against the centrality of death, and instead sees a kind of universal revulsion for blood as involved.

the menstruating women or new mothers impure is simply a way of protecting them when they are physically and emotionally vulnerable (e.g., by prohibiting their husbands from engaging in sexual intercourse).[27]

(Read 13:1–8, 45–52.) As with bodily discharges, it is not difficult to see why certain skin ailments might make a person impure, especially if such ailments were feared to be communicable (13:1–46). Although these diseases have traditionally been labeled as leprosy, apparently a variety of dermatological conditions apply, and we do not know a precise diagnosis for many. The text describes "a swelling or an eruption or a spot" (13:2). One could think of chicken pox or shingles or psoriasis, among other possibilities. The category of "scale disease" could even include something like skin peeling off as a result of sunburn. Such dermatological defilement results in quarantine: those infected must publicize their condition with how they dress, must verbally warn people away by crying, "Unclean!" and must live outside the camp until healed (13:45–46). Again, the way various skin ailments might make the skin appear to be dead (which, again, is what happens simply with sunburn), suggests another association between defilement and death. The similar appearance of mold or mildew in clothing or on a wall also renders these substances impure (13:47–59; 14:34–53). The association may seem strange to us until we recall that many people have a strong ambivalence about fungus—we eat fungi in the form of mushrooms, but most others we spray with fungicide!

(Read 11:9–12; another list appears in Deuteronomy 14.) Perhaps the most well-known substance that defiles a person is food. Many people today are aware that some Jews (and Muslims) will not eat pork, and may even know that the same people will not eat shrimp, lobster, clams, or oysters. That eliminates a lot from the standard seafood restaurant menu! Again, to understand the dietary laws, we must keep in mind the overarching concern for holiness. The effect, if not also the intent, of the holiness laws includes the separation of Israel from other peoples. The strict dietary limitations alone could have accomplished such distinction: Israel's selective diet reflects Israel's status as God's select people (cf. 11:47). You are what you eat (or do not eat). As Hendel puts it, "What one eats and with whom one shares food are visible expressions of social bonds and boundaries."[28] To take pork as an example, it may be that Israelites avoided it because they associated it with Philistine culture, where it was a prominent dietary staple. Thus "holiness was endangered by taking pork into the Israelite body, just as Philistine culture was a threat to the wholeness of the Israelite social body."[29] More broadly, we repeat a question we raised at the outset:

---

27. Levine (*Leviticus*, 223), suggests that *pure* and *impure* are the equivalents of *immune* and *susceptible*. Behind such protective measures also probably is the primitive fear of demonic powers that would take the life of the mother and/or the newborn. No reason is given for the differences between giving birth to male or female infants

28. Hendel, *Remembering Abraham*, 22, with references to the work of Mary Douglas.

29. Ibid. See also See Milgrom, *Leviticus 1–16*, 651–52; Milgrom, *Leviticus: Book of Ritual*, 116. The cultural distinction may well be one among others, e.g., animal locomotion. See below.

how does the production and consumption of food reflect one's spiritual values? Or, how does eating correspond to the religious beliefs that a community claims to hold? After all, other than the need for air and water, there is nothing more basic to life than eating. What makes eating holy?

The most basic expression of the holiness of food is the ritual acknowledgment that all food comes from God and thus must be, in a sense, shared with God. To borrow feudal language, God is the Lord or sovereign of the manor, and Israel is Yahweh's fief. Ps 50:10–11 puts it well: "every wild animal of the forest is mine, the cattle on a thousand hills. I know all the birds of the air, and all that moves in the field is mine." Thus, alongside the other functions of sacrificial offerings (e.g., for atonement), they acknowledge Yahweh's manorial ownership. The refusal to acknowledge that ownership would amount to poaching. Showing gratitude for God's provision of food is a regular part of worship. In addition to various seasonal sacrifices outlined in Leviticus 23, Priestly ordinances in the book of Numbers require *daily* offerings: two lambs per day, along with grain, oil, and a "drink offering" (Num 28:1–8)—in short, a complete meal (albeit without vegetables). God even calls the sacrifices "the *food* for my offering by fire, my pleasing aroma" (Num 28:2; cf. Lev 3:11, 16). But does God need food? As is often the case, literalism is the enemy. More than likely, the priestly authors of the ordinances understand food for God symbolically. Just as the tabernacle constitutes God's dwelling, so the offerings are the meals served there.[30] Human dependence on

"daily bread" is acknowledged by offering *God* daily bread. Giving to God is always giving *back* to the donor of creation. Thus the psalm quoted above ridicules the notion of God's requiring food as a *lack* of true thanksgiving (Ps 50:8–15).[31]

Aside from the offerings of food to God, there is the question of what food Israelites may eat and how to prepare it. The answer to this question is in the so-called dietary laws. Just as some interpreters would see the quarantine of the person with skin disease as simply a version of public health policy, so some would see the dietary laws as examples of food hygiene. The ban on eating pork would help prevent the possibility of contracting trichinosis. But such nutritional concerns are probably far from the primary interest here. Rather, the various prohibitions almost certainly reflect symbolically the ancient worldview that undergirds them. The distinction between foods perhaps appears most clearly with seafood. If you ask someone, "What lives in the ocean?" probably the first answer would be, "Fish." And if you asked the person to draw a picture of a fish, it would probably look like that little medallion that some people put on their car bumpers to indicate that they are Christians (or the counter medallion that champions the name of Charles Darwin!). With greater

---

30. Anderson ("Introduction to Israelite Religion," 279–80) stresses the importance of this symbolism for understanding sacrifice.

31. The legitimacy of covenant making with God by sacrifice is acknowledged in v. 5, and sacrifice explicitly is *not* the substance of divine rebuke (v. 8). Vv. 10–11 graphically describe God's sovereignty over the world (God's "manor"). Note also that adultery is part of the indictment (v. 18), behavior that clearly disqualifies one from approaching God in priestly legislation.

detail, the picture would show a creature that "has fins and scales," precisely the one that Leviticus declares ritually edible. But why would one not want to eat a crab cake, or Oysters Rockefeller, or Lobster Newburg? Well, they don't have fins and scales. They don't *look* like fish. It is a matter of locomotion. Fish swim, but shrimp seem to jump up and down, crabs and lobsters crawl along, and oysters don't go *anywhere*. Thus the equation is, seafood = fish = fins-and-scales. Anything else is *not* sea*food*, even if it is a sea creature. It is odd, weird, atypical.

If, in fact, locomotion is the primary criterion for seafood (and the matter, like many others in Leviticus, is highly debatable), then we are probably dealing with a classification system of animal life that makes sense within the author's understanding of the created world. Locomotion is also involved in the classification of land animals (11:1–3), and possibly winged insects (11:20–23; a gourmet dinner of locusts is approved), although birds probably involve different criteria (11:13–19).[32] However, it is important to note that all of these regulations have to do with food for humans. Nowhere does the text suggest that eating such foods is *nutritionally* harmful, much less that there is something bad about the banned creatures. We must remember that the same school of authors that produced Genesis 1 (the Priestly school) is at work here, and no doubt agrees with the creation account when God declares that everything created is "very good," including "every living creature that moves," "creeping things and wild animals of the earth of every kind" (Gen 1:21–22, 31). Thus though certain creatures are "detestable" or an "abomination" *as food* for Israelites (11:9, 13, 20, 23), they are not detestable within the order of God's creation (even unclean animals are passengers on Noah's ark, Gen 7:2!).[33] The dietary laws are the way Israelites may live a life of holiness, which, in this case, means a life in accordance with the integrity of creation. As Houston so aptly puts it, "It is only when each creature observes its place in the cosmic order, and humanity, in dominion over them all, preserves the place of each, that justice and harmony can be maintained in the world."[34] Contemporary views of what constitutes cosmic order may well be different from the view of Leviticus, but the question of what to eat remains a religious and moral one (see Appendix 5).

---

32. Milgrom (*Leviticus: Book of Ritual*, 117; cf. *Leviticus 1–16*, 655, 720) suggests that "all other animal species" in ch. 11 in addition to sea creatures are classified by "their means of locomotion." However, all of the prohibited birds appear to be birds of prey, which, of course, eat other dead animals, including their blood, thus again possibly involving the specter of death. Additional reasons may apply to some creatures. Friedman (*Torah*, 347–48) argues for various explanations, including similarity or difference from the human form.

33. Clearly the prohibition against eating all sorts of wildlife would have the effect of protecting the species. Douglas, in fact, most recently argues that it is the very vulnerability of many species that makes them "unclean," i.e., the law is intended to protect them, e.g., sea creatures that cannot quickly escape predators because they do not have fins with which to swim away, with insects being the most vulnerable (*Leviticus as Literature*, 169, 171).

34. Houston, "Towards an Integrated Reading," 160. As he notes on 161, "the integrity of creation" was coined by the World Council of Churches to address how Christians (among others) should live faithfully and responsibly in the world.

(Read Lev 17:1–4, 10–13.) Finally with regard to food, it is not only *what* one may eat, but also *how* food is to be prepared, that involves holiness. Here the concern narrows to three requirements on the consumption of meat. First, the list of permitted animals is quite small, primarily domestic livestock—sheep, goats, and cattle, with occasional wild game.[35] Second, blood must be drained completely from the meat before eating, and, third, probably all meat must first be sacrificed on the altar.[36] The priest performs the sacrifice, but only after the layperson kills the animal, thus joining slaughter and sacrifice as one spiritual action. Indeed, if one does *not* sacrifice the animal before eating meat, one is guilty of murder ("bloodshed"; Lev 17:4)! The

combination of these three regulations constitutes what it means to eat meat in holiness.

The blood prohibition actually does not originate here but goes back to the postflood decree of God to Noah, when God decided to allow humans to be carnivorous and no longer vegetarians (Gen 9:1–5; cf. 1:29–30). Still, that concession carried the caveat that no one should "eat flesh with its life, that is, its blood." The prohibition imposed on Noah is thus universal and not limited to Israel (as is Leviticus). After all, the whole world is Yahweh's manor (cf. Ps 19:1), and as sovereign of the manor, Yahweh gives permission for humans to kill animals for food. Draining the blood acknowledges this. The rationale appears again even more explicitly in Lev 17:11: "For the life of the flesh is in the blood." The result is a remarkable statement of the bond between *animals* and *humans*, such that one can really speak of a mutuality that the two separate words obscure—all are *fauna*—all share the life of the flesh in the blood. In fact, Milgrom suggests that "both animals and people have a *nefeš*, a 'soul,' . . . the life essence of both human and beast as distinct from the body."[37] Draining the blood from meat before consumption shows the deepest respect for the life of the animal as one of God's creatures. Moreover, in Lev 17:11 the "life" of animals is inextricably connected to their use as *sacrificial* animals: "For the

35. See 11:2b–8 and Deut 14:3–8, where specific wild game is allowed as well, on which cf. Lev 17:13. Though such game is not brought for sacrifice, the blood prohibition remains.

36. The latter is debatable and turns on the meaning of the word *šaḥat* (17:3), which can be both "sacrifice" and "slaughter." Alternatively, it is only *sacrifices* "in the open field" that are forbidden. Milgrom opts for "slaughter": 17:3–7 "demands that meat for the table initially be offered up as a sacrifice" (*Leviticus 17–22*, 1453; cf. *Leviticus: A Book of Ritual*, 189); so also Alter (*Five Books*, 616) and Friedman (*Torah*, 371). Levine offers a detailed discussion and opts for "sacrifice" (*JPS Torah Commentary*, 112–13; so also Kaiser, *Book of Leviticus*, 1118). In contrast, the Deuteronomic regulations allow the nonsacrificial butchering of meat at one's home, since otherwise it would have to be brought to one central sanctuary (later, Jerusalem; Deut 12:20–27; cf. Tigay, *Deuteronomy*, 124 and Excursus 14). Still, the blood prohibition remains in effect (v. 23). It seems most likely to me that the Deuteronomic legislation is a revision, and thus that "slaughter" is the meaning in Lev 17:3. At any rate, the spiritual nature of eating meat remains, almost literally, given that the word *nefeš* in 17:11 can mean "spirit" (see below).

37. Milgrom, *Leviticus: A Book of Ritual*, 190. See the discussion above in ch. 1 of Gen 2:4b— 3:24. Both humans and animals are characterized as "living beings" (*nefeš ḥayyah*), although there the physiological connection is with the breath. The word *nefeš* is also used for "person" in vv. 10 and 12.

life [*nefeš*] of the flesh is in the blood; and I have given it to you for making atonement for your lives [*nefeš*, plural] on the altar; for, as life [*nefeš*], it is the blood that makes atonement." If all meat must be offered as a sacrifice, there is no secular slaughter of meat. Aside from its function in securing atonement for *sin*, therefore, animal sacrifice is fundamentally an act of expiation for the very killing itself that consumption requires.[38] Thus all production and eating of meat is intrinsically spiritual. Every meal is a sacred meal. Every dinner is a thanksgiving dinner.

Modern readers who recoil at the notion of animal sacrifice would do well to consider the spiritual significance attached to it, but also compare the way meat in particular is produced in modern industry. See Appendix 5.

> "Cooking today is an almost limitless enterprise involving, for extreme practitioners, liquid nitrogen, soy lecithin and syringes, and our modern food rules and taboos can rival Leviticus: We want ours free-range, macrobiotic, meatless, wheat-less, raw, local, organic, wild."[39]

3. ATONEMENT

The text that prohibits the consumption of animal blood at the same time provides one of the few comments regarding the role of blood in making sacrifices for atonement (17:11). While there are numerous functions of sacrifice (e.g., thanksgiving, well-being, communion with God, petition for blessing), expiatory sacrifice provides the primary answer to a question raised by much of the above discussion of defilement: what is the remedy for it? While the focus in 17:11 is on the blood of sacrifices, not all sacrifices involve animals; some are cereal or grain sacrifices, and these too are expiatory. Thus, as Milgrom states, "*it is the altar, not the blood, that expiates.*"[40]

Although there are aspects of sin as defilement that make it seem impersonal, in fact it functions as a distortion of the *relationship* between Yahweh and Israel. The narrative context transforms defilement from a "pre-ethical" apprehension of holiness to one based on a covenantal ethic.[41] Impurity is not intrinsically harmful or lethal to the one who becomes unclean. For example, sexual intercourse renders a man and woman unclean only for the remainder of the day on which it occurs, after which defilement runs its course, and a person is again pure. One need only bathe to mark the end of the impurity (e.g., 15:16–18; cf. 13:6). The real problem with defilement is thus not that of a power that works automatically against the one who is impure. Rather, the problem comes when the one who is

---

38. See Milgrom (*Leviticus: A Book of Ritual*, 185): the sacrifice is required "to ransom his life for spilling the life-blood of the animal in order to enjoy its meat."

39. Caruso, "The Food Issue," *The Smithsonian* 43/3 (June 2012) 39.

40. Milgrom, *Leviticus: A Book of Ritual*, 192 (italics original).

41. Ricoeur, *Symbolism of Evil*, 28.

temporarily unholy comes into potential contact with the sacred, for example, by entering the tabernacle precinct or partaking of consecrated food. Such a violation moves from the passive state of defilement into sinful *actions* that could be avoided.

The greatest threat of all is that impurity will penetrate the sanctuary and incur the wrath of Yahweh, who would abandon the sanctuary. Some impurity is so serious that it also requires expiatory sacrifice, that is, atonement—or, as it is often signified, at-one-ment. Sacrifice is the means to reconciliation between Yahweh and Israel. Here the analogy of stain is again helpful. Atonement accomplished through sacrifice is to impurity as cleansing is to stain.[42] But the ultimate object of sacrificial atonement is not only the community or the individual person; it is the sanctuary, the sanctity of which is threatened by the people's impurity.[43] As a result, sacrifice provides the means by which the tabernacle will continue to function as the place in which Yahweh continues to "tent" with Israel.

Precisely how the authors understood sacrifice to effect atonement remains unclear. Nowhere do we find an elaborate theological explanation of the process. Almost certainly, there are magical vestiges involved, yet the ritual is not a mechanical device that can be manipulated at will. The text insists that the ritual is a gift of God (17:11), not a human invention. Some notion of a ransom is at play, since God has given the life of the animal for the life of the human, a transference suggested by the laying on of hands (e.g.,

3:2, 8, 13). "As a result of the performance of certain rites, God grants expiation or atonement. In such instances, expiation, forgiveness, etc. are not the direct physical effects of the rites performed. Such acts are prerequisite, but not causational. It is God who grants the desired result!"[44]

Also, sacrifices do not provide the cure for various ailments; rather, they signify that a cure has happened and mark the transition back to normalcy (e.g., scale-disease, 14:1–4). The effectiveness of sacrifice is limited almost exclusively to unintentional violations (cf. 5:15, 17) and thus at first does not seem to extend to such deliberate acts as murder, adultery, and apostasy.[45] Someone who deliberately eats food that causes impurity or eats sanctified food while in a state of impurity or eats meat not already sacrificed will be excommunicated (7:20–27; 17:4, 9–10, 14).[46] Yet, in the end, "since all sins, however grave, can be classed as unwitting if remorse and repentance follow, a benign technicality allows them all to be forgiven."[47] This blanket amnesty is the purpose behind the Day of Atonement (see below).

---

42. See Levine, *In the Presence*, 57.

43. Milgrom, *Leviticus: A Book of Ritual*, 30.

44. Levine, *In the Presence*, 65–66.

45. Ibid., 90–91; Bamberger in Plaut, *Torah*, 768 and 861. In addition, as Milgrom notes (*Leviticus: A Book of Ritual*, 59), repentance on the part of the worshiper is a precondition in the ritual texts.

46. Literally, "cut off from their kin," the meaning of which is unclear. It may refer to the afterlife (contrast being "gathered to one's kin," e.g., Gen 25:8) or to a lack of offspring.

47. Douglas, *Leviticus as Literature*, 126. Cf. also Milgrom, *Leviticus: A Book of Ritual*, 58. A sterling example is the exoneration of a confessed perjurer, which normally would have required the death penalty (6:1–7; cf. Exod 20:7; Deut 5:11).

As with the effectiveness of the ritual, so with its significance: it does not lie in the ritual itself but derives from the narrative context in which the ritual is prescribed. As we have already seen, the first sacrifice on the altar secured the atonement for Aaron and the people (9:7). In its present narrative context, that event signified both the consecration of the sacrificial ritual and the consummation of the process of forgiveness for the sin of the calf that began in Exodus 32. With the establishment of ongoing sacrifice, atonement is a continuing possibility. Within the entire pentateuchal narrative the sacrificial rituals of Leviticus provide *the first and only* means for reconciliation between God and humankind that is both formal and repeatable.[48] Thus the nature of the ritual as a divine gift is crucial to its meaning. Elsewhere Yahweh specifies punishments for breach of covenant; only here in Leviticus does Yahweh authorize a procedure that will protect the covenant community from its own sin. Thus the laws of Leviticus present the unique instance in which God issues commandments of how to live in a proper relationship and offers a means by which that relationship may be restored once it has been broken.

All the various references to atonement come together in the regulations for the Day of Atonement" in ch. 16 (cf. 16:29–30; Yom Kippur is the contemporary Jewish holy day; compare Ash Wednesday). In this annual ritual, the high priest (here Aaron) enters the Holy of Holies and sacrifices a bull to secure atonement on behalf of himself and his sons, then a goat on behalf of the people as a whole. "He shall make atonement *for the sanctuary*, because of the impurity of the people of Israel, and because of their transgressions, all their sins" (v. 16, AT) . Then, in what appears to be a kind of repetition, Aaron places his hands on a *second* goat, thereby apparently transferring "all the iniquities of the people," and sends the goat out of the camp into the wilderness. Although the second goat provides the origin for our word *scapegoat*, the sacrifice of the first goat more appropriately fits with that word.[49] Now all of Israel is "clean before Yahweh" (16:30, AT).

In short, Leviticus offers not only a way righteousness may be followed, but also a way unrighteousness may be remedied. It holds before Israel the command, "You must be holy," but also the promise, "atonement shall be made for you" (16:30). The new way of righteousness now includes a way out of sin.

4. "THE LAND IS MINE"

(Read 18:1–6, 19–30.) If Israel is a "holy nation," it must also live in a holy land. While the expression "holy land" does not occur in Leviticus, the theology of holiness imbues its entire understanding of the land. The holiness of Canaan is prominent in the two companion chapters, 18 and 20, and especially in the framework texts, 18:2–5, 24–30;

---

48. Repentance (e.g., Deuteronomy 30) does not seem to involve a particular ritual; also confessions of sin, such as we see in the Psalms, may be involved (e.g., Psalm 51, especially vv. 2, 7, and 10). Deut 31:9–13 calls for a regular covenant reading and renewal every seven years, but it does not involve repentance and forgiveness.

49. The figure of Azazel is variously explained. Many see in it the vestige of a wilderness goat demon or satyr (cf. 17:7).

20:22–26. Since Israel is "separated" from the other peoples, Israel is not to live according to their customs, and particularly not the customs of the present inhabitants of the land of Canaan. The nature of those customs is spelled out explicitly in ch. 18, where the Canaanites are identified with various forms of sexual immorality, which, of course, is understood in terms of defilement. Here, as elsewhere, "Canaanite" is more of a pejorative stereotype than an historical description (cf. Gen 9:20–27). The offenses include various types of incest, but also child sacrifice and male homosexuality (on the latter, see Appendix 6). Now we learn that the land too may become defiled (vv. 24–30). Again the physical connotations of defilement are salient; the impurity of the inhabitants means that iniquity has infected the land itself, and the land must be purged. The result is literally physical revulsion—the land "vomits out" its inhabitants. Defilement is both poisonous and emetic. Thus Israel is warned to avoid those native customs that cause defilement, lest Israel too be vomited out of the land.

(Read 19:1–20, 32–37.) In ch. 19, we can see how holiness extends beyond personal matters into the entire socioeconomic life of the community, introduced by the verse we have already cited: "You shall be holy, for I, Yahweh your God am holy" (AT). Some of this chapter echoes the Ten Commandments: reverence for parents (v. 3), prohibitions against idols (v. 4), stealing, false testimony (vv. 10–11), and profaning God's name (v. 12; cf. Exod 20:1–18). And then there are some rather peculiar offenses, including fortune telling, hairstyles, and tattoos (vv. 16b–28). But several regulations reflect a broad economic policy. *Economy* means "household rule," and here we have some of *God's* household rules, all framed by divine self-identification—"I am Yahweh" (vv. 4, 37). Thus cheating in business by using false measuring devices is forbidden (vv. 35–36), a practice that apparently exploited the poor in particular (cf. Amos 8:4–6). Similarly, concern for hired help appears in the prohibition against withholding their wages at the end of the work day (v. 13b). Protection of people with disabilities governs v. 14, and the aged, v. 32. Surely one of the most arresting regulations concerns limitations on private property (vv. 9–10; 23:22). Farmers are not allowed to harvest all of their crops, but must leave some "for the poor and the alien," a kind of biblical "workfare." Israelites, who are sharecroppers on God's manor, must share their crop (see on 25:23 below). Indeed, imbedded within all of these regulations, obscure as some may seem, lies the Golden Rule: "you shall love your neighbor as yourself" (v. 18), a principle that is extended in v. 34 by demanding rights for aliens (non-Israelites) equal to full citizens, and such equality is rooted in the story of *Israel's* being an alien in Egypt (cf. v. 36).[50]

The inclusion of ch. 19 along with the previous chs. on defilement shows how crucial it is to read Leviticus as a book rather than a disconnected assemblage of rules. Holiness embraces what we tend to place in different categories—the ritual and the moral. Ethics—the rule of God's economy—includes both and, in fact, refuses to value one over the other. It is just as important to respect

50. References to resident aliens presupposes Israel's settlement in Canaan, rather than the wilderness setting.

the harmony of creation (e.g., abstaining from eating shrimp) as it is to love one's neighbor (e.g., not harvesting one's entire crop). Ecojustice is as important as social justice. As Houston says, "The dietary laws do not symbolize, but exemplify, justice and righteousness."[51] And everything together defines who God is: "I am Yahweh" (twelve times in ch. 19). God is the one who brought Israel out of Egypt, *and* the one who demands honest (or "right") business practices (vv. 35–36).[52] The scales on the counter also measure the holiness of the merchant.

Chs. 21–24 focus on the nature of the priesthood, offerings, the various annual festivals, and offer a few notes on tabernacle furnishings and the disturbing incident of the man executed for blasphemy.[53] Previous descriptions of the festivals appeared in Exodus,[54] and these "holy days" (the etymology for *holiday*)

flesh out what holiness means temporally, adding to what we know spatially. That is, just as the tabernacle marks off sacred space, so the various festivals (including the weekly Sabbath), mark off sacred time ("holy convocations," 23:2). Although these festivals are connected chronologically with the exodus story and thus history (e.g., 23:43), clearly the more fundamental connection is to nature, i.e. to agriculture and the cyclical time of the seasons. As with the eating of certain foods, celebrating these festivals is a way of maintaining harmony with the world as God's creation (cf. Gen 1:14; 2:3).[55]

(Read 25:1–12, 25–28.) The personification of the land that concluded ch. 18 reappears in the legislation for the sabbatical year and the year of jubilee in ch. 25, where God's peculiar economy appears most prominently.[56] The primary purpose of the former (every seven years) is not to provide rest for human beings, but rather for the land (v. 4). In this year there is to be no sowing of crops or even pruning of vines. Thus the land can "rest" from the work it has done in providing food for human beings, and it is thus protected from ruthless exploitation. As with the dietary laws, we must be careful not to interpret this instruction in purely practical terms, although it would clearly have some ecological benefit. In the first place, it is not clear to what extent the custom was practiced;[57] and in the second place, a fundamental theological issue is at stake. While we may detect some associations

---

51. Houston, "Theology of the Sacrifice," 161. This does not mean that contemporary readers must not eat shrimp, but it does mean that eating should not be unduly harmful to the created world (or "the environment"). See Appendix 5 on "Sacrifice and Slaughter."

52. The word for righteousness, honesty, integrity—*ṣedek*—appears three times in v. 36.

53. This incident is shocking to most readers, for whom blasphemy may be immoral but certainly not deserving of stoning. For the author, blaspheming "the Name" (vv. 11, 16, note capitalization in NRSV) is the most radical expression of defiance and thus defilement, a kind of linguistic violation of the Holy of Holies, and the radical punishment fits the crime. Otherwise, the life of the entire community is endangered. Christians who are uncomfortable with this story should remember that there is a saying of Jesus in which blasphemy against the Holy Spirit is condemned as an unforgivable "eternal sin" (Mark 3:28–30; cf. Luke 12:10; Acts 5:1–11).

54. Exod 23:14–19; 34:21–23; cf. Numbers 28–29; Deut 16:1–17.

55. Cf. Olson, *Numbers*, 172.

56. Cf. Exod 23:10–11.

57. See Bamberger in Plaut, *Torah*, 941, for positive evidence regarding the Second Temple period and the Common Era.

with relatively primitive understandings of the land in relation to divine powers of fertility in the soil, the literary context has suppressed such views. At the outset (vv. 1–2) the law is rooted in the narrative setting of a gift from Yahweh to Israel at Sinai. As with the people themselves, the sanctity of the land is not intrinsic but derives from the relationship rendered by this narrative. Just as the people represent God's new community on earth by conforming to the order of nature and the pattern of rest established by the creator,[58] so must the land be allowed its Sabbath to conform to this pattern as well.

The tripartite relationship of God, land, and people appears much more succinctly in v. 23: "for the land is mine; with me you are but aliens and tenants." This is perhaps the most remarkable statement of the manorial theology that governs Israel's relationship to God, especially when one realizes the meaning of the words "alien" and "tenant" (sometimes translated "sojourner"). As we have seen before, these terms refer not to permanent, native inhabitants, but to temporary residents. Ever since Abraham and Sarah, the Israelites have been resident aliens, with little more than a burial plot to call their own. Now in a startling reformulation of the pentateuchal theme, the text insists that Israel's status in the land will *always* be that of an alien! The point, of course, is that Israel does not possess the land as owner but as sharecropper. As the sovereign of the manor, Yahweh may evict Israel if Israel proves to be an undesirable tenant. This text thus represents the first

explicit statement of a conditional formulation of the land promise, one that becomes more prominent in ch. 26 and in the rest of the Pentateuch. As an alien, Israel does not possess the land as an inalienable right.

The statement of Israel's alien status in v. 23 serves as the motivation for the central commandment of the Jubilee year (every forty-nine years): since the land belongs to Yahweh alone (v. 23), it cannot be bought and sold like any other commodity; it is not private property.[59] On the other hand, particular plots of land are understood to belong to particular families (or at least extended families), and while that property, in a sense, may be leased, it belongs to that family forever, and at each Jubilee year they may reclaim it.[60] Presumably this ownership goes back to the original gift of the entire land of Canaan by Yahweh to Israel, which in v. 38 is portrayed as the purpose of Israel's release from Egyptian bondage. The land was to be parceled out by lot, with each tribe receiving an "inheritance," which, in turn, would be subdivided among the individual families within the tribe (cf. Numbers 34). The legislation of the Jubilee year thus intends to protect this gift of Yahweh to each family. As a gift of God, it is not to be commercialized, for this would deny its very character as gift. The

---

58. Gen 2:1–3; Exod 31:12–17; 35:1–3, and see the discussion at the end of the previous chapter.

59. Cf. above on 19:9–10; 23:22.

60. The indentured-servitude section (25:39–43) differs dramatically from its counterparts in Exod 21:2–6 and Deut 15:12–18, in that servants are released only in the Jubilee year, thus serving for fifty years (virtually a lifetime), rather than six. The concern in Leviticus is primarily preserving the family (from permanent servitude or from loss of property), not the individual. See Tigay, *Deuteronomy*, Excursus 16.

land as gift also suggests why the above contradiction is more apparent than real; the land of Canaan as a whole belongs to Yahweh alone and is Yahweh's to give (or retract), but individual segments of that land are given as property to individual tribes. Thus the individual tribes may be understood as landed tenants, even while the nation as a whole retains the tenuous status of resident alien. Radical as the Jubilee year may seem (indeed, utopian),[61] at least in theory it solves a problem that bedevils capitalist economies: "It ensures that there will be no gross inequality of wealth-holding."[62]

(Read 26:1–5, 14–16, 31–46.) The contingency of the people's relationship to the land becomes all the more radical when it appears in terms of blessing and curse. We have already seen indications that the sacerdotal view of the "holy nation" in Leviticus understands the sanctuary as the locus of blessing, mediated to the people by the priests. Thus at the climactic consecration of the sacrificial altar and the priests at the end of ch. 9, the blessing pronounced on the people by Aaron and Moses has a prominent role (vv. 22–23). However, seen in the larger context of the whole book of Leviticus, the sanctuary and priests are not an automatic or unconditional source of divine blessing; rather, that blessing—or its opposite, the curse—is determined by obedience or disobedience within the covenant relationship between Yahweh and the people. The elaboration of this contingency of blessing and curse, and thereby of the relationship of the people to the land, is spelled out graphically in ch. 26 (cf. Deuteronomy 27–28). Perhaps the most telling detail is the warning that if Israel repeatedly disobeys, Yahweh will no longer "smell your pleasing odors" of sacrifice (26:31), thus negating the efficacy of virtually all of Leviticus 1–16, presumably even the Day of Atonement—at least, apparently, but see below.

Ch. 26 would be a more fitting conclusion to the book than ch. 27 and perhaps was originally intended as such. In fact, the summary statement in 26:46 seems to include all of Exodus 19 through Leviticus, namely, the time that Israel spent at Sinai (cf. 27:34). It is true that Israel does not leave Sinai until Numbers 10, but, as we shall see in the next chapter, Numbers 1–10 really has a different focus than Leviticus (it is interested in "Israel on the march"), and thus is rightly separated from it. Moreover, since a list of blessings and curses traditionally concludes a treaty, ch. 26 fits here at the end of that time in which Yahweh first promulgated the statutes of the treaty with Israel. If the entire Sinai period is in view at the end of the book (27:34), then the legal process of covenant making has become the structure for the plot of the narrative. Story and Torah are one.

Ultimately, Leviticus directs the reader not only to the hoary past when Yahweh spoke to Moses from the tent of meeting at Mount Sinai, but also to the far distant future, beyond the occupation of the land, to a time when the promises of nationhood, land, and blessing all will have been both fulfilled and then destroyed by sin and the resultant

61. So Alter (*Five Books*, 656) who points out how rabbinic interpretations in effect nullified the Jubilee after the disappearance of tribal territory in postexilic Israel (655).

62. Douglas, *Leviticus as Literature*, 243; similarly Friedman, *Torah*, 402–3.

curse (26:27–39). Thus the text projects an Israel which waits in exile "beyond the Jordan," just as the Israel within the narrative has yet to reach the Jordan. Yet it also projects, even in that situation, a synchronic movement of human repentance and divine forgiveness that together point to a horizon of hope (26:40–45). This is the way Deuteronomy will end and thus the way the Torah will end. For even though the curse may come in all its fury, Yahweh will not break the covenant with the ancestors, which here includes both those of Genesis (v. 42) as well as the Exodus generation (v. 45). Yahweh will remain Israel's sovereign. This is who Yahweh *is*: "I am Yahweh" (26:45).

FOUR

Numbers

In the Wilderness

1. NUMBERS AS NARRATIVE

NUMBERS CONTAINS A BEWILDER-
ING variety of literary materials: on
the one hand, detailed regulations, lists,
and rules (most of chs. 1–10 and 26–36);
on the other hand, dramatic stories of
a woman miraculously turned into a
leper, an earthquake that swallows a surly
mob, a rod that produces almonds, and
a charismatic wizard with his talking
donkey (within chs. 11–25).[1] There are
texts that make contemporary readers
cringe: God kills over thirty thousand
people by plague (11:33; 14:37; 16:49;
25:9), dispatches poisonous snakes that
kill off yet more (21:6), orders the execution of a man who breaks the Sabbath
blue law (15:32–36), sanctions genocidal
holy war (21:1–3; 31:1–20), and imposes

a misogynistic trial by ordeal on women
(5:11–31). Yet the book contains one of
the most beautiful and popular benedic-
tions that has blessed innumerable worshipers through the ages (6:24–26).

In the present text narrative material is framed on either end by what we
might call legislative pronouncements.
However, as we have already seen in the
latter part of Exodus and in Leviticus,
such a distinction cannot be made without qualification, for there is also legislative material imbedded within chs. 11–25
(cf. chs. 15, 18, 19), and stories within the
otherwise nonnarrative texts (e.g., 9:1–8
and chs. 27, 32). Moreover, as William
Hallo notes, "the legislative portions of
Numbers are set in and directly derived
from the narrative context to an extent
found nowhere else."[2] In fact, materials

---

1. For a survey of interpretation and bibliography see Dozeman, *Numbers*, 22. A study that
emphasizes the final form of the text is Olson's
Death of the Old; more recently, see his commentary (*Numbers*).

2. Hallo in Plaut, *Torah*, 1019–20. On the
other hand, Dozeman (ibid., 12) sees the legislative framework in 1:1 and 36:13 as converting
the book more into "divine law" rather than
"an episode in a larger history." One confusing

that are not technically legislative—such as the census lists in Numbers 1 and 26—also are part of the warp and woof of the narrative, so much so that they provide structure and meaning to the whole book *as* a narrative.

That Numbers deserves to be a book may at first sight appear questionable. There are so many connections with Exodus and Leviticus that Numbers might seem to be little more than an addendum. All three books share similar sacerdotal regulations and concerns. Large portions of Exodus and Numbers, as well as the whole book of Leviticus, take place "in the wilderness of Sinai," and some of the controversy stories in Numbers appear déjà vu after Exodus.[3] These stories at some point were placed within two units (Exod 15:11—18:28; Num 11:1—20:13) to form a framework for the massive Sinai narrative that comes in between (Exodus 19—Numbers 10).

However, despite all of this overlapping, there is a salient transition at Num 10:11–13 where a redactor has given us a precise date for the day on which the people of Israel broke camp and started their journey away from "the wilderness of Sinai." This turning point in the narrative has influenced the whole book of Numbers; in fact, it clearly provided the theme around which a collection of often disparate literary traditions became a "book." That theme we may designate as

"the way to the land." The book of Numbers is essentially the story of what happened to the people of Israel in between the wilderness of Sinai and the land of Canaan. It is for this reason—that is, primarily on the basis of narrative structure—that we have three books (Exodus, Leviticus, and Numbers), and not two or even one.[4] The three books in their canonical shape have distinctively different orientations: Exodus concentrates on the liberation from Egypt and the constitution of the covenant and sacral community of Israel; Leviticus focuses on the detailed instructions for the sacral community, highlighted by the ordination of the priesthood and consecration of the sacrificial altar (chs. 8–9); and Numbers emphasizes those events encountered by Israel on the march from Sinai to Canaan. Whereas Leviticus focuses on the *order* of holiness for the sacral community, Numbers focuses on that community in terms of its *marching* orders.

Numbers thus deals with space and time that is in between—in between Egypt and Canaan, slavery and full citizenship, promise and fulfillment. The Hebrew title to the book (taken from 1:1) is most appropriate: "in the wilderness." To many contemporary people, wilderness may bring to mind snow-capped peaks, lush green meadows, crystal-clear lakes, and roaring streams, but that is not the connotation of wilderness in Numbers. The very barrenness of this land and the strange animals that inhabit it make it an object of dread. It is a "great and terrible wilderness, with fiery serpents and scorpions, and thirsty ground where there is no water" (Deut 8:15; cf. Num 21:6; 20:2).

---

chronological date appears in 7:1, which seems to go back to the tabernacle construction of Exodus 40.

3. Manna and quail, administrative assistants (Exodus 16; 18; Numbers 11), water from a rock (Exod 17:1–7; Num 20:1–13). However, what appear as reasonable complaints in Exodus now connote rebellion entailing divine judgment.

4 Cf. Clines, *Theme of the Pentateuch*, 87.

> ### Table 5: The Structure of Numbers
>
> 1:1–10:36 Marching orders and departure from Sinai
>
> 11:1–20:13 Rebellion in the camp
>
> > 11:1–14:45 Prophetic controversies and fate of the wilderness generation
> >
> > 15:1–41 Legislative interlude
> >
> > 16:1–20:13 Priestly controversies and fate of Moses and Aaron
>
> 20:14–25:18 Passage through the nations
>
> 26:1–36:13 The inheritors of the land

In short, it is "a land through which no one can pass" (Jer. 2:6). Yet it is precisely this land through which Israel now must pass on the way to Canaan. It is no wonder, therefore, that the departure from Sinai is fraught with a sense of danger, and that numerous passages betray anxiety over the provision of guidance for such a perilous journey. Perhaps it was to mark this anxiety that the redactors placed an account of the Passover celebration near the end of the opening unit (9:1–14), for that ritual dramatizes the people's liminal situation in between the past and the future.[5] The way to the land is not only a geographical journey, it is also a spiritual journey, and the wilderness is both a place and a condition. The rigors

of this journey will test the integrity and endurance of the people and their leaders such that the "wilderness journey" will become a companion metaphor for the "dark night of the soul."

Just as the redactors had good reason to constitute Numbers as a book, so they provided it with four sections, each with a distinctive integrity, yet each linked to the preceding to produce a narrative with impressive literary artistry and theological depth.

2. MUSTERING THE TROOPS (CHS. 1–10)

(Read 1:1–5, 44–54; 2:1–2, 17, 34; 6:22–27; 9:1–2, 15–23; 10:11–13, 29–36.[6]) The distinct focus of Numbers is evident in the opening verses. As in Leviticus, so in Numbers Yahweh speaks to Moses from

---

5. For the redactor, apparently the literary context of the passage is more important for its significance than chronology (cf. 9:1; 10:11; 1:1). For a bibliography and discussion on the liminal significance of the wilderness stories, see Cohn, *Shape of Sacred Space*, ch. 2. Note also that 9:13 ("not on a journey") presupposes settlement in the land of Canaan, as does the reference to resident aliens.

6. Much of the material not suggested here in chs. 3–8 deals with priestly matters of various kinds, some of which is comparable to parts of Leviticus (e.g., 5:1–4 on skin disease and bodily discharges).

the tent of meeting, but the concern is not with liturgical offerings. Yahweh's order is for a draft registration of "all in Israel who are able to go forth to war" (v. 3; cf. 20, 22, etc.). Whereas Exodus and Leviticus focused on Israel as a vassal and a congregation governed by the commanding and sanctifying presence of Yahweh, Numbers focuses on Israel as a military force marching behind Yahweh as vanguard. Israel is an army about to take the field.[7] The primary purpose of Numbers 1–9 is the mobilization of this fighting force for the departure from Sinai and the "order of march" (10:28) through the wilderness.

The result of the military census in ch. 1 is impressive—603,550 fighting men! While this may not have been the original figure, in the present text the number represents a formidable array.[8] In addition, when we add women and children, the number clearly suggests that Israel has indeed been fruitful and multiplied (Gen 1:28; cf. Exod 1:7; Deut 1:10–11). Israel begins the march to Canaan as a people blessed and an invincible army.

Of course the sacral dimension of this army is not lost in Numbers—if anything, it is accentuated. The tribe of the Levites is singled out as the custodian of all the appurtenances of the tabernacle (1:47–54; cf. chs. 3–4; 8). The entire camp of the people is to be in the form of a concentric circle, with the tabernacle in the center, then the Levites around it, and then each of the other tribes (in order of prominence), with all tents facing inward toward the tabernacle. The inner circle of the Levites provides a protective barrier to prevent any improper encroachment on the sanctuary, and even they are not allowed to touch or even look at the furnishings directly.[9] Consequently, when camp is broken, those tribes on the east of the camp will depart first, then those on the south, followed by the Levites bearing the tabernacle, the tribes on the west, and finally those on the north. The camp and order of march reflect the centrality of the divine presence, a theological picture distinct from the older sources in which the tent or tabernacle is outside the camp (e.g., Exod 33:7; Num 11:16, 26; 12:4). Moreover, as with the laws of holiness in Leviticus, the "perfect ordering of the people around God's dwelling place is a realization of the created order in history."[10]

Just as Numbers emphasizes the tabernacle as the center of a military

---

7. This bellicose image assumes that Israel eventually conquered the land of Canaan by military force. Historians suggest that this picture is certainly exaggerated, and that the actual settlement of those known as Israel also involved peaceful assimilation or a kind of internal revolution. For various models of the settlement in Canaan, see Mann, *Book of the Former Prophets*, 24.

8. It appears that the number originally was 6,000; the word formerly thought to mean "hundred" probably means "platoon." Cf. Hallo and Plaut in *Torah*, 1019, 1034–35. On the other hand, I would agree with Harrelson ("Guidance in the Wilderness," 28) that the authors were aware of the incredibility of the figure but used it for irony (with respect to the spy story in chs. 13–14)—"A fighting force of more than 600,000 men has been entirely cowed by the report of ten scouts."

9. Cf. 8:19. In ch. 4, where the Kohathites are a subdivision of the Levites, only Aaron and sons (the priests) are allowed to touch the ark and other holy furnishings, and they must cover them before the Kohathites take over the transportation (note especially vv. 15 and 20).

10. Fretheim, *Creation, Fall, and Flood*, 26.

camp, so it focuses on the divine presence as military escort. The cloud and fire that led Israel through the sea and defeated the Egyptians will now lead Israel through the wilderness: "It was always so: the cloud covered [the tabernacle] by day, and the appearance of fire by night. Whenever the cloud lifted from over the tent, then the Israelites would set out; and in the place where the cloud settled down, there the Israelites would camp" (9:16–17).[11]

Although much of the material in chs. 1–10 may not make for exciting reading, the redactors have constructed the unit to drive toward a dramatic moment—the departure of Yahweh's army from Sinai:

> In the second year, in the second month, on the twentieth day of the month,[12] the cloud lifted from over the tabernacle of the covenant. Then the Israelites set out by stages from the wilderness of Sinai; and the cloud settled down in the wilderness of Paran. They set out for the first time at the command of Yahweh by Moses. (10:11–13, AT)

For the author, this moment was as exciting as the launching of the lunar spacecraft was for many Americans. After all, what is being "launched" from Sinai is, in effect, the new model of human community before God.

The manifestation of Yahweh's presence that began with the burning bush (Exodus 3), that wrought victory at the sea (Exod 13:21—14:31), that confronted the people at the sacred mountain (Exodus 19–34), that encamped in the tabernacle among the people (Exodus 40), and that sanctified the worshiping community (Leviticus 8–9) now has stirred once again. The Levites—who carry the tabernacle on the march—are consecrated in 8:5–26, followed by the Passover service. Then the cloud lifts up over the tabernacle and moves off in the direction of Canaan. If there had been any question that Yahweh belonged only to "the mountain of God,"[13] it is now negated: Yahweh will be with Israel as protector and guide.

Such is the picture of Israel that we gain in the first unit of Numbers: the holy nation is now the army of Yahweh, hundreds of thousands strong, marching rank on rank, led by the cloud of the Holy Warrior who overthrew Pharaoh and all his host. It is a community completely ordered by the divine will and responsive to its human leadership, for it begins its march "at the command of Yahweh by Moses" (10:13). What enemy could possibly defeat such a mighty force? How could such an army fail? We cannot help but approach the second unit of Numbers with such questions in mind.

---

11. There is some inconsistency regarding the vanguard of this line of march in that various leaders are reported: the cloud, the ark, and Moses' father-in-law, Hobab (10:11, 29–36; alias Ruel, Exod 2:18; alias Jethro, Exod 3:1). Presumably, when the cloud ascends, the tabernacle is dismantled and the line of march forms behind the cloud. On the divine vanguard motif, see my *Divine Presence and Guidance*. Ch. 8 deals specifically with Numbers 1–10.

12. The chronology is somewhat confused by other notices involving flashbacks (7:1; 9:1), but the arrangement of the material in 7:1–10:10 emphasizes preparation for the departure in 10:11.

13. Cf. Exod 32:1, 34; 33:1–6. See my *Divine Presence and Guidance*, ch. 9.

3. MUTINY AND DOOM (11:1—20:13)

(Read 11:1–35; 12:1–26; 13:1–3, 17–33; 14:1–45; 16:1–17:13; 20:1–13.) The contrast between the mighty force described in chs. 1–10 and the sniveling, recalcitrant mob whom we now meet is overwhelming. Chapters 11–20 present a series of rebellions in the Israelite camp, each of which depicts the people in a very negative light, yet each of which might be understandable if not excusable. However, the context of chs. 1–10 foils any attempt to sympathize with the people. The discrepancy is perhaps nowhere greater than at the immediate juncture. In 10:36 we hear Moses' typical call to the divine warrior to return from victory over Israel's enemies: "Return, O Yahweh of the ten thousand thousands of Israel!" (AT).[14] Yet immediately in 11:1 we confront what is typical of the whole second unit: "Now the people complained in the hearing of Yahweh about their misfortune" (AT).

It is significant that this otherwise obscure incident (11:1–3) was placed here at the beginning of the second unit. It is an etiology of the place-name Taberah, but it does not tell us what "misfortune" is the subject of the people's complaint. Thus what internally is already puzzling becomes in context completely inexplicable, and the divine judgment that follows is not surprising. Finally, the intercessory role of Moses is also crucial; only his intervention prevents Yahweh's fiery wrath from enveloping the entire camp. This brief and enigmatic passage thus functions as a paradigm for the stories that follow: Israel complains, Moses intervenes, Yahweh's care is elicited, or righteous indignation curtailed.

After the introductory episode in 11:1–3, the narrative takes on a much more serious quality when the people question the adequacy of the gracious gifts of Yahweh and implicitly charge that Moses' mission has failed. They are tired of the manna, the "bread from heaven" that Yahweh had provided for their sustenance (see Exodus 16). Now they want a good steak—"Who will give us meat to eat?" (v. 4).[15] Moreover, the bland and spartan diet of the wilderness makes them long for the succulent vegetables and subtle flavors of Egyptian cuisine. Apparently those who are now free but poorly fed would rather be slaves and well fed—"Surely it was better for us in Egypt!" (v. 18). Fear of the wilderness and the understandable need for food have aroused a romantic idealization of the past. Fear has blinded them from seeing Yahweh's presence, resulting in an unthinking distortion of divine grace, and Moses rightly uncovers the theological dimensions of their complaint: "You have rejected Yahweh, who is among you . . . , saying 'Why did we come out of Egypt?'" (v. 20, AT). Nevertheless, the people's rebellion here is only implicit, only expressed in the form of a surly question, and thus at this stage it represents only a foreshadowing of what is to come (chs. 13–14).

If the people's querulous refusal to recognize divine grace has a familiar ring

---

14. Probably a reference to the "hosts" that the divine warrior commands, associated with the ark. Cf. 1 Sam 4:4; Ps 80:1; 99:1.

15. This story is thus at odds with Exod 16:12a and 13a and the implication in Leviticus that the people had ample livestock for sacrifices! Cf. Num 11:22; Exod 12:32.

to it (cf. already Exod 14:10–12), so too does the way it involves Moses' role as leader. This is the primary focus of the second narrative thread in ch. 11.[16] Moses' appeal to Yahweh in light of the people's complaint is as bold as it is pathetic (vv. 10–15). "Why have you treated your servant so badly? Why have I not found favor in your sight, that you lay the burden of all this people on me?" (cf. Exod 5:22–23). Moses' lament has a tone of desperation that we have not seen before, and he closes his appeal with the wish to die. There follows a reaffirmation of Moses' leadership as well as a demonstration of his magnanimity. The cloud appears at the tent of meeting,[17] and some of the prophetic spirit that resides with Moses is transferred to others (v. 25). Precisely how this is to help Moses out of his predicament is not made clear (especially given its ephemeral nature; see the end of v. 25), but what is clear is that Moses is the fountainhead of the prophetic spirit. Moreover, Moses affirms the freedom of that spirit to affect people not officially authorized (11:26–30). With the leadership question solved, the narrative then resolves the demand for meat, and with a vengeance (11:31–35). God has already predicted that those hungry for meat will soon grow even more tired of it than they are of manna (11:20); and, sure enough, the quail arrive in overabundance, form-ing a ring around the camp some three feet deep! Moreover, for those whose craving started the rebellion, the first bite of meat brings death (11:31–35).[18]

The questions surrounding divine presence and human leadership are hardly resolved in ch. 11, notwithstanding the quails and the great charismatic awakening. In ch. 12 questions of leadership reappear, again couched in the form of prophetic legitimacy. Here the challenge to Moses' leadership is more direct. While the role of Moses' wife in the incident (v. 1) remains ambiguous, the question posed by Miriam and Aaron is quite clear: "Has Yahweh indeed spoken only through Moses? Has he not spoken through us also?" (v. 2, AT). The issue concerns the authoritative media of revelation, the legitimate spokespersons of Yahweh—in short, an issue similar to that in ch. 11: the extent of the prophetic office. Indeed, elsewhere both Aaron and Miriam are identified as prophets (Exod 7:1; 15:20), and here their challenge could include the accusation that Moses' marriage to a foreigner is unorthodox (cf. Exod 34:11–16). But whereas in ch. 11 God distributed Moses' spirit to others, here God declares Moses' role as prophet to be unique.[19]

The story wastes little time in reaffirming Moses' authority. First, in a rare biographical comment, the narrator tells us that Moses was the most humble man on earth (a comment notoriously difficult

---

16. There seem to be two stories intertwined here, one of the provision of meat, another on the provision of assistants to Moses (on the latter, cf. Exodus 18).

17. Cf. 11:17, 25. In this tradition, the cloud (or glory) appears occasionally at critical moments at the tent door rather than hovering over the tabernacle permanently (so also 12:5, 10; 14:10; 16:19, 42; 20:6).

18. Verse 35 seems to refer only to those in v. 4a, who are distinguished as non-Israelite "riffraff" (cf. Alter, *Five Books*, 735).

19. Cf. Dozeman, *Numbers*, 108–9, who suggests that in both stories prophecy breaks traditional boundaries (inside/outside the camp, endogamy/exogamy).

to square with the Mosaic authorship of the Pentateuch!). Then Yahweh once again appears in the cloud at the tent of meeting and rebukes Miriam and Aaron (but punishes only Miriam!). Whereas Moses was the fountainhead of the prophetic spirit in chapter 11, here his authority goes beyond that of the prophet, for only Moses speaks with Yahweh "mouth to mouth" (an unusually bold metaphor), and only Moses is addressed by Yahweh as "my servant" (vv. 6–8; cf. 7:89). Moreover, while the emphasis in Yahweh's speech is on the "word" shared between them,[20] the end of the story also demonstrates Moses' authority when his intercession saves Miriam from permanent skin disease.[21]

One would think that these indications of Yahweh's presence among the people, and direct divine confirmations of Moses' leadership, would prevent any further complaining. But in chs. 13–14 the complaining escalates into full-scale revolt, and a crisis develops that can be compared only with the flood story (Gen 6:5–8) and the golden-calf incident (Exodus 32). "Now Yahweh said to Moses, 'Send men to spy out the land of Canaan, which I am giving to the Israelites'" (13:1–2, AT). Israel stands at a watershed that separates the past from the future, the wilderness from the land of promise. To look behind is to look through the beginnings of the march on the way, through all the preparations of the camp, through the epochal events at Sinai and in

Egypt, through three generations of the ancestors, all the way back to those words spoken to Abram at the very beginning of Israel's story: "Go from your land . . . to the land that I will show you" (Gen 12:3). Now, that charge and promise, whose fulfillment had at best been adumbrated to the ancestors, are about to be realized.

Chapter 13 thus presents us with what was to have been Israel's D-Day, yet it proves to be a day of infamy and defeat, a day that sealed the doom of the whole wilderness generation of Israel. The reason is not difficult to find; it is the same reason that stood behind the incident of the golden calf. Israel's greatest enemy was not the Canaanite force, not even the giants among them (13:32–33); Israel's greatest enemy was the enemy within— Israel's lack of trust. This threat from within does not emerge until the spies have returned with their report. There is no problem with the land itself, for "it flows with milk and honey," and they have brought an enormous cluster of grapes to demonstrate its fertility.[22] But the cities are heavily fortified, and the spies even saw the descendants of Anak—the legendary giants—there. The sudden dis-

---

20. The root *dabar* is used four times here for "word," "speak," and "speech." Cf. the visual dimension of Moses' uniqueness in Exod 33:21–23.

21. NRSV "leprosy," but see text note z and Leviticus 13.

22. Chs. 13–14 clearly combine at least two sources. It is possible to see two different reasons for the revolt: (1) a spy story involving fear of the military power of the Canaanites; and (2) a geographical survey involving a negative report about the value of the land itself (e.g., Dozeman, *Numbers*, 120–26, ascribing the second to P; cf. Campbell and O'Brien, *Sources of the Pentateuch*, 80–82, 153–55; Lohfink, *Theology of the Pentateuch*, 110–12; Levine, *Numbers 1–20*, 358). It is a tribute to the redactor that separating these sources at some points requires considerable ingenuity! In any case, both sources describe a wish to return to Egypt (14:2–3) and Yahweh's avowal to refuse entry to the current generation (14:23 and 26–30).

quiet in the camp is momentarily silenced by Caleb (one of the spies), who is certain of Israel's superior military capability. But the other spies quickly dispel Caleb's confidence; now the mighty army of Yahweh seems "like grasshoppers" in the face of the Canaanite force (13:33). This "bad report" triggers the usual complaint from the people, but this time their utter panic drives them into outright mutiny: "Let us choose a captain, and go back to Egypt!" (14:4).

As in the account of the golden calf in Exodus 32, so in this instance the seriousness of Israel's disobedience leads to the threat of total destruction. Yahweh threatens to annihilate the people and begin again with Moses. In both cases Moses' intercession prevents Yahweh's wrath from running its full course. Nevertheless, here Yahweh appears to execute the punishment postponed in Exodus 32:34.[23] Israel as a nation will survive, but the entire wilderness generation will die outside of the land of promise (except for Joshua and Caleb, and, presumably at this point, Moses and Aaron). Perhaps the punishment in Numbers 14 is also much more severe than in Exodus 32 not only because here we have the crescendo of repeated rebellions, but also because here there is an attempt to reverse completely Yahweh's earlier act of liberation. In Exodus 32 the Israelites may commit idolatry, but at least they want gods to lead them on their way; now they want to *reverse* that way by electing a captain to lead them back to Egypt. Accordingly,

a measure-for-measure punishment dominates the section in 14:26–35. Those who complained that they would die in the wilderness will die in the wilderness, yet their children—whom they thought would die—will live and enter the land;[24] the spy mission that took forty days will have its counterpart in a new wilderness wandering of forty years. Throughout the section the redactor hammers out a stark contrast between death in the wilderness and life in the land.

Once the wilderness generation has brought about its own doom, one would think that the spy story would have run its course, but there is yet another incident that adds a note of irony. When the people are informed of their fate, they suddenly become as courageous as they had before been cowardly. Now they think that a confession of sin will turn them into conquerors (14:40). Moses warns them that precisely what they unjustifiably feared was the case before, is the case now: "Yahweh is not among you . . . Yahweh will not be with you" (vv. 42–43, AT). Nevertheless, the people set out on a campaign into the land, unaccompanied by Moses (their legitimate human leader) or the ark (the representation of divine presence; cf. 10:35). The result is a decisive defeat. In this final act of foolishness, the people justify the sentence Yahweh had already declared; theirs is not to be the generation of the land. What they persistently and stupidly described as divine purpose has now become the result of human irresponsibility: Yahweh has brought them

---

23. There Yahweh had promised to send his angel before the people to Canaan, but also had warned that, at some time in the future, punishment would be invoked for the sin of the calf.

24. Thus, although God does not clear "the guilty," God also does *not* visit "the iniquity of the parents upon the children," counter to 14:18.

out to die in the wilderness (Exod 14:11; 16:3; 17:3; Num 14:2).

To summarize, in their present shape chs. 11–14 resume a thematic tension that began as early as Exodus 3. In almost all cases, the immediate question has to do with the people's refusal to recognize Moses as their legitimate leader. Due to the mixture of traditions, the focus shifts from the relationship between Moses' authority and the prophetic office (ch. 12) to Moses' abilities as a field commander (ch. 14). Correlated with this challenge to Moses' authority, and indeed inseparable from it, is the Israelites' increasingly bitter and ultimately irrational refusal to recognize Yahweh's saving presence among them. Here the very identity of Yahweh as defined by the preceding narrative ("I am Yahweh your God, who brought you out of the land of Egypt,") is radically distorted. In fact, at the very moment of potential fulfillment of the promise of the land, the people throw that promise into question: "Why does Yahweh bring us into this land, to fall by the sword?" Thus the denouement of this episode (v. 11: "How long will they not trust in me?") stands in stark contrast to that in Exodus 1–14, where the people finally "trusted in Yahweh, and in Moses his servant" (14:31, AT). Moreover, within the context of Numbers 1–14, chs. 11–14 betray an additional irony. It is the people who set out on the way to the land "at the command of Yahweh by Moses" (10:13) who in the end "transgress the command of Yahweh" (14:41). It is the invincible force of "ten thousand thousands," led by the ark and Yahweh of hosts (10:35–36) who in the end see themselves "as grasshoppers" and are abandoned by

the ark and Yahweh and defeated by their enemy (14:44–45). Such is the wilderness generation, the generation who must die outside the promised land.

(Read 16:1–17:12; 18:1, 7; 19:1–3, 9–13; 20:1–13.) It is tempting to suggest that ch. 15 was placed in its present position simply to allow the reader to recover from the devastating conclusion of chs. 11–14. At first it is difficult to discern any other reason for the insertion of this collection of regulations. But the contextual significance of the chapter is striking: immediately after the wilderness generation is doomed to die *outside* the land, Yahweh gives instructions to Moses for life *in* the land (vv. 2, 18).[25] With chs. 16–20 the redactor has shaped material of unusually complex and diverse origins into a narrative unit with impressive integrity.[26] To do so he seized on recurrent catchwords in order to enhance a thematic homogeneity, not only in chs. 16 and 17, but to the end of the unit at 20:13. While some of these catchwords are more obvious in Hebrew, most are apparent even in English:

"to draw near" (*qarab*), 16:5, 9, 10, 40; 17:13; 18:3, 4, 7, 22

"holy" or "sanctify" (*qadash*), 16:3, 5, 7, 37, 38; 18:9, 10, 32; 20:12, 13

"to choose" (*bahar*), 16:5, 7; 17:5

"to die/put to death" (*mwt*), 16:13, 29, 41, 48; 17:10, 13; 18:3, 7, 22, 32; 19:11, 13, 14, 16, 18; 20:1, 3, 4

25. The peculiarity of ch. 15 is accentuated by the redactional slip in vv. 22–23, where the editor refers to Moses in the third person in the context of a direct address by Yahweh to Moses

26. For more details, see my study, "Holiness and Death."

Taken together, these catchwords produce the central theme of the unit: holiness and death.

The narrative that begins at 16:1 combines two originally separate incidents relating generally to Moses' leadership.[27] In yet another incredibly ironic accusation (cf. 14:3), Dathan and Abiram suggest that Moses has led them "*out* of a land flowing with milk and honey," in order to kill them in the wilderness. At the same time, they accuse him of pretending to be "prince over us" without authority (16:13, AT). Such complaints, of course, resume the controversy that can be traced all the way back into the book of Exodus (cf. Exod 2:14). This narrative thread is resolved when Moses as wonder worker bids God to open the earth and swallow the rebels alive (16:28–34).[28] However, when we look at the unit 16:1—20:13 as a whole, we find that the controversy has taken on a peculiar configuration. General complaints about Moses' leadership have been subsumed under the more specific topic of Moses's— and Aaron's— relationship to the priesthood, and, eventually, their relationship to the holy God of Israel.

The unit gets underway with the initial challenge to Moses and Aaron, led by Korah: "You have gone too far! For all the congregation are holy, every one of them, and Yahweh is among them; why then do you exalt yourselves above the assembly of Yahweh?" (16:3, AT). More specifically, the chief rebel, Korah, is a Kohathite, among those Levites charged with transporting the tabernacle furnishings, but expressly forbidden to touch the uncovered furnishings themselves, on pain of death (4:1–20).[29] Thus Korah and company apparently confuse the call for everyone to be holy (Exod 19:6; Lev 11:45; 19:2) with a denial of the *gradations* of holiness of the camp and personnel, especially their own limited status vis-à-vis the Aaronide priests. There are echoes of the "unholy fire" offered by Nadab and Abihu in Leviticus 10. To this Moses responds that Yahweh "will show who is Yahweh's, and who is holy" (AT) by choosing the one who is to "come near" to Yahweh, referring to the one who is to have immediate access to the holy God of the sanctuary. Others may not so approach, and those who do so without divine authorization will die. Consequently, in the ensuing narrative (16:35), fire consumes the rebels, just as it did in Lev 10:1–2. Moreover, when the "whole congregation" defends the rebels and revolts, it takes Aaron's authorized offering of incense to prevent their complete destruction (16:41–50). The sacerdotal legitimacy of the Aaronide priests is then confirmed with the sprouting almond rods in ch. 17. In the face of such power, it is no wonder that the whole people fears death (17:12–13).

The narrative thread is maintained well into ch. 18, where the issue of the priestly authority of Moses and particularly of Aaron is finally resolved,

---

27. Although skillfully intertwined, one can detect separate stories, one about Korah and two hundred fifty rebels, the other about Dathan and Abiram.

28. Baden (*Composition*, 164–65) compares this wonder to that of the prophet Elijah in 1 Kgs 18:36–37 (fire from heaven), both stories confirming prophetic leadership.

29. Ibid, 161. Baden sees a story about priesthood combined with another about the "national prophetic leadership of Moses" (163).

both with respect to contentious groups (the Levites), as well as the whole people. The redactor has also linked the material in chs. 16–18 with the final incident in 20:1–13 by using the key word "perish" in a strategic retrospective reference (root *gwʾ* 17:12–13 and 20:3). We may thus construe the whole unit as a narrative expression of an issue central to the preceding book of Leviticus: the ultimate danger inherent in the presence of holiness—the presence of Yahweh—among the people. Holiness cannot bear what is unholy, either by defilement, or by unauthorized encroachment on the divine sphere (cf. again Exod 19:12–13; Lev 10:1–7). In such a confrontation, either the holy one must withdraw, or the unholy must die, and it is clearly the latter alternative that is taken in chs. 16–18.

It is also this intrinsic connection between holiness and death that provides the reason behind the insertion of ch. 19 into its present position. Since the priests emerge in chs. 16–18 as the inner circle who prevent the congregation from encroaching on the realm of the holy and thus from inviting death, what better place to insert legislation in which the priests are the manufacturers of a substance that counteracts the effects of contact with the dead? This is particularly the case if we understand death as the ultimate form of defilement and thus the extreme opposite of holiness.[30]

We may now turn to the final incident in the unit, the story about water from the rock in 20:1–13. Apparently Moses and Aaron are faulted here because they disobey Yahweh's order to speak to the rock, and angrily strike it instead

with the rod. The absence of any judgment here over the people's complaint about water only highlights the leaders' anger and failure.[31] While to us the fault may seem trivial, and the punishment unnecessarily severe, from the author's perspective, Moses is entrusted with the responsibility of a unique mediation of the divine will, and thus his failure to execute Yahweh's command to the letter meets with a correspondingly serious punishment. But our purpose is to focus on the way the sentence handed down to Moses and Aaron provides a surprising conclusion to the unit 11:1—20:13.

Looked at internally, one can easily see that 16:1—20:13 ends in a bitter irony, one that is directly connected to the interplay of holiness and death. The challenge of the rebels to Moses and Aaron ("everyone is holy—why do you exalt yourselves?") at first leads to the death of the rebels and to the exaltation of the leaders (along with their party, the priests). But in the end, the controversies lead to the humiliation of Moses and Aaron, and to a divine verdict of death outside the land of promise, a verdict that is seen as necessary because the holy ones (16:5, 7) failed to sanctify *the* Holy One (20:12–13).

The irony is all the more salient when we compare this unit with the preceding one (11:1—14:45; ch. 15). As already indicated there, the initial unit turns, not on controversies involving leadership and priesthood, but on disputes regarding leadership and prophecy (cf. 11:26–30 and especially 12:6–8). Seen in this light,

30. Mann, "Holiness and Death," n. 30.

31. Cf. Dozeman, *Numbers*, 160b. Olson (*Numbers*, 126–27) presents no less than five possible interpretations of Moses' question in v. 10.

the complaint in 12:2 is the precise thematic counterpart to that in 16:3: "Has Yahweh indeed spoken only through Moses? Has he not spoken through us also?" (12:2, AT); "all the congregation are holy . . . , why then do you exalt yourselves above the assembly of Yahweh?" (16:3, AT). Moreover, whereas the initial unit issues in a verdict of death outside the land for the whole people (except their children, of course, and Caleb and Joshua; chs. 13–14), the final unit issues in a verdict of death outside the land for the leaders. The contrast is highlighted by a glance at the motif of "trust." Whereas in the first unit it is Moses who is "entrusted with all [Yahweh's] house" (12:7, AT), and it is the people who refuse to trust in Yahweh (14:11), in the final unit it is Moses and Aaron who do not trust in Yahweh (20:12). Thus the theme of holiness and death, which constitutes a distinct thread uniting 16:1—20:13, ultimately links this unit with the preceding in the form of an ironic contrast.

The story of water from the rock has a dramatic effect on the portrait of Moses in the subsequent pentateuchal narrative. All the endeavors of Moses that follow—and those endeavors will be considerable— will be achieved in the face of and in spite of the inevitable doom that hangs over his life. Despite all he will do to deliver the Israel of the future to the banks of the Jordan River, he himself will not be allowed to cross over into the land of promise. Thus, for the figure of Moses, the rest of the pentateuchal narrative is marked by a note of tragedy. "The tragic hero has normally had an extraordinary, often a nearly divine, destiny almost

within his grasp,"[32] only to prove himself all too fallible a human being. So it is with Moses, at least in this story (see below on Deut 3:26).

4. BLESSING TURNED TO CURSE (20:14—25:18)

(Read 21:1–9, 33–35.) A redactor has sewn together the third unit in the book in part by the use of itinerary notices (e.g., 20:22; 21:4, etc.), which take Israel all the way from Kadesh in the "Wilderness of Zin," to "the plains of Moab beyond the Jordan at Jericho" (20:1; 22:1).[33] Thus, at the end of this unit, and indeed, throughout the remainder of the Pentateuch, Israel stands at the door to the promised land, on the east bank of the Jordan river (cf. Num 36:13; Deut 1:1–5).

The unit opens with a subsection (20:14—21:35) that seems to suggest that Israel is really "on the way." Despite being repulsed by the Edomites, and despite yet another questioning of their mission (the incident of the serpents), the section as a whole presents at last an Israel victorious over her foes, the king of Arad, and Sihon and Og. Thus Israel's military confrontations in the passage through the peoples are relatively successful: no defeats, one retreat, and three victories. Yet Israel has at best gained a foothold on territory that will have an ambiguous status vis-à-vis

32. Frye, *Anatomy of Criticism*, 210.

33. The itinerary notices begin at 1:1, then resume at 11:3, 34–35; 12:16, etc. While some interpreters use the itinerary notices as indicators of the structure of the book, the notices do not function that way in the final redaction. See Olson, *Death of the Old*, 34–35.

Canaan.[34] The promised land still lies ahead, and the rest of the unit presents two quite different kinds of confrontations between Israel and the peoples: one in which—unbeknownst to Israel—the enemy attempts to employ a powerful secret weapon (a sorcerer's curse), and one in which the same enemy appears as a religious subversive, inviting Israel to an ecumenical festival of worship. As we shall see, it is the second confrontation that proves to be the more insidious, and spells disaster.

(Read chs. 22–24.) Initially, the story of Balaam in chs. 22–24 presents a confrontation between the power of Yahweh and the power of a pagan diviner, one who theoretically could discern the will of the gods, especially through the examination of the organs of sacrificial animals. Balaam is represented as a diviner of considerable reputation and ability,[35] for he is brought all the way from his homeland in Mesopotamia, and Balak, his Moabite employer, expresses his confidence in Balaam by saying, "Whomever you bless is blessed, and whomever you curse is cursed" (22:6). Thus the pentateuchal theme of blessing and curse is posed quite sharply, and in the form of a challenge to the blessing that the priests have been charged to pronounce over Israel (6:22–27). This challenge is not unprecedented, for Balak reminds us of the Pharaoh when he fears that Israel is "too mighty for me" (22:6; cf. Exod 1:9–10),

and the employment of a diviner recalls the magicians of Pharaoh's court. Moreover, as in Exodus, the outcome of the plot is predetermined; there will be no contest because, in the very first words he utters, Balaam avers that he will do and say what Yahweh tells him![36] What a striking coincidence: here is the pagan sorcerer, brought by the enemy, Moab, to curse Israel, and the sorcerer declares at the outset that he follows the orders of the *God* of Israel. It would be somewhat like asking a diplomatic ambassador to help plan the attack on his or her own country. Moreover, in his first consultation with God Balaam is told explicitly, "You shall not curse the people, for they are blessed" (22:12). With this, the plot of the story is hardly disclosed before its outcome is decided. The deck is stacked in Israel's favor. The one whom Yahweh has blessed cannot be cursed—at least, not without Yahweh's approval.

There are other indications that Balaam steps to the beat of a different drummer. While his reputation seems to be that of a diviner, and he orders the customary sacrifices (22:40; 23:1, 29), his decisions are not based on such ritual procedures but on direct communication with Yahweh (cf. 23:1–7). In fact, it seems to be part of the redactor's purpose to emphasize Balaam's status as a spokesperson—indeed, a prophet—of Yahweh! Thus in the end any pretense of the use of omens is abandoned, and Balaam,

34. See ch. 32 and Josh 22:7–34.

35. A similar figure with this name appears in texts from the area of Moab from the eighth century BCE. For references see Dozeman, *Numbers*, 178. In other biblical traditions, Balaam is called the "son of Beor" and executed as an enemy (31:8; Josh 13:22).

36. See 22:8, 19, 38. Cf. Exod 3:19–20; 7:1–5. There is an inconsistency in the story in that at first God orders Balaam to go, then is angry with him for doing so, then orders him to resume his journey (22:20, 22, 35). The entire fable (22:22–35), with its humorous critique, could be an insertion.

overwhelmed by the Spirit of God, delivers oracles of what he has seen and heard in a direct, visionary encounter (24:1–4).

The way the character of Balaam changes from pagan sorcerer to charismatic prophet of Yahweh suggests that the story does have a movement, even if the outcome of the plot is predetermined. After Balaam's initial encounter with Yahweh, the reader is relieved of the necessity to maintain the question, will Israel be blessed or cursed? and is increasingly prompted to raise a different set of questions: what is the nature of the blessing that is Israel's, and what is to happen to Moab? These two questions, of course, are inextricably intertwined. Moving through the four oracles there is a gradual development from the possibility of a curse placed on Israel by the enemy to the likelihood of a blessing on Israel to the confirmation of a blessing on Israel and a curse on the enemy (which also includes Edom, 24:18). From a self-confident employer of an internationally famous sorcerer, Balak becomes a compromising and ultimately impotent pawn in a cosmic game, forced to stand by outraged and helpless as his hireling turns the curse upon him and his own people. Thus Balak is at first shocked by the implicit blessing upon Israel (23:11), then, after the second oracle, he makes a desperate attempt at least to keep Balaam neutral—"If indeed you do not curse them, at least do not bless them" (23:25; AT). But his plea goes unheeded, and, as I have implied, the third oracle becomes even more explicit—"Blessed be every one who blesses you, and cursed be every one who curses you" (24:9). With this, Balak becomes furious, and orders

Balaam to flee, only to hear him turn the curse explicitly against his own people, the Moabites (24:10–14).

Undoubtedly we are intended to read the Balaam story with a sense of humor. Here is a diviner who, at one point, is less capable of discerning the divine will than is his donkey. Here is a shrewd king whose lavish bribes and elaborate magical rites reveal him to be a fool. But the meaning of the story is obviously not limited to such comic twists. The most obvious function of the story can be seen in the way it serves as an extended illustration and confirmation of the blessing originally placed on Abraham and Sarah, a blessing that again involves political sovereignty over Moab, Edom (traditionally the descendants of Lot and Isaac respectively), and other peoples. Here we have a clear resolution to the question that has appeared a number of times in the pentateuchal narrative: what is to happen to the offshoots of the Abrahamic line? Edom (Num 20:14–21) and Moab (Numbers 22–24) have both proved to be inimical to Israel, the people blessed by Yahweh, and thus have brought upon themselves the curse (cf. especially 24:15–19).[37] Their refusal to seek their own blessing through the blessing placed on Abraham (Gen 12:3) also stands in ironic contrast to the attitude of Balaam, who echoes the ancestral blessing and wishes it upon himself: "Who can count the dust of Jacob, or number the dust-cloud of Israel? Let me die the death of

---

37. Deuteronomy presents a different story, in that God forbids Moses from attacking either Edom or Moab, much less taking their land (Deut 2:1–13). Friedman (*Torah*, 502) points out that in the Balak story Israel has made no aggressive intentions against Moab.

the upright, and let my end be like his!" (Num 23:10; cf. Gen 13:16; 28:14).

A second function of the Balaam story is perhaps less obvious, namely, it illustrates once again that the blessing on Israel is completely derived from unmerited grace. Here the meaning of the story lies in its immediate literary context, especially its juxtaposition with ch. 25, and will involve us again with the pentateuchal theme of the problem of Israel's responsibility. Indeed, this aspect of the Balaam story provides the major focus for the entire unit, 20:14—25:18.

Perhaps the perspective that will best illuminate the contextual meaning of the Balaam story is that provided by the narrator at the moment when Balak and Balaam first join forces: "On the next day Balak took Balaam and brought him up to the Heights of Baal, and from there he saw the nearest of the people [of Israel]" (22:41, AT). Picture, for a moment, this scene, portrayed with the barest of details. Here is the Moabite king and his hired sorcerer, standing on a high ridge named for the pagan god Baal, looking down on the encampment of Israel, which is so vast that only a portion is visible. What is most interesting about this scene (and about the entire story that follows) is that only the two characters—and we, the readers—know it is happening. Israel knows nothing. Nestled in their camp in the valley, apparently safe and secure from all danger, the people are not aware that a drama is being played out on the heights above, a drama whose outcome will destine them to either blessing or curse, life or death. In fact, even once the drama has run its course, and Balaam and Balak return to their respective homes, Israel is not informed of what has happened. The people are blessed without even knowing the danger of the curse.

The irony of the Balaam story, and indeed of Israel's stay "in the plains of Moab" as a whole, thus turns on the contrast between the blessing Yahweh has pronounced upon Israel without the people's knowledge, and the curse the people bring down upon themselves. When God's work is done, Israel's is begun (ch. 25). When Yahweh was confronted with the Moabites, Yahweh turned their curse into a blessing on the victim, and a curse on the culprit. When the Israelite people are confronted with the Moabites, they turn their own blessing into a curse.

(Read 25:1–3, 9.) The story is composite[38] but focuses on the apostasy described in the opening lines: "While Israel was staying at Shittim [the place of their encampment in the plains of Moab] the people began to have sexual relations with the women of Moab. These invited the people to the sacrifices of their gods, and the people ate and bowed down to their gods. Thus Israel yoked itself to the

38. There are two stories interwoven here: one about Moabite women (25:1–5) and the other about a Midianite woman (vv. 6–15), fused by vv. 16–18. The second praises Eleazar, the grandson of Aaron, for his ruthless (indeed grisly) zeal, and probably over against the passivity of Moses (v. 6), who, after all, was married to a Midianite and advised by her father (10:29; cf. 2:15–22, ch. 18, etc.)! Despite the conflation (and confusion), most references elsewhere focus on the first story and the apostasy to the "Baal of Peor" and the punishment by plague (31:16; Deut 4:3–4; Josh 22:17; Hos 9:10). The Midianite part has a gruesome sequel in ch. 31 (based in part on the implication of Midianite complicity with Moab in 22:4, 7). For a much more positive story about a Moabite woman, see the book of Ruth!

Baal of Peor." Here the Israelite men succumb to the pandering of the Moabite women, and the illicit sexual relations lead to *religious* infidelity—worshiping "the Baal [Lord] of Peor." Once again there is an outrageous breach of covenant (often celebrated with ritual eating, Exod 24:11; Gen 31:54). What was to have been Israel's passage *through* the peoples has become Israel's immersion *in* the peoples. Thus the explicit warning of the covenant law regarding mixing with the native population has been disregarded: "Take care not to make a covenant with the inhabitants of the land . . . [when] someone among them will *invite* you, and you will *eat* of the *sacrifice* . . . and their *daughters* . . . will make your sons also *prostitute* themselves to their gods" (Exod 34:12, 15–16).[39] The holy nation has become defiled by participation in pagan "abominations" (cf. Leviticus 18). Indeed, it is possible that direct defilement of the tabernacle is involved in the second story, if that is the referent for "the tent" (v. 8).[40] As a consequence, "the an-

ger of Yahweh was kindled against Israel" (25:3, AT), and the result is the death of twenty-four thousand by plague (v. 9).[41] Indeed, as becomes clear in ch. 26, that spells the end of the wilderness generation: those who will not enter the land. But in the wider narrative context, death by plague also involves an irony. In terms of physical disease, plague is the direct opposite of the blessing that God has pronounced over Israel (6:22–27), and death is the opposite of well-being (*šalom*). In other words, plague is the physical form of Yahweh's curse (cf. Lev 26:21; Deut 28:58–62; 29:26–28). Thus the juxtaposition of the Balaam story with that of Baal Peor is drawn even more sharply. Unknowingly redeemed from the curse of the Moabites that would have brought defeat and death, Israel mixes with the Moabites (the text bluntly calls it fornication, 25:1) and brings on the curse of the covenant. Such is the bitter end of Israel's passage through the peoples. The greatest threat in that passage is not the armies of the peoples, but rather their religion and culture.

From the incident of the golden calf at the foot of Mt. Sinai to the incident of Baal Peor at the door to the promised land, the story of Israel as the covenant people is the story of repeated breach of covenant, a wanton, reckless,

39. The word for "have sexual relations" here is the same as "prostitute themselves" in Num 25:1. Note the parallels to the italicized words in Num 25:1–2; cf. also Exod. 20:3; 23:24; and the militant warning in Deuteronomy 7. Prostitution often serves as a metaphor for religious apostasy (cf. "infidelity"). Levine (*Numbers* 21–36, 258) argues that no sexual relations are involved here at all. Meyers (*Discovering Eve*, 70–71) argues that the preservation of virgins in 31:18 points to a need for exogamy to maintain population growth.

40. Any reading is complicated by the word (*qubbah*), which is unique to this passage. Friedman (*Torah*, 513–14) suggests that it refers to "the inside of the Tabernacle," and thus that the offense involved is not simply miscegenation but that the couple has entered the sacred space forbidden to anyone but priests, and then used that space for sex, compounding the defilement

(Lev 15:18; cf. Amos 2:6–8)! It is a ritual offense, however barbaric the punishment may seem to us. This violation also explains the reason for the plague in v. 9 (cf. 8:19). For a different view, see Levine (previous note).

41. Two other punishments ordered by God and Moses seem to go unexecuted (vv. 4–5). On the other hand, Dozeman (*Numbers*, 198–99) suggests that Moses punishes only the guilty (25:5), thus following God's similar decision with the spy incident (14:20–25).

and ultimately disastrous invocation of Yahweh's curse, in defiance of the blessing originally pronounced on Abraham and held out to the covenant people as the possibility of their future. It is for this reason that the rest of the pentateuchal narrative—from Numbers 26 to the end of Deuteronomy—will portray the people of Israel as if frozen in space and time, encamped "in the plains of Moab by the Jordan at Jericho" (36:13). It is this Israel of the broken covenant who must now be reassessed, recommissioned for the task of entering the land and, above all, instructed in how to go into the land that Yahweh swore to their ancestors.

5. THE INHERITORS OF THE LAND (CHS. 26–36)

(Read 26:1–3a, 63–66; 36:13.) The final literary unit in Numbers is dominated by rather arcane matters having to do with sacerdotal and civil legislation, but it is clear from numerous references to the preceding units that the redactors were self-consciously adding to an ongoing narrative, and not simply compiling lists. The primary concern of this material involves the danger Israel's past behavior poses for the possession of the land by the next generation.

This concern is immediately evident in the redaction of the census list in ch. 26. Originally, the list probably began with v. 4b: "The Israelites, who came out of the land of Egypt, were . . ." To this superscription the redactor added vv. 1–4a, creating some literary awkwardness. The purpose of this editing is clearly to tie the taking of the census to the immediately preceding incident of Baal Peor and the

plague (25:9; 26:1). What this already implies is made even more explicit at the end of the census, with vv. 63–65: "Among these there was not one of those enrolled by Moses and Aaron the priest, who had enrolled the Israelites in the wilderness of Sinai" (v. 64). In effect, this serves as a corrective to v. 4b. The census is not of those "who came out of the land of Egypt," but rather of the new generation who has reached the age of military service (twenty years; v. 2). Moreover, the focus here is not on military conscription but on tribal boundaries within the land (26:51–56).[42] Thus an originally independent census has been altered to fit the narrative context; it is a new census that is to be understood as the counterpart to that taken in Numbers 1 (note especially 1:3).

The reason for the alteration in ch. 26, of course, was also provided by narrative necessity. All of the exodus generation had died, in fulfillment of Yahweh's punishment for the mutiny at Kadesh (chs. 13–14, especially 14:29; cf. 26:65). Only the new generation can be the inheritors of the land (26:53); only a new commander (Joshua) can lead them *into* the land (27:12–23). This is the major justification for our determination of the final unit of the book as chs. 26–36. Both this unit and chs. 1–25 begin with a military census, but the latter leads ultimately to the death of the entire wilderness generation, whereas chs. 26–36 create a completely new literary horizon. The one focuses on the past, and how Israel's sin led to disaster; the other focuses on the future, and how renewed obedience to

42. Olson, *Numbers*, 163; Alter, *Five Books*, 821.

Yahweh can lead to the fulfillment of the promise. In short, the one represents the grim reality of Yahweh's curse; the other offers the possibility of Yahweh's blessing.[43]

This relationship between the past as warning and the future as possibility—and both with reference to the promise of land—dominates the redaction of chs. 26–36. Here, perhaps more than anywhere else in the Pentateuch, the redactors go beyond their role as narrators and become commentators as well; that is, they speak directly to the reader, and offer a theological interpretation of the events within the narrative. Thus in 26:63–65 the redactors explain why there was a new census, and in 26:9b–11 the redactor not only inserts a narrative summary of the sin of Dathan, Abiram, and Korah, but also steps outside the narrative mode and directly admonishes the reader that the story serves as a pedagogical sign (v. 10b). The NRSV appropriately translates the word for "sign" as "warning." The sin of the past has become a warning for the future.[44]

The sin of the wilderness generation and its legacy for the future is not limited to the corporate inheritors of the land but also extends to the individual leaders, Moses and Aaron. One of the clear indications of redaction as we near the end of the pentateuchal narrative is the way time

is being stretched, that time in which Israel encamps "in the plains of Moab," looking over to the promised land. The most poignant effect of this stretching of time can be seen in the fate of Moses. In 27:12–14 and again in 31:1–2, the reader receives the clear impression that Moses' death outside the land is imminent. In the former passage, Moses is reminded by Yahweh of his breach of faith (Num 20:1–13), and in the latter the reader is led to expect Moses' death at the end of the chapter, after revenge has been taken on the Midianites. And yet, Moses' death does not occur there; in fact, it does not occur until the very end of the Pentateuch, in Deuteronomy 34.

The reason that the apparently imminent death of Moses has been prolonged in the pentateuchal redaction is twofold. First, a successor (Joshua) had to be appointed for Moses, just as there had been one (Eleazar) for Aaron (for the latter, cf. 20:23–29). But this actually takes place already in 27:15–23.[45] Thus the major reason for the prolongation of Moses' death has to do with the preparation of the people as a whole—the new generation—as the inheritors of the land. This is the reason Moses' death could not come at the end of Numbers 31, or even at the end of the book. Even aside from the admonitory passages discussed above, most of chs. 26–36 has to do with instructions for how to live in the land of the promise: tribal allotments (ch. 26); rules of inheritance of the land, especially for females (27:1–11; ch. 36); a festival calendar for the land (chs. 28–29); the

---

43. Olson has developed this reading most fully, as indicated in the title of his book *The Death of the Old and the Birth of the New: The Framework of the Book of Numbers and the Pentateuch.* He traces numerous parallels between the two parts of the book suggesting a deliberate editorial structuring (see the convenient summary list in his *Numbers,* 5–6).

44. Cf. 16:40, where the same incident is described as a "reminder." Note also 32:7–15.

45. Note the variant tradition in Deut 31:14–15, 23, which now appears to confirm Joshua's appointment.

boundaries of the land (ch. 34); Levitical cities and cities of sanctuary in the land (ch. 35). Given the way Israel's past history has been over and over again a history of the broken covenant, and the way the continued breaking of covenant led Israel to the brink of destruction, here "in the plains of Moab" it is absolutely crucial that the new Israel be instructed as to the way that lies ahead. That way is not simply geographical—the way across the Jordan River, into the land of Canaan. That way also is and always has been theological—the way of Torah. Thus the time Israel spends "beyond the Jordan" is, without exaggeration, the most critical time in the pentateuchal narrative. It is truly an hour of decision, in which Israel stands between promise and fulfillment, between blessing and curse, between the wilderness and the new land. Within the pentateuchal narrative there was only one individual who possessed the stature and authority to instruct Israel in this way of Torah, the one through whom the Torah had been given to Israel in the first place, the one who knew Yahweh "face-to-face," the one who talked with Yahweh "mouth to mouth," the prophet without equal—Moses, "the servant of Yahweh."

FIVE

Deuteronomy

Beyond the Jordan

1. DEUTERONOMY AS NARRATIVE

SOMETIMES ONE CAN UNDERSTAND a great deal about people by knowing what stories out of their past they remember, which stories they choose to retell, and the way they go about the retelling. In the opening chapters of Deuteronomy, the authors have repeated several stories from Israel's past that they obviously consider crucial to Israel's identity. That they have retold these stories in a separate book rather than editing the original versions in their place, suggests the self-consciousness with which the authors were working as interpreters.[1] As a result, Deuteronomy is both the conclusion of

the pentateuchal narrative and the definitive commentary on that part of the narrative that precedes it. As Mosaic torah, Deuteronomy is "the hermeneutical key to the Pentateuch as a whole."[2]

As the epilogue to the pentateuchal narrative, Deuteronomy presents us once again with a rather strange notion of what narrative is, for there is very little action in the book. Moses delivers several lengthy speeches, his leadership of the people is transmitted to Joshua, and then Moses dies. The dearth of events is reflected by the reticence of the redactors to speak in the narrative mode. In fact, the redactors *as narrators* come to the fore in only a few passages in the beginning and near the end (note esp. 1:1–5; 4:41—5:1a; frequently in chs. 27–34).[3] Even here the

---

1. Of course, every pentateuchal redactor was an interpreter, but this is more overtly the case with the Deuteronomic editors. For example, P apparently embellished a J narrative in the manna story (Exodus 16) and the spy story (Numbers 13—14), whereas the Deuteronomist chose a fresh retelling of these stories mixed with commentary (chs. 8 and 1 respectively). See Levinson, *Deuteronomy*, 146–47.

2. McBride, "Introduction and Annotations to Deuteronomy," 266.

3. Other examples within the introductory chapters are usually understood as explanatory glosses (2:10–12, 20–23; 3:9, 11, 13b–14; 10:6–7, [8], 9).

content of the narration (with the notable exception of ch. 34) is little more than a reminder of who is speaking: "Then Moses said" (e.g., 29:2; 31:1, 7, 9–10). *Indirectly* through Moses' comments or from a rare comment by the narrator we learn that a few other things happen: the people pledge their allegiance to Yahweh (26:16–19), and the Levites receive a copy of the covenant law (31:9). But these little scenes are momentary at best, and some of them do not even occur "on stage." If one were to dramatize the book, one would need really only one actor—the rest of the cast would be walk-ons. Indeed, even God would enjoy only a bit part, appearing just a few times at the end. The show really belongs to Moses alone.

In dramatic terms, therefore, Deuteronomy is essentially a soliloquy, just as most of Leviticus was a soliloquy, but here it is a man and not God who is talking. The difference is striking. Whereas Leviticus opens with Yahweh speaking to Moses from the tent of meeting, and the phrase "Yahweh said to Moses" occurs repeatedly throughout, Deuteronomy opens with Moses speaking to Israel and, with few exceptions (all at the end), Yahweh never speaks.[4] The reason for this remarkable shift from divine to human speech lies in the Deuteronomic emphasis on Moses' office established at Mt. Sinai (or Horeb, in Deuteronomic parlance). In chs. 4–5 the Deuteronomist repeats the story from Exodus 19–20, adding an interpretation of the significance of the events. In ch. 4 the emphasis falls on v. 12: "Yahweh spoke to you out of the midst of the fire; you heard the sound of words, but saw no form; there was only a voice" (AT). The rest of the chapter is a passionate homily on this verse. Since the people saw no form in Yahweh's self-revelation, they should make no form, no physical representation (the second commandment, cf. 5:8–10). The only way to re-present the reality of Yahweh is to recite Yahweh's words (and deeds); the only appropriate response to this reality is obedience to the words.

In the context of the wider pentateuchal narrative the emphasis on Yahweh's words rather than on a visible form takes on a greater significance. From the moment Israel left Egypt until the end of the book of Deuteronomy (31:15), Yahweh's guidance has been marked by the visible phenomena of cloud and fire. But those phenomena will cease when Israel crosses the Jordan. Then there will be only the ark of the covenant, the ark that contains Yahweh's words.[5] As much of Deuteronomy will insist, the future of Israel—either for good or for ill—will be determined by the extent to which they follow the guidance (torah) of these words. Thus the traditional Hebrew title for the book is highly appropriate: "these are the words" (1:1).

Chapter 5 describes the revelation of the Decalogue and, just as important,

---

4. Lev 1:1–2a, as frequently. Cf. Num 1:1; 2:1; 3:5, 11, etc., predominantly in Numbers 1–10; 26–36. In Deuteronomy, there is no direct speech by God until ch. 31, then at the end of ch. 32 and in ch. 34. The only divine speeches of any length are 31:16–21 and 32:48–52. (Of course, Yahweh often speaks indirectly in the narration of Moses.)

5. The cloud makes another brief appearance at the consecration of Solomon's temple (1 Kgs 8:11), in a passage related to Exodus 40. On the torah of Moses as guidance see immediately Josh 1:7–8; cf. the role of the ark in the crossing of the Jordan in Joshua 3–4.

the legitimation of Moses' office. At the height of the theophany, the people draw back and ask Moses to be their mediator: "Go near, you yourself, and hear all that Yahweh our God will say; and speak to us all that Yahweh our God will speak to you; and we will hear and do it" (v. 27, AT). Again, the author repeats an incident from Exodus (20:18–19) but amplifies it, here with a divine speech in response (vv. 28–31). The divine affirmation of the people's election of Moses accentuates the authority he now bears, and thus authorizes the words of Moses that follow *in the rest of the book*. In fact, the "commandments, statutes, and ordinances" that Yahweh had earlier given to Moses on Mt. Sinai (v. 31), Moses is only now delivering to Israel (chs. 6–26).[6] Because Moses is the spokesperson for Yahweh, Moses' words are Yahweh's words, and the following speeches of Moses are fresh revelations of Yahweh. Subsequently, Moses' office is identified as that of the prophet, a mediator of God's will, unlike Canaanite "soothsayers and diviners" (18:14), and unlike pretenders who are fakes (18:15–22). The figure of the "prophet like Moses" (18:15) makes the office of the monarchy seem relatively subordinate (17:14–20), a role that will be confirmed in the Former Prophets, the books of Joshua through 2 Kings.[7]

So far we have concluded that Deuteronomy is essentially a series of speeches by Moses. In fact, the redactors have divided the book into four speeches.[8] Chapters 4 and 5 are placed at the juncture of the first and second speeches as conclusion and introduction respectively. Obviously the story of Yahweh's self-revelation at Horeb, of the gift of the covenant and the Decalogue, is of central importance to the authors. In fact, it is possible to construe the book more in terms of a legal document than a narrative. Thus the core (chs. 12–26) is a law code dealing with everything from the covenantal responsibility of the king to whether or not one may eat a buzzard. Moreover, the form of the book can be compared to the form of a political treaty, moving from historical prologue (chs. 1–5) to blessings and curses (chs. 27–28; see Appendix 3).[9] Similarly, the book may reflect the *liturgical* order of a covenant-making or renewing ceremony (cf. 29:10–15; 31:10–13).[10] In fact, since chs. 6–26 represent newly disclosed commandments of Yahweh, and since at the end of the pronouncement of these commandments the people accept them (26:16–19), we can understand Deuteronomy as the *completion* of a covenant-making process stretching back to the original events at Sinai. From this perspective, the best term to describe the content of the book is that of "consti-

6. Cf. Moran, "Deuteronomy," §§229e and Weinfeld, *Deuteronomy 1–11*, 241. Thus contradicting the tradition in Exodus 20–24 where Moses reported the various statutes and ordinances to the people (esp. 24:3).

7. Though later prophets clearly functioned in ways compatible with the office of Moses in Deuteronomy, the author of 34:10 presents Moses as imcomparable. The criterion for true prophecy in 18:22 is impractical, to say the least.

8. Moran, "Deuteronomy," 223c (4:44; 29:1; 33:1). For another division, see Plaut, *Torah*, 1289.

9. Including general commandments (chs. 6–11), specific stipulations (chs. 12–26), summons to witnesses (4:26; 30:19; 31:26, 28), deposit of the treaty document (31:24–26).

10. For the role of public recitation of the law, see the study of Weeks, *Reading Law*.

tution" or "polity," the latter combining both sacerdotal and civic connotations of government.[11] In this sense, Deuteronomy represents the polity of the realm of God, the order for the Great Society ruled by the Great Commandment (see below).

Still, the legal delineations do not sufficiently consider the framework of the book or the dominating presence of the figure of Moses. As much as Deuteronomy may be compared to Exodus 19–24, and may even be a completion of a process begun there, the redactors have set it apart as a distinct document: "the book is cast in the form of Moses' last will and testament."[12] More specifically, the book is the *story* of how Moses pronounced his last will and testament. In effect, Deuteronomy as a whole seems to be a combination of two traditional forms—the deathbed blessing and the charge. A clear precedent occurs in the portrayal of Jacob's deathbed pronouncements at the end of Genesis, marking a major transition in the Pentateuchal narrative.[13]

In Deuteronomy, however, the charge is not limited to the specific command regarding the deposit of the "book of the torah" (31:26, ṣivah), but in fact extends to all of chapters 1–33. This is indicated in part by the inordinate number of references to Moses' impending death, beginning with 1:37.[14] The Deuteronomist has a very different understanding of why

Moses was not allowed to enter Canaan from that given in Numbers 20 (the fault lies with the people, not with Moses),[15] but the effect of the repeated references to Moses' imminent death is to emphasize not so much *why* Moses may not enter as *that* he may not enter. Particularly in the opening chapters, the references impress upon Moses' audience that these are Moses' *final* words of instruction. When the people enter the land, they will no longer have Moses with them—they will have only his words. Just as Yahweh's words now replace his previous guidance in the forms of fire and cloud, so now the "book of the torah of Moses" takes the place of Moses (cf. Josh 1:1–8). Thus, overall, Deuteronomy as a book is the *narrative* of Moses' farewell address, the address that constitutes his last will and testament to the new generation of Israel, the people who wait "beyond the Jordan" for the fulfillment of the promise. On the one hand, ever since the failure of Adam and Eve, the Pentateuch has been a search for the genuinely righteous person, the human being who comes as close as humanly possible to representing the divine will. Moses is that person. Yet it is not Moses himself but Moses' words, his *torah*, that arrests Israel's attention and claims Israel's allegiance.

One way to construe the structure of the book is as follows:

Prologue	1:1—4:43
General Commandments	4:44—11:32

---

11. McBride, "Polity of the Covenant People."

12. McBride, "Yoke of the Kingdom," 288 and see n. 30 there. Cf. Knierim, "Composition," 359.

13. Gen 47:29—49:33; cf. 27:1; Joshua 23–24; 1 Kgs 2:1–4.

14. See 1:34–39; 3:23–28; 4:21–22; then near the end, 31:1–2, 14, 16. The Priestly tradition is maintained in 32:48–52.

15. See my previous study, "Theological Reflections on the Denial of Moses." For an extensive analysis of Deuteronomy from this perspective, see Olson, *Deuteronomy and the Death of Moses.*

We cannot, of course, discuss all the material in detail. Instead we shall focus on the way the redactors have used paradigmatic stories in conjunction with *torah* at key points within the first three units.

The introduction to the first address of Moses (1:1—4:43) provides the key for unlocking the combination of torah and narrative that pervades the entire book. In the opening verses, a redactor has set the scene of the book as Moses' testamentary address "beyond the Jordan, in the land of Moab," almost forty-one years after Israel left Egypt. On this occasion, the redactor says, "Moses undertook to expound this law [torah], saying, . . ." What is the torah Moses sets out to explain? It is not torah in the strict sense of "law." Moses is not expounding here the "commandments, statutes, and ordinances." Moses is retelling a portion of the preceding pentateuchal narrative (to begin with, the rebellion at Kadesh, Numbers 13–14). At the same time, Moses' narration is intricately laced with interpretation and commentary on the story's meaning for his present audience. He is not simply retelling, but also expounding the torah. Moses is both a skilled storyteller and a passionate preacher. As a result, the narration itself *is* torah, a form of instruction.[16]

Yet it is more than that. It is significant that the redactor uses the word *torah* and not some other word for teaching (e.g., *limmad*, as in 4:1, 5, etc.). In the context of what will unfold in Deuteronomy, the retelling of the story as instruction makes a demand of Moses' listeners, for narrative as torah cannot be understood apart from the covenantal context of Moses' testament. In fact, the basic purpose of his narration, as we shall see, is to lead up to the Great Commandment that Yahweh as the covenant sovereign places upon Israel, the covenant vassal.[17] Ultimately, the telling of the story demands that the audience either accept or reject this Great Commandment, and the covenant itself. Thus listening to the story cannot be (from the redactor's point of view) a passive act; it demands a response. One cannot listen to the story and simply conclude that it is interesting, or even that it is profound. After hearing the story, one must respond in either of two ways: because of this story, I accept the covenant; or, despite this story, I reject the covenant. Acceptance or rejection will finally determine whether one receives blessing or curse, hence the gravity of the response that is demanded. The significance of the narration in Deuteronomy is eviscerated if this demand for responsibility is ignored.

Moses' explanation of torah and its relationship to narrative (i.e., the

---

16. See Lohfink, "Darstellungskunst und Theologie," 105–34.

17. The expression "Great Commandment" is an English translation of the title of a major work by Lohfink: *Das Hauptgebot*.

pentateuchal narrative) is by no means limited to the first address, crucial as the interpretive key in 1:5 may be. In fact, all of chs. 1–11—which lead up to the specific covenant stipulations in chs. 12–26—are anchored in stories from Israel's past that serve as the motivation for Israel's future, and thus are "law" (torah; cf. 4:44).[18] The context stretches from creation (4:32) to Yahweh's oath to the ancestors (e.g., 4:31; 6:23) to the exodus (e.g., 6:21; 7:8) to Israel's present situation. Moreover, the placement of the stories is also significant. A story of rebellion opens and closes chs. 1–11 (Kadesh, ch. 1; and the golden calf, 9:6—10:11), while the encounter at Mt. Sinai stands in between the two subsections (chs. 4–5). In addition, the specific laws themselves are studded with references to previous stories, and the collection concludes with a liturgical recitation summarizing events from Genesis 12 up to that time in the future when Israel will have entered the land (ch. 26). Because these stories provide the stuff of Israel's identity, they are the torah for her future.

2. THE GREAT COMMANDMENT (CHS. 1–11)

(Read ch. 1; 2:8b–9, 16–10, 31–35; 3:23–29; 4:1–20, 44–45; 5:1–21; ch. 6; 7:1–11; ch. 8; 9:6–8; 10:12–22; 11:26–29; 12:1–7; 15:1–18.)

Ch. 1 opens with a grim warning, creating a sense of urgency that remains unrelieved throughout the rest of the book. The redactor wishes us to read Moses' testament in light of the story that brought Israel to the brink of destruction and condemned both the wilderness generation and Moses to die outside the promised land—the story of the rebellion at Kadesh (Numbers 13–14). At the outset, the author emphasizes how this story could have ended in the fulfillment of the promise to the ancestors: "See, I have set the land before you; go in and take possession of the land that I swore to your ancestors, to Abraham, to Isaac, and to Jacob, to give to them and to their descendants after them" (v. 8). Similarly, Moses affirms in vv. 10–11 that the blessing on Abraham has been fulfilled ("you are as numerous as the stars of heaven" [Gen 15:5]), and that an even greater blessing awaits Israel in the future. But by an artful rearrangement of the narrative sequence, the author also provides an interpretation of why the promise of land and blessing came to ruin: Moses reports the rebellion of the people immediately after the good report from the spies, and before any indication of the opposing military forces (vv. 25–28). The point is to illustrate a fatal lack of trust in the God who had led them through the wilderness (vv. 32–33) that results in an irrational fear and disastrous rejection of the ancestral promise and of Yahweh. In a shocking formulation, the author even has the people turn their redemption into damnation: "Because Yahweh hated us he has brought us out of the land of Egypt!" (AT). Thus the Deuteronomic retelling of the story has rightly been labeled as the representation of an "anti-exodus" and an "anti–holy war."[19]

---

18. Here (with v. 45) torah includes the "decrees" (i.e., the Ten Commandments) and the "statutes and ordinances" (chs. 12–26 [cf. the concluding formula in 26:16]).

19. Moran, "Deuteronomy," §226d.

The Deuteronomist has naturally retained that element of the story in which the people who came out of Egypt are doomed to die outside of the land. That, after all, is the major thrust of the message for the present generation, Moses' audience. The situation throughout Deuteronomy is thus comparable to that at the end of Numbers (chs. 26–36). The old generation has died (Deut 2:14–16), and the new generation stands in their place, full of hope but also confronting the same temptations to which their parents succumbed. Although the "you" whom Moses addresses would often seem to be the old generation (e.g., frequently in chs. 1–10), it is in fact the new; for they, along with every subsequent generation, are included with those who stood at Sinai and received the covenant (cf. 4:3; 5:3; 29:10–15). Israel has also stood at the door to the land before—as Moses' audience does now—and refused to go in, or tried to go in on their own terms (1:41–46). The rest of the book is Moses' final instruction on how to go into the land as responsible heirs of the promise. From here to the end, the subject of "when you go into the land" is always to be read in light of this harrowing story, and is thus a subject to which the Deuteronomist returns again and again with the utmost seriousness (e.g., 6:1, 3, 10; 7:1; 8:7, etc.).

Between the story of Kadesh and the story of Horeb, Moses recounts Israel's passage through the peoples—chs. 2–3 (cf. Num 20:14—25:18; ch. 32). Close comparison with the accounts in Numbers reveals some striking differences. The Deuteronomist has subjected his material to a systematic interpretation upholding Yahweh's beneficent attitude and promises to the extracovenantal ancestors of Abraham—the Ammonites, Moabites, and Edomites. They too possess a specific geographical territory as a divine gift (2:5, 9, 19). There are now, in effect, four promised lands, each of which is to remain inviolate, a fulfillment of the promise to Abraham that, in conjunction with the blessing pronounced upon him, at least these peoples also will receive blessing. The realm of Yahweh is not geographically limited to Israel's land, even though Israel may be the only covenant people of Yahweh. It is ultimately Yahweh who establishes the boundaries of all peoples, because all of humanity, and all of the earth, are Yahweh's (cf. Deut 32:8–9; Exod 19:5; cf. Ps 24:1). At the same time, there are those, such as Sihon and Og (2:24—3:11), who unknowingly seek a curse because of their hostility to the chosen people. They will be dispossessed of their lands. And there are those who now inhabit what is to be Israel's land. They too will be dispossessed, for reasons explained in ch. 7.[20]

After recounting his appeal to enter the land, and Yahweh's denial (3:23–28), Moses brings his audience full circle, back to that temporal *now* so fraught with theological urgency (3:29—4:1).The opening speech has taken us from Horeb to Kadesh to the east bank of the Jordan, and now to Horeb again (ch. 4). The second part of the prologue (4:44—11:32) also begins and ends with Horeb, and thus with an obvious irony; the story of covenant making opens the section (ch. 5), while the story of covenant breaking closes the section (9:7—10:11).

20. Cf. already in Exod 23:23–33; Lev 18:24–30; see further below and excursus 3.

Accordingly, the prologue as a whole begins with the disaster of Kadesh and ends with the golden calf—the covenant of Horeb stands in the center.

As we have seen, chs. 4 and 5 authorize Moses' words as a continuation of Yahweh's self-revelation. Thus, what immediately follows is of the utmost importance. All of chs. 1–5 have been a preparation for this revelation, and all that follows in the rest of the book can be understood as a development of this revelation.

After an exhortative introduction (6:1–3), Moses pronounces what is appropriately called the Great Commandment, the commandment which, above all others, stands at the theological center of his testament. It is the traditional Shema of Judaism (the Hebrew word means "hear," but *listen!* might be better): "Hear, O Israel! Our God is Yahweh, Yahweh alone! And love Yahweh your God with all your heart, with all your life, indeed with all your capacity!"[21] This commandment stands behind the "Greatest Commandment" of Jesus (Matt 22:34–40, etc.) and the central tenet of Islam.[22] In effect, the Shema is an extension of the first of the Ten Commandments (5:6–7). There are two primary foci: first, the confession that only Yahweh can be Israel's God (rather than that Yahweh is the only God); and second, that this confession carries with it the demand to love Yahweh (hence the continuation of the imperative mood in v. 5). "Love" here is in no sense sentimental; although it connotes endearment, it is also technical treaty language for loyalty. And that is precisely what the Great Commandment commands—undivided loyalty to Yahweh. This is the heart of the covenant, the bedrock of Israel's responsibility to Yahweh. The exclusivity of the demand is accentuated by the final phrase: "with all your heart, with all your life, indeed with all your capacity!" With climactic progression, the Shema emphasizes that the total person—and the total community—must pledge its allegiance to Yahweh, and to no other. The words of the Shema are of such central importance that they must be communicated constantly, day and night; bound on one's forehead; and written on every doorpost and city gate (vv. 6–9).

> "We maintain our preliminary concerns as if they were ultimate. And they keep us in their grasp if we try to free ourselves from them. Every concern is tyrannical and wants our whole heart and our whole mind and our whole strength. Every concern tries to become our ultimate concern, our god."[23]

---

21. The translation is McBride's, "Yoke of the Kingdom," 274, and "Introduction and Annotations," 279. For other possible readings, see Nelson, *Deuteronomy*, 89–90; Weinfeld, *Deuteronomy 1–11*, 337–38.

22. For Islam, "There is no god but God [Allah]." Cf. the rest of the Shema (heart, life, capacity) with the comment of Volf (*Allah*, 29, citing another book he has edited): this tenet "'reminds Muslims that their hearts, their individual souls and all the faculties and power of their souls . . . must be totally devoted and attached to God.'" He goes on to note how love of neighbor is combined with devotion to Allah.

23. Tillich, *New Being*, 157–58.

3. DEUTERONOMIC ORTHODOXY

Another traditional translation of the Shema says that "Yahweh is one."[24] Whether translated as "one" or "alone," the Hebrew word *'ehad* signifies an insistence on unity and uniformity that pervades the book. The phrase *e pluribus unum*—"from many, one"—that graces American currency provides an ideological parallel, especially when referring to a joining of separate states (originally colonies) within a federal unity (compare tribes and "all Israel"). For Deuteronomy, the emphasis clearly is on the *unum* and not the *pluribus*, the one and not the many. This means, not only that Yahweh is a single deity, but also that there is a singular way to *interpret* what Yahweh's sovereignty demands of Israel. There is a right way and a wrong way, what is good in God's eyes (12:25, 28) versus what is good in one's own eyes (12:8), and the authors leave no doubt that *their* way is the right way. In short, the word *alone* points to the claim of orthodoxy over against heterodoxy.[25]

The issue here is by no means limited to ancient Israel. Virtually every culture and political system has to find a balance within the tension between uniformity and diversity, community and individualism, national interests and local interests. Two systemic examples appear in communism and libertarianism.

Deuteronomic orthodoxy is the product of religious reformations accomplished by two kings: Hezekiah and Josiah. These reforms are reported in 2 Kgs 18:4–5 and 22:1—23:25 and especially in the latter, one can easily see the king enacting what is prescribed in Deuteronomy. Indeed, when one of Josiah's priests is renovating the temple, he discovers "the book of the law," which many scholars believe to be at least the core of Deuteronomy (2 Kgs 22:8). It is quite likely that much of Deuteronomy was written with the *intention* of instituting a reformation and imposing the authors' view of orthodoxy. Moreover, since the primary agent of the reforms was the king, Josiah, it is impossible to separate completely the political motives from the religious. In fact, the religious reform complemented Josiah's attempt to regain independence from the imperial power of Assyria, a revolutionary act that illustrates the political dimension of the Shema (absolute allegiance to Yahweh). The religious establishment centered in the temple helped establish the monarchy centered in the palace.[26] If the "law of Moses" is saying there is one way to believe, one way to worship, one way live, and that way happens to correspond to the *king's* way, then political power en-

24. See note n to the NRSV text. Some scholars suggest that the reference is to different manifestations of Yahweh at different shrines. Deities were often associated with local holy places. Note the story of the place Bethel ("House of God") in Genesis 28 and the title "God of Bethel" in Gen 31:13. Examples of such Yahwistic shrines may be "Yahweh in Hebron" (2 Sam 15:7) and "Yahweh at Gibeon" (2 Sam 21:6). Each local shrine could easily have its own interpretations of the nature of the deity. However, several scholars argue that this reading is conjectural and unwarranted (McBride, "Yoke of the Kingdom," 294–96; Tigay, *Deuteronomy*, 438–40).

25. For a thorough discussion see McBride, "Essence of Orthodoxy," and Miller, *Religion of Ancient Israel*, 46–62.

26. See Blenkinsopp, *Treasures*, 61–62.

joys an enormous endorsement. Josiah's campaign for a *national* revival benefited from the Deuteronomic *religious* revival. Of course, the reverse may be true, and indeed *was* in Israel's history: more often kings were deemed *heterodox* by the Deuteronomists. Ultimately, therefore, those who dictated (or interpreted) the law stood above those who ruled, which is why Deuteronomy requires the king to *read* the law every day, a far more limited role than King Josiah himself was willing to play.[27]

We can summarize Deuteronomic orthodoxy in the phrase *one God, one people, one land, and one sanctuary*. God and people are inseparable in covenant theology, as stated in the formulary "I will be your God and you shall be my people" (e.g., 26:17–18; 29:13; cf. Lev 26:12; Exod 6:7). That Yahweh *alone* is Israel's God means that Israel may worship no other gods, nor may Israel manufacture any kind of "idol" that might compete for devotion to Yahweh. In both regards, the Deuteronomic reformation was attempting to eliminate previous forms of piety for which other gods were quite acceptable and the use of sacerdotal objects was uncontroversial. The deities were primarily Baal and the female Asherah, and the objects included stylized wooden trees and stone pillars, both of which

Deuteronomy forbids (16:21).[28] Deuteronomic theology is thoroughly auditory and not visual, a limitation rooted in God's *speaking* the words of the covenant and not appearing in any visible form (ch. 4, especially vv. 15–18; 5:8–10).

Israel's status as the one people of Yahweh meant that Yahweh had chosen them "out of all the peoples" of the earth (10:14–16; cf. Exod 19:5–6; Deut 7:6). God's selection of Israel was not based on merit—on being powerful or lovable—but solely on God's grace—on being loved (over *against* Israel's stubbornness, 9:4–7; 7:7–8). Israel's responsibility as the elect was to live *apart* from the other native peoples and their deities as a "countercultural society."[29] This way of life appears, for example, in the dietary laws, which emphasize Israel's "holiness" (ch. 14; cf. Leviticus 11). Above all, Israel is forbidden to mimic the worship practices of the other Canaanite peoples, and prohibited from intermarrying with them (7:1–5; 12:29–31; 18:9–14). On the one hand, such exclusivity prevents any wishy-washy anything-goes spirituality, or any idolatry, in which competing centers of value vie for the place of God (contemporary secular examples would include success and consumerism).[30] Indeed, the banned Canaanite practices may have

27. Thus the king is a very different figure in Deuteronomy than in the Deuteronomistic historian's account of Josiah. The very limited "law of the king" (17:14–20) seems to exclude the major functions of a monarch common in the ancient Near East: commander-in-chief, chief justice, and ecclesiastical high priest. Here the king is little more than a scribe! See Levinson, *Deuteronomy*, 95–96, 138–43, 153. For other differences between Deuteronomy and the Josianic reform, see Nelson, *Deuteronomy*, 148–50.

28. See the NRSV text note. "Asherah" can be the name of a sacramental object or the name of the deity. Deuteronomy demands that all such "Canaanite" objects and shrines be demolished (7:1–6, 25). See Appendix 4.

29. Nelson, *Deuteronomy*, 94, who refers to the likely historical background of Assyrian culture in the 7th century (98–99).

30. I have discussed this more benign reading of 7:1–26 as "Keeping Apart from the Joneses" (*Deuteronomy*, 62–67).

included the horrific—child sacrifice (12:31; 18:10).[31] On the other hand, at its most virulent, this exclusive orthodoxy led to nothing short of divine authorization for genocide (7:2; 20:16–18; 2:34; 3:6).[32] One people living in its own land meant that other peoples could not live in that land.[33] Similarly, measures insuring "national security" internally have a chilling, even totalitarian dimension (13:1–18; 17:2–7).[34] For the authors such intolerance was required by the covenant (or "treaty") model, under which any relations with the peoples would lead to disloyalty to Yahweh, and thus to their own destruction, subject to the curses of the covenant (7:4, 26; 8:19–20; 28:15–68; see Appendix 3). The enduring strengths of Israel's covenant theology, of enormous positive influence on Western civilization, must not blind us to its dark side, which has had "savage results" throughout history.[35]

One people worshipping one God in one country has yet another focus in that there is to be only one sanctuary: "the place that Yahweh your God will choose out of all your tribes to put his name there, to tent it" (12:5, AT). There is a chosen place for the chosen people to worship.[36] Although the geographical scale and religious makeup is incomparable, imagine all the religious communities in the United States—all the churches, synagogues, mosques, and ashrams—being forced to close and all worshipers required periodically to attend the National Cathedral in Washington, DC. In

31. For discussion of the various interpretations of these verses, see Tigay, *Deuteronomy*, excursus 15.

32. See Appendix 3 for the covenant context. As appalling as such proscriptions are, they are fictional representations of what the authors *wished* had happened, not what actually happened. See Tigay, *Deuteronomy*, excursus 18; Weinfeld, *Deuteronomy* 1–11, 51–52, and *Promise of the Land*, ch. 4. Levinson (*Deuteronomy and Innovation*, 149) suggests that Deuteronomic orthodoxy stereotypes former orthodoxy as "foreign and odious" in order to replace it. For a discussion of how the biblical portrayal of the "conquest" of Canaan and its indigenous people figures in American history, see Hawk, "Truth About Conquest," especially 137–40.

33. As we have seen, other peoples had their own "promised land," notably Edom, Moab and Ammon (2:1–25), here because of their Abrahamic lineage. Similarly, such nations had their own deities; in the case of Moab, it was Chemosh (Num 21:29; Judg 11:24). But, for historical reasons, no Moabite or Ammonite was allowed in the "assembly of Yahweh" (23:3–4, AT).

34. Loyalty to the central authorities over against family and friends appears in a similar way in Assyrian vassal treaties. See Pritchard, *ANET*, 535, Numbers 6 (73) and 10 (108). However, the draconian strictures of ch. 13 might appear in a different light if viewed from the perspective of resistance to the occupying power of Assyria. One might compare how far people were willing to go in resisting occupation by Nazi Germany (including destroying those swastikas!).

35. The phrase is McBride's ("Essence of Orthodoxy," 134), and is set over against Deuteronomy's "theological acuity." For example, as he suggests elsewhere, "egalitarian justice is the crux of theocratic government . . . [and] the single most important contribution of Deuteronomic constitutionalism to our political heritage" ("Polity of the Covenant People," 28). See the section below on "a poor person's coat."

36. For a thorough discussion of the possible reasons behind the centralization, see Tigay, *Deuteronomy*, excursus 14, who concludes that all other sanctuaries were simply considered to be "inherently pagan" (464). Nelson (*Deuteronomy*, 147) suggests that no good reason is offered; it is "simply a fait accompli." For a comprehensive analysis of how Deuteronomy adapts customs and laws to centralization, see Levinson, *Deuteronomy and Innovation*.

contrast to the implications of an older law in which God may be worshiped in numerous places (Exod 20:24), in Deuteronomy there is only the one place. The Deuteronomic "name theology" attempts to affirm God's presence in the sanctuary without questioning God's transcendence ("in heaven"; cf. 26:15; 1 Kgs 8:27–30), employing the same root word *šakan*, "to tent, encamp," that we have seen used for the tabernacle (*miškan*), connoting mobility rather than permanence.[37] Thus Passover, which elsewhere is a household celebration, here must be observed at the central sanctuary, as must the other annual religious festivals (ch. 16; contrast Exod 12:1–7).[38] Similarly, unresolved judicial cases must be taken to the central place (17:8–9), and the ruling there is binding (17:10–13). In order to counteract inconveniences involving the slaughter of meat, now people may slaughter meat locally so that only *sacrificial* slaughter must be at the central place (12:15–27).[39] Similarly, agricultural tithes may by paid at the sanctuary in money instead of produce (14:22–26). Although the narrative setting of the book, before Israel's entrance into Canaan, does not allow naming the central sanctuary as the temple in Jerusalem, it is surely what the authors have in mind. Nevertheless,

Deuteronomy's portrayal of Israel's faith differs remarkably from that of the Jerusalem priesthood as represented in the book of Leviticus, with its preoccupation with ritual and defilement.[40]

Finally, one people worshiping one God in their own country at one sanctuary is the rule for Israel, the orthodox word, allowing for no exceptions or supplementation (4:2; 12:32; cf. 5:22b). Here the text approaches the status of canonical Scripture (remembering that *canon* comes from the Latin for "rule"). What better way to ensure that one's *interpretations* of law and tradition will remain authoritative than to have the stamp of divine approval, excluding all subsequent interpretations from canonical status?[41] On the other hand, Deuteronomy clearly includes reinterpretations of various traditions and laws,[42] and it affirms the necessity for and legitimacy of new interpretations to meet the need of subsequent generations (cf. 17:11).[43] An orthodox

---

37. As Friedman suggests (*Torah*, 605), the name is "almost a tangible entity." For the subtlety, see Nelson, *Deuteronomy*, 152–53.

38. Imagine American households being forbidden to celebrate Thanksgiving dinner in their homes and being required, instead, to have the meal at an officially designated site.

39. This apparently contradicts the position of Lev 17:3–4, where all slaughter must be sacrificial. See n. 36 in ch. 3, and Tigay, *Deuteronomy*, 461–62.

40. Exceptions include the dietary laws in ch. 14.

41. Cf. Nelson, *Deuteronomy*, 225, who refers to Deuteronomy's self-image as a "protocanonical book" (17:18). Just as cultural exclusivity poses dangers, so does canonicity, namely, the danger that words (instead of physical images) can, in effect, become idolatrous.

42. A good example is the law on indentured servitude. Compare Deuteronomy 15 with Exod 21:2–11; 22:25 (for details see Nelson, *Deuteronomy*, 197–98). For a thorough discussion of Deuteronomy's adaptations to older traditions see Levinson, *Deuteronomy*, with summaries on 20–22 and 144. As he points out (153) it is "a major irony of literary history" that the compilers of the Pentateuch incorporated Deuteronomy along with texts which it was attempting to supplant (e.g., the Covenant Code of Exodus 20–23).

43. See Tigay, *Deuteronomy*, xxvii, 43–44, 165. Such openness presents a tension with the

text thus authorizes an orthodox process whereby the meaning of the text is open to change.

4. TORAH AND NARRATIVE

Clearly, if the Shema in 6:4–5 is the Great Commandment and the heart of the covenant, it must also be the heart of torah—perhaps even the heart of *the* Torah. What, then, is the relationship between this, the greatest commandment, and the Torah as narrative? This question is answered as we come to the end of the chapter, where it is posed in a different form by a child: "What is the meaning of the testimonies and the statutes and the ordinances which Yahweh our God has commanded you?" (6:20, AT). In other words, what is the meaning of the Great Commandment, and, indeed, what is the meaning of torah? The child is asking for no less than the ground of all ethical behavior, the ethos of the community called Israel.

What response does Moses have the parent give? He does not provide a philosophical or systematic argument on the meaning of torah, or merely authoritarian custom—"Because Yahweh said so, it is enough to do it." Instead Moses suggests that the parent do what he himself has been doing all along in his testament; he suggests that the parent tell the child a story. Of course, it is not just any story, it is the story that provides Israel's communal identity, the story that begins, "We were Pharaoh's slaves in Egypt" (6:21; cf.

26:5–8). This is also the narrative that renders the identity of the one who is confessed, witnessed to, in the Shema. To say, "Yahweh is our God" and "We were Pharaoh's slaves in Egypt" is to state Israel's identity in exact correspondence to Yahweh's identity: "I am Yahweh your God, who brought you out of the land of Egypt, out of the house of slavery" (Deut 5:6 [AT]; Exod 20:2).

Nowhere is the relationship between torah and narrative put so succinctly. The connection between the narration (plus interpretation) in Deuteronomy 1–11 and the laws in chs. 12 and following suggests what is, without exaggeration, the most important aspect of the understanding of torah. Torah is not heteronomous, an imposition of divine will out of the blue, so to speak. Rather, as Paul Ricoeur puts it, torah is "connected to the founding events" in such a manner that "the legislative genre is in a way included in the narrative genre. And this in turn signifies that the memory of deliverance [from Egypt] qualifies the instruction in an intimate way."[44] The meaning of torah lies in the narrative itself, and the narrative (if one genuinely responds to it) leads to the responsibility of torah (v. 24). It is not primarily a responsibility to torah—this is the significant addition in v. 25—but to *Yahweh*, who is the ultimate subject of the narrative. It is this responsibility to Yahweh, manifested in obedience to the commandments, that Moses designates as "righteousness." To be righteous is to live out the implications of one's narrative identity ("We were Pharaoh's slaves in Egypt") in response to the one who is the primary agent of that narrative ("I am

insistence of sole authenticity against competing claims, as Tigay (339) emphasizes in his comment on the eulogistic exaltation of Moses' prophetic uniqueness (34:20–12).

44. Ricoeur, *Essays*, 82–83.

Yahweh your God, who brought you out of the land of Egypt"). The reciprocity of law and story is now transparent; obedience to law is rooted in the recital of and identification with a story, an identification that is vacuous without obedience to law.

The rest of the prologue is preoccupied with three future situations when the Israelites will be in the land and will be tempted to forget their narrative identity and abandon absolute allegiance to Yahweh. In each case, remembering the story is posed as the only means to avoid disloyalty and the resultant punishment (cf. 7:17–18; 8:17–18; 9:4, 7). In the first case, the Israelites will be tempted to forget their status as Yahweh's holy people and instead to fuse indistinguishably with Canaanite culture (7:1–11). If the motivation for cultural assimilation is, in part, fear of the Canaanites' military superiority, Israel must remember the story of Yahweh the Holy Warrior and his victory over the Egyptians (7:17–26).

In the second case (ch. 8), Israel is warned against the presumption of self-sufficiency, as if the land and all its rich blessings were a result of human achievement alone. Affluence is not inherently evil, but it is inherently dangerous. The way to avoid an attitude in which materialism replaces allegiance to Yahweh is to remember the story of the wilderness journey, and especially the provision of manna. Israel's greatest treasure is not gold and silver, but the memory of a time of poverty that demonstrated God's love and humankind's dependence.

"If our heartes shall turne away soe that wee will not obey, but shall be seduced and worship . . . other Gods, our pleasures, and profitts, and serve them; it is propounded unto us this day, wee shall surely perishe out of the good Land whither wee passe over this vast Sea to possess it."[45]

The third case is almost a reverse of the first: the Israelites are warned against the assumption that their imminent victory over the Canaanites will be a sign of their relative "righteousness" (9:4–5)—their integrity, virtue, or rectitude. In contrast, Moses calls them to remember the story of the golden calf that exemplifies their *un*righteousness "from the day you came out of the land of Egypt until you came to this place" (9:7). Thus, in terms of narrative referents, the prologue concludes with that story that brought Israel to the brink of destruction (9:8, 14, 19), just as it began with that story that described the doom of the entire wilderness generation. If the concluding story of the golden calf is not sufficiently negative reinforcement to instill obedience to the specific laws that follow, the larger context provides more, for Israel's narrow escape resulted only from Moses'

45. The concluding lines of John Winthrop's classic sermon, "A Modell of Christian Charity," delivered on board the ship *Arbella*, about to land in America in 1630 (quoted also in Appendix 4). Winthrop applies the covenant theology of Deuteronomy to the settlers' relationship with God in the New World. For the complete text (widely anthologized) see Bellah, *Habits of the Heart*, 22–27.

intervention with Yahweh, but when Moses has finished with his testament, Israel will have him no more. They will have only his words.

The transitional material in 10:12—11:32 reiterates the paramount call of the Shema (10:12–13) but also introduces a completely new aspect that will dominate much of chs. 12–25. The Great Commandment demanding the love of Yahweh also demands the love of other people; it has a horizontal as well as a vertical dimension. Israel is to love Yahweh because Yahweh first loved Israel (10:15), but Yahweh also loves the poor, the weak, and the defenseless (the widow, the orphan, and the resident alien ["sojourner"]); and therefore Israel is to love them too (10:18–19). The later Jewish, Christian, and Muslim correlations of the love of God and neighbor have their origin here. The heritage of this Golden Rule stands in stark contrast to the intolerance we have already noted (ch. 7). The transitional material intends to move us from the Great Commandment to the Great Society, for these two belong together just as, and for the same reason that, narrative and torah belong together.

6. MEMORY: A POOR PERSON'S COAT AND A BASKET OF FRUIT (CHS. 12–26)

(Read 24:10–22; 26:1–11, 16–18; 28:1–2, 15; 30:15–20; 31:14–15; ch. 34.)

We have seen that the transitional material introducing the legal corpus provides a sociological extension of the Great Commandment. Israel is commanded not only to love Yahweh, but also to love the widow, the orphan, and the resident alien (or "stranger").[46] Since aliens are non-Israelites, the command to love them stands in obvious tension with the command to destroy Canaanites elsewhere (e.g., 7:1–2; see above). The widow, orphan, and alien are often mentioned together because they constitute the clearest examples of those who were helpless in the ancient world. References to these people, as well as to others within Israelite society who are helpless (the poor, the hired servants), are concentrated in a series of laws in 24:10–22. Here we also find repeated what is crucial for our understanding of the commandment to "love the stranger" in 10:19—the motivation attached to the commandment: "for you were strangers in the land of Egypt." We have noted in passing a similar injunction in Exod 22:21. While other ancient Near Eastern law codes protected the widow and the orphan, only in ancient Israelite law was there legislation on behalf of the alien.[47] The reason has to do with the central core of Israel's narrative identity. What ch. 24 adds to the earlier motivation in Exodus is the specific command to remember: "remember that you were a slave in Egypt" (vv. 18, 22; cf. 5:15; 15:15).

46. The NRSV variously translates the word *ger* as "stranger" (10:18–19) and "resident alien" (24:17). Another traditional translation is "sojourner." The term refers to anyone who, for various reasons, would not enjoy the same rights and privileges as ordinary citizens. See the comparable ordinance in Lev 19:33–34, which, in effect, prohibits a distinction between alien and citizen.

47. Hallo in Plaut, *Torah*, 371. For ancient Near Eastern law codes, see Pritchard, *ANET*, section 2, especially the "Code of Hammurabi," 163–79.

> "Employers through the [American] South relied on debt to coerce . . . hundreds of thousands of black families [to be] tied to white land-owners by tenant farming and share cropping."[48]

There are many motivations for obedience to torah in Deuteronomy and elsewhere: sanctions, such as capital punishment (24:7); the promise of reward (22:7), often closely associated with divine blessing (15:6); the threat of a divine curse (chs. 27–28); requirements due to Israel's holiness (14:1–2); and appeals to humanitarian concern (24:6). But the basic motivation for obedience to torah is remembering the narrative that provides Israel's identity: "You were Pharaoh's slaves in Egypt." We have seen this to be the case in a more strictly theological dimension with the narrative that renders the meaning of torah and the Great Commandment in 6:20–25. Now we see it applied explicitly on the horizontal level.

The specific commandments to remember suggest that the narrative providing Israel's communal identity is also the bedrock for justice in the wider society. There is an inherently ethical dimension to remembering the story, and to the love of Yahweh that results from that memory. As Paul Tillich has written, "Justice is the structural form of love without which it would be sheer sentimentality."[49] Israel cannot genuinely love Yahweh without also loving the widow, the orphan, the alien, the poor, and the hired servant. The reason for the motivation is imbedded in the meaning of the narrative: because you were once aliens or slaves in Egypt, and were the beneficiaries of divine justice (redemption), therefore you must be agents of justice in society. The way this works out in specific circumstances can include not only proscriptions of injustice, but also prescriptions of the way in which the helpless are to be treated. A hired servant must be given his or her wages on the day they are earned (24:15); indentured servants must be released after six years, and sufficiently provisioned upon release to prevent recurrent dependence (15:12–18).[50] Israelites must leave part of their crops for the poor to glean (24:19–22); in making a loan to a widow, an Israelite may not demand her "garment" (the basic overcoat) in pawn (24:17); Israelites may not demand interest on any loans to fellow Israelites (23:19); and one law even suggests that the loan itself (i.e., the principal) is cancelled every seven years (15:1–2; imagine if this were applied to today's student loans!). However much we may emphasize the motivation for such laws, we must not ignore their substance: "From the topics and terms of the instructions we are able to derive an actual socioeconomic content for Israel's understanding of 'deliverance from

---

48. Pollard, *Slavery by Another Name*. Contrast the purpose of biblical laws, as Nelson puts it (*Deuteronomy*, 190): "to rob debt of its tyrannical power, to limit human misery, and to avoid a paralysis of economic life that would stunt the blessings of productivity."

49. Tillich, *Systematic Theology* 2:174.

50. Jer 34:8–22 records an incident when the wealthy of Jerusalem disobeyed such legislation, and God's verdict of judgment as a result.

bondage' or 'national liberation.'"[51] Obedience to these laws is as much an expression of Israel's identity as remembering the story—indeed, helping the helpless is the ethical form of memory.

> "Let His Honor the mayor hear the word of his servant: your servant was reaping in the field, and had finished; and I gathered in about a bushel before my rest. When I had finished reaping, there came Hashabiah the son of Shobai, and he took your servant's overcoat. And all of my fellows will witness on my behalf, they who reap with me in the heat of the sun, my fellows will witness on my behalf that truly I am free of guilt. Restore my overcoat. Do not leave me helpless."[52]
>
> "You shall give the pledge [of a poor person] back by sunset, so that your neighbor may sleep in the cloak and bless you." Deut 24:13

The connection between law and motivation is the connection between torah and narrative. That connection, and the way remembering the story impinges on every aspect of society having to do with justice, has been eloquently expressed by André Neher: "It is as though the law, in a desire to prevent the petrification of the Exodus and its relegation into past history, demanded from man when faced with his neighbor, that he put himself back in the situation when the breach was first made: to rediscover the experience of passing from degradation to dignity in all its freshness."[53] Being an alien is not simply an aspect of who Israel was; it is a permanent aspect of who Israel is (cf. Lev. 25:23). This is the horizontal dimension of torah and narrative; identification with the ancient story of oppression requires identification with the oppressed in any age. Genuine response to the story entails not only love of Yahweh but also active pursuit of human rights for all. If ever human beings are properly to attempt to be "like God" (Genesis 3–11) it is in this imitation of divine redemption.

"Justice, and only justice, you shall follow, that you may live and inherit the land which Yahweh your God gives you" (16:20; AT). In the chapters preceding the corpus of laws, we have seen that the inheritance of the land is conditional on a number of basic attitudes, all of which are part of a proper righteousness: trust, loyalty, gratitude, humility. While the laws in chs. 12–26 contain a great deal of other meanings that we have not pursued, one of the basic concerns is to demonstrate that inheritance of the land is also conditional on the maintenance of justice in society. "It will be righteousness for you" when the story is properly remembered and loyalty to Yahweh is maintained (6:20–25, AT). Just so, Israel will be "in the right" when a poor person is not denied a coat overnight (24:10–13). Just as worshipers are not to appear before God "empty-handed" (Deut 16:16), so they are

---

51. Gottwald, *Tribes of Yahweh,* 59.

52. Adapted from a seventh-century BCE ostracon (a shard of pottery with an inscription, the ancient medium for a memo); "A Letter from the Time of Josiah," translated by W. F. Albright (*ANET,* 568).

53. Neher, *Moses,* 97.

not to leave the disadvantaged "empty-handed" (15:13).

We turn now to the conclusion of the legal corpus in ch. 26. The final verses (16–19) represent the completion of the laws as well as the covenant agreement between Yahweh and Israel. The latter covenant-making process is extended by the ceremony at Shechem (ch. 27), blessings and curses (ch. 28), final covenant instructions (chs. 29–30), and deposit of the covenant document (ch. 31). Then comes Moses' "song" in ch. 32, his formal blessing of the tribes in ch. 33, and his death in ch. 34.

The position of 26:1–15 is thus pivotal, coming at the end of the treaty stipulations and leading into the declaration of covenant agreements. The two ceremonies described here have to do with the agricultural produce of the land. We shall focus on the firstfruits ceremony in vv. 1–11. The passage as a whole is provided with a framework that focuses the reader's attention on the land as Yahweh's gift to Israel. The passage opens with a temporal clause—"When you have come into the land that Yahweh your God is about to give you" (AT)—and closes with a suggested invocation of God—"Look down from your holy habitation, from heaven, and bless your people Israel and the ground that you have given us, as you swore to our ancestors—a land flowing with milk and honey" (v. 15). Moreover, five times in vv. 1–15 the passage emphasizes that the land is Yahweh's gift (*natan*), and two times refers to the "ground" ('*adamah*), i.e. arable soil.

The central focus on the land is matched by a renewed emphasis on the relationship between torah and narrative.

The *ritual action* commanded for the celebration of the annual first harvest (vv. 1–4) is supplemented by another commandment, that the participants recite the *narrative* that provides their identity as the covenant people (vv. 5–10a). The story that the participants are to recite is, in effect, a summary of the entire pentateuchal narrative from Genesis 12 to the end. In fact, it goes beyond the end, for it deals with a time in the future of Moses' audience when they can say, in the past tense, "Yahweh brought us into the land" (vv. 9–10, AT). The ritual law is also intended to apply to all subsequent generations who will celebrate the festivals of firstfruits and agricultural tithes.[54]

Here we shall focus not so much on the credo in vv. 5–9 but on the shorter declaration in the ceremony in vv. 1–4. On presenting the firstfruits, the participants are to say, "I declare this day that I have come into the land" (v. 3b, AT). Here the native becomes an immigrant, reenacting the entry into the land. Moreover, the effect of the opening temporal clause ("When you come into the land," v. 1) is to accentuate the temporal and spatial tension that underlies and is intrinsic to ritual participation. Whereas in the *ceremony* the declaration expresses fulfillment ("I have come into the land"), in the *text* the introduction expresses promise ("When you come into the land"). In other words, by projecting into the future what has already occurred long ago, the entrance formula catapults subsequent generations back to a time and place "beyond the

54. This assumes that the ceremony of firstfruits (vv. 1–4) is to be an annual event, rather than once and for all. Cf., in context, Exod 22:29; 23:19; 34:26; Lev 23:9–14. So also Tigay, *Deuteronomy*, 238.

Jordan." Entrance into the land becomes a perennially *potential* reality, even though the participant declares that the reality has already been realized—"I have come into the land."

The text as a whole therefore revolves around the opening temporal clause and the declaration within the entrance ceremony: "When you come into the land . . . ; I have come into the land." This tension between introductory formula and liturgical confession must not be broken. In particular, the declaration cannot and must not ignore the temporal clause. The experience of "now" (v. 10) cannot be valid without the remembrance of "when" (v. 1). In short, the effect created by the opening clause is the placing of the liturgical festival within a temporal, as well as narrative nexus. This, to be sure, is accomplished also by the credo in vv. 5–9, but while the credo moves from past to present, it does not *suspend* that movement as does the entrance formula. The tension introduced by this formula is both temporal and spatial, summoning Israel to recognize the inseparable relationship among past, present, and future, and between life in the wilderness and life in the land. The tension is thereby theological as well, for the festival's location within historical narrative serves as a reminder that the festival is rendered solely to the God who is the subject of that narrative, the God who is "about to give" the land, that is, "Yahweh alone."

Thus, like the social law protecting the alien, this ritual law also prevents the "petrification" of Israel's story into merely past history. Liturgy is another form that gives shape to narrative memory. Indeed, the ritual and ethical bond is reflected by the juxtaposition of vv. 12–15, where the third year tithe of produce from the land is given "to the Levites (landless priests), the resident aliens, the orphans, and the widows." Memory is the fulcrum for theology (chs. 1–11), for ethics (chs. 12–25), and for worship (ch. 26).

Both the social and the ritual laws we have examined introduce a subtle aspect of inconclusiveness to Israel's narrative identity. Israel is the community of the redeemed, but only if also a redemptive community. Israel is the people who will soon possess the land, but only if they continue to recognize and remember their status as aliens. This sense of inconclusiveness is not incidental to these laws; on the contrary, it pervades the book of Deuteronomy, and is nowhere more striking than at its end.

SIX

Conclusion

The Way of Torah

THE MEANING OF A story is often significantly determined by the way it ends, and this is certainly the case for the pentateuchal narrative. What meaning should we infer from the fact that the Pentateuch concludes with the picture of all Israel standing "beyond the Jordan," looking over to the promised land? Why did the editors, along with subsequent tradition, opt for a Pentateuch rather than a Hexateuch (Genesis through Joshua)? Why does the narrative that establishes Israel's identity not include the occupation of the land that has been a driving motivation ever since Genesis 12?[1]

"All plots have something in common with prophecy, for they must appear to educe from the prime matter of the situation the forms of a future."[2] Commenting on the deposit of the book of the

torah in the ark (Deut 31:26), William Moran suggests that "the *torah* itself becomes prophetic."[3] While by torah he did not mean the Pentateuch, the extension is appropriate. Perhaps it is not merely coincidental that "the Law" ends with an encomium to Moses as the unique prophet of Israel (34:10–12), whereupon the collection that tradition knows as the Former Prophets begins with Joshua. In other words, perhaps at its end the redactors of the Pentateuch are saying that this narrative—so much of which relates Moses' words and deeds—is, in fact, the source from which all other prophetic books derive, much as Moses' prophetic spirit was the source of communal prophecy in the wilderness (Num 11:25).[4]

Moran's categorization of the torah as prophetic is based in part on the way it is construed as a "witness" for the future (Deut 31:26; cf. vv. 19, 21, referring to the

---

1. Indeed, in his study of the Pentateuch, Clines has suggested that there is really one theme, namely, "the partial fulfillment—which implies also the partial nonfulfillment—of the promise to or blessing of the patriarchs" (*Theme of the Pentateuch*, 29).

2. Kermode, *Sense of an Ending*, 83.

3. Moran, "Deuteronomy," §238d.

4. Cf. Blenkinsopp, *Prophecy and Canon*, 89; and Polzin, *Moses and the Deuteronomist*, 19, 56–57, 72.

song of ch. 32). As a prophetic document, the Torah does not simply recount ancient history; it opens up a path for each new generation. The end of the Torah thus points us toward the *way* of Torah. On the other hand, as prophecy the Torah is not merely a crystal ball; rather, it performs a critical function within the ongoing life of the people. It provides the criterion by which their present is informed and judged in terms of their past, and the way their future is determined by that critical evaluation. The incompleteness of the Pentateuch as plot can be seen as a temporal expression of the same conditionality of occupation of the land otherwise couched in the social terms of "aliens and tenants" (Lev 25:23). Israel is never the owner; rather, Israel is always subject to eviction *by* the owner, either because of infidelity or injustice.[5]

Two further observations on the incompleteness are in order. First, there is no indication anywhere in the pentateuchal narrative that would lead us to suspect that the end of the Pentateuch results in an annulment of the themes we have traced—especially the theme of land and nationhood. For example, many Christian hymns refer to heaven in such terms as "Canaan's fair and happy land." While the symbolic extension is not inappropriate, any suggestion that the pentateuchal theme of the land refers only to an otherworldly realm would turn the narrative into an allegory.[6] While the connection between divine will and the claim of human territorial sovereignty presents enormous theological (and political!) problems, it does affirm the fundamental need for security that virtually all people in some way experience (cf. 2 Sam 7:10; Mic 4:1–4). As Brueggemann suggests, "A literal sense of the term [land] will protect us from excessive spiritualization, so that we recognize that the yearning for land is always a serious historical enterprise concerned with historical power and belonging."[7]

Second, our emphasis throughout this book on the meaning of the text apart from continual references to authorial situations does not mean that we can ignore that situation in which the Pentateuch as a separate document almost certainly came into existence. I refer, of course, to the exile of 587 BCE and its aftermath. With the exile came the loss of land and nationhood, and the apparent onslaught of God's curse, understood as a result of Israel's irresponsibility to the divine will. While a significant number of the exiles would return to the land within a generation, there would be no independent state for four hundred years. Moreover, never again would those who called themselves Israelites—or, more properly now, Judeans—be limited to the land of Canaan.

---

5. The great dangers are the presumption of ownership due to autonomy (Deut 8: 17) or virtue (Deut 9:4). Brueggemann (*Land*, 192–93) reminds us that the prophetic heritage of Israel championed the "*dispossessed*" over against "the landed" (italics original): "We have yet to face how odd and discomforting is the biblical affirmation that God wills land for his people and he will take it from others for the sake of the poor."

6. Cf. Clines, *Theme of the Pentateuch*, 94–95, 99–100. Slaves in nineteenth-century America understood that the promised land (along with heaven) could refer to freedom in the North, not only a blessed state after death. The heavenly movement is already apparent in Heb 11:13–16.

7. Brueggemann, *Land*, 2–3. On the development of spiritualization of the land in early Judaism, see Weinfeld, *Promise of the Land*, 213–21.

The exile marked the beginning of the diaspora, the spread of Jewish communities of increasing size and importance from Babylon to Alexandria and beyond. In the context of this tumultuous epoch—from about 600 to 450 BCE—the Pentateuch was born.

The inconclusiveness of the Pentateuch made it immediately applicable to those who had experienced the exile, and subsequently to those who lived outside the land or even those who had returned to the land but not as an independent nation. "Wherever exilic Jewry opens the Pentateuch it finds itself."[8] Moreover, all future generations who also stand "beyond the Jordan" can identify with the Torah. Because of the way the story of the Pentateuch ends (or does not end), the story is about them, not just about ancient Israel. Even more remarkable, the resultant process of identification with the Israel in the Torah was not one of doleful resignation. On the contrary, to identify with the Israel who stood "beyond the Jordan" was to grasp one's election as God's chosen people from among all the peoples of the world. Thus, "through the Torah, Israel passed from a nation in destitution to a religious community in dispersion which could never be destroyed."[9] In fact, we can extend the application beyond the implied Jewish community and say that largely (but not only) because of the way the story ends, it is also about everyone. That is, the story can be about all human beings because it remains open ended, and this open endedness evokes a dimension of the human condition. In short, perhaps the most remarkable feature of the Torah is its correspondence to "the narrative quality of experience," the way every human being is an uncompleted story, a nexus of past, present, and future. Personal identity is a combination of "the chronicle of memory and the scenario of anticipation."[10]

The inconclusiveness of the Pentateuch emerges in a context that has appeared at a number of key places within the narrative—the context of departure. Another quotation from Frank Kermode's *The Sense of an Ending* will prove helpful here in considering the end of the Pentateuch as a moment of departure:

> All . . . plotting presupposes and requires that an end will bestow upon the whole duration and meaning. To put it another way, the interval must be purged of simple chronicity, of the emptiness of *tock-tick*, humanly uninteresting successiveness [i.e., *chronos*]. It is required to be a significant season, *kairos* [a pregnant moment] poised between beginning and end. It has to be, on a scale much greater than that which concerns the psychologists, an instance of what they call "temporal integration"—our way of bundling together perception of the present, memory of the past, and expectation of the future, in a common organization. Within this organization that which was conceived of as simply successive becomes charged with past and future: what was *chronos* becomes *kairos*.[11]

In terms of departure, we shall emphasize two key phrases from the

8. Clines, *Theme of the Pentateuch*, 98.

9. Sanders, *Torah and Canon*, 51.

10. Crites, "Narrative Quality of Experience," 303; see 291–311, esp. 302–3.

11. Kermode, *Sense of an Ending*, 46.

above quotation—an "interval . . . poised between beginning and end," and a way of "bundling together perception of the present, memory of the past, and expectation of the future."

The Pentateuch does not end with an arrival, but with a suspension of the moment before departure. The suspension of such a moment is not unique to the end of the narrative. The bridge between the primeval cycle and the ancestral saga of Genesis (12:1–3) is constructed on the foundation of Yahweh's charge to Abram before his departure from Haran. Jacob becomes the heir to Abram's promise on the night before his escape from Esau (28:10–17); he receives the name Israel and a divine blessing on the night before his return to Canaan (32:22–32); and he receives a renewal of the promise of nationhood on the night before his departure for Egypt (46:1–7). The traditional name of the book of Exodus ("a going forth") speaks for itself, and includes not only the departure from Egypt, but the expectation of Israel's departure from Sinai (Exodus 32–33), an expectation realized in Numbers 10. Similarly, Israel stands on the verge of departure from the wilderness to the promised land in Numbers 13–14, only to step back in diffidence and defeat.

As we have previously seen, the Passover celebration represents a liturgical expression of the suspended moment of departure, a classic rite of passage, and we may now see it as suggesting a sense of the end of the Pentateuch.[12] Passover is "a night of watching for Yahweh" (Exod 12:42), and, by extension, it is a night of watching for Israel. Passover celebrates

salvation, but not by placing the celebrants on the other side of the Sea; the celebrants are poised on the night in between slavery and freedom. Even while it celebrates salvation as past, it portrays salvation as future. This sense of departure as *kairos*, as an urgent moment full of hope as well as danger, pervades the end of the Pentateuch. Just as in the Passover liturgy the celebrants have not crossed the Red Sea, so at the end of the Pentateuch, the Israelites (and we the readers) are not deposited on the other side of the Jordan, but suspended "beyond the Jordan," waiting to enter the land. The Torah leaves the reader at a moment of temporal tension, not only at the end, but also at the beginning, of an adventure.[13]

On the other hand, one can make too much of the inconclusiveness of the Pentateuch. This happens when one distorts its narrative dimension by construing it apart from its political (i.e., "constitutional") dimension. At the same time that the themes and plot render a story, they also render *torah*—instruction, guidance, and law. If the end of the Pentateuch is inconclusive, it is not premature but, in fact, entirely appropriate to the function of the Pentateuch as *the* Torah, the guidebook of Israel. As both story and law, the Pentateuch is inconclusive but not incomplete, and the resultant tension is an essential part of its significance.

From the moment God drove Adam and Eve from the garden, the Pentateuch has portrayed Yahweh as a deity in search of community, a God whose primary purpose is the restoration of the order among

---

12. See my study, "Passover."

13. See Clines, *Theme of the Pentateuch*, 107–11. Cf. the originally suspended ending of the Gospel of Mark (9:8).

creator, creature, and world that existed before the first human beings broke the first commandment. The Pentateuch is a narrative description of that process of restoration—or better, re-creation—as it took shape in the sacral community known as Israel. At the end of the Pentateuch, that community—as a possibility—is now complete. Through the agency of Moses, God has finished the work that began with the charge to the ancestors, that continued with the salvation of Israel from Egypt, and that completed in the formation of the covenant community gathered around the tabernacle. Israel is a people with a divinely given polity, "a constitutional theocracy" with a complete system of government.[14] Near the end of Moses' last will and testament, therefore, Moses can declare: "*this day* you have become the people of Yahweh your God" (27:9). The Israel that stands "beyond the Jordan" represents a complete model of reality, the way human beings can live in conformity to the will of God. While it is true that the eternal-covenant tradition established with Abraham grounds the hope of remaining God's people in God's unconditional promise, the dominating position of Deuteronomy at the end of the Pentateuch focuses our attention on

the Sinai/Horeb covenant and the possibility of conforming to God's will.[15] Thus the Israel who becomes God's people "this day" outside the land (27:9) presents the model for anyone who wishes to be part of that community in any time and in any place.[16]

With this description of the new community of God, the Pentateuch has reached its true end—its *telos*—its goal and purpose. The pentateuchal narrative renders a new world. But as it was "in the beginning," so it is now; while that world exists as a reality in terms of what God has done, it exists only as a possibility in terms of what Israel will do. The Torah ends very much the way it began. Just as God placed the earth before Adam and Eve and offered it to them as their dominion, so God places the land of Canaan

14. See McBride, "Polity of the Covenant People," 27. He is referring specifically to Deuteronomy, but we may expand the designation to cover the entire Pentateuch. Baden (*Composition*, 229) argues that the absence of land occupation demonstrates that the final shape of the Pentateuch is that of "law book." Cf. Weeks, *Reading Law*: "In contrast to the literary complaint that the narrative plot has not been concluded, the persuasive rhetoric of the Pentateuch suggests that this story never ends" (154). The Pentateuch is "a rhetorically complete unit" even though it does not conform to any one genre (including narrative and law [156]).

15. The "eternal covenant" dominates the Priestly source (e.g., Gen 9:16; 17:7) and quite likely is intended to counter the Sinai/Horeb covenant. See Appendix 3. Cf. Lohfink (*Pentateuch*, 172), who emphasizes that for P only punishment will result in Israel's disobedience, but never *God's* breaking covenant. The eternal covenant appears briefly in Deuteronomy (4:31), but even here it is the grounds for Israel's repentance (vv. 29–30). The language of repentance (literally "return") appears repeatedly in 30:1–5, where the initiative of restoration seems to lie with Israel (v. 6 there represents a more desperate theology of divine imposition, in line with Jer 31:33; Ezek 11:19; 36:26).

16. As Tigay suggests (*Deuteronomy*, 180), the absence of a conquest story "expresses the absoluteness of the covenant and its independence of the land . . . The promised land is ahead of us, but our duties to God are now." Cf. Dozeman (*God at War*, 180): "God, country, and people are never merged in Torah . . . God is always on the move three days ahead (Num 10:33–34)." Cf. LaCocque (*Trial of Innocence*, 265): "Israel in diaspora mirrors the diasporic soul of humanity and its striving toward the rest and peace of rejoining its center, called Eden."

before Israel and offers it to them. Just as God provided for Adam and Eve a commandment, obedience to which would mean continued blessing, but disobedience to which would entail a curse, so God has blessed Israel as God's special people, but warned them of the curse that leads to death. Just as Adam and Eve could be genuinely human only in responsibility to the divine will, so Israel can be God's holy nation only in responsibility to God's torah.

Here again the Pentateuch is at once complete and open-ended. Although it renders the new world created by God—the work God has finished, the covenant community that is "very good"—it ends with the death of Moses, and with the challenge of his testimony. The Torah ends with a charge, and thus with a question: will Israel *be* the new community God has created, or not? The way of Torah lies open, but it is a straight and narrow path:

> I call heaven and earth to witness against you this day, that I have set before you life and death, blessing and curse; therefore choose life, that you and your descendants may live, loving Yahweh your God, obeying his voice, and cleaving to him; for that means life to you and length of days, that you may dwell in the land which Yahweh swore to your fathers, to Abraham, to Isaac, and to Jacob, to give them. (Deut 30:19–20, AT)

APPENDIX 1

The Redactional Process in Genesis

IT IS QUITE POSSIBLE that the connective function of God's promise of the land of Canaan derives from one or more authors and reflects an intention to pull together stories or cycles of stories that originally may have had little or nothing to do with each other (e.g., Gen 12:7; 26:2–4; 28:3–4; 35:12; 50:24). Some have argued that a version of the land promise is an early kernel for the existing one, reflecting a universal longing for the security that territorial possession provides; others argue that the land promise is a much later addition reflecting the longing of sixth-century exiles in Babylon, and designed to tie in the originally independent traditions of Israel's settlement in Canaan (i.e., the book of Joshua).

There are certainly three cycles of stories focusing on the figures of Abraham, Jacob, and Joseph (the character of Isaac does not enjoy such a lengthy collection). Thematically, all three are distinct, and we can characterize them alliteratively by the words *progeny, presence,* and *Providence.* The Abraham stories (chs. 12–24) focus on the promise of a son and legitimate heir—*legitimate* meaning that he is a son of both Sarah and Abraham, thus excluding the servant Eliezer and Abraham's son by Hagar, Ishmael (Gen 15:3–4; 17:18–19). This plot is resolved with the birth (and near death!) of Isaac (chs. 21–22) and his proper marriage (ch. 24). The Jacob stories (chs. 25–36) focus on Jacob's journey to his mother's homeland, his acquisition of children and property there, and his return to Canaan, stories that are framed by divine appearances (28:13–15; 35:9–12; cf. 46:4). The Joseph cycle, often called a novella, focuses on the sibling rivalry between Joseph and his brothers, on his abduction to Egypt, and subsequent rise to power there, and the reconciliation with his brothers and reunion with his father (chs. 37; 39–50). Throughout this story, God is "with Joseph," as God was with Jacob, and for both this presence resulted in "success" (30:27–30; 39:2, 23); but the divine presence in the Joseph story is more like a discrete, invisible Providence, guiding events from behind the scenes. God never "appears" to Joseph, as God did to Abraham (12:7), and certainly not (as God appeared to Jacob) in the persona of a sweaty championship wrestler (32:24)! In short, the distinct themes of progeny, presence, and Providence point to originally separate, if not independent, narrative cycles, and those cycles themselves may well be composites of originally shorter, independent stories. In turn, the individual cycles reflect rather different pictures of God, despite numerous similarities.

We can use the story of Jacob's dream in Gen 28:10–22 as an example of a short story within a larger cycle, connected editorially with other cycles. Jacob is on his way to find a wife among his kinfolk far away in Haran. Two different motivations for this search occur in the narrative. On the one hand, Jacob's mother, Rebekah, urges him to *flee* to Haran because his brother, Esau, wants to kill him (27:41–45; for understandable reasons—27:1–40!). Jacob is a fugitive from fraternal vengeance. On the other hand, Rebekah complains to Abraham about "the women of the land" (i.e., Canaan) and suggests that Jacob not marry among them but go to her kinfolk (27:46—28:5; here the place is called Paddan-aram). Jacob is a romantic suitor in search of a suitable wife. Probably two

separate literary sources explain the different motivations (J in 27:41–45 and P in 27:46—28:9). *In combination*—i.e., redactionally—it makes Rebekah's complaint seem deceptive (deception seems to be a family trait!), although we cannot ascribe this to the intention of the editor who joined the sources.[1]

Jacob's dream occurs while he is on the way to Haran. One likely analysis of the passage sees at least two strands: (1) an original story about how Jacob discovered a holy place made numinous by divine presence (a theophany involving "angels of God"), naming the place Bethel, which means "house of God" (or "of El"; vv. 10–12, 16aα [through "his sleep"], 17–19). He commemorates the place by converting his stone pillow into a sacramental pillar (or monument). Such a story appears often as a sanctuary-foundation legend or etiology (cf. 12:6–7; 16:7–14; 22:11–14). A rough American analogy would be the legendary landing of Pilgrims at Plymouth Rock, the first mention of which occurs over one hundred and twenty years after the supposed event.

(2) Another writer added vv. 13–15, 16aβb inserting an appearance of God (not just angels) *as Yahweh*, identified as the "God of Abraham your father [i.e., his grandfather, cf. 29:5] and the God of Isaac," and a divine *speech*. Yahweh now promises Jacob offspring and territorial possession of the land in which Bethel is situated, concluding with a promise of protection on the journey. Thus this addition presents three major alterations—theological (El to Yahweh), genealogical

---

1. See Baden, *Composition*, 178, 234, and, in general, 226–29.

(Jacob is Abraham's grandson), and geo-political (Bethel to Canaan). Similarly, the addition of a vow in vv. 20–22 refers to Yahweh as "my god," and also provides a second etiology: the ten-percent tithe.

There are many variations on such an analysis, but at least there do seem to be two separate layers here. One could stand on its own as the etiology of the sacred space Bethel (a northern site), with angels and probably El as the divine presence. The dream story may not originally have had any connection with the narratives about Isaac or Abraham. The other literary strand incorporates the first into the overarching divine *promises* made by *Yahweh* to the *ancestors*, thus tying the Bethel etiology into a continuous narrative involving three generations, claiming the whole land of Canaan, and connecting Jacob's dream within the universal context of "all the families of the earth" (v. 14; cf. 12:1–3). Again, from a redactional viewpoint, the dream story connects with another Bethel story in 35:1–15 to frame the entire account of Jacob's journey with appearances of God.

There are theological consequences to this combination of sources: a local holy site is absorbed into the *land* of Canaan, so that a *natural* sacred space becomes sanctioned *political* territory. The focus on numinous divine presence in a *place* shifts to divine presence on the *way*, as well as an historical divine promise.[2]

The original identity of God as *El*, who is also a Canaanite deity, becomes fused with the national (southern) God *Yahweh* (see appendix 2). What is more, *someone* benefits from that ten-percent tithe!

The political dimensions of the story (especially its second layer) are compounded if we connect it with the time in the tenth century BCE when the northern part of the Davidic/Solomonic empire split off from the southern, and the new northern king, Jeroboam I, constructed a sanctuary at Bethel. The story of *Jacob's* founding the place may well be a counter to the Deuteronomic Historian's censorious account of *Jeroboam's* founding it in 1 Kgs 12:25–33. From another perspective, scholars who see an exilic background for such narratives would suggest that the story holds out the promise to exiles that God is with them wherever they go, and that a return to the land of Canaan is possible.

While we cannot present such a detailed analysis of every passage in the Pentateuch, some such development often stands behind the present, canonical text of the narrative.

2. There is a similar combination at 12:6–7, where what was no doubt a sacred, oracular tree (*moreh*) has lost significance to the divine promise of land (cf. 18:1; 35:4; Josh 24:26). For a penetrating analysis of the role of such natural subjects in the theology of J (over against the traditional scholarly dichotomy of nature versus history and the God of a place versus the God of the fathers), see Hiebert, *Yahwist's Landscape*, 9–12, 104–12.

APPENDIX 2

The Names of God[1]

Most people do not think of God as having a name—at least the God of Judaism and Christianity. We use the word *God* (with the capital *G*) either to address God directly or to refer to God in the third person. A close reading of the book of Genesis, however, will begin to uncover a more complicated picture. Genesis 1 refers simply to "God," but Genesis 2–3 uses "the Lord God," and Gen 4:26 tells us that only with Adam and Eve's grandchildren do people begin "to invoke the name of the Lord." Then in Gen 14:22 Abraham addresses "the Lord, God Most High, maker of heaven and earth," and in 17:1 the Lord says to Abraham, "I am God Almighty." But Abraham calls "on the name of the Lord, the Everlasting God" (21:31), and God later says to Jacob "I am the God of Bethel" (31:13). How do we explain all these names of God?

There are at least three Hebrew names used for God in the foregoing examples: *Yahweh, 'Elohim,* and *'El.* Most scholars agree that Yahweh was one of the personal names of God, and ultimately obscured other names. The NRSV follows ancient convention in rendering the name with "the LORD" (and in all-capital letters). This gesture of reverence derives from the notion that God's name is too holy to pronounce. Indeed, the tradition is already in the Hebrew Bible, where the name simply appears with the consonants *yhwh* (called the Tetragrammaton) and the *vowels* that are in the word *'adonay* ("my lords," a plural of majesty).[2] The name is derived from the verb that means "to be, to become" (*yhwh* from the root *hyh*), and probably means "he causes to be," "brings to life." Some Jews will not say or even write the full name. In reading the Hebrew text, when they come to the consonants *yhwh* they will say "Adonay" or even *hashem* ("the name").[3] Similarly,

---

1. Some of this material comes from excursus 3 in my *Book of the Former Prophets,* 57–64.

2. The English invention *Jehovah* combines the two, interchanging *y/j* and *w/v.*

3. A precedent for the latter is in the rather macabre story of Lev 24:10–23 where someone who blasphemes "the Name" is executed (note how the NRSV capitalizes the *n* in vv. 11 and 16). The story illustrates the utter seriousness with which ancient Israel understood God's holiness.

some translations abbreviate it as YHWH or Yhwh. Nevertheless, God does have a personal name, and sometimes it is crucial in understanding the text. "Lord," after all, is a title, not a personal name. People in England, where there still are lords, will recognize the difference more easily. *Lord* is also masculine, with the feminine being *lady*, a title that you will definitely *not* see used for Yahweh. Thus to say "the Lord is God" seems like a tautology, but to say "Yahweh is God" is to make a claim about a specific deity over against other contenders. (Compare "the leader is president" over against, say, "Obama is president," and you will see the difference!) In quoting the NRSV I will use "the Lord." However, in my own translations I will often use the name Yahweh, with all due respect to traditional sentiment. In doing so, I appeal to our Taoist friends who, in the *Tao Te Ching*, say at the outset, "The name that can be named / is not the eternal Name. // The unnameable is the eternally real. / Naming is the origin / of all particular things."[4]

Alongside Yahweh, the most prominent name is the generic word for God, *elohim*. Actually, the word is another plural noun of majesty, probably meaning something like "power, exaltation" (we might compare the so-called royal plural of English—when monarchs use the pronoun *we* to refer to themselves—and everyone else says "your majesty" [cf.

Gen 1:26]). As a plural noun, the word *elohim* sometimes actually refers to a plurality of gods (e.g., the "other gods" in the Ten Commandments, Exod 20:3; see appendix 4), but more often simply means "God."[5] Closely related to the word *elohim* is the word *el*. The word *el* can mean simply "god," or it can be a personal name, El, something like the way we use *god* (or *God*) in the third person and *God* as a form of personal address. (The Muslim name for the divine, Allah, is etymologically related [literally *al* + *ilah*, "the God"].) The word *El* appears in several of the names for God that we have already noted: "God Most High" is *el 'elyon* (pronounced "el el-yone"); "God Almighty" is *el šaddai* (pronounced "el shah-die"); "God Everlasting" is *el 'olam* (pronounced "el oh-lahm"); and "God of Bethel" is *el beth-'el* (pronounced "el beth-el," which is something of a tautology literally meaning "God of the House of God"). There is no doubt that ancient Israelites worshiped God by the *personal* name El. Indeed, the very name Israel is a composite using the divine name El (probably meaning "El reigns").[6] We also know that the name was used by people other than those who came to identify themselves as Israelites. Indeed, the Canaanite king Melchizedek praises El Elyon in blessing Abram, and Abram identifies El Elyon as "the Lord" (i.e.,

---

Similarly, in a saying of Jesus, blasphemy against the Holy Spirit is the one unpardonable sin (Matt 12:32; Mark 3:29; Luke 12:10).

4. Translated by Mitchell, *Tao Te Ching*, 1. Cf. the statement of Nicholas of Cusa (15th century) regarding *Father*, *Son*, and *Holy Spirit*: "God 'infinitely excels and precedes all such names'" (quoted by Volf, *Allah*, 51).

5. The word *god* or *gods*, uncapitalized, in effect represents a theological criticism of the deities of non-Israelites as unreal, but that is a philosophical problem beyond our purpose here.

6. Traditionally interpreted as, "he who strives with God" (Gen 32:28). Many English names use the same word: Samuel, Daniel, Michael, and so forth.

Yahweh, Gen 14:19–22), the first evidence of ecumenism.[7]

Much of our knowledge about El (and other gods) comes from a remarkable collection of cuneiform texts dated to the late fourteenth century BCE and discovered at the ancient city of Ugarit, near the Mediterranean coast in what is now Syria.[8] We do not see the kind of mythological stories about the gods in the Hebrew Bible that we see in Ugaritic literature,[9] and there are significant differences in *how* the gods are portrayed.[10] Nevertheless, there are many similarities between the biblical El and the Ugaritic El.

In Ugaritic mythology, El is the head of the pantheon and presides over the council of gods.[11] Often El was not only the high god of mythology but also the personal god of a family, referred to as "the God of my father," who cared for and guided the family, a role prominent in the stories of Genesis.[12] Even Yahweh uses the self-referent of "El Shaddai" (Gen 35:11; traditionally "God Almighty" but probably "God of the Mountain"). *Translating* the word *ʾel* as "God," rather than *transliterating* it as "El" tends to hide the personality behind the title, thereby obscuring the fact that El and Yahweh originally were two separate deities. (In a similar way, rendering *Yahweh* with "the Lord" obscures God's personality.) Thus, early in Israel's history, some Israelites worshiped the "other god," El, even though later generations would not remember El's original independence.

Yahweh's self-referent as El becomes developmentally significant in the exodus story. There Yahweh says explicitly that *before* the exodus Yahweh was known *only* as El Shaddai (6:2–3), even though the name Yahweh obviously appears repeatedly in the book of Genesis, including as

---

7. Cf. the archaic oracle in Num 24:16 where three names appear: El, Elyon, and Shaddai (NRSV: God, Most High, and Almighty).

8. The texts include myths, epics and liturgical and administrative documents. Especially interesting to biblical scholars have been the myths about Baal, El, Anat, and Athirat (Asherah), along with the gods of chaos, Yam (Sea) and Mot (Death). (On some of these, see appendix 4). There are also epic texts about figures named Keret and Aqhat. While these texts are enormously informative, one must remember that they predate most biblical texts by at least four hundred years. How the Ugaritic theology and anthropology might have developed in that time we cannot know.

9. Cf. Pardee, *Ritual and Cult,* 236: "there are only traces of polytheism visible in the Hebrew Bible in contrast with the full-blown Ugaritic polytheism." For some major exceptions, see below on Psalm 82 and Deut 32:8–9; see also Gen 6:1–4. Also the cosmic battle between Yahweh and the chaos monster sometimes approaches mythical status (as conflict between divine powers); cf. Isa 27:1; 51:9. However, Israel almost always adapts such myth to apply it to Israel's history (e.g. Isa 51:10–11 where the defeat of the sea dragon results in Israel's release from exile).

10. For example, there are Ugaritic stories about Baal having sexual intercourse with a cow, and El getting falling-down drunk at a party. However, Wyatt, *Religious Texts,* 405 warns that those who see El's behavior here as shameful "import an alien ethic (indeed an absurdly moralistic posturing) . . . and misconstrue the symbolic parameters of this kind of mythology." Cf. Smith, *Early History,* 203–4.

11. Smith, *Origins,* 78, points out that Israelite theology used the council model for construing divine community rather than a familial model, whereas at Ugarit there were both (i.e. El as father of other gods). Only in an earlier stage might Israelite theology have seen El as the father of Yahweh (again, Deut 32:8, see below and n. 14).

12. Cf. Smith, *Memoirs,* 22; Miller, *Religion,* 62–63.

a self-referent (e.g., Gen 28:13). The Exodus text (from the Priestly author) seems to reflect a process in which the separate deities El and Yahweh merged into one; some group who experienced the exodus seems to be behind the merger.[13] There are a few passages that suggest that Israelites once understood El as the head of the council of gods, precisely as the Ugaritic texts do:

> El has taken his place in the divine council; in the midst of the gods he holds judgment. (Ps 82:1, AT)[14]

And in another text, Yahweh appears as a subordinate to El:

> When El Elyon apportioned
>   the nations,
> when he divided humankind,
> He fixed the boundaries
>   of the peoples,
> according to the number
>   of the gods;
> Yahweh's portion was his people,
> Jacob, his allotted inheritance.
>   (Deut 32:8, AT)

Here there is the clear vestige of a kind of pantheon involving the senior deity, El, a junior deity, Yahweh, and other deities as well. Reading this text is like looking back in time, back to a time when Israel (Jacob) clearly believed in other gods,

believed that the God El had determined their destiny, even as they confessed that the God Yahweh was appointed as their patron deity.[15] Eventually the figure of El was fused with that of Yahweh, an easy transition since *ʾel* could mean "god" to begin with. Thus worshiping El was the same as worshiping God, leaving primarily the figure of Baal as God's chief competitor. The result was a theology that we call monotheism, as evidenced in the words of the sixth-century-BCE prophet known as Second Isaiah: "I am Yahweh, and there *is* no other; besides me there is no god" (45:5, AT).

---

13. This exodus tradition is consistent with various texts (including Judg 5:4) that point to the area south of Canaan as the origin of belief in Yahweh. However, it is also quite possible that El originally was the God of the exodus story, as some texts indicate. Cf. Num 23:8, 19, 22, 23; 24:4, 8, 16 (three verses also with Yahweh). See, among others, Smith, *Origins*, 146–147.

14. The text continues, "You are gods, sons of El Elyon," whereupon El condemns them to mortal status. This is a good example of how polytheism was adapted by Israel, especially in a concern for social justice.

15. Smith, *Memoirs*, 109, notes that the poem also reflects later developments when it refers to the "no-gods" whom Israel worshiped (32:17) and describes Yahweh as the "only god" (v. 39). That latter verse sounds very much like Second Isaiah (e.g., 43:10–13). For a different view, in which El Elyon and Yahweh here are identical from the outset, see Nelson, *Deuteronomy*, 371.

Appendix 3

Two Covenants

A covenant (Hebrew: *berit*) is simply one type of formal agreement between two or more parties. There are numerous types of agreements. Abraham and Abimelech come to an agreement that involves well rights. Several key terms appear here: integrity, honesty, or loyalty (*ḥesed*); swearing an oath; covenant; and witness (Gen 21:22–34). Abraham's son Isaac makes a similar agreement with another Abimelech (presumably the son of the former), also involving a covenant and oath as well as a banquet (Gen 26:26–33). Jacob and his father-in-law, Laban, come to an agreement that is essentially a non-aggression pact also involving a covenant, witnesses, and a meal, as well as a kind of monument. They also invoke God by various names to oversee the agreement (Gen 31:43–54).

Just as covenants serve to structure relationships between individuals or groups, so ancient Israel used covenant relationships as theological models for the divine/human relationship, either with an individual or, more generally, with the people as a whole. Some such

model is virtually inescapable for understanding human relationship to the divine, and covenant is only one among numerous possibilities (e.g., parent/child [e.g., Hosea 11; Deut 32:5–6], marriage [e.g., Hosea 2; Jer 2:2, 23–25, 32], lover/ beloved [Deut 7:7–8; 10:15], or, in Eastern religion, atman/Brahman). Within the biblical texts, two types of covenant predominate: what we will call the grant and the treaty. (We could also use the names "ancestral covenant" and "Sinai covenant.") The grant is concentrated in the ancestral saga of Genesis but reappears at critical points later in the pentateuchal narrative as well. The treaty appears when Israel escapes from Egypt and encounters God at the mountain called Sinai, and this type of covenant undergirds especially Exodus 19–24, 32–34; and Deuteronomy 4–30. The treaty model also informs much of the redaction of the following Former Prophets (the books of Joshua through 2 Kings).

1. THE GRANT MODEL[1]

Like the treaty model, the grant model derives from legal or diplomatic practices that we know from various ancient Near Eastern documents outside the Bible—in this case, from the grant of land by a ruler to a subject as a reward for loyal service. In one such document, the grantor (the Hittite Muršiliš II) says to the grantee: "I have given you the Šeḫa-River-Land and the Land Appawiya." In another, the grantor includes successive generations as the grantees: "After you, your son and grandson will possess it [and] . . . nobody will take away from the descendant of Ulmi-Tešup either his house [i.e., dynasty] or his land in order to give it to a descendant of someone else."[2]

The covenant with Abraham clearly reflects such practices, if not also such documents: "On that day the Lord made a covenant with Abram, saying 'To your descendants I give this land, from the river of Egypt to the great river, the river Euphrates'" (15:18). The covenant making begins with a reference to a "reward" for Abram (15:1), and later in the Abraham story, his obedience is rewarded with a renewed promise of numerous offspring who "shall possess the gate of their enemies" (22:17). Here and elsewhere, the reward is, in effect, inherited by all subsequent generations through the merit of Abraham (22:14; 26:5; Exod 32:13; Deut 1:8; 9:4–5, 27; 2 Kgs 13:23). In a sense, the covenant in ch. 15 is simply a ritual confirmation of the oath or promise of land made more vaguely at the outset (12:1), then more specifically (12:7), and completed with a sign in ch. 17, where it is also called "an everlasting covenant" (17:7, 13, 19). The language of the covenant with Noah and all creatures after the flood resembles that of the land grant: an everlasting covenant promising that God will never again destroy the earth with a flood (Gen 9:8–17), and granting humans in particular dominion over the earth and all its creatures (9:1–7). Beyond the Pentateuch, the land-grant model also has an even stronger resemblance to the covenant between God and King David and his dynasty: "Your house [i.e., dynasty] and your kingdom shall be made sure forever before me; your throne shall be established forever" (2 Sam 7:16). Moreover, future generations benefit from the grant to David just as with the grant to Abraham, sometimes even when they don't deserve it (1 Kgs 11:12–13, 32–39; 2 Kgs 20:5–6; Isa 55:3). Chronologically, it is possible that the Davidic grant stands behind the Abrahamic, but the exact relationship is difficult to determine; the dating of such texts may be related to the dates of the ancient Near Eastern texts in question.

The grant is everlasting in part because it is unconditional, not dependent on compliance by the grantee to any stipulations. In the case of the ancient Near Eastern document quoted above, the grant is promised to the grantee's descendants even if one of them "sins."[3] Just so, the grant of a dynasty to David is permanent; even if a member of the

1. A somewhat different version of the following is in my *Former Prophets*, excursus 1.

2. Weinfeld, *Deuteronomic School*, 72, 79, citing two different documents; see also Weinfeld, *Promise of the Land*, ch. 9, especially on the land grant. For examples from thirteenth-century-BCE Ugarit, see Hallo, *The Context of Scripture* 3:256–58. Some of the latter grants involve some kind of commercial service as a condition; others specifically do not make such a requirement.

3. Weinfeld, *Deuteronomic School*, 79.

dynasty "commits iniquity" requiring punishment, *God's* commitment to the relationship will continue "forever" (2 Sam 7:14–15).

Clearly, a grant of land to one individual or people means that someone else does *not* have title to the land.[4] In the covenant statement in Genesis 15, the land is specifically identified as the land of numerous peoples, including the Canaanites (15:19–21). This people, along with the Amorites, are the most frequently mentioned as those who are to be displaced. One might rightly ask, why should the grantee possess the land and not the others (especially if the others were there first!)? There are numerous dimensions to an answer. As we have already seen, the grant is a reward for some meritorious behavior of the grantee. Presumably, the grantor holds overall title to the land (a claim which may beg the question!). In Israel's theological model, the lands of all peoples went along with the appointment of their titular deities granted by the chief God, called Most High (Elyon), probably the creator (cf. Gen 14:19). Israel was assigned to Yahweh and the land of Canaan (Deut 32:8–9). This text probably represents an early tradition before Elyon (an epithet of El) and Yahweh were fused into one deity (see appendix 2). This ancient tradition is reflected in the much more recent text of Deuteronomy 1–4. There God commands Israel to "take possession" of the land of the Amorites and Canaanites (1:6–8), but the lands of Moab and Ammon are off limits because God has given *them* their respective territories as well (2:9, 19). Again, such multiple land grants

are attested in the same ancient Near Eastern documents mentioned above.[5]

Still, the question of why some people would be *displaced* remains. The biblical texts have another answer for that question, namely, "the iniquity of the Amorites" (Gen 15:16). The native peoples are judged to be morally unfit to inhabit the land. We have already seen this judgment implied in the story of the cursing of Canaan (Gen 9:20–27), but it becomes much more explicit in 15:16 and especially later, in the book of Leviticus. There God warns Israel not to follow the customs of the Canaanites (18:3–4), which are largely judged to be sexual deviances (18:6–23). Because the Canaanites allegedly engaged in such behavior, they defiled the land, and God cast them out—or, more graphically, the land "vomited" them out (18:24–25; cf. 20:22–24). Such revulsion for and animosity toward the Canaanites becomes a leitmotif in the Deuteronomic literature (e.g., Deut 7:1–6; 9:4–5; 1 Kgs 11:1–13; 2 Kgs 17:7–20; cf. Jer 2:20–25).[6] Clearly this antagonism toward Canaanites approaches xenophobia (see further below), but it has a flip side: Israel does *not* possess the land because of Israel's own inherent superiority, but purely out of the grace of God, the grantor (cf. Deut 7:7–8; 9:4); and, just as important, Israel may *lose* the land if the people become corrupt (here the land

4. Some royal land grants at Ugarit specify from *whom* land is taken to be given to another; see Hallo, *The Context of Scripture* 3:256–58.

5. Thus the grant quoted from Muršiliš immediately refers to lands granted to two other beneficiaries (ibid., 72). The grants to Moab and Ammon are due to their relationship to Abraham through his nephew, Lot (Gen 19:30–38). See the story in Judg 11:12–28, where there is a reference to Moab's land and patron deity, Chemosh (v. 24).

6. For further discussion of such xenophobia, see the section on "Deuteronomic Orthodoxy" in ch. 5.

grant is fused with the treaty model; see below).

Another problem with the anti-Canaanite bias in such texts is the historical and cultural question of what makes one a Canaanite instead of an Israelite. Much recent scholarship suggests that, in fact, the distinction between the two was not nearly as clear-cut as the texts make out. Increasingly, *Canaanite* became a kind of ethnic stereotype similar to our word *pagan*, or even *infidel*, to designate people whose religious preferences were deemed unorthodox by those who wrote the biblical texts. The result was a kind of demonizing. Indeed, some scholars would go so far as to say that the difference between ancient Israelites and Canaanites was a fictional invention intended deliberately to legitimate a particular political claim on the land, a fiction that in effect simply denied the existence of peoples (both ancient and modern) whom we should more properly call Palestinians.[7] On the other hand, some scholars argue that stories of the ancestors in Genesis portray not settlement by conquest from the outside but indigenous assimilation of Palestinian peoples involving peaceful resolutions of conflicts that included making covenants or treaties.[8]

Americans—that is, Euro-Americans—must be careful not to throw stones at the glass house of Israel constructed on the basis of the land grant. Our own history contains a close analogy in the "letters patent" that authorized the possession of land in America, and thus the *dispossession* of Native Americans. Here is an example of such a patent:

25 March 1584

Letters Patent to Walter Raleigh

Elizabeth by the grace of God. . . . We have gyuen and graunted and by thes presents for vs our heyres and successors doe geve and graunte to our trusty and welbeloved servaunte Walter Raleighe Esquier and to his heyres and assignes for ever . . . to discover search fynde out and viewe such remote heathen and barbarous landes Contries and territories not actually possessed of any Christian Prynce and inhabited by Christian people . . . to haue holde occupy and enioye to him his heyres and assignes for ever.[9]

Queen Elizabeth assumes the right and authority, no doubt God-given, to grant certain lands to Walter Raleigh, although not encroaching on any land currently possessed by any "Christian people." Other peoples, namely, Native Americans, have no rights. Indeed, part of the colonization process involved the "conversion" of Native Americans to Christianity, since they were considered to be "infidels and

---

7. See Whitelam, *Invention of Ancient Israel,* who argues that biblical scholarship has been complicit in the denial of Palestinians' history and their contemporary right to land. "The irony of this situation is that for the past there is a Palestine but no Palestinians, yet for the present there are Palestinians but no Palestine" (58). Note the analogy he draws to American history and Native Americans on p. 70.

8. Cf. Gen 21:22–34 and 26:12–33. Clearly the exodus/conquest model dominates the canonical structure and content of the Pentateuch, including numerous outright contradictions (e.g., making covenants with "natives," Exod

34:15–16; Deut 7:2–6). For a convenient listing of the differences between the proposed ancestral versus exodus blocks of tradition, see Dozeman, "Commission of Moses," 129.

9. Quoted in Quinn, *The Roanoke Voyages,* 82.

salvages [*sic*, for 'savages']" incompatible with "humane civilitie."[10] Such language is only part of a larger discourse in which the European settlers saw themselves as a new Israel (hence founding towns like New Canaan, Connecticut). Some, of course, dissented—notably Roger Williams, who was expelled from the Massachusetts Bay Colony for questioning the authority of the King of England and denouncing the charters granted to settlers "as an unlawful expropriation of lands rightfully belonging to the Indians."[11]

2. THE TREATY

The perceptive reader no doubt has already noticed that the notion of *Israel* being displaced from the land (noted above regarding Leviticus) seems to contradict the very notion of the land grant as an everlasting covenant, indeed, one that God will not nullify even in the face of sin. In fact, this apparent contradiction points to a deep tension between the land grant and the second type of covenant: the treaty. More accurately called a suzerainty treaty, this type of document records an agreement between an overlord (suzerain) and a lesser monarch (the vassal). We have numerous examples of such treaties in ancient Near Eastern literature, especially from the seventh century BCE.[12] Although there are elements of the

treaty form in Exodus 19—24, the closest resemblance is in the book of Deuteronomy. The major parts of these treaties include the following, with Deuteronomic parallels indicated:

- a preamble, identifying the parties (Deut 1:1–5)

- a historical prologue, describing the suzerain's acts of beneficence (Deuteronomy 1–4)

- stipulations—the rules and regulations required of the vassal (Deuteronomy 5—26)

- storing and periodic public recitation of the treaty document (Deut 27:1–13; 30—31)

- witnesses (Deut 31:19–29)

- blessings and curses—i.e., rewards for obedience, punishments for disobedience (Deut 27:15–28:68)

There are numerous differences between the land grant and the suzerainty treaty, but the categorization of Moshe Weinfeld points to the central one: "While the 'grant' constitutes an obligation of the master to his servant, the 'treaty' constitutes an obligation of the servant, the vassal, to his master the suzerain."[13] While the land grant is a reward for service performed by the grantee, the treaty is a list of stipulations required of the vassal in gratitude for past protective actions performed by the suzerain. Obedience to the stipulations will ensure the continued protection by the suzerain (blessings), but disobedience will bring punishment (curses), the ultimate of which is

10. Barbour, *Jamestown Voyages*, 25.

11. Ahlstrom, *Religious History of the American People*, 154. For a discussion of how the biblical so-called conquest of Canaan figures into American history, see Hawk, "Truth about Conquest."

12. For examples see "Vassal Treaties of Esar-Haddon," in *ANET*, 534–41. For examples of specific parallels of language, compare p.

535, Numbers 6 (73) and 10 (108), with Deut 13:6–11.

13. Weinfeld, *Deuteronomic School*, 74; cf. Weinfeld, *Deuteronomy 1–11*, 6–9, 58.

destruction and, in numerous instances, *exile* from the vassal's land. Beginning with Exodus 19, this model becomes the dominant one for much of the rest of the Pentateuch, and, as suggested above, the ideology behind the Former Prophets. The very name *Torah* refers to the *law* that constitutes the stipulations, using *constitute* in a rather literal sense: the Torah represents the political constitution of the covenant people.[14]

The most important stipulation is the demand for absolute fidelity to the suzerain, prohibiting any such treaty agreements with other rulers who would thereby compete for the people's allegiance and alter the social order. Treaties often refer to this allegiance as "loving" the suzerain. Such "love" refers more to covenant loyalty than to an emotion: "You [the vassal] shall love Assurbanipal [the suzerain] . . . king of Assyria, your lord, as yourself. You shall hearken to whatever he says and do whatever he commands, and you shall not seek any other king or other lord against him. This treaty . . . you shall speak to your sons and grandsons, your seed and you seed's seed which shall be born in the future."[15] Such covenant love is the heart of Israel's relationship with God: "Love Yahweh your God with all your heart . . . and keep these words that I am commanding you today in your heart. Recite them to your children" (Deut 6:5–6, AT). Thus the "love of God"

so central to Western religions has it roots here.[16]

Just as human overlords would punish rebellious vassals who switched allegiance to "other lords," so Yahweh[17] will punish Israel when they switch allegiance to "other gods."[18] Indeed, the model of covenantal reward and punishment is widely assumed not only in the Pentateuch and Former Prophets but also in the writing Prophets.[19] The abiding relevance of the model is its insistence on absolute allegiance to God, over against any contenders, whether gods in the theistic sense or those powers that are socioeconomic or political.[20] This model is potentially subversive of *any* power that would claim ultimate authority (e.g., a human ruler of Israel or an occupying empire). In effect, the biblical authors adopted the treaty language but replaced the "king of Assyria" (see above) with Yahweh. Such replacement contains the seed of revolution. Thus swearing allegiance to "Yahweh alone" (Deut 6:4) had political and well as theological

14. One of the most concise discussions of this is that of McBride, "Polity of the Covenant People."

15. Quoted by Römer, *So-Called Deuteronomistic History*, 75, citing the study of Younger on Assyrian annals. For an informative review of covenants, treaties, and the political meaning of love, see Kugel, *How to Read the Bible*, 243–47, 348–50, 353–55.

16. The groundbreaking study of this is by Moran, "Ancient Near Eastern Background." Cf. also Weinfeld, *Deuteronomic School*, 81, among other scholars. Cf. Matt 22:36–40; Mark 12:28–34; Luke 10:25–28.

17. On the name, see appendix 2. Here is a good example of when knowing the personal name helps to understand the contrast with other gods.

18. On the identity of these other gods, see appendix 4. The annals of the Assyrian overlords in the ninth century BCE record their devastating punishment of vassal kings who broke the terms of their treaties and rebelled against them.

19. For the classic formulation in the Former Prophets, see 2 Kgs 17:5–8; in the prophets cf. Jer 34:13–17; Hos 2:2–13; Amos 4:6–12.

20. See the quotations at the end of appendix 4.

implications—loyalty to Yahweh could entail treason against the colonial power. In fact, the Deuteronomic reformation, reflected in the book of Deuteronomy and in the national revival of King Josiah in the seventh century BCE, probably was connected with a revolt against Assyria as the dominant superpower of the era.

We must recognize, however, that the treaty model poses theological problems as well. One has to do with the xenophobia about Canaanites to which we referred above. At its worst, covenant loyalty to God demands the extermination of other peoples, for which we should not hesitate to use the term *genocide* (Deut 7:2, 22–24; 20:16–18; 2:34; 3:6).[21] We certainly cannot excuse such a theology, but we can understand the logical connection with the treaty model. Other peoples in Canaan are threats to Israel's very existence because they provide the temptation to become alternative covenant partners (Deut 7:2) worshiping alternative gods (Deut 7:4), thus eliciting Yahweh's covenant curses.

The tension between the land-grant and the treaty models will seem to come to the breaking point as we near the end of the Pentateuch (as it already does in Leviticus 18). But we will see how the biblical authors could appeal to both models when it would seem that the future of Israel is hopeless: on the one hand, "if you return to the Lord your God . . . and obey him with all your heart," then God will "restore your fortunes" (Deut 30:1–2)—the treaty model; on the other hand, "you will return to Yahweh your God . . . *because* . . . [Yahweh] will not forget the covenant sworn to with your *ancestors*" (Deut 4:30–31, AT)—the grant model.[22]

Theologically, both covenant types have strengths and weaknesses. The grant is an act of pure grace that offers an unconditional promise of divine blessing, providing the grounds for hope, but *because* it is unconditional the grant could lead to a kind of divine permissiveness and human irresponsibility. The treaty stipulations require an undivided commitment to God and a community ethos for which social justice is central, but the conditionality of blessing and curse could lead to a rigid rewards-and-punishment understanding of human fortune and calamity that cannot explain apparently undeserved suffering or offer hope beyond human failure. One can easily see why for some biblical authors *both* covenant models are needed.[23]

---

21. For discussion of the problem of such mass killing in the book of Joshua and elsewhere see my *Book of the Former Prophets*, 20–24, including examples from contemporary history. The term *ethnic cleansing* applies, but only loosely, as the basis for extermination is not ethnic identity.

22. In terms of the history of traditions, one could argue that the eternal covenant of the land grant (predominantly from the Priestly author) serves as a corrective to the contractual basis of the treaty, rooting hope beyond punishment (especially exile) in God's remembering the ancestors (e.g. Exod 32:13). For one such reading, see Blenkinsopp, *Treasures Old and New*, 162–63, 172–73.

23. The combination appears in such texts as Gen 26:3–5, where the grant originally to Abraham is extended to Isaac "*because* Abraham obeyed" the commandments, statutes, and laws of God—the latter phrase using the language of stipulation from the treaty model (e.g., Deut 4:44–45). For a brief discussion of the tension involved, see my *Deuteronomy*, 154–58, on Deut 30:1–20.

APPENDIX 4

God and the "Other Gods"[1]

CENTRAL TO THE COVENANT or treaty model of Israel's relationship to Yahweh is the first commandment of the Ten Commandments: "you shall have no other gods before me." As the NRSV note to Exod 20:3 and Deut 5:7 says, "before" could be translated with "besides." More literally, the expression means, "in my face," and has the same connotation of aggression or infringement of personal space carried by the English idiom. Originally the prohibition may have referred to statues of other gods placed in the presence of Yahweh in the sanctuary (where, of course, Yahweh's presence was invisible). Indeed, the connection between worshiping other gods and using an idol, whether of other gods or representing Yahweh, is so close that the second commandment against idolatry merges with the first: "you shall not bow down to *them*" (Exod 20:5; Deut 5:9, AT).

What other gods are involved? The answer assumes the background of the names of God discussed in appendix 3, (i.e., that the deity El originally was separate from Yahweh but became identified to the extent that El was not considered as an alien deity). Within Israel's Palestinian environment, that leaves primarily two other deities—Baal and Asherah. Baal (more technically, *ba'al*, pronounced "bah-all") plays a prominent role in Canaanite mythology, where he is a subject of El. He is a storm deity, manifesting his power in clouds, lightning, thunder, and rain, as does Yahweh (e.g., Exod 13:21; 14:19; 19:9, 16). As the provider of rain, Baal is also connected with fertility of the land. Baal battles with the forces of chaos (personified in Yam ["Sea"] and Mot ["Death"]), and in conquering them assumes sovereignty. As rainmaker, Baal competed with Yahweh for the people's devotion. The rivalry is only hinted at within the Torah (e.g., the Baal of Peor, Num 25:1–5), but takes center stage

1. The following is adapted from excursus 3 in my *Book of the Former Prophets*.

within the Former Prophets (especially the stories of Elijah, 1 Kings 16–19). It is quite likely that some early Israelites worshiped Baal in some form (e.g., Judg 6:25), but, especially in the Deuteronomic reformation (seventh century), Baal became the primary other god, whose name was anathema.

The second major deity who represented an other god was the female Asherah, also associated with fertility. Since the word *asherah* can be used not only as a proper name but a noun referring to a stylized wooden tree or pole, it is often not clear which is involved (or perhaps both; cf. Deut 16:21). Similar to such poles (although not associated with Asherah) were pillars, usually steles made of stone.[2] Again, it is likely that, prior to the Deuteronomic reformation (and, indeed, after!), worship of Asherah was not unusual. The popular or family-oriented religion of ancient Israel at times called for the worship of other deities and used sacramental objects in ways that the official religion promoted by the Deuteronomic movement tried to stamp out.[3] There is even a highly controversial extrabiblical text that refers to Yahweh and "his *asherah*."[4] In addition to Asherah, there were other female deities worshiped

at various times, including the consort of Baal, Astarte (also known as Ashtaroth or Ishtar, and also called "the queen of heaven": Jer 7:18).

In addition to Baal and Asherah, there is Molech (Milcom), who is especially associated with child sacrifice (Lev 18:21; 20:2–5).

Two kings are especially singled out for introducing (or condoning) the worship of other deities: Solomon (1 Kgs 11:1–8) and Manasseh (2 Kgs 21:1–9). Manasseh was considered the antithesis to his grandson, Josiah, who instituted reforms (2 Kings 22).

For contemporary readers, the phrase "other gods" may make little sense in *theistic* terms, but it makes a great deal of sense in terms of what one values above all else and for what one is willing to sacrifice everything.[5] In a classic sermon that appropriated covenant language and applied it to English settlers approaching the shores of New England in 1631, John Winthrop warned of "other gods" who threatened to "seduce" the settlers into infidelity. But they were not gods in the usual sense; they were "our pleasures and our profits"—in short, materialism, greed, and wealth.[6] Hundreds of years later, we can hear an echo of Winthrop's terms in the admission of a man named Brian: "I was operating as if *a certain value* was of the utmost importance to me. Perhaps it was success. Perhaps it was fear

---

2. Jacob erects one in Gen 28:18–22, as does Moses, Exod 24:4! For the prohibition, see Lev 26:1; Deut 16:22; cf. 7:5; 12:3. Yet another sacramental object subject to Deuteronomic condemnation was the household god (e.g. those household gods belonging to Rachel's father, Laban, Gen 31:30–35; cf. Judg 17:5; 1 Sam 19:13, etc.).

3. For numerous essays discussing this issue see Miller et al., *Ancient Israelite Religion*.

4. For discussion of this text and the scholarly debate, see my *Book of the Former Prophets*, 61–62.

5. The theologian Paul Tillich used the term "ultimate concern." That which is one's ultimate concern functionally is one's god. See Tillich, *Dynamics of Faith*, 1–4.

6. The sermon, "A Modell [sic] of Christian Charity," is widely available; see Bellah, *Habits of the Heart*, 22–27. An excerpt is in my *Book of the Former Prophets*, 14–15.

of failure, but I was extremely success-oriented, to the point where everything would be *sacrificed* for the job, the career, the company."[7]

---

7. One of those interviewed in Bellah, *Habits of the Heart*, 5 This book and its companion book of primary readings, is one of the most perceptive investigations of the role of covenantal language and identity in American experience. Note especially pp. 28–35.

APPENDIX 5

Holiness and Food

CONTEMPORARY READERS WHO GREW up non-Jewish and non-Muslim often find the dietary laws of Leviticus irrelevant.[1] They have trouble seeing a connection between what they eat and what they believe, between food and faith. They enjoy their shrimp cocktails, crab cakes, and pork-loin roasts without any sense of religious or moral problems. Just so, the very notion of animal sacrifice may well seem primitive to modern readers, especially when we read of how the animal is killed and dismembered, drained of blood and eviscerated (e.g., Lev 1:5–9). However, the *principle* involved in what to eat and how to prepare it in Leviticus presents some arresting challenges to our own dietary customs.

In Leviticus, the major principle behind what to eat lies in honoring the order and harmony of the created world as it was perceived. Sea creatures that did not fit with the order of fins-and-scales should not be sea*food*. Thus Israelites abstained from eating shrimp. Although our view of the natural order may differ from that of Leviticus, there may be other reasons why we might abstain from eating shrimp, e.g., ecological or moral reasons. For example, a program on PBS revealed how workers in the shrimp industry in Thailand are sometimes kept in virtual slavery and exploited.[2] In this case, social injustice and ecojustice might demand that we at least find out the source of the shrimp that we eat, and that we abstain from eating shrimp from these particular industries (or seek the reform of these industries). We could make similar arguments for abstaining from eating endangered species like Atlantic halibut or bluefin tuna.

As for animal sacrifice, we have seen that (in Leviticus, at least) all meat that was slaughtered for food had to be sacrificed. Here again the principle

---

1. Christians may point to the saying of Jesus that all foods are "clean" (Mark 7:14–22), but that saying from the first century CE needs to be placed alongside contemporary religious and moral reasons for abstaining from certain foods (see below).

2. Sapienza, "Thai Shrimp Industry Exploits Workers."

involves respecting the order of creation but specifically lies in honoring animals as gifts from God and as creatures whose life is consecrated and holy, as is human life (Lev 17:2, 11). Other cultures both ancient and modern have held similar views: "'The Aleuts believed that everything, animate and inanimate, had it own soul, its own spirit . . . Everything in life was connected with everything else, depended on everything else . . . The salmon knew it was food and accepted the fact that it would die so that the People would live . . . When a hunter went hunting, he did so in new clothes . . . to show respect for the salmon's sacrifice.'"[3]

The biblical restrictions on the preparation of meat evolved to form the elaborate kosher system which, among other criteria, ensures that animals are slaughtered with the least amount of pain possible. Friedman puts it well: "when we take animals' lives in order to support our own, we should remember that both their lives and ours are part of a common creation, and that both are treated in the Torah as sacred."[4] Arguably, industrial meat production goes far from showing such respect. One major study of the beef industry by Jeremy Rifkin opens with a first chapter titled, "Sacrifice to Slaughter."[5] This title suggests how the modern beef industry has turned the ancient reverence for animals as a divine gift into a marketplace calculation of animals as mercantile commodity.

3. Spoken by a character in the novel *Play With Fire*, by Dana Stabenow, 167–68.

4. Friedman, *Torah*, 317.

5. Rifkin, *Beyond Beef*. The shift in meaning would be more difficult to convey in Hebrew, since the same word can be translated "sacrifice" or "slaughter." See n. 36 in ch. 3.

Most cattle now are raised on enormous tracts of land and processed in huge factories. Near the end of their lives, cattle are herded into feed lots where they are fed all sorts of grains and some things far worse. They are then hauled sometimes for great distances in cramped trucks often without water. Those that survive the journey are marched single file into the slaughterhouse. They are stunned by a pneumatic gun, and then the butchers go to work with their knives: "the animal is mechanically hoisted from the platform and hung upside down over the slaughterhouse floor. Men in blood-soaked gowns, handling long knives, slit each steer's throat, thrusting the blade deep into the larynx for a second or two, then quickly withdrawing the knife, severing the jugular vein and carotid artery in the process."[6]

The feedlot and the slaughterhouse are only part of the problem with the beef industry. Others include the following: massive soil erosion; loss of rainforests to pasture, especially in Third World countries; water pollution from the runoff of animal waste, pesticides, and herbicides; extensive use of fossil fuels; and groundwater depletion—not to mention health problems that result from people eating animal fat. Indeed, some recent studies confirm the suspicion that red meat is carcinogenic, especially if cooked at high heat.[7] Moreover, many Third World people have been forced off their land so that wealthy landowners can raise cattle. In Brazil, the standard food of peasants—black beans—"are becoming more expensive, as farmers have switched to growing

6. Ibid., 14.

7. Baklar, "Risks"; "Six Reasons."

soybeans for the more lucrative international feed market."[8] Rifkin poses the moral issue most sharply: "The question of consuming beef, then, extends far beyond the simple issue of 'taste' to include the most complex issues of social justice and equity. . . . Consumption by a privileged few of grain-fed beef while millions go without the minimum daily caloric requirements."[9] The prophet Amos would recognize the behavior (Amos 6:4–6; 5:11).

Thus, as with abstaining from eating certain seafood, one might abstain from eating red meat for moral and religious reasons. Ironically, in such abstentions, one might be avoiding foods which, in Leviticus, are perfectly legitimate, but the abstention would be grounded in the Levitical principle of respect for creation. Abstention would be an expression of holiness—being apart from a society's normal eating customs. One Whole Foods store in Greensboro, North Carolina, describes its coffee as "organic, rainforest alliance, shade grown, fair trade, bird safe, reforestation-driven, farmer connected, and wind powered." Here is a contemporary Kosher list based on the criteria of what is ecologically sustainable and economically just.

Of course, eating red meat or shrimp is only one small part of what one author rightly calls "the Omnivore's Dilemma."[10]

Reading Leviticus may compound that dilemma by raising questions about whether what people eat and how they grow and prepare their food are commensurate with their religious beliefs.

> "We killed two trout. It's strange to kill your dance partners, but that's what we did. We did it because the world is strange—because this is a world where no matter who you are or where you live or what you eat or whether you choose or don't choose to understand and be grateful, it is sacrifice—sweet, bleeding sacrifice—that sustains you. So we killed two trout, but knew no sacrificial prayers, and so simply knelt by the river, commended them on how well they'd fought, whispered, 'Swim, little soul. Go be a bird, or a singing mouse, or a whale,' then broke their bodies to sustain our own."[11]

8. Rifkin, *Beyond Beef,* 148.

9. Ibid., 156.

10. Pollan, *Omnivore's Dilemma.* The state of California has passed a controversial law prohibiting the sale of foie gras, a liver delicacy produced by force-feeding ducks through tubes down their throats, several times a day for several weeks. One suspects that the authors of Leviticus would applaud.

11. Spoken by a character in Duncan, *The River Why,* 282.

APPENDIX 6

Homosexuality and the Bible

HOMOSEXUALITY IS ONE OF the most controversial issues in American culture, and especially in religious communities.[1] The problem is firmly rooted in the book of Leviticus, as well as in other passages, including some in the New Testament. How to read and apply such texts for our contemporary time presents an interesting case study in the process of interpretation. As I write these words, my state (North Carolina) has just passed an amendment to the constitution limiting marriage to that between one man and one woman, an act supported by many churches and clergy. Yet I am a member of a local church within the United Church of Christ that is "open and affirming," welcoming gays and lesbians (and other sexual minorities), including celebrations of holy union between partners.

For many people, a union between same-sex partners simply cannot *be* holy because of the so-called holiness laws in Leviticus: "You shall not lie with a male as with a woman; it is an abomination" (18:22). And later we find the punishment: "If a man lies with a male as with a woman, both of them have committed an abomination; they shall be put to death; their blood is upon them" (20:13).

First, we notice that these two passages fit with the pattern of offense/punishment typical of chs. 18 and 20. The punishment here is the death penalty. If contemporary readers consider the offense to be against the will of God (as stated in the text), do they then think that the penalty should apply as well? Most people would reject the penalty as barbaric.[2] But then how should one distinguish between which law from God is to be followed and which not? Even if the penalty *is* followed, then should one

1. Two books that contain arguments on both sides of the issue are Balch, *Homosexuality*; and Siker, *Homosexuality in the Church*.

2. There are, of course, flagrant examples of such barbarity throughout history, notably in Nazi Germany, but also incidents of torture and murder of homosexuals in the United States. One preacher recently suggested imprisoning all homosexuals (male and female) within an electrified fence so that, eventually, they would die off. See Woodroof, "When Gay-Bashing Goes Viral."

also agree to the death penalty for children who curse their parents (20:9) or for adultery (20:10) or incest (20:11–12)? Again, what criteria govern which laws to follow or not follow?

Second, we notice how limited such prohibitions against homosexuality are, compared to how vociferous the modern debate! Only these two verses in the Hebrew Bible address the issue. Moreover, there is no mention of lesbianism (although female bestiality is forbidden, 18:23). The text (as throughout this section) is addressed to males (masculine singular suffix for *you*). Thus only male homosexual acts are forbidden, and, for that matter, a literal reading suggests that only *one* male homosexual act, i.e. anal intercourse (sodomy, on which see below). Thus the law does not explicitly prohibit other forms of sexual relations between two men, although it probably intends to do so.

The word *sodomy* comes from the story of Sodom and Gomorrah in Genesis 19. Many people simply assume that this story illustrates a negative view of male homosexuality. What the story describes, however, is by no means a loving relationship between two men committed to each other; rather, it describes attempted homosexual gang rape, and against male angels, no less! A similar story in Judges 19 reveals the same picture, only more horrific in that it ends in heterosexual rape of a woman to the point of death. Just as one would not use the latter story to condemn heterosexual acts, so one should not use the Sodom story to condemn homosexual acts between consenting adults. Indeed, it would be ironic to do so since the real sin of Sodom is inhospitality!

The law in Lev 18:22 describes sexual intercourse between two men as "an abomination" or "detestable" (*šeqeṣ*). The same term is used to condemn eating forbidden seafood, certain insects, and "swarming" creatures (Lev 11:9, 20, 41; cf. 7:21), as well as eating third-day leftovers of a sacrifice (19:7). Deuteronomy has no law against homosexuality but tends to use a different word for "abomination" (*toʿebah*), which applies to numerous other matters. The general rule for foods is, "You shall not eat any abhorrent thing" (*toʿebah*), (14:3). The various forbidden foods here generally match those in Leviticus 11. But other categories of behavior also apply. A woman who wears "a man's apparel . . . is abhorrent [*toʿebat*, feminine adjective] to the Lord your God" (22:5). No pantsuits! Again, a man who has divorced his wife and then wants to remarry her after *she* has remarried and been divorced, is not allowed to do so. It would be an abomination (*toʿebah*; 24:4), because she has become "defiled" or "unclean" (why is not explained). Love is *not* better the second time around!

Clearly, many people in contemporary American culture would enjoy a dinner of shrimp and oysters without feeling defiled (on this, see appendix 5). Many people do not condemn women for wearing pants (although there was a time when it was at least frowned upon) and might well see the second marriage of a previously divorced couple as charmingly romantic. So which offenses in the biblical regulations should we consider to be abominations and which not? More generally, there are numerous other customs prohibited by biblical purity laws but that we find completely innocuous: interbreeding of animals, sowing two kinds of seeds in the same field, making clothing by blending cotton and wool (Lev 19:19). Probably the reason behind such thinking in Leviticus had in part to do with unwillingness to fuse two different types within the perceived order of creation: e.g. cotton and wool blends vegetable and animal.

Some would say that we can distinguish between purity laws and moral laws, and that the former are no longer applicable, while the latter are—the latter supposedly including the prohibition against male homosexuality. Some Christians in particular appeal to the rejection of purity laws in a passage like Mark 7:14–22, where Jesus says that what goes into the body cannot defile, only what comes out, including "fornication, theft, murder, adultery," and the like. Indeed, the author of Mark then concludes, "Thus he declared all foods clean."

But this story and its implications can work another way. In the book of Acts, we hear of the controversy among early Christians as to which of the laws in the Hebrew Bible applied to them. Above all, could Gentiles (non-Jews) be admitted to the church (originally founded by Jews) even though they did not conform to most Jewish regulations? Table fellowship—what one eats and with whom—was at the center of this controversy.

In Acts 10:1–16, there is a story about the Apostle Peter, who was opposed to Gentiles, having a dream in which a voice from heaven orders him to eat various foods: "all kinds of four-footed creatures and reptiles and birds of the air." Peter says he will not do this because he has "never eaten anything that is profane or unclean" (cf. Leviticus 11). But the voice replies, "What God has made clean, you must not call profane." Immediately who should show up seeking membership in the church but a Gentile, one Cornelius, and Peter interprets his dream: "God has shown me that I should not call anyone profane or unclean" (10:28). Peter does not say "any food," but "anyone," thereby radically shifting the significance of the vision. "The issue, as it turns out, is not simply about 'unclean' food but also about 'unclean' people, about who shall sit at our table."[3]

This story involves a fascinating process of tradition and interpretation. In order to say, "What God has made clean, you must not call profane," the early church also had to say that what *had* been God's word at one time was no longer God's word for *their* time. That is, the purity laws in the Hebrew Bible, which are presented as the *words* of God, no longer functioned as the *word* of God: as the authoritative rule for faith. Some of what God said in Leviticus and Deuteronomy (e.g., Lev 11:1) was contradicted by what God said to Peter in his dream. Thus what Scripture had claimed as a past revelation was replaced by the claim of a new revelation.[4] Moreover, the revelation about dietary custom was interpreted to

---

3. Willimon, *Acts*, 98.

4. It is critical here to acknowledge that outside of a mechanically literal interpretation of biblical texts, we are always dealing with fictive literature in which an author has invented dialogue for God. Thus what is "revealed" is itself a product of human imagination and interpretation. Cf. Patrick (*Rhetoric of Revelation*, 71): "at some point in the formation of the tradition, someone placed these words in YHWH's mouth." I have discussed this regarding "natural theology" in my *God of Dirt*, 6–7.

apply to social justice.[5] The result was to welcome people into the church who previously were not only not welcome but considered to be unworthy.

One can argue that the same process could be applied to the issue of homosexuals in the church. One cannot separate ritual law and moral law into totally distinct categories. Holiness encompasses both.[6] Thus the prohibition against mixing different types of seeds stands back-to-back with the Golden Rule, which undergirds all of social ethics (Lev 19:18–19). The story of Peter and Cornelius refutes the argument that one can ignore the law against eating shrimp and oysters but must continue to abide by the law prohibiting homosexuals. Some of what God said in Leviticus (e.g. 18:1, 22) no longer functions as the word of God for today. Indeed, some Christians now argue that God is still speaking and is saying that no one may now call profane those whom God made to be homosexual. Moreover, the theological claim about creation corresponds to considerable biological research that sees homosexuality as innate rather than as a lifestyle choice that one makes arbitrarily. The *experience* of homosexuals who understand their orientation as natural—as who they were created to be—should be part of the process of ongoing interpretation.

Of course, some Christians opposed to homosexuality appeal to other New Testament passages, notably 1 Cor 6:9–10 and 1 Tim 1:9–10.[7] Of the two terms used in these texts (NRSV here), one, "male prostitutes" is as irrelevant as would be "female prostitutes." The other term ("sodomites" in the NRSV) is subject to differing translations and interpretations. Some scholars basically agree with the NRSV and see a condemnation similar to that in Leviticus. Others see another reference to some form of sexual exploitation, probably of young boys, which would also be irrelevant. The other text is Rom 1:26–27, in which Paul refers to "unnatural" intercourse, which again raises the question of what is natural and what is unnatural (see above). Even if the Romans text contains a blanket prohibition, as with the Leviticus texts, one could employ the same process of interpretation involved in the Cornelius story. One could, in the end, extend another (more liberal) text from Paul—"There is no longer Jew or Greek, there is no longer slave or free, there is no longer male and female; for all of you are one in Christ Jesus" (Gal 3:28)—to also include the categories of gay and straight.[8]

The change represented in the Cornelius story, in fact, is rooted in the Hebrew Bible itself, especially when we understand Scripture as both process and product (see the Introduction to this

---

5. Although not referring to the Acts story, the discussion of "Open Commensality" by Crossan (*Historical Jesus*, 262) is relevant: "An open table and an open menu offend alike against any cultural situation in which distinctions among foods and guests mirror social distinctions, discriminations, and hierarchies."

6. Houston ("Integrated Reading," 158) suggests that the Holiness Code author of Leviticus "draws no distinction as we are used to between 'ritual' and 'moral' commands." Both have to do with holiness (cf. 20:22–26 on sexual crimes and clean/unclean animals).

7. Among the other offenders listed here are liars and the greedy, which would seem to implicate a lot more people than homosexuals!

8. Note also Rom 14:14: "Nothing is unclean in itself; but it is unclean for anyone who thinks it unclean."

book). The law in Lev 18:22 is embedded in a list of prohibitions regarding marriage and the family (18:6–23).[9] Various relationships, some of which we too would consider incestuous, are forbidden, largely because of the tensions that they would create in extended families, where people live in close proximity. Sociologically, the laws concern a relatively small number of people. In particular, as Shenker states, "The social horizon of the prohibition of homosexuality here refers to a limited group of persons, i.e., the extended family group and the totality of extended families in the village and in the region."[10] The prohibition is not applied explicitly to all humankind.[11]

9. Some scholars think that Leviticus disapproves of male homosexuality because it wastes semen and thus represents a loss of potential life (especially since semen was thought to be a homunculus, not sperm needing an egg). This would also explain why lesbianism is *not* condemned. Others think that the marking off of social boundaries is predominant, functioning much like the dietary laws at a time when maintaining Jewish identity was critical.

10. Schenker, "What Connects," 182. Cf. Milgrom (*Leviticus: A Book of Ritual*, 197): Lev 18:22 and 20:13 do "not cover all male-male liaisons, but only those within the limited circle of family." Given the various qualifications, Milgrom concludes that more than 99 percent of homosexual men ("namely, non-Jews") are excluded from the prohibition (*Leviticus 17–22*, 1787). However, the redactional framework to Leviticus 18 and 20 suggests that the various sexual prohibitions applied to non-Israelites as well. The centrality of procreation is apparent in that normally sex with one's brother's wife is forbidden (Lev 18:16; 20:21), but if the brother dies, one is obligated to have sex with the widow in order to produce children for the deceased brother (Deut 25:5–6).

11. The editorial framework of Leviticus does accuse the native Canaanites of all the defilements prohibited in ch. 18, part of the general

In terms of changing customs, it is interesting to note how the laws in Leviticus 18 contradict the marital relationships we see elsewhere in the Hebrew Bible. Abraham claims that his wife Sarah is his half sister (Gen 20:12, contrast Lev 18:1; cf. 2 Sam 13:13). Abraham also married Sarah's slave girl, Hagar, and had a child by her, then later married yet another wife and had children by her (Gen 25:1–3). Jacob married sisters (Genesis 29; contrast Lev 18:18), and had children by both of their slave-girls. Thus, though not against prohibitions in Leviticus, bigamy was commonplace. The priest Elkanah had two wives (1 Samuel 1). David had at least six wives, along with concubines (by whom he also had children; 1 Chr 3:1–10), and Solomon— that proverbial paragon of wisdom—was reputed to have seven hundred wives and three hundred concubines (1 Kgs 11:3)! The changes in marital customs simply reflect many other changes apparent in different legal sources. These changes center on different issues in the texts. For example, regarding preparation of the Passover lamb, see Exod 12:9 versus Deut 16:7, where a word often rendered "cook" means "boil"; also compare secular versus only-sacral meat slaughter (Lev 17:1–4; Deut 12:15); or treatment of indentured servants (Exod 21:2–11; 22:25; 23:10–11;

pejorative stereotype. Milgrom (*Leviticus 17–22*, 1788) argues that the homosexuality prohibition applies only to inhabitants of Canaan (i.e., the "Holy Land"), and thus is not universal. There is no evidence that the Canaanites practiced rampant homosexuality or held fertility cult rituals. The juxtaposition of Lev 18:22 with the child-sacrifice prohibition in v. 21 is also probably a deliberate attempt to apply guilt by association. On this see Bird, "Bible in Christian Ethical Deliberation," 158–61.

Deut 15:1–18). Indeed, slavery in principle is never condemned in Scripture but is now universally rejected. As Kaiser says, "sometimes the circumstances alter what is often perceived at face value to be an unalterable view."[12] As a further contemporary example, one can note how acceptable divorce has become for many people, even though a saying of Jesus virtually rules it out (Matt 5:31–32).[13]

Certainly the biblical authors were not accustomed to experiencing same-sex partners who were committed to each other in love—people who may even have children by adoption, former heterosexual relationships, or other means (e.g., artificial insemination). They could not see gay or lesbian couples living harmoniously with their extended family and friends. The purity laws reflect marital and family relationships from a culture radically different from our own. As with much of Scripture in general, those laws contain moral values that continue to be recognized universally—like the "Golden Rule"—but also contain rusty iron rules so corroded that they are no longer reasonable, civil, or just.[14]

---

12. Kaiser, *Leviticus*, 1072, not referring to homosexuality, on which he takes an equivocal position.

13. Note that part of the saying—"whoever marries a divorced woman commits adultery"—would, under the purity law of Lev 20:10, require the death penalty for both the man and the woman.

14. Friedman (*Torah*, 377–78), speaking from a Jewish perspective, suggests that contemporary wisdom must determine the issue (following Deut 17:8–9), and concludes that "the period in which this commandment [Lev 18:18] was binding has come to an end."

Bibliography

Alter, Robert. *The Art of Biblical Narrative*. New York: Basic Books, 1981.

———. *The Five Books of Moses*. New York: Norton, 2004.

Abram, David. *Becoming Animal: An Earthly Cosmology*. New York: Pantheon, 2010.

Ahlstrom, Sidney. *A Religious History of the American People*. New Haven: Yale University Press, 1972.

The American Heritage College Dictionary. 4th ed. Boston: Houghton Mifflin, 2002.

Anderson, Gary A. "Introduction to Israelite Religion." In *The New Interpreter's Bible*, edited by Leander E. Keck et al., 1:272–83. 12 vols. Nashville: Abingdon, 1994.

Anderson, Herbert. *The Family and Pastoral Care*. Theology and Pastoral Care Series. Philadelphia: Fortress, 1984.

Auerbach, Eric. *Mimesis: The Representation of Reality in Western Literature*. Translated by Willard R. Trask. 50th anniversary edition, with a new introduction by Edward Said. Princeton: Princeton University Press, 2003.

Baden, Joel S. *The Composition of the Pentateuch: Renewing the Documentary Hypothesis*. New Haven: Anchor Yale Reference Library. Yale University Press, 2012.

Bakalar, Nicholas. "Risks: More Red Meat, More Mortality." *New York Times*, March 12, 2012, D6. Online: http://www.nytimes.com/2012/03/13/health/research/red-meat-linked-to-cancer-and-heart-disease.html?_r=0/.

Balch, David. L., editor. *Homosexuality, Science, and the "Plain Sense" of Scripture*. Grand Rapids: Eerdmans, 2000.

Barbour, Philip L. *The Jamestown Voyages under the First Charter: 1606–1609*. Volume 1. 2 vols. Works issued by the Hakluyt Society, 2nd series, 136. London: Cambridge University Press, 1969.

Barnes, Brooks. "At 97, He Has a Book (or 2) Left." *The New York Times*, November 13, 2012, C1, 5.

Barth, Karl. *Church Dogmatics*. IV/1, *The Doctrine of Reconciliation*. Edited by G. W. Bromiley and T. F. Torrance. New York: Scribner, 1956.

Barton, John. *Reading the Old Testament: Method in Biblical Study*. Rev. ed. Louisville: Westminster John Knox, 1996.

Beal, Timothy. *The Rise and Fall of the Bible: The Unexpected History of an Accidental Book*. Boston: Houghton Mifflin Harcourt, 2011.

Bellah, Robert N. *The Broken Covenant: American Civil Religion in a Time of Trial*. The Weil Lectures, 1971. New York: Seabury, 1975.

———. "Civil Religion in America." In *American Civil Religion*, edited by Russell E. Richey and Donald G. Jones, 21–44. New York: Harper & Row, 1974.

——— et al. *Habits of the Heart: Individualism and Commitment in American Life*. Berkeley: University of California Press, 1985.

Berry, Wendell. *The Art of the Commonplace: Agrarian Essays*. Washington DC: Counterpoint, 2002.

Bird, Phyllis A. "The Bible in Christian Ethical Deliberation concerning Homosexuality: Old Testament Contributions." In *Homosexuality, Science, and the "Plain Sense" of Scripture*, edited by David L. Balch, 142–76. Grand Rapids: Eerdmans, 2000.

Blenkinsopp, Joseph. *Treasures Old and New: Essays in the Theology of the Pentateuch*. Grand Rapids: Eerdmans, 2004.

Book of Worship. New York: United Church of Christ, Office for Church Life and Leadership, 1986.

Bronstein, Hebert, editor. *A Passover Haggadah: The New Union Haggadah*. Prepared by the Central Conference of American Rabbis. 2nd rev. ed. New York: Viking, 1982.

Brooks, David. "The Age of Possibility." *The New York Times*, November 16, 2012, A29.

Brooks, Geraldine. *Caleb's Crossing*. New York: Viking, 2011.

Brown, William P. *The Seven Pillars of Creation: The Bible, Science, and the Ecology of Wonder*. Oxford: Oxford University Press, 2010.

Brueggemann, Walter. *The Book of Exodus*. In *The New Interpreter's Bible*, edited by Leander E. Keck et al., 1:677–981. 12 vols. Nashville: Abingdon, 1994.

———. *Genesis*. Interpretation. Atlanta: John Knox, 1982.

———. *Theology of the Old Testament: Testimony, Dispute, Advocacy*. Minneapolis: Fortress, 1997.

Brueggemann, Walter, and Hans W. Wolff. *The Vitality of Old Testament Traditions*. Atlanta: John Knox, 1975 [2nd ed. 1982].[1]

Buber, Martin. *Moses: The Revelation and the Covenant*. Harper Torchbooks. New York: Harper, 1958.

Campbell, Antony F., and Mark. A. O'Brien. *Rethinking the Pentateuch: Prolegomena to the Theology of Ancient Israel*. Louisville: Westminster John Knox, 2005.

Carr, David M. *Reading the Fractures of Genesis: Historical and Literary Approaches*. Louisville: Westminster John Knox, 1996.

Caruso, Michael, editor. "The Food Issue." *The Smithsonian* 43/3 (June 2012).

Childs, Brevard S. *The Book of Exodus: A Critical, Theological Commentary*. Old Testament Library. Philadelphia: Westminster, 1974.

Clements, Ronald. E. *The Book of Deuteronomy*. In *The New Interpreter's Bible*, edited by Leander E. Keck et al., 2:271–538. 12 vols. Nashville: Abingdon, 1998.

Clines, David J. A. *The Theme of the Pentateuch*. JSOTSup 10. Sheffield: Department of Biblical Studies, Sheffield University, 1978 [2nd ed., 1997].

Coats, George W. *Genesis, With an Introduction to Narrative Literature*. Forms of the Old Testament Literature 1. Grand Rapids: Eerdmans, 1983.

———. "The King's Loyal Opposition: Obedience and Authority in Exodus 32—34." In *Canon and Authority: Essays in Old Testament Religion and Theology*, edited by George W. Coats and Burke O. Long, 91–109. Philadelphia: Fortress, 1977.

———. *Moses: Heroic Man, Man of God*. JSOTSup 57. Sheffield: Sheffield Academic, 1988.

———. *The Moses Tradition*. JSOTSup 161. Sheffield: Sheffield Academic, 1993.

———, editor. *Saga, Legend, Tale, Novella, Fable: Narrative Forms in Old Testament Literature*. JSOTSup 35. Sheffield, England: JSOT Press, 1985.

———. "The Yahwist as Theologian? A Critical Reflection." *JSOT* 3 (1976) 33–42.

Cohn, Robert. *The Shape of Sacred Space: Four Biblical Studies*. Studies in Religion 23. Chico, CA: Scholars, 1981.

Cotter, David W. *Genesis*. Berit Olam. Collegeville, MN: Liturgical, 2003.

Cragg, Kenneth, and R. Marston Speight. *Islam from Within: Anthology of a Religion*. The Religious Life of Man. Belmont, CA: Wadsworth, 1980.

Crites, Stephen. "The Narrative Quality of Experience." *JAAR* 39 (1971) 291–311.

Cross, Frank M. *Canaanite Myth and Hebrew Epic: Essays in the History of the Religion of Israel*. Cambridge: Harvard University Press, 1973.

Douglas, Mary. *Leviticus as Literature*. Oxford: Oxford University Press, 1999.

Dozeman, Thomas B. *The Book of Numbers*. In *The New Interpreter's Bible*, edited by Leander E. Keck et al., 2:1–268. Nashville: Abingdon, 1998.

———. "The Commission of Moses and the Book of Genesis." In *A Farewell to the Yahwist?: The Composition of the Pentateuch in Recent European Interpretation*, edited by Thomas B. Dozeman and Konrad Schmid, 107–29. SBL Symposium Series 34. Atlanta: Society of Biblical Literature, 2006.

---

1. In this bibliography, brackets surround more recent or accessible editions, even though these editions were not consulted for this book.

———. *God at War: A Study of Power in the Exodus Tradition*. New York: Oxford University Press, 1996.

———. *God on the Mountain: A Study of Redaction, Theology, and Canon in Exodus 19–24*. SBL Monograph Series 37. Atlanta: Scholars, 1989.

Dozeman, Thomas B., and Konrad Schmid, editors. *A Farewell to the Yahwist?: The Composition of the Pentateuch in Recent European Interpretation*. SBL Symposium Series 34. Atlanta: Society of Biblical Literature, 2006.

Duncan, David James. *The River Why*. San Francisco: Sierra Club Books, 1983.

Fackenheim, Emil. *God's Presence in History: Jewish Affirmations and Philosophical Reflections*. The Deems Lectures, 1968. New York: New York University Press, 1970.

Fantalkin, Alexander, and Oren Tal. "The Canonization of the Pentateuch: When and Why? (Part I)." *Zeitschrift für die alttestamentliche Wissenschaft* 124 (2012) 1–18.

Fisher, Loren R. *Genesis: A Royal Epic*. 2nd ed. Eugene, OR: Cascade Books, 2011.

Fokkelman, J. P. *Narrative Art in Genesis: Specimens of Stylistic and Structural Analysis*. Assen: Van Gorcum, 1975. [2nd ed., Biblical Seminar 12. Sheffield: JSOT Press, 1991.]

Fretheim, Terence E. *The Book of Genesis*. In *The New Interpreter's Bible*, edited by Leander E. Keck, et al., 1:319–674. 12 vols. Nashville: Abingdon, 1994.

———. *Creation, Fall, and Flood: Studies in Genesis 1–11*. A Tower Book. Minneapolis: Augsburg, 1969.

———. *Exodus*. Interpretation. Louisville: John Knox, 1991.

Freedman, David Noel, editor. *The Anchor Bible Dictionary*. 6 vols. New York: Doubleday, 1992.

Friedman, Richard Elliott. *Commentary on the Torah: With a New English Translation*. San Francisco: HarperSanFrancisco, 2001.

———, editor. *The Creation of Sacred Literature: Composition and Redaction of the Biblical Text*. Near Eastern Studies 22. Berkeley: University of California Press, 1981

———. "Torah (Pentateuch)." In *The Anchor Bible Dictionary*, edited by David Noel Freedman, 6:612–16. 6 vols. New York: Doubleday, 1992.

Frei, Hans. *The Eclipse of Biblical Narrative: A Study in Eighteenth and Nineteenth Century Hermeneutics*. New Haven: Yale University Press, 1974.

Frye, Northrop. *The Anatomy of Criticism*. Princeton: Princeton University Press, 1957.

———. *The Great Code: The Bible and Literature*. San Diego: Harcourt Brace Jovanovich, 1981.

Gardner, Anne. "Ecojustice: A Study of Genesis 6.11–13." In *The Earth Story in Genesis*, edited by Norman C. Habel and Shirley Wurst, 118–22. Earth Bible 2. Cleveland: Pilgrim, 2000.

Gilkey, Langdon. "The Political Dimensions of Theology." *Journal of Religion* 59 (1979) 154–68.

Greenberg, Moshe. *Understanding Exodus*. Heritage of Biblical Israel 2. New York: Behrman House, 1969. [2nd ed., Eugene, OR: Cascade Books, 2013.]

Greene, Brian. *The Elegant Universe: Superstrings, Hidden Dimensions, and the Quest for the Ultimate Theory*. New York: Vintage, 1999.

Good, Robert McClive. *The Sheep of His Pasture: A Study of the Hebrew Noun AM(M) and Its Semitic Cognates*. Harvard Semitic Monographs 29. Chico, CA: Scholars, 1983.

Gottwald, Norman K. *The Tribes of Yahweh: A Sociology of the Religion of Liberated Israel*. Maryknoll, NY: Orbis, 1979.

Gunn, David M. *The Fate of King Saul: An Interpretation of a Biblical Story*. JSOTSup 14. Sheffield: Department of Biblical Studies, University of Sheffield, 1980.

Halbe, Jörn. *Das Privilegrecht Jahwes, Ex. 34,10–26: Gestalt und Wesen, Herkunft und Wirken in vordeuteronomischer Zeit*. FRLANT 114. Gottingen: Vandenhoeck & Ruprecht, 1975.

Hallo, William W., editor. *The Context of Scripture*. Vol. 3, *Archival Documents from the Biblical World*. 3 vols. Leiden: Brill, 2002.

Hallo, William W., and J. J. A. van Dijk. *The Exaltation of Inanna*. Near Eastern Researches 3. New Haven: Yale University Press, 1968.

Harrelson, Walter. "Guidance in the Wilderness: The Theology of Numbers." *Interpretation* 13 (1959) 24–36.

Hastings, Max. *Inferno: The World at War, 1939–1945*. New York: Knopf, 2011.

Hawk, L. Daniel. "The Truth about Conquest: Joshua as History, Narrative, and Scripture." *Interpretation* 66 (2012) 129–40.

Hendel, Ronald. *Remembering Abraham: Culture, Memory, and History in the Hebrew Bible*. Oxford: Oxford University Press, 2005.

Henninger, Daniel. "Our Un-Presidential Debates." *Wall Street Journal*, October 27, 2011, A17. Online: http://online.wsj.com/article/SB10001424052970204777904576653432518503552.html/.

Herberg, Will. "America's Civil Religion: What It Is and When It Comes." In *American Civil Religion*, edited by Russell E. Richey and Donald G. Jones, 76–88. New York: Harper & Row, 1974.

Heym, Stefan. *The King David Report: A Novel*. New York: Putnam, 1973.

Hiebert, Theodore. *The Yahwist's Landscape: Nature and Religion in Early Israel*. New York: Oxford University Press, 1996.

Holladay, Carl R. "Contemporary Methods of Reading the Bible." In *The New Interpreter's Bible*, edited by Leander E. Keck et al., 1:124–49. 12 vols. Nashville: Abingdon, 1994.

Hopkins, David C. "Life in Ancient Palestine." In *The New Interpreter's Bible*, edited by Leander E. Keck et al., 1:213–27. 12 vols. Nashville: Abingdon, 1994.

Houston, Walter J. "Towards an Integrated Reading of the Dietary Laws of Leviticus." In *The Book of Leviticus: Composition and Reception*, edited by Rolf Rendtorff and Robert A. Kugler, 142–61. VTSup 93. Leiden: Brill, 2003.

Jensen, Robin M. *The Substance of Things Seen: Art, Faith, and the Christian Community*. Grand Rapids: Eerdmans, 2004.

Jenson, Philip Peter. *Graded Holiness: A Key to the Priestly Conception of the World*. JSOTSup 106. Sheffield: Sheffield Academic, 1992.

Kaiser, Walter C., Jr. *The Book of Leviticus*. In *The New Interpreter's Bible*, edited by Leander E. Keck et al., 1:983–1191. 12 vols. Nashville: Abingdon, 1994.

Kearney, Peter J. "Creation and Liturgy: The P Redaction of Ex 25—40." *Zeitschrift für die alttestamentliche Wissenschaft* 89 (1977) 375–86.

Kermode, Frank. *The Sense of an Ending: Studies in the Theory of Fiction*. Mary Flexner Lectures, 1965. New York: Oxford University Press, 1967.

Kierkegaard, Søren. *Fear and Trembling*, and *The Sickness unto Death*. Translated with introductions and notes by Walter Lowrie. Garden City, NY: Doubleday, 1954.

Kikawada, Isaac M., and Arthur Quinn. *Before Abraham Was: The Unity of Genesis* 1–11. Nashville: Abingdon, 1985.

King, Martin Luther, Jr. "I Have a Dream." In *The Voice of Black America*, edited by Philip S. Foner, 971–75. New York: Simon & Schuster, 1972.

Knierim, Rolf P. "The Composition of the Pentateuch." In *The Task of Old Testament Theology: Substance, Method, and Cases*, 351–79. Grand Rapids: Eerdmans, 1995.

Kugel, James L. *How to Read the Bible: A Guide to Scripture, Then and Now*. New York: Free Press, 2007.

LaCocque, André. *Onslaught against Innocence: Cain, Abel, and the Yahwist*. Eugene, OR: Cascade Books, 2008.

———. *The Trial of Innocence: Adam, Eve, and the Yahwist*. Eugene, OR: Cascade Books, 2006.

Lambdin, Thomas O. *Introduction to Biblical Hebrew*. New York: Scribner, 1971.

L'Engle, Madeleine. *Questions of Faith 5: What Gives You Faith?* Video. Nashville: Ecufilm, 1999.

Levinson, Bernard M. *Deuteronomy and the Hemeneutics of Legal Innovation*. New York: Oxford University Press, 1997.

Levine, Baruch. *In the Presence of the Lord*. Studies in Judaism in Late Antiquity 5. Leiden: Brill, 1974.

———. *Leviticus*. JPS Torah Commentary. New York: Jewish Publication Society, 1989.

Lohfink, Norbert. *Das Hauptgebot: Eine Untersuchung literarischer Einleitungsfragen zu Dtn* 5—11. Analecta Biblica 20. Rome: Pontifical Biblical Institute Press, 1963.

———. "Darstellungskunst und Theologie in Dtn 1, 6—3, 29." *Biblica* 41 (1960) 105–34.

———. *Theology of the Pentateuch: Themes of the Priestly Narrative and Deuteronomy*. Translated by Linda M. Maloney. Minneapolis: Fortress, 1994.

Mann, Thomas W. "'All the Families of the Earth': The Theological Unity of Genesis." *Interpretation* 45 (1991) 341–53.

———. *The Book of the Former Prophets*. Eugene, OR: Cascade Books, 2011.

———. *Deuteronomy*. Westminster Bible Companion. Louisville: Westminster John Knox, 1995.

————. *Divine Presence and Guidance in Israelite Traditions: The Typology of Exaltation.* 1977. Reprinted, Eugene, OR: Wipf & Stock, 2010.

————. *The God of Dirt: Mary Oliver and the Other Book of God.* Cambridge: Cowley, 2004.

————. "Holiness and Death in the Redaction of Num 16:1—20:13." In *Love and Death in the Ancient Near East: Essays in Honor of Marvin H. Pope,* edited by John H. Marks and Robert M. Good, 181–90. Guilford, CT: Four Quarters, 1987.

————. "Passover: The Time of Our Lives." *Interpretation* 50 (1996) 240–50.

————. "Stars, Sprouts, and Streams." In *God Who Creates: Essays in Honor of W. Sibley Towner,* edited by William P. Brown and S. Dean McBride Jr., 135–51. Grand Rapids: Eerdmans, 2000.

————. "Theological Reflections on the Denial of Moses." *Journal of Biblical Literature* 98 (1979) 481–94.

Massey, James Earl. "Reading the Bible as African Americans." In *The New Interpreter's Bible,* edited by Leander E. Keck et al., 1:154–60. 12 vols. Nashville: Abingdon, 1994.

Mathews, Donald G. *Religion in the Old South.* Chicago History of American Religion. Chicago: University of Chicago Press, 1977.

Margulis, Lynn. "Talking on the Water." *Sierra* 79 (1994) 72.

McBride, S. Dean, Jr. "Biblical Literature in Its Historical Context." In *Harper's Bible Commentary,* edited by James L. Mays et al., 14–26. San Francisco: Harper & Row, 1988.

————. "The Essence of Orthodoxy: Deuteronomy 5:6–10 and Exodus 20:2–6." *Interpretation* 60 (2006) 123–51.

————. "Introduction and Annotations to the Book of Deuteronomy." In *The HarperCollins Study Bible.* Edited by Wayne E. Meeks et al., 266–325. New York: HarperCollins, 1993.

————. "Polity of the Covenant People: The Book of Deuteronomy." In *Constituting the Community: Studies on the Polity of Ancient Israel in Honor of S. Dean McBride, Jr.,* edited by John T. Strong and Steven S. Tuell, 17–33. Winona Lake, IN: Eisenbrauns, 2005.

————. "The Yoke of the Kingdom: An Exposition of Deuteronomy 6:4–5." *Interpretation* 27 (1973) 273–306.

McEvenue, Sean. *The Narrative Style of the Priestly Writer.* Analecta Biblica 50. Rome: Pontifical Biblical Institute Press, 1971.

McFague, Sallie. *The Body of God: An Ecological Theology.* Minneapolis: Fortress, 1993.

————. *Super, Natural Christians: How We Should Love Nature.* Minneapolis: Fortress, 1997.

Mettinger, Tryggve N. D. *The Dethronement of Sabaoth: Studies in the Shem and Kabod Theologies.* Coniectanea biblica. Old Testament Series 18. Lund: Gleerup, 1982.

Meyers, Carol. *Exodus.* New Cambridge Bible Commentary. Cambridge: Cambridge University Press, 2005.

Miles, Jack. *God: A Biography.* New York: Knopf, 1995.

Millard, A. R., and D. J. Wiseman, editors. *Essays on the Patriarchal Narratives.* 1983. Reprinted, Eugene, OR: Wipf & Stock, 2008.

Milgrom, Jacob. *Leviticus 1–16.* Anchor Bible 3. New York: Doubleday, 1991.

————. *Leviticus 17–22.* Anchor Bible 3A. New York: Doubleday, 2000.

————. *Leviticus: A Book of Ritual and Ethics.* Continental Commentaries. Minneapolis: Fortress, 2004.

————. "Sacrifices and Offerings, OT." In *Interpreter's Dictionary of the Bible, Supplementary Volume,* edited by Keith Crim et al., 763–71 Nashville: Abingdon, 1976.

Miller, Patrick D. *Genesis 1–11.* JSOTSup 8. Sheffield: JSOT Press, 1976.

————. *The Religion of Ancient Israel.* Library of Ancient Israel. Louisville: Westminster John Knox, 2000.

Miller, Patrick D. et al., editors. *Ancient Israelite Religion: Essays in Honor of Frank Moore Cross.* Minneapolis: Fortress, 1987.

Mitchell, Stephen, translator. *Tao te Ching: A New English Version, with Foreword and Notes.* New York: Harper & Row, 1988.

Moberly, R. W. L. *At the Mountain of God: Story and Theology in Exodus 32–34.* JSOTSup 22. Sheffield: JSOT Press, 1983.

Moran, William L. "The Ancient Near Eastern Background of the Love of God in Deuteronomy." *Catholic Biblical Quarterly* 25 (1963) 77–87.

————"Deuteronomy." In *A New Catholic Commentary on Holy Scripture,* edited by Reginald C. Fuller et al., 256–76. Rev. ed. London: Nelson, 1969.

Muir, John. *Nature Writings.* New York: Library of America, 1997.

Neher, André. *Moses and the Vocation of the Jewish People.* New York: Harper, 1959.

Nelson, Richard D. *Deuteronomy: A Commentary.* Old Testament Libray. Louisville: Westminster John Knox, 2002.

Neusner, Jacob. *The Way of Torah: An Introduction to Judaism.* Religious Life of Man. Belmont, CA: Dickenson, 1970

Niditch, Susan. "Genesis." In *The Women's Bible Commentary,* edited by Carol A. Newsom and Sharon H. Ringe, 13–29. Louisville: Westminster John Knox, 1998.

———. *Oral World and Written Word: Ancient Israelite Literature.* Library of Ancient Israel. Louisville: Westminster John Knox, 1996

Noth, Martin. *The Deuteronomistic History.* JSOTSup 15. Translated by J. Doull. Sheffield: University of Sheffield, Department of Biblical Studies, 1981.

———. *A History of Pentateuchal Traditions.* Translated by Bernhard W. Anderson. Englewood Cliffs, NJ: Prentice-Hall, 1972.

O'Connor, Flannery. *Mystery and Manners: Occasional Prose.* Selected and edited by Sally and Robert Fitzgerald. New York: Farrar, Straus & Giroux, 1969.

Oliver, Mary. *New and Selected Poems.* Boston: Beacon, 1992.

Olson, Dennis T. *The Death of the Old and the Birth of the New: The Framework of the Book of Numbers and the Pentateuch.* Brown Judaic Studies 71. Chico, CA: Scholars, 1985.

———. *Deuteronomy and the Death of Moses: A Theological Reading.* Overtures to Biblical Theology. Minneapolis: Fortress, 1994.

———. *Numbers.* Interpretation: A Bible Commentary for Teaching and Preaching. Louisville: John Knox, 1996.

Osiek, Carolyn. "Reading the Bible as Women." In *The New Interpreter's Bible,* edited by Leander E. Keck et al., 1:181–87. 12 vols. Nashville: Abingdon, 1994.

Otto, Rudolf. *The Idea of the Holy.* New York: Oxford, 1958.

Pannenberg, Wolfhart. "Zur Theologie des Rechts." *Zeitschrift für evangelische Ethik* 7 (1963) 17–20.

Pardee, Dennis. *Ritual and Cult at Ugarit.* Writings from the Ancient World 10. Atlanta: Society of Biblical Literature, 2002

Parker, Simon B. "Ancient Near Eastern Literary Background of the Old Testament." In *The New Interpreter's Bible,* edited by Leander E. Keck et al., 1:228–43. 12 vols. Nashville: Abingdon, 1994.

Patrick, Dale. *The Rhetoric of Revelation in the Hebrew Bible.* Overtures to Biblical Theology. Minneapolis: Fortress, 1999.

Plaut, W. Gunther et al. *The Torah: A Modern Commentary.* New York: Union of American Hebrew Congregations, 1981 [Revised edition, 2005].

Pollan, Michael. *The Omnivore's Dilemma: The Natural History of Four Meals.* New York: Penguin, 2006.

Pollard, Samuel D., director. *Slavery by Another Name.* PBS documentary. Airdate: 13 February 2012, (based on a book by the same title by Doug Blackmon). Boston: PBS Distribution, 2012.

Polzin, Robert. "'The Ancestress of Israel in Danger' in Danger." *Semeia* 3 (1975) 82–83.

———. *Moses and the Deuteronomist: Deuteronomy, Joshua, and Judges.* A Literary Study of the Deuteronomic History. New York: Seabury, 1980 [2nd ed., Indiana Studies in Biblical Literature. Bloomington: Indiana University Press, 1993].

Price, Reynolds. *A Palpable God: Thirty Stories Translated from the Bible, with an Essay on the Origins and Life of Narrative.* New York: Atheneum, 1978.

Pritchard, James B., editor. *Ancient Near Eastern Texts Relating to the Old Testament.* Princeton: Princeton University Press, 1950.

Pury, Albert de. "The Jacob Story and the Beginning of the Formation of the Pentateuch." In *A Farewell to the Yahwist?: The Composition of the Pentateuch in Recent European Interpretation,* edited by Thomas B. Dozeman and Konrad Schmid, 51–72. SBL Symposium Series 34. Atlanta: Society of Biblical Literature, 2006.

Quinn, David Beers, editor. *The Roanoke Voyages: 1584–1590.* Volume 1. Works issued by the Hakluyt Society ; 2nd ser., no. 104. London: Hakluyt, 1955.

Rad, Gerhard von. *Genesis: A Commentary*. Translated by John H. Marks. Old Testament Library. Phila-delphia: Westminster, 1961 [Rev. ed. 1972].

―――. *Old Testament Theology*. Vol. 1. Translated by D. M. G. Stalker. New York: Harper & Row, 1965.

Redford, Donald B. *A Study of the Biblical Story of Joseph (Genesis 37–50)*. VTSup 20. Leiden: Brill, 1970.

Rendtorff, Rolf. *Das Überlieferungsgeschichtliche Problem des Pentateuch*. BZAW 147. Berlin: de Gruyter, 1977 [English ed.: *The Problem of the Process of Transmission in the Pentateuch*. Translated by John J. Scullion. Sheffield: JSOT Press, 1990].

Rendtorff, Rolf, and Robert A. Kugler, editors. *The Book of Leviticus: Composition and Reception*. VTSup 93. Leiden: Brill, 2003.

Richey, Russell E., and Donald G. Jones, editors. *American Civil Religion*. Harper Forum Books. New York: Harper & Row, 1974.

Ricoeur, Paul. *Essays on Biblical Interpretation*. Philadelphia: Fortress, 1980.

―――. *The Symbolism of Evil*. Translated by Emerson Buchanan. Religious Perspectives 17. Boston: Beacon, 1967.

Rifkin, Jeremy. *Beyond Beef: The Rise and Fall of the Cattle Culture*. New York: Dutton, 1992.

Römer, Thomas. *The So-Called Deuteronomistic History: A Sociological, Historical, and Literary Introduc-tion*. London: T. & T. Clark, 2007.

Rosenberg, Joel W. "Introduction and Annotations to Genesis." In *The HarperCollins Study Bible. New Revised Standard Version*. New York: HarperCollins, 1993.

Ruwe, Andreas. "The Structure of the Book of Leviticus in the Narrative Outline of the Priestly Sinai Story (Exod 19:1—Num 10:10*)." In *The Book of Leviticus*, edited by Rolf Rendtorff and Robert A. Kugler, 55–78. VTSup 93. Leiden: Brill, 2003.

Sanders, James. *Torah and Canon*. Philadelphia: Fortress, 1972 [2nd ed., Eugene, OR: Cascade Books, 2005].

Sapienza, Stephen. "Thai Shrimp Industry Exploits Workers to Whet Global Appetite for Cheap Shrimp." Public Broadcasting Service in collaboration with the Pulitzer Center on Crisis Reporting. *PBS Newshour*, aired on September 20, 2012. Online: http://www.pbs.org/newshour/bb/world/july-dec12/thaishrimp_09-20.html/.

Sarna, Nahum M. *Genesis*. JPS Torah Commentary. Philadelphia: Jewish Publication Society, 1989.

―――. *Understanding Genesis*. New York: Schocken, 1966.

Sasson, Jack. "The Tower of Babel as a Clue to the Redactional Structuring of the Primeval History (Gen. 1—11:9)." In *The Bible World*, edited by Gary Rendsburg et al., 211–38. New York: Ktav, 1980.

Schenker, Adrian. "What Connects the Incest Prohibitions with the Other Prohibitions Listed in Leviticus 18 and 20?" In *The Book of Leviticus*, edited by Rolf Rendtorff and Robert A. Kugler, 162–85. VTSup 93. Leiden: Brill, 2003.

Schmid, Konrad. "The So-Called Yahwist and the Literary Gap between Genesis and Exodus." In *A Farewell to the Yahwist? : The Composition of the Pentateuch in Recent European Interpretation*, edited by Thomas B. Dozeman and Konrad Schmid, 29–50. SBL Symposium Series 34. Atlanta: Society of Biblical Literature, 2006.

Scholes, Robert, and Robert Kellogg. *The Nature of Narrative*. London: Oxford University Press, 1966.

Seuss, Dr. *Yertle the Turtle and Other Stories*. New York: Random House, 1950.

Siker, Jeffrey S., editor. *Homosexuality in the Church: Both Sides of the Debate*. Louisville: Westminster John Knox, 1994

Silva, Moisés. "Contemporary Theories of Biblical Interpretation." In *The New Interpreter's Bible*, edited by Leander E. Keck et al., 1:107–24. 12 vols. Nashville: Abingdon, 1994.

"Six Reasons to Eat Less Red Meat." *Nutrition Action Healthletter* June 2013. Online: http://cspinet.org/new/pdf/cover_-_eat_less_red_meat.pdf/.

Smith, Mark S. *The Early History of God: Yahweh and the Other Deities of Ancient Israel*. 2nd ed. Biblical Resource Series. Grand Rapids: Eerdmans, 2002.

―――. *The Memoirs of God: History, Memory, and the Experience of the Divine in Ancient Israel*. Minneapolis: Fortress, 2004.

―――. *The Origins of Biblical Monotheism: Israel's Polytheistic Background and the Ugaritic Texts*. New York: Oxford University Press, 2001.

Speiser, E. A. "The Creation Epic." In *Ancient Near Eastern Texts Relating to the Old Testament*, edited by James B. Pritchard, 60–72. 3rd ed. Princeton: Princeton University Press, 1969.

Stabenow, Dana. *Play With Fire. A Kate Shugak Mystery*. New York: Berkley Prime Crime, 1995.

Stegner, Wallace. *Crossing to Safety*. New York: Random House, 1987.

Stroup, George W. *The Promise of Narrative Theology: Recovering the Gospel in the Church*. Atlanta: John Knox, 1981.

Toorn, Karel van der. "Cultic Prostitution." In *Anchor Bible Dictionary*, edited by David Noel Freedman, 5:510–13. 6 vols. New York: Doubleday, 1992.

Terrien, Samuel. *The Elusive Presence: Toward a New Biblical Theology*. 1978. Reprinted, Eugene, OR: Wipf & Stock, 2000.

Tigay, Jeffrey J. *Deuteronomy*. JPS Torah Commentary. Philadelphia: Jewish Publication Society, 1996.

Tillich, Paul. *The Dynamics of Faith*. New York: Harper & Row, 1957.

———. *The New Being*. New York: Scribner, 1955.

———. *Systematic Theology*. 3 vols. Chicago: University of Chicago Press, 1951–63.

Tinker, George E. "Reading the Bible as Native Americans." In *The New Interpreter's Bible*, edited by Leander E. Keck et al., 1:174–80. 12 vols. Nashville: Abingdon, 1994.

Van Seters, John. *Abraham in History and Tradition*. New Haven: Yale University Press, 1975.

———. *The Life of Moses: The Yahwist as Historian in Exodus–Numbers*. Louisville: Westminster John Knox, 1994.

Van Wijk-Bos, Johanna W. H. *Making Wise the Simple: The Torah in Christian Faith and Practice*. Grand Rapids: Eerdmans, 2005.

Volf, Miroslav. *Allah: A Christian Response*. New York: HarperOne, 2011.

Wellhausen, Julius. *Prolegomena to the History of Ancient Israel*. Cleveland: World, 1957 [1878].

Ward, Peter D. *The Flooded Earth: Our Future in a World without Ice Caps*. New York: BasicBooks, 2010.

Watts, James W. *Reading Law: The Rhetorical Shaping to the Pentateuch*. Biblical Seminar 59. Sheffield: Sheffield Academic, 1999.

Weinfeld, Moshe. *Deuteronomy 1–11*. Anchor Bible 5. New York: Doubleday, 1991.

———. *Deuteronomy and the Deuteronomic School*. Oxford: Clarendon, 1972.

———. *The Promise of the Land: The Inheritance of the Land of Canaan by the Israelites*. The Taubman Lectures in Jewish Studies. Berkely: University of California Press, 1993.

Westermann, Claus. *Genesis 1–11: A Commentary*. Translated by John J. Scullion. Continental Commentaries. Minneapolis: Augsburg, 1984.

White, Hugh C. "French Structuralism and OT Narrative Analysis: Roland Barthes." *Semeia* 3 (1975) 99–127.

———. *Narration and Discourse in the Book of Genesis*. Cambridge: Cambridge University, 1991.

Whitelam, Keith W. *The Invention of Ancient Israel: The Silencing of Palestinian History*. London: Routledge, 1996.

Whybray, R. N. *The Making of the Pentateuch: A Methodological Study*. JSOTSup 53. Sheffield: Sheffield Academic, 1987.

Wicker, Brian. *The Story-Shaped World: Fiction and Metaphysics: Some Variations on a Theme*. Notre Dame: University of Notre Dame Press, 1975.

Williams, Tennessee. *A Streetcar Named Desire*. New York: New Directions, 1980 [First ed., 1947].

Willimon, William H. *Acts*. Interpretation. Atlanta: John Knox, 1988.

Wilson, E. O. *Anthill: A Novel*. New York: Norton, 2010.

Woodroof, Martha. "When Gay Bashing Goes Viral." Guest Voices. *Washington Post*. June 3, 2012. Online: http://www.washingtonpost.com/blogs/guest-voices/post/when-gay-bashing-goes-viral/2012/06/03/gJQAIGBoBV_blog.html/.

Wyatt, Nicolas. *Religious Texts from Ugarit*. 2nd rev. ed. Biblical Seminar 53. London: Sheffield Academic, 2002.

Zevit, Ziony. "The Priestly Redaction and Interpretation of the Plague Narrative in Exodus." *Jewish Quarterly Review*, ns 66 (1976) 193–211.

Scripture Index[1]

---

1. Restricted to primary discussion of particular passages.

Made in the USA
Middletown, DE
09 August 2016